Ancient Egyptian Coffins

ANCIENT EGYPTIAN COFFINS

PAST • PRESENT • FUTURE

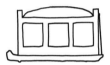

Edited by

HELEN STRUDWICK and JULIE DAWSON

OXBOW | books
Oxford & Philadelphia

Published in the United Kingdom in 2019 by
OXBOW BOOKS
The Old Music Hall, 106–108 Cowley Road, Oxford, OX4 1JE

and in the United States by
OXBOW BOOKS
1950 Lawrence Road, Havertown, PA 19083

Typeset by Nigel Strudwick.
Computer hieroglyphs by Cleo Huggins.

Hardcover Edition: ISBN 978-1-78570-918-0
Digital Edition: ISBN 978-1-78570-919-7 (epub)

A CIP record for this book is available from the British Library

Library of Congress Control Number: 2018964769

Printed in Malta by Melita Press Ltd

For a complete list of Oxbow titles, please contact:

UNITED KINGDOM
Oxbow Books
Telephone (01865) 241249
Email: oxbow@oxbowbooks.com
www.oxbowbooks.com

UNITED STATES OF AMERICA
Oxbow Books
Telephone (800) 791-9354, Fax (610) 853-9146
Email: queries@casemateacademic.com
www.casemateacademic.com/oxbow

Oxbow Books is part of the Casemate Group

Front cover: The cartonnage mummy case of Nakhtefmut (Fitzwilliam Museum, E.64.1896) photographed in visible light and using visible-light induced luminescence (VIL). © The Fitzwilliam Museum.

Contents

Introduction

Over the last decade, the pace and intensity of study of ancient Egyptian coffins has increased dramatically. At the Fitzwilliam Museum, a project to investigate all aspects of coffins in the collection grew out of the research and conservation work associated with the redisplay of the Egyptian galleries from 2004–2006. In 2016, as one of Museum's major events in celebration of its bicentenary and in recognition of the importance of Egyptian coffin studies, an exhibition was staged: *Death on the Nile: Uncovering the Afterlife of ancient Egypt*. It was devoted entirely to coffins, their manufacture, development and use, showcasing both the Museum's own research and the broader context of coffin studies within which that sits.

The culmination of the exhibition was a conference *Ancient Egyptian Coffins: Past • Present • Future*, held from 7 to 9 April 2016. Over one hundred delegates from seventeen countries attended, including nine colleagues from Egypt funded through the generosity of the Fitzwilliam Museum's Marlay Group. This book presents many of the papers given at the conference, together with abstracts of the posters that were presented. Papers were arranged broadly chronologically and by site to enable the maximum cross-fertilisation of ideas between subject specialists (such as Egyptologists, archaeologists, conservators, technologists and scientists), and this arrangement has been preserved in these proceedings.

The conference was preceded by a three-day event entitled *The Coffin Workshop*. This was a practical seminar for twenty participants, and looked in detail at some of the key features of wooden coffin construction and decoration together with the imaging and analytical techniques used to investigate them.

One aspect which provoked much discussion, especially at the Workshop, was terminology. Within this publication, we have encouraged authors to standardise the terminology they used. Two terms, in particular, require some explanation:

The word "paste" has been adopted in preference to "plaster". The latter is often used rather loosely, when describing Egyptian objects, to mean both true plasters (made from lime or gypsum cements) and pastes made from a binder (such as animal glue) mixed with calcium sulphate (often called gesso) or with calcium carbonate (often called whiting). Sometimes all these materials are mixed together, with the addition of clay minerals and vegetable fibres. Thus, the term "paste" has been used, as it implies no particular chemistry or technology.

The lower part of an anthropoid coffin is referred to many different ways in the literature; for example, base, case or trough. Within this publication, where the authors have so agreed, the term "box" has been adopted.

In addition, use of the terms "proper right" and "proper left" has, with our encouragement, been accepted by most contributors. The latter terms are widely used in the art world, but they provoked the most lively discussion at both the workshop and the conference.

Our thanks go to Tim Knox, then Director of the Fitzwilliam Museum, for his support both of the Egyptian coffins project generally, and of the *Death on the Nile* exhibition and this conference in particular. We owe a great debt to many other colleagues at the Museum for their support, especially Lucilla Burn, former Keeper of Antiquities, who was unfailingly supportive of the coffin project and provided invaluable advice during the planning and installation of the exhibition. Thanks also go to

Melanie Pitkin, the Museum's Coffins Project Research Associate, who has provided invaluable assistance with the editing of contributions.

The departure of two key members of staff in the Antiquities Department at the Fitzwilliam, together with other difficulties, have caused considerable delay in the preparation of these proceedings. We are grateful to our colleagues at the Museum and our contributors to this volume for all they have done to get it to the final stages of preparation. We are indebted especially to Nigel Strudwick who has typeset the book, in addition to carrying out further editing of the papers. Our greatest thanks, however, go to Oxbow Books for producing this volume for us. We hope its appearance will amply repay their patience.

Helen Strudwick and Julie Dawson

Bibliography

Abbreviations:

LÄ = Helck, Wolfgang and Wolfhart Westendorf (eds). 1975–1992. *Lexikon der Ägyptologie*. Wiesbaden: Otto Harrassowitz.

LGG = Leitz, Christian (ed.). 2002–2003. *Lexikon der ägyptischen Götter und Götterbezeichnungen. Volumes 1–7* (Orientalia Lovaniensia analecta 110–116) and *Lexikon der ägyptischen Götter und Götterbezeichnungen. Volume 8. Register* (Orientalia Lovaniensia analecta 129). Leuven: Peeters.

PM = Porter, Bertha and Rosalind L.B. Moss; Ethel W Burney, Jaromír Málek. 1927–. *Topographical bibliography of Ancient Egyptian hieroglyphic texts, reliefs, and paintings*. Oxford: Clarendon Press.

PN = Ranke, Hermann. *Die ägyptischen Personennamen, Bd. 1: Verzeichnis der Namen*. Glückstadt: J.J. Augustin.

Wb = Erman, Adolf and Hermann Grapow (eds) 1926–1963. *Wörterbuch der Aegyptischen Sprache*. Leipzig: J.C. Hinrichs.

Abbas, Eltayeb Sayed. 2014a. *Ritual Scenes on the Two Coffins of P3-dj-imn in Cairo Museum* (BAR International Series 2603). Oxford: British Archaeological Reports.

——— 2014b. "The Significance of a ritual scene on the floor board of some coffin cases in the Twenty-First Dynasty". In: Pischikova, Budka and Griffin 2014, 419–438.

Accorsi, Gianluca, Giovanni Verri, Margherita Bolognesi, Nicola Armaroli, Catia Clementi, Costanza Miliani and Aldo Romani. 2009. "The exceptional near-infrared luminescence properties of cuprorivaite (Egyptian blue)". *Chemical Communications* 23: 3392–3394.

Altenmüller, Hartwig. 1976. *Grab und Totenreich der Alten Ägypter*. Hamburg: Hamburgisches Museum.

Ambers, Janet. 2004. "Raman analysis of pigments from the Egyptian Old Kingdom". *Journal of Raman Spectroscopy* 35: 768–773.

Amenta, Alessia. (ed.) 2013. *Vatican Coffin Project, Protocollo indagini scientifiche. Analysis Protocol.* Città del Vaticano: Musei Vaticani.

Amenta, Alessia. 2014 "The Vatican Coffin Project". In: *Thebes in the First Millennium BC*, edited by E. Pischikova, J. Budka and K. Griffin, 483–499. Newcastle upon Tyne: Cambridge Scholars Publishing.

Amenta, Alessia and Hélène Guichard (eds). 2017. *Proceedings of the First Vatican Conference 19–22 June 2013*. Città del Vaticano: Edizioni Musei Vaticani.

Anđelković, B. and Elias, Jonathan. 2015. "Inscriptions on the Interior of the 30th Dynasty Coffin of Nefer-renepet from Akhmim". *Issues in Ethnology and Anthropology* (Belgrade), n.s. 10 issue 3.

Andreau, Guillemette. 2002. *Les Artistes de Pharaon. Deir el-Médineh et la Vallée des Rois*. Paris: Réunion des musées nationaux.

Asensi Amorós, Maria Victoria. 2017. "The wood of the Third Intermediate Period coffins: The evidence of analysis for the Vatican Coffin Project". In: Amenta and Guichard 2017, 45–50.

Assmann, Jan (ed.). 1991. *Das Grab des Amenemope TT 41. Theben 3*. Mainz am Rhein: Verlag Philipp von Zabern.

Aston, David A. 1999. *Elephantine XIX: Pottery from the Late New Kingdom to the Early Ptolemaic Period*. Mainz am Rhein: Verlag Philipp von Zabern.

——— 2004. "Amphorae in New Kingdom Egypt". *Ägypten und Levante* 14: 175–213.

——— 2009. *Burial assemblages of dynasty 21–25: Chronology, typology, developments* (Denkschriften der Gesamtakademie, Bd. 56). Wien: Verlag der Österreichischen Akademie der Wissenschaften.

Aubert, M.-F. 1997. *Louvre Guide du visiteur, Les Antiquités égyptiennes II, Egypte romaine, art funéraire Antiquités coptes*. Paris: Réunion des Musées Nationaux.

Ayora Cañada, María José, Ana Domínguez Vidal, Yolanda de la Torre and Alejandro Jiménez-Serrano. 2015. "On-site spectroscopic investigation of pigments in archaeological Egyptian funerary artefacts at Qubbet el Hawa necropolis (Aswan)". Poster presented at the 8th International Conference on Advanced Vibrational Spectroscopy (July 12–17, 2015), Vienna, Austria.

Baba, Masahiro and Ken Yazawa. 2015. "Burial assemblages of the Late Middle Kingdom: Shaft-tombs in Dashur North". In: Miniaci and Grajetzki 2015, 1–24.

Baba, Masahiro and Sakuji Yoshimura, 2010. "Dahshur North: intact Middle and New Kingdom coffins". *Egyptian Archaeology* 37: 9–12.

Balanda, S.Z. 2009. "The title '*ḥry-sštꜣ*' to the end of the New Kingdom". *Journal of the American Research Centre in Egypt* 45: 319–348.

Barta, Winfried. 1968. *Aufbau und Bedeutung der altägyptischen Opferformel.* Glückstadt: Augustin.

Barwik, Miroslaw. 2003. "New data concerning the Third Intermediate Period cemetery in the Hatshepsut temple at Deir el-Bahari". In: Strudwick and Taylor 2003, 122–130.

Bell, M. 1985. "Gurob 605 and Mycenaean Chronology". In: *Mélanges Gamal Eddin Mokhtar*, edited by P. Posener-Kriéger, 64–77. Le Caire: L'Imprimerie de l'Institut français d'archéologie orientale.

Berman, Lawrence M. 1992. "Funerary Equipment". In: *Egypt's Dazzling Sun: Amenhotep III and his World*, edited by Arielle P. Kozloff and Betsy M. Bryan, 305–310. Cleveland: The Cleveland Museum of Art.

Betrò, M. 2013. "Firenze inv. Nr. 9477: the coffin of Qenamon (TT93)". *Egitto e Vicino Oriente* 36: 15–20.

Bettum, Anders. 2013. *Faces within faces: the symbolic function of nested yellow coffins in Ancient Egypt.* Oslo: University of Oslo.

Bettum, Anders and Lucy Skinner. 2015. "The Amarna Coffins Project: Coffins from the South Tombs Cemetery". In: Kemp, Barry (ed.). "Tell el-Amarna, 2014–15". *Journal of Egyptian Archaeology* 101: 337–342.

Bianchetti, P., F. Talarico, M.G. Vigliano and M.F. Ali. 2000. "Production and characterization of Egyptian blue and Egyptian green frit". *Journal of Cultural Heritage* 1 (2): 179–188.

Bianchi, Robert S. 1983. "Glass Inlays". *Bulletin of the Egyptological Seminar* 5, 9–29.

——— 2011. *Ancient Egypt, art and magic: Treasures from the Fondation Gandur pour l'Art.* St Petersburg, Florida: Museum of Fine Arts. Published in conjunction with the exhibition of the same name, shown at the Museum of Fine Arts St. Petersburg, Florida, 17 December 2011–20 April 2012.

Bickel, Susanne and Elina Paulin-Grothe. 2014. "KV40: a burial place for the royal entourage". *Egyptian Archaeology* 45: 21–24.

Billing, Nils. 2002. *Nut: The Goddess of Life in Text and Iconography* (Uppsala Studies in Egyptology). Uppsala: Department of Archaeology and Ancient History, Uppsala University.

Biondi, E., T. Cavaleri, M. Nervo, M. Pisani and M. Zucco. 2015 "A hyperspectral imager based on a Fabry-Perot interferometer as a tool in cultural heritage studies". In: *Color and Colorimetry. Multidisciplinary Contributions, Vol. XI B, atti della XI Conferenza del colore, Milan, 10–11 september 2015*, edited by M. Rossi and D. Casciani, 173–182. Milan: Gruppo del Colore – Associazione Italiane Colore.

Bleiberg, Edward (ed.). 2008. *To Live Forever.* New York: D. Giles Limited in association with the Brooklyn Museum of Art.

Boeser, P.A.A. 1916. *Beschreibung der Aegyptischen Sammlung des Niederländischen Reichsmuseums der Altertümer in Leiden. Mumiensärge des Neuen Reiches.* Milano: Cisalpino-Goliardica.

——— 1917. *Beschreibung der Aegyptischen Sammlung des Niederländischen Reichsmuseums der Altertümer in Leiden. Mumiensärge des Neuen Reiches. Zweite Serie.*, Milano: Cisalpino-Goliardica.

Bogoslovsky, E.S. 1973. "Monuments and documents from Dêr el-Medîna in museums of the USSR. Part VI. 20. Sarcophagus No 1, Voronezh Museum of Fine Arts". *Vestnik Drevnei Istorii* 1973/2: 70–102.

Borojevic, K., R. Mountain. 2013. "Microscopic identification and sourcing of ancient Egyptian plant fibres using longitudinal thin sectioning". *Archaeometry* 55: 81–112.

Botti, Giuseppe. 1958. *Le casse di mummie e i sarcophagi da el Hibeh nel Museo Archeologico di Firenze.* Florence: L.S. Olschk.

Bragg, Laura M. 1914. "Exhibits at the museum: Egyptian mummy". *Bulletin of the Charleston Museum* 10 (No. 6): 49–51.

Brech, Ruth. 2008. *Spätägyptische Särge aus Achmim. Eine Typologische und chronologische Studie.* Gladbeck: PeWe-Verlag.

Bresciani, Edda, Sergio Pernigotti and Maria Paola Giangeri Silvis. 1977. *La tomba di Ciennehebu, capo della flotta del re* (Biblioteca degli studi classici e orientali 7). Pisa: Giardini.

Broekman, Gerard P.F., Robert Johannes Demarée and Olaf E. Kaper (eds). 2009. *The Libyan Period in Egypt: Historical and Cultural Studies into the 21st–24th Dynasties: Proceedings of a Conference at Leiden University 25–27 October 2007.* Leuven: Peeters.

Brunetto, A. 2004. *L'utilizzo della Strumentazione laser per la pulitura delle superfici nei manufatti artistici.* Saonara: Il Prato.

Bruno, Lisa. 2014. "On not exhibiting a corpse: the Mummy Chamber, Brooklyn Museum". *Understanding Egyptian Collections: Innovative display and research projects in museums, Ashmolean Museum, Oxford University, 1–2 September 2014.* Podcast of a talk given in September 2014: https://podcasts.ox.ac.uk/not-exhibiting-corpse-mummy-chamber-brooklyn-museum (accessed 28 April 2018).

Bruwier, M.-C. 1998. "Présence et Action d'Anubis sur le coffret d'un prêtre Héracléopoltain». In: *Egyptian religion: The last thousand years: Studies dedicated to the memory of Jan Quaegebeur* (Orientalia Lovaniensia analecta; 84–85), edited by Willy Clarysse, Antoon Schoors and Harco Willems, 61–79. Leuven: Peeters.

Bruyère, Bernard. 1925. "Un jeune prince ramesside trouvé à Deir el Médineh». *Bulletin de l'Institut Français d'archéologie orientale* 25: 147–165.

——— 1929. *Rapport sur les fouilles de Deir el Médineh (1928)* (Fouilles de l'Institut français d'archéologie orientale 6). Le Caire: L'Imprimerie de l'Institut français d'archéologie orientale.

——— 1937. *Rapport sur les fouilles de Deir el Médineh (1933–1934)* (Fouilles de l'Institut français d'archéologie orientale 14). Le Caire: L'Imprimerie de l'Institut français d'archéologie orientale.

Budge, E.A. Wallis. 1887. "Excavations made at Aswan by Major-General Sir F. Grenfell during the years 1885 and 1986". *Proceedings of the Society for Biblical Archaeology* 10: 4–40.

——— 1893. *A catalogue of the Egyptian collection in the Fitzwilliam Museum, Cambridge.* Cambridge: University Press.

——— 1924. *British Museum: A Guide to the first, second and third Egyptian rooms.* London: Trustees of the British Museum.

Budka, J. 2008. "Neues zu den Nutzungsphasen des Monumentalgrabes von Anch-Hor, Obersthofmeister der Gottesgemahlin Nitokris (TT 414)". *Ägypten und Levante* 18: 61–85.

——— 2010. "Varianz im Regelwerk. Bestattungsabläufe im Monumentalgras von Anch-Hor, Obersthofmeister der Gottesgemahlin Nitokris (TT 414)". *Ägypten und Levante* 20: 49–66.

Buhl, Marie-Louise. 1959. *The Late Egyptian anthropoid stone sarcophagi* (Nationalmuseets Skrifter. Arkaeologisk-historisk raekke, VI). Kobenhaven: Nationalmuseet.

Buscaglia, P., M. Cardinali, T. Cavaleri, P. Croveri, G. Ferraris di Celle and A. Piccirillo. 2015. "Materiali riempitivi per il risarcimento di lacune di manufatti lignei: sperimentazione di tinture e leganti innovativi per cariche cellulosiche". In: *Atti del XIII Congresso Nazionale IGIIC–Lo Stato dell'Arte 15 (Venaria Reale 22–24 October 2015)*, 507–515. Florence: Nardini Editore.

Calza, Cristiane, M.J. Anjos, S.M.F. Mendonça de Souza, Antonio Brancaglion Jr. and Ricardo Lopes. 2007. "X-Ray microfluorescence analysis of pigments in decorative paintings from the sarcophagus cartonnage of an Egyptian mummy". *Nuclear Instruments and Methods in Physics Research B* 263: 249–252.

Calza, Cristiane, Renato Freitas, Antonio Brancaglion Jr. and Ricardo Lopes. 2011. "Analysis of artifacts from ancient Egypt using an EDXRF portable system". *International Nuclear Atlantic Conference–INAC 2011*: 1–13.

Cardoso, Isabel Pombo. 2006. "18th century church altarpieces in the Algarve, Portugal: a comparison of the historical documents to the results of the microscopical analysis". *infocus Magazine* 4: 64–86.

Carrara, Nicola, Alessandra Menegazzi and Susanna Moser. 2010 "Collezionismo egittologico all'Università di Padova: i reperti dei Musei di Scienze Archeologiche e d'Arte e di Antropologia". *Bollettino del Museo Civico di Padova* XCIX: 7–26.

Cartwright, Caroline R. 1997. "Egyptian mummy portraits: examining the woodworkers' craft". In: *Portraits and masks: burial customs in Roman Egypt*, edited by Maurice Bierbrier, 106–111. London: British Museum Press.

——— 2001. "Cedrus libani under the microscope; the anatomy of modern and ancient Cedar of Lebanon wood". *Archaeology and History in Lebanon* 14: 107–113.

——— 2013. "Identifying the woody resources of Diepkloof Rock Shelter (South Africa) using scanning electron microscopy of the MSA wood charcoal assemblages". *Journal of Archaeological Science* 40: 3463–3474.

——— 2015. "The principles, procedures and pitfalls in identifying archaeological and historical wood samples". *Annals of Botany* 116 (1): 1–13.

——— 2016. "Wood in ancient Egypt: choosing wood for coffins". In: Strudwick and Dawson 2016, 78–79 and 251.

Cartwright, Caroline R., Lin Rosa Spaabæk and Marie Svoboda. 2011. "Portrait mummies from Roman Egypt: ongoing collaborative research on wood identification". *British Museum Technical Research Bulletin* 2: 49–58.

Cartwright, Caroline R. and John H. Taylor. 2008. "Wooden Egyptian archery bows in the collections of the British Museum". *British Museum Technical Research Bulletin* 2: 77–83.

Catullo, T.A. 1836. "Relazione dei doni fatti dal consigliere Cav. Acerbi, già console generale di S.M.I.R.A. in Egitto, al Gabinetto di Storia Naturale dell'I.R. Università di Padova". *Biblioteca Italiana ossia giornale di letteratura, scienze ed arti compilato da una società di letterati* 83.

Cavaleri, T., M. Pisani and M. Zucco. 2015. "A new hyperspectral imager for studying Egyptian coffins". In: *Colours 2015: Bridging science with art, Evora, 24–26 September 2015*, book of abstracts, 69.

Cavillier, Giacomo. 2017. "The Butehamun Project: Research on the Funerary Equipment". In: Amenta and Guichard 2017, 97–100; 576–577.

Chaballe, L. Y. and J.-P. Vandenberghe. 1982. *Elsevier's Dictionary of Building Tools and Materials: In five languages: English/ American, French, Spanish, German and Dutch.* Amsterdam: Elsevier Science.

Champollion, Jean-François and Sylvie Guichard. 2013. *Notice descriptive des monuments égyptiens du musée Charles X.* Paris: Éditions Khéops.

Chassinat, Emile. 1909. *Catalogue général des antiquités égyptiennes du Musée du Caire. La seconde trouvaille de Deir el-Bahari (sarcophages) (CG 6001–6029).* Le Caire: L'Imprimerie de l'Institut français d'archéologie orientale.

Chassinat, Emile. 1932. *Le temple de Dendara* volume 1. Le Caire: Institut français d'archéologie orientale.

Cleopatra y la fascinación de Egipto. 2015. Milano: Skira. Published in conjunction with the exhibition of the same name, shown at the Centro de Exposiciones Arte Canal, Madrid, Spain, 3 December 2015 – 8 May 2016.

Cooney, Kathlyn M. 2007. *The cost of death: The social and economic value of ancient Egyptian funerary art in the Ramesside Period.* Leiden; Nederlands Instituut voor het Nabije Oosten.

——— 2012. "Objectifying the body: the increased value of the ancient Egyptian mummy during the socioeconomic crisis of Dynasty Twenty-one". In: *The Construction of Value in the Ancient World*, edited by J. Papdopoulos and G. Urton, 139–159. Los Angeles: Cotsen Institute Press.

——— 2011. "Changing burial practices at the end of the New Kingdom. Defensive adaptation in tomb commissions, coffin commissions, coffin decoration, and mummification". *Journal of the American Research Center in Egypt* 47: 3–44.

——— 2014. "Ancient Egyptian funerary arts as social documents: social place, reuse, and working towards a new typology of 21st Dynasty coffins". In: Sousa 2014a, 45–66.

Cooper, M. 1998. *Laser Cleaning in Conservation: An Introduction.* London: Butterworth-Heinemann.

Corcoran, Lorelei. 2016. "The color blue as an animator in ancient Egyptian art". In: *Essays in global color history: interpreting the ancient spectrum*, edited by Rachael B. Goldman, 41–63. Piscataway, New Jersey: Gorgias Press.

Corkhill, Thomas. 1979. *A Glossary of Wood: 10000 terms relating to timber and its use, explained and clarified.* London: Stobart Davies.

Cornell, Rochelle and Udo Schwertmann. 2006. *The Iron Oxides: Structure, Properties, Reactions, Occurrences and Uses.* 2nd edition. New York: John Wiley & Sons.

Cremonesi, P. and E. Signorini. 2004. "L'uso dei solventi organici neutri nella pulitura dei dipinti: un nuovo test di solubilità". *Progetto Restauro* 31: 2–15.

Crevatin, Franco and Duilio Bertani [*et al.*]. 2008. *Il libro dei morti di Ptahmose (Papiro Busca, Milano) ed altri documenti egiziani antichi* (Biblioteca degli "Studi di egittologia e di papirologia" 6). Pisa: F. Serra.

Crevatin, Franco and Marzia Vidulli Torlo (eds). 2013. *Collezione egizia del Civico Museo di Storia ed Arte di Trieste* [with contributions by Susanna Moser and members of "Casa della Vita" Association]. Trieste: La Collezione Egizia, LuglioEditore.

Crivellaro, A. and F.H. Schweingruber. 2013. *Atlas of Wood, Bark and Pith Anatomy of Eastern Mediterranean Trees and Shrubs.* Berlin Heidelberg: Springer-Verlag.

Croveri, P., A. Giovagnoli, A. Piccirillo, T. Cavaleri, I. Clonier, A. De La Sayette and V. Girardin. 2014. "New natural dyes for restoration of textiles: morphological, physical and chemicals analyses of woollen threads (INNOCOLORS project)". In: *Proceedings of ART'14 11th international conference on non-destructive investigation and microanalysis for the diagnostics and conservation of cultural and environmental heritage, Madrid, June 2014*, 1–9. Madrid: AIPnD MAN END.

Dąbrowska-Smektała, E. 1966. "Coffin of Tay-akhuth, Chantress of Amun-Re". *Rocznik Orientalistyczny (Warsaw)* 30.2: 7–17.

Dallongeville, S., N. Garnier, C. Rolando, and C.Tokarski. 2016. "Proteins in art, archaeology, and paleontology: From detection to identification". *Chemical Reviews* 116 (1): 2–79.

D'amicone, E. 2008. "Schiaparelli e gli scavi nella Valle delle Regine". In: *Ernesto Schiaparelli e la tomba di Kha*, edited by B. Moiso, 145–166. Torino: AdArte.

Daniels V., R. Stacey and A. Middleton. 2004. "The blackening of paint containing Egyptian blue". *Studies in Conservation* 49 (4), 217–230. DOI: 10.1179/sic.2004.49.4.217.

Daressy, Georges E. 1900. "Les sépultures des prêtres d'Ammon à Deir el-Bahari». *Annales du service des antiquités de l'Egypte* 1: 141–148.

——— 1902. *Catalogue général des antiquités égyptiennes du Musée du Caire. Fouilles de la Vallée des Rois 1898–99.* Le Caire: L'Imprimerie de l'Institut français d'archéologie orientale.

——— 1907. "Les cercueils des prêtres d'Ammon (deuxième trouvaille de Deir el-Bahari)». *Annales du service des antiquités de l'Egypte* 8: 3–38.

——— 1909. *Catalogue général des antiquités égyptiennes du Musée du Caire. Cercueils des cachettes royales (CG 61001–61044).* Le Caire: L'Imprimerie de l'Institut français d'archéologie orientale.

Daudin-Schotte, M., M. Bisschoff, I. Joosten, H. van Keulen and K.J. van den Berg. 2013. "Dry cleaning approaches for unvarnished paint surfaces". In: *New Insights into the Cleaning of Paintings: Proceedings from the Cleaning 2010 International Conference Universidad Politécnica de Valencia and Museum Conservation Institute*, edited by Marion F. Mecklenburg, A. Elena Charola and Robert J. Koestler, 209–219. Washington: Smithsonian Institution Scholarly Press.

Daumas, F. 1988. *Valeurs phonétiques des signes hiéroglyphiques d'Epoque Gréco-Romaine* volume 1. Montpellier: Université Paul-Valery, Institut d'Egyptologie.

D'Auria, Susan, Peter Lacovara and Catharine H. Roehrig. 1992. *Mummies and Magic: The Funerary Arts of Ancient Egypt.* Boston: Museum of Fine Arts. [Reprint]

Dautant, Alain, Thomas Boraud and Bernard Lalanne. 2011. "Le cercueil d'Iténéferamon au musée d'Aquitaine", *Égypte Nilotique et Méditérranéenne* 4: 233–272.

David, A. Rosalie. 2007. *The two brothers: death and the afterlife in Middle Kingdom Egypt.* Bolton: Rutherford Press.

Davies, Nina M. 1938. "Some representations of tombs from the Theban Necropolis". *Journal of Egyptian Archaeology* 24: 25–40.

Davies, W.V. 1995. "Ancient Egyptian timber imports: An analysis of wooden coffins in the British Museum". In: *Egypt, the Aegean and the Levant. Interconnections in the Second Millennium BC*, edited by W.V. Davies and L. Schofield, 146–148. London: British Museum Press.

——— (ed.) 2001. *Colour and Painting in Ancient Egypt.* London: British Museum Press.

Davis, R., 2005. "Radiography: archaeo-human and animal remains Part I: Clinical Radiography and Archaeo-Human Remains". In: *Radiography of Cultural Material*, edited by Andrew Middleton and Janet Lang, 130–154. London: Routledge.

Dawson, Julie, Christina Rozeik and Margot M. Wright (eds). 2010. *Decorated surfaces on ancient Egyptian objects: technology, deterioration and conservation.* London: Archetype Publications in association with the Fitzwilliam Museum and Icon Archaeology Group.

Dawson, Julie, Jennifer Marchant, Eleanor von Aderkas, Caroline Cartwright, Rebecca Stacey, 2016. "Egyptian Coffins: Materials, Construction and Decoration". In: Strudwick and Dawson, 75–111.

Dawson, Warren R. 1926. "A note on the Egyptian mummies in the Castle Museum, Norwich". *Journal of Egyptian Archaeology* 15, No. 3/4 (November): 186–190.

Dawson, Warren R. and Peter Hugh Ker Gray. 1968. *Catalogue of Egyptian antiquities in the British Museum: 1. Mummies and human remains.* London: The British Museum.

Defernez, C. 2001. *La céramique d'époque perse à Tell El-Herr. Étude Chrono-typologique et comparative (Cahier de recherches de l'Institut de papyrologie et d'égyptologie de Lille).* 2 volumes. Supplément no. 5. Lille: Université Charles-de-Gaulle Lille III.

Derrick, M.R., D. Stulik and J.M. Landry. 1999. *Infrared Spectroscopy in Conservation Science.* Los Angeles: Getty Conservation Institute.

Desroches-Noblecourt, Christiane (ed.). 1976. *Ramsès le grand.* Paris: Galeries nationales du grand palais.

Deutsches Institut für Normung. 1978. *DIN 68252-1:1978-01 Begriffe für Schnittholz; Form und Maß.* Berlin: DIN.

——— 1992. *DIN 406-10:1992-12 Technische Zeichnungen; Maßeintragungen*; Berlin: DIN.

——— 1995. *DIN EN 844-1:1995 Rund- und Schnittholz – Terminologie – Teil 1: Gemeinsame allgemeine Begriffe über Rundholz und Schnitzholz; Deutsche Fassung EN 844-1:1995.* Berlin: DIN.

——— 1997. *DIN EN 844-2:1997 Rund- und Schnittholz – Terminologie – Teil 2: Allgemeine Begriffe über Rundholz; Deutsche Fassung EN 844-2:1997.* Berlin: DIN.

——— 2016. *DIN 68150-1:2016-09 Holzdübel – Maße, Technische Lieferbedingungen.* Berlin: DIN.

Devéria, *Théodule.* 1855. "Noub, la déesse d'or des égyptiens". *Mémoires de la société des antiquaires de France* 22: 150–175.

Di Marco, Simona. 2000. "Frederick Stibbert: the man, his time, his dream". In: *Frederick Stibbert. Gentiluomo, collezionista e sognatore*, edited by K. Aschengreen Piacenti, 25–32. Firenze: Polistampa Edizioni.

Dils, P. 1991. In: *Van Nijl tot Schelde/Du Nil à l'Escaut*, edited by E. Gubel, 253. Brussels: Banque Bruxelles Lambert 1991. Published in conjunction with the exhibition of the same name, shown at Banque Bruxelles-Lambert, 5 April–9 June 1991.

Dobrowolska, K. 1970. "Génèse et evolution des boîtes à vases-canopes". *Études et Travaux* 4: 74–85.

Dodson, Aidan. 1994. *The canopic equipment of the kings of Egypt* (Studies in Egyptology 20). London/New York: Kegan Paul International.

——— 1998. "On the burial of Maihirpri and certain coffins of the Eighteenth Dynasty". In: *Proceedings of the seventh international congress of Egyptologists. Cambridge, 3–9 September 1995* (Orientalia Lovaniensia analecta 82), edited by Christopher J. Eyre, 331–338. Leuven: Peeters.

Donadoni Roveri, Anna Maria. 1969. *I sarcofagi egizi dalle origini alla fine dell'antico regno* (Serie Archeologica 16). Roma: Università di Roma, Istituto di Studi del Vicino Orienti.

——— 1989. *Dal museo al museo: passato e futuro del Museo egizio di Torino*. Torino: U. Allemandi.

Dreyfus, Renée. 2007. *Selected Works: Legion of Honor*. San Francisco and London: Fine Arts Museum of San Francisco, in association with Scala.

Dreyfus, Renée and Jonathan P. Elias. No date. *Mummy by the Bay: Irethorrou, an Egyptian Priest of the Early Persian Period.* Blog post: https://www.famsf.org/blog/mummy-bay-irethorrou-egyptian-priest-early-persian-period (accessed 03/05/2018).

Drusini, A., M. Rippa Bonati, P.P. Parnigotto, G.P. Feltrin and D. Fiore. 1982 "Indagine radiografica e con CT della mummia egiziana dell'Istituto di Antropologia di Padua". *Quaderni di Anatomia Pratica* s. XXXVIII, nn. 1–4: 53–66.

Duarte, Cássio de Araújo. 2014. "Crossing the landscape of eternity: parallels between Amduat and funeral procession scenes on the 21st Dynasty coffins". In: Sousa 2014a, 81–90.

Duhme, Andreas and Sonja Senge. 2015. *Die Baumportraits. 55 Werkstatthölzer – von Apfelbaum bis Zirbelkiefer.* Hanover: Vincentz Network.

Dulíková, V., Odler, M. and Havelková, P. 2011. "Archeologický výzkum hrobky lékaře Neferherptaha (Excavation of the physician Neferherptah's tomb). Preliminary report about the excavations in Abusir during autumn 2010". In: *Pražské egyptologické studie VIII (Prague Egyptological Studies VIII)*, 9–16. Prague: Charles University.

Dyer, J., G. Verri and J. Cupitt. 2013. *Multispectral Imaging in Reflectance and Photo-Induced Luminescence Modes: A user manual.* London: The British Museum.

Earl, G., P.J. Basford, A.S. Bischoff, A. Bowman, C. Crowther, M. Hodgson, K. Martinez *et al.* 2011. "Reflectance Transformation Imaging systems for ancient documentary artefacts". In: *EVA London 2011: Electronic Visualisation and the Arts* edited by J.P. Bowen, S. Dunn and K. Ng, 147–154. London: BCS.

Edel, Elmar. 2008. *Die Felsgräbernnekropole der Qubbet el-Hawa bei Assuan*, edited by Karl-J. Seyfried and Gerd Vieler. Paderborn: Ferdinand Schöningh.

Edwards, I.E.S. 1938. *A Handbook to the Egyptian Mummies and Coffins exhibited in the British Museum.* London: The British Museum.

Egner, Roswitha and Elfriede Haslauer. 1994. *Särge der Dritten Zwischenzeit I. Corpus Antiquitatum Aegyptiacarum. Kunsthistorisches Museum Wien, Lieferung 10.* Mainz am Rhein: Verlag Philipp von Zabern.

Elias, Jonathan P. 1993. *Coffin inscription in Egypt after the New Kingdom: a study of text production and use in elite mortuary preparation.* PhD dissertation, University of Chicago.

Emmett, T., 2015. *The Manufacture of 'Egyptian Blue' Pigment: Technical Issues*, 1–29. Cambridge: The Fitzwilliam Museum. Unpublished research report.

el-Enany, Khaled. 2010. "Un carré de lin peint au Musée de l'Agriculture du Caire (inv.893)". *Bulletin de l'Institut Français d'archéologie orientale* 110: 35–45.

Englund, Gertie. 1974. "Propos sur l'iconographie d'un sarcophage de la 21e dynastie". In: *From the Gustavianum Collections in Uppsala* (Boreas 6), edited by Sture Brunnsåker and Hans-Åke Nordström, 37–69. Uppsala: Almqvist & Wiksell.

Erman, Adolf. 1894. *Ausführliches Verzeichniss der aegyptischen Altertümer, Gipsabgüsse und Papyrus.* Berlin: Spemann and Königliche Museen zu Berlin.

Etcheverry, Marie-Pierre, Max Schvoerer and Françoise Bechtel. 2001. "Bleu égyptien: mise en évidence de deux processus de formation de la cuprorivaïte". *Revue d'Archéométrie* 25: 87–100.

European Committee for Standardisation. 1995. *DIN EN 844-3:1995 Rund- und Schnittholz – Terminologie – Teil 3: Allgemeine Begriffe über Schnittholz; Deutsche Fassung EN 844-3:1995.* Berlin: DIN.

——— 2001. *DIN EN 844-12:2001-03 Rund- und Schnittholz – Terminologie – Teil 12: Zusätzliche Begriffe und allgemeiner Index; Deutsche Fassung EN 844-12: 2000.* Berlin: DIN.

Falck, Martin von. 1987".Ein ägyptischer Holzsarg im Archäologischen Museum der Universität Münster". *Boreas. Münstersche Beiträge zur Archäologie* 10: 176–198, pl. 23–24.

Farrell, E.F., Snow, C. and Vinogradskaya, N. 2006. "The study and treatment of Pa-di-mut's cartonnage mummy case". *Journal of the American Institute of Conservation* 45: 1–15.

Faulkner, Raymond O. and Carol Andrews. 1972. T*he Ancient Egyptian Book of the Dead*, London. Guild Publishing, UK.

Ferrarato, B., F. Zenucchini, G. Ferraris di Celle, A. Piccirillo and M. Gulmini. Forthcoming. "Pulitura del blu egizio su superfici archeologiche". In: *Aplar 6: Applicazioni Laser nel restauro.* proceeding of conference held in Firenze 14–16 September 2017. Abstract of paper available at www.apla.eu/pdfs/libro_abstracts_APLAR_6.pdf .

Fischer, Henry George. 1977. *The orientation of hieroglyphs. Part I: Reversals.* New York: Metropolitan Museum of Art.

Fotakis, C., D. Anglos, V. Zafiropulos and S. Georgiou and V. Tornari. 2007. *Lasers in the preservation of cultural heritage. Principles and applications.* London & New York: Taylor & Francis Group.

Gaetani, Maria Carolina, Ulderico Santamaria, and Claudio Seccaroni. 2004. "The use of Egyptian blue and lapis lazuli in the Middle Ages: the wall paintings of the San Saba church in Rome". *Studies in Conservation* 49(1): 13–23.

Gale, R., P. Gasson, F.N. Hepper and G. Killen. 2000. "Wood". In: Nicholson and Shaw 2000, 334–371.

Galerie Antiker Kunst N. u. Dr. S. Simonian 1978. No title. *Apollo Sep-Oct.* [Advertisement]

Galil, J. and D. Eisikowitch. 1968. "On the pollination ecology of *Ficus sycomorus* in East Africa". *Ecology* 49 (2): 259–269.

——— 1974. "Further studies on pollination ecology in Ficus sycomorus ii. Pocket filling and emptying by Ceratosolen arabicus Mayr". *New Phytologist* 73: 515–528.

Galliano, Geneviève and Musée des beaux-arts. 2011. *Un jour j'achetai une momie. Émile Guimet et l'Égypte antique.* Paris: Hazan. Published in conjunction with the exhibition of the same name, shown at the Musée de Beaux Arts de Lyon, 30 March–2 July 2012.

Ganio, Monica, Johanna Salvant, Jane Williams, Lynn Lee, Oliver Cossairt and Marc Walton. 2015. "Investigating the use of Egyptian blue in Roman Egyptian portraits and panels from Tebtunis, Egypt". *Applied Physics A* 121: 813–821.

Gänsicke, Susanne. 2010. "The conservation of decorated organic Egyptian surfaces: a literature review". In: Dawson, Rozeik and Wright 2010, 66–77.

García-Fernández, Pablo, Miguel Moreno and Jose Antonio Aramburu. 2016. "Origin of the Anomalous Color of Egyptian and Han blue Historical Pigments: Going beyond the Complex Approximation in Ligand Field Theory". *Journal of Chemical Education* 93(1): 111–117.

Garstang, John. 1907. *The burial customs of ancient Egypt as illustrated by the tombs of the Middle Kingdom.* London: A. Constable & Co., Ltd.

Gasse, Annie. 1996. *Les sarcophages de la troisième* période *intermédiaire du Museo Gregoriano Egizio* (Aegyptiaca gregoriana; v. 3). Città del Vaticano: Monumenti, musei e gallerie pontificie.

Gauthier, Henri. 1927. *Dictionnaire des noms géographiques contenus dans les textes hiéroglyphiques* volume IV. Le Caire: L'Imprimerie de l'Institut français d'archéologie orientale pour la Société royale de géographie d'Égypte.

Geiger, T. and F. Michel. 2005. "Studies on the polysaccaride JunFunori used to consolidate matt paint". *Studies in Conservation* 50 (3): 193–204.

Germer, Renate. 1998. *Das Geheimnis der Mumien. Ewiges Leben am Nil.* München: Prestel.

——— 2004. "Wann, wie und warum begannen die Ägypter ihre Verstorbenen zu balsamieren?" *Sokar* 8 (1/2004): 18–19.

——— 2008. *Handbuch der altägyptischen Heilpflanzen.* Wiesbaden: Otto Harrassowitz.

Germer, Renate, Hannelore Kischkewitz and Meinhard Lüning. 2009. "Mumien der Grabung in Abusir el-Meleq". In: Kischkewitz, Germer and Lüning 2009, 179–190.

Germer, Renate, Thomas Nickol, Frank Schmidt and Walter Wilke. 1995. "Untersuchungen der altägyptischen Mumien des Ägyptischen Museums der Universität Leipzig und des Museums für Völkerkunde Leipzig". *Zeitschrift für Ägyptische Sprache und Altertumskunde* 122: 137–154.

Grajetzki, Wolfram. 2014. *Tomb treasures of the late Middle Kingdom. The archaeology of female burials.* Philadelphia: University of Pennsylvania Press.

Grothe-Paulin, E. 1988. "Der ägyptische Sarg in Helsinki". *Studia Orientalia (Helsinki, The Finnish Oriental Society)* 64: 7–75.

Grosser, Dietger. 1977. *Die Hölzer Mitteleuropas. Ein mikrophotographischer Lehratlas.* Berlin Heidelberg: Springer-Verlag.

Guilhou, Nadine and Annie Perraud. 2010. *Le sarcophage du muséum d'Histoire naturelle de Perpignan. La momie de Ioufenkhonsou, Jw=f-n-Hnsw.* Sant-Estève: Presses Littéraires.

Güney, A., D. Kerr, A.Sökücü, R. Zimmermann and M. Küppers. 2015. "Cambial activity and xylogenesis in stems of *Cedrus libani* A. Rich at different altitudes". *Botanical Studies* 6: 1–10.

Guzzon, E. 2017. "The wooden coffins of the late Third Intermediate Period and Late period found by Schiaparelli in the Valley of the Queens (QV43 and QV44)". In: Amenta and Guichard 2017, 191–198.

Győry, Hedvig 2006. "On the Collars of the Gamhud Coffins". *Bulletin de musée hongrois des Beaux-Arts* 101: 7–30.

el-Hadidi, Nesrin M.N. 2015. "Changing research trends in the field of archaeological wood at the Conservation Department, Faculty of Archaeology, Cairo University". *Studies in Conservation* 60: 143–154.

Hannig, Rainer. 2006. *Die Sprache der Pharaonen. Großes Handwörterbuch Ägyptisch-Deutsch (2800 bis 950 v. Chr.).* 4th edition. Mainz am Rhein: Verlag Philipp von Zabern.

van Harlem, Willem M. 1995. *Corpus Antiquitatum Aegyptiacarum. Fascicle III.* Amsterdam: Allard Pierson Museum.

Haslauer, Elfriede 2013. "Teilkartonage an Mumien aus Gamhud in der Ägyptischen Sammlung des Kunsthistorischen Museum, Wien". In: *Florilegium Aegyptiacum – Eine wissenschaftliche Blütenlese von Schülern und Freunden für Helmut Satzinger zum 75. Geburtstag am 21. Jänner 2013, GM Beihefte* 14, edited by Roman Gundacker, Julia Budka and Gabriele Pieke, 125–144. Göttingen: Seminar für Ägyptologie und Koptologie der Georg-August-Universität.

Haslauer, Elfriede and Roswitha Egner. 2009. *Särge des Dritten Zwischenzeit II. Corpus Antiquitatum Aegyptiacarum. Kunsthistorisches Museum Wien, Lieferung 12.* Mainz am Rhein: Verlag Philipp von Zabern.

Hassan, Selim. 1941. *Excavations at Gîza III (1931–1932).* Cairo: Faculty of Arts, Fouad I University.

Hatton, G.D., A. Shortland and M. Tite. 2008. "The production technology of Egyptian blue and green frits from second millennium BC Egypt and Mesopotamia". *Journal of Archaeological Science* 35: 1591–1604.

Hayes, William C. 1978. *The Scepter of Egypt. A Background for the Study of the Egyptian Antiquities in the Metropolitan Museum of Art. Volume I: From the Earliest Times to the End of the Middle Kingdom.* New York: Harper & Brothers, in co-operation with the Metropolitan Museum of Art.

——— 1959. *The Scepter of Egypt. A Background for the Study of the Egyptian Antiquities in the Metropolitan Museum of Art. Volume II: The Hyksos Period and the New Kingdom (1675–1080 B.C.).* New York: Harvard University Press.

Heyne, A. 1998. "Die Szene mit der Kuh auf Särgen der 21. Dynastie". In: *Ein ägyptisches Glasperlenspiel. Ägyptologische Beiträge für Erik Hornung aus seinem Schülerkreis,* edited by Andreas Brodbeck, 57–68. Berlin: Gebr. Mann.

Hollis, S.T. 1987. "The cartonnage case of Pa-di-mut Harvard Semitic Museum 2230". In: *Working with no data: Semitic and Egyptian studies presented to Thomas O. Lambdin,* edited by David M. Golomb, 165–179. Winona Lake, Indiana: Eisenbrauns.

Horie, C.V. 1987. *Materials for conservation. Organic consolidants, adhesives and coatings.* London: Butterworths.

Hornung, Erik. 1982. *Der ägyptische Mythos von der Himmelskuh. Eine Ätiologie des Unvollkommenen* (Orbis Biblicus et Orientalis 46). Freiburg: Universitätsverlag Freiburg.

——— 1984. "Der ägyptische Sarg im Heimatmuseum Appenzell". *Innerrhoder Geschichtsfreund* 28: 31–39.

——— 1999. *The Ancient Egyptian Books of the Afterlife*. New York-Ithaca: Cornell University Press.

Hornung, Erik and Betsy M. Bryan (eds). 2002. *The Quest for Immortality: treasures of ancient Egypt*. Washington DC: National Gallery of Art. Published in conjunction with the exhibition of the same name, shown at the National Gallery of Art, 12 May – 2 September 2002.

Ikram, Salima and Aidan Dodson. 1998. *The Mummy in Ancient Egypt: Equipping the dead for eternity*. London: Thames and Hudson.

Ikram, Salima, Carlos Prates, Sandra Sousa and Carlos Oliveira. Forthcoming. "A medley of mummies from Deir el-Bahari". *Deir el-Bahari Studies* 2.

InsideWood. 2004 onwards. http://insidewood.lib.ncsu.edu/search (accessed 3/1/2017).

International Organisation for Standardisation. 1974. *ISO 1032:1974 Coniferous sawn timber; Sizes; Terms and definitions*. Geneva: ISO.

Jagiella, Christian and Harals Kürschner. 1987. *Atlas der Hölzer Saudi-Arabiens: Die Holzanatomie der Wichtigsten Bäume und Sträucher Arabiens mit einem holzanatomischen Bestimmungsschlüssel*. Wiesbaden: Reichert Verlag.

Jaksch, H., W. Seipel, K. Weiner and A. el-Goresy. 1983. "Egyptian blue – cuprorivaite. A window to ancient Egyptian technology". *Die Naturwissenschaften* 70: 525–535.

Jamen, France. 2016. *Le cercueil de Padikhonsou au musée des Beaux-Arts de Lyon (XXIe dynastie)*. Wiesbaden: Harrasowitz Verlag.

Jansen-Winkeln, Karl. 2007a. *Inschriften der Spätzeit, Teil I: die 21. Dynastie*. Wiesbaden: Harrasowitz Verlag.

——— 2007b. *Inschriften der Spätzeit, Teil II: die 22.-24. Dynastie*. Wiesbaden: Harrasowitz Verlag.

——— 2009. *Inschriften der Spätzeit, Teil III: die 25. Dynastie*. Wiesbaden: Harrasowitz Verlag.

——— 2017. "'Libyerzeit' oder 'Postimperiale Periode'? Zur historischen Einordnung der Dritten Zwischenzeit". In: Jurman, Bader and Aston 2017, 203–238.

Jiménez Serrano, Alejandro. 2011. "Das Projekt Qubbet el-Hawa der Universidad de Jaén (Spanien). Neue Annäherungen an die Bestattungssitten des alten Ägypten". In: *Zwischen den Welten. Grabfunde von Ägyptens Südgrenze*, edited by L.D. Morenz, M. Höveler-Müller and A. el-Hawary, 182–197. Rahden: Verlag Marie Leidorf.

——— 2013. "Los nobles de la VI Dinastía en Qubbet el-Hawa". In: *Séptimo Centenario de los Estudios Orientales en Salamanca* (Estudios filológicos 337), edited by Ana Agud, 29–37. Salamanca: Ediciones Universidad de Salamanca.

——— 2015. "A unique funerary complex in Qubbet el-Hawa for two governors of the late Twelfth Dynasty". In: Miniaci and Grajetzki 2015, 169–176.

Jiménez Serrano, Alejandro, Juan Luis Martínez de Dios and Juan Manuel Anguita Ordóñez 2008. "Proyecto Qubbet el-Hawa: La tumba nº 33. Primera campaña (2008)". *Boletín de la Asociación Española de Egiptología* 18: 35–60.

Jiménez Serrano, Alejandro, Juan Luis Martínez de Dios, Marta Valenti Costales, Francisco Vivas Fernández, Yolanda de la Torre Robles and Juan Manuel Anguita Ordóñez. 2009. "Proyecto Qubbet el-Hawa: Las tumbas nº 33, 34 y 34h. Segunda campaña (2009)". *Boletín de la Asociación Española de Egiptología* 19: 41–75.

Jiménez Serrano, Alejandro, Inmaculada Alemán Aguilera, Miguel Cecilio Botella López, Carolina Cardell Fernández, Juan Luis Martínez de Dios, María Cruz Medina Sánchez, Israel Mellado García, *et al.* 2010. "Proyecto Qubbet el-Hawa: las tumbas Nº 33, 34 y 34h. Tercera Campaña (2010)". *Boletín de la Asociación Española de Egiptología* 20: 65–98.

Jiménez Serrano, Alejandro, Marta Valenti Costales, Juan Luis Martínez de Dios, Mª Luisa Gónzalez García, Yolanda De La Torre Robles, Teresa López-Obregón Silvestre, Linda Chapón, José M. Alba. "Cuarta campaña (2012) de excavaciones en las tumbas 33 y 34 de la necrópolis de Qubbet el-Hawa (Asuán, Egipto)". *Informes y trabajos* 9 (Excavaciones en el exterior 2011): 102–123.

Jiménez Serrano, Alejandro, Inmaculada Alemán Aguilera, Miguel Botella López, Catalina Calero, Linda Chapón, Luisa García González, Teresa López-Obregón Silvestre *et al.* 2013. "Proyecto Qubbet el-Hawa: las tumbas 31 (Sarenput), 33 y 34. Quinta Campaña". *Boletín de la Asociación Española de Egiptología* 22: 7–85.

Jiménez Serrano, Alejandro, Juan Luis Martínez de Dios, Yolanda De La Torre Robles, Vicente Barba Colmenero, Martina Bardonova, Eva Montes, Luisa M. García González, *et al.* 2014. "Proyecto Qubbet el-Hawa: Las tumbas 33, 34aa y QH34bb. Sexta campaña (2014)". *Boletín de la Asociación Española de Egiptología* 23: 7–48.

Jiménez Serrano, Alejandro and J.C. Sánchez León. 2015a. "A forgotten governor of Elephantine during the Twelfth Dynasty: Ameny". *Journal of Egyptian Archaeology* 101: 117–130.

——— 2015b. "Sattjeni: Daughter, Wife and Mother of the Governors of Elephantine during the End of the Twelfth Dynasty". *Zeitschrift für Ägyptische Sprache und Altertumskunde* 142: 154–166.

Johnson-McDaniel, Darrah and Tina T. Salguero. 2014. "Exfoliation of Egyptian blue and Han blue, two alkali earth copper silicate-based pigments". *Journal of Visualized Experiments* 3791(86), 51686. doi:10.3791/51686.

Jones, Dilwyn. 2000. *An index of ancient Egyptian titles, epithets and phrases of the Old Kingdom* (BAR International Series 866). Oxford: Archaeopress.

Jones, Jana, Thomas F.G. Higham, Ron Oldfield, Terry P. O'Connor and Stephen A. Buckley. 2014. "Evidence for Prehistoric Origins of Egyptian Mummification in Late Neolithic Burials". *PLoS ONE* 9(8): e103608. https://doi.org/10.1371/journal.pone.0103608 (accessed 22 March 2018).

Jurman, Claus, Bettina Bader and David Aston (eds). 2017. *A true scribe of Abydos: essays on First Millennium Egypt in honour of Anthony Leahy* (Orientalia Lovaniensia analecta 265), 445–490. Leuven: Peeters.

Kamal, Ahmed. 1902. "Fouilles à Deir-el-Barsheh". *Annales du service des antiquités de l'Egypte* 2: 14–43.

——— 1908. "Fouilles à Gamhoud". *Annales du service des antiquités de l'Egypte* 9: 8–30.

Kamal, Moharram. 1938. "Gift of His Majesty King Farouk 1st (1937) to the Egyptian Museum". *Annales du service des antiquités de l'Egypte* 38: 1–20.

Kanawati, Naguib. 1989. *The rock tombs of El-Hawawish. The cemetery of Akhmim.* Volume 9. Sydney: Australian Centre for Egyptology.

Kariya, Hiroko, Lisa Bruno, Jakki Godfrey and Tina March. 2010. "Treatment of a Dynasty 18 painted coffin, 37.47Ea-e (Abbott Collection 405A)". In: Dawson, Rozeik and Wright 2010, 97–105.

Karlstrom, Ann Heath and Henrik Kam. 2013. *Legion of Honor: Inside and Out.* San Francisco: Fine Arts Museums of San Francisco.

Karner, S., N.C. Schellmann, A. Schäning, W. Baatz. 2015. "Die Konservierung und Restaurierung des Sargdeckels der But-har-chonsu, Teil 1: Ein dreidimensionales Puzzle". In: *Ein ägyptisches Puzzle*, edited by S. Haag and R. Hölzl, 27–37. Wien: Kunsthistorisches Museum.

Killen, Geoffrey. 1994. *Egyptian Wood Working and Furniture.* Princes Risborough: Shire Publications Ltd.

Kischkewitz, Hannelore, Renate Germer and Meinhard Lüning. 2009. *Berliner Mumiengeschichten: Ergebnisse eines multidisziplinären Forschungsprojektes.* Berlin: Schnell & Steiner.

Kitchen, Kenneth A. 1973. *The Third Intermediate Period in Egypt (1100–650 B.C.).* Warminster: Aris and Phillips Ltd.

——— 1990. *Catalogue of the Egyptian Collection in the National Museum, Rio de Janeiro.* Warminster: Aris & Phillips.

Koch, Carola. 2012. *"Die den Amun mit ihrer Stimme zufriedenstellen": Gottesgemahlinnen und Musikerinnen im thebanischen Amunstaat von der 22. bis zur 26. Dynastie* (Studien zu den Ritualszenen altägyptischer Tempel 27). Dettelbach: J.H.Röll Verlag.

Koefoed-Petersen, Otto. 1951. *Catalogue des sarcophages et cercueils égyptiens.* Copenhague: [Bianco Lunos Bogtrykkeri].

Kondo, Jiro, Michinori Ohshiro and Tadashi Kikugawa (eds). 2004. *The Gateway to Ancient Egypt through the Kikugawa Egyptian Collection in Japan.* Tokyo: Bungeisha.

Kong, J. and S. Yu. 2007. "Fourier transform infrared spectroscopic analysis of protein secondary structures". *Acta Biochimica et Biophysica Sinica* 39(8): 549–559.

Koss, A. and J. Marczak. 2015. *Lasers in Conservation of Artworks and Monuments. Principles, Exploitation and Safety.* Warsaw: Institute of Conservation and Restoration of Works of Art. Academy of Fine Arts, Warsaw.

Kóthay, Katalin Anna (ed.) 2012a. *Art and Society: Ancient and Modern Contexts of Egyptian Art. Proceedings of the International Conference held at the Museum of Fine Arts, Budapest, 13–15 May 2010.* Budapest: Museum of Fine Arts.

——— 2012b. "The Gamhud Artisans". In: Kóthay 2012a: 235–256.

Kóthay, Katalin Anna and Éva Liptay, 2010. *Egyptian Artefacts of the Museum of Fine Arts, Budapest*, Budapest, 2010.

Kueny, Gabrielle and Jean Yoyotte. 1979. *Grenoble, musée des Beaux-Arts. Collection égyptienne*, Paris: Réunion des musées nationaux.

Küffer, Alexandra. 2007. "Aus dem Museumsshop von Kairo: Sarg mit Mumie einer anonymen Person im Museum für Völkerkunde Burgdorf". In: Küffer and Siegmann 2007, 176–182.

Küffer, Alexandra and Marc Renfer. 1996. *Das Sargensemble einer Noblen aus Theben.* Bern: Bernisches Historisches Museum.

Küffer, Alexandra and Renate Siegmann. 2007. *Unter dem Schutz der Himmelsgöttin: Ägyptische Särge, Mumien und Masken in der Schweiz.* Zürich: Chronos.

Kurth, Dieter. 2010. *A Ptolemaic sign-list. Hieroglyphs used in the temples of the Graeco-Roman period of Egypt and their meanings.* Hützel: Backe-Verlag.

Kyalangalilwa, B., J.S. Boatwright, B.H. Daru, O. Maurin and M. van der Bank. 2013 "Phylogenetic position and revised classification of Acacia s.l. (Fabaceae: Mimosoideae) in Africa, including new combinations in *Vachellia* and *Senegalia*". *Botanical Journal of the Linnean Society* 172: 500–523.

Lacau, P. (1906). *Catalogue general des antiquités égyptiennes du Musée Du Caire: Sarcophages antérieurs au Nouvel Empire (Nos 28087–28126).* Le Caire: L'Imprimerie de l'Institut français d'archéologie orientale.

Lacovara, Peter, Selima Ikram, Bob Brier, Margaret Leveque and Renée Stein. 2015. "An Egyptian Mummy of the Late Old Kingdom in the Michael C. Carlos Museum, Emory University". *Journal of the American Research Center in Egypt* 51: 65–74.

Lakomy, Konstantin C. 2016. *"Der Löwe auf dem Schlachtfeld": das Grab KV 36 und die Bestattung des Maiherperi im Tal der Könige.* Wiesbaden: Dr. Ludwig Reichert Verlag.

Lavrentyeva, Nika V. 2015. "The Coffin of the Priestess of Amun Ius-ankh in the Collection of the Pushkin State Museum of Fine Arts (I.1.a.6800)". In: *Peterburgskie egiptologičeskie čtenija. 2013–2014* (Trudy Gosudarstvennogo Ermitaža 76), 107–121, pl. VI–X. [In Russian]

Lee, Lorna and Stephen Quirke. 2000. "Painting materials". In: Nicholson and Shaw 2000, 104–120.

Leemans, Conradus. 1867. *Monumens égyptiens du Musée d'Antiquités des Pays-Bas à Leide. IIIe partie. Monumens funéraires. M. Momies et cercueils de momie, fasc. 4, fasc. 6.* Leiden: H.W. Hazenberg.

Lefebvre, Gustave. 1920. "Le tombeau de Petosiris». *Annales du service des antiquités de l'Egypte* 20: 41–121.

——— 1923. *Le tombeau de Petosiris. Deuxième partie: les textes.* Le Caire: Publications du Service des Antiquités de l'Egypte.

——— 1924. *Le tombeau de Petosiris. Première partie: description.* Le Caire: Publications du Service des Antiquités de l'Egypte.

Leitz, Christian 2011. *Der Sarg des Panehemisis in Wien* (Studien zur spätägyptischen Religion 3). Wiesbaden: Harrassowitz.

Limme, L. 2009. "Cercueil d'Irethorerou". In: *Antiquités Égyptiennes au Musée Royal de Mariemont,* edited by Claire Derriks and Luc Delvaux, 351–355. Morlanwelz: Musée royal de Mariemont.

Lipke, P. and Ahmed Y. Moustafa. 1984. *The Royal Ship of Cheops: A retrospective account of the discovery, restoration and reconstruction. Based on interviews with Hag Ahmed Youssef Moustafa* (British Archaeological Reports Internationl Series 225). Oxford: B.A.R.

Liptay, Eva. 1992. "Deux fragments de cercueil de la XXIème dynastie». *Bulletin du Musée Hongrois des Beaux-Arts* 76: 3–13.

——— 2000. "Fragment du cercueil d'un prêtre d'Amon de Thèbes de la XXIème dynastie». *Bulletin du Musée Hongrois des Beaux-Arts* 92–93: 7–22.

——— 2002. "Bandeau sur la tête. Aspects religieux d'un motif iconographique de la 21e dynastie». *Bulletin du Musée Hongrois des Beaux-Arts* 96: 7–30.

——— 2003. "Between heaven and earth. The motif of the cow coming out of the mountain". *Bulletin du Musée Hongrois des Beaux-Arts* 99: 11–30.

——— 2008. "*'My face is (that of) Ra'* 1. The inner decoration of a Twenty-First Dynasty Coffin in Budapest". *Bulletin du Musée Hongrois des Beaux-Arts* 108–109: 11–13.

——— 2011. *Coffins and Coffin Fragments of the Third Intermediate Period.* Budapest: Museum of Fine Art.

Lipińska, Jadwiga. 1977. *The Temple of Tuthmosis III. Architecture (Deir el-Bahari).* Warsaw: PWN-Éditions Scientifiques de Pologne.

López-Grande, Maria J. 2016. "Cerámicas halladas en la tumba QH33 de Qubbet el-Hawa. Estudio preliminar de recipientes del Tercer Periodo Intermedio y de los Periodos Saíta y Persa". *Boletín de la Asociación Española de Egiptología* 25: 113–141.

López-Grande, Maria J. and Marta Valenti Costales. 2008. "Qubbet el-Hawa (Asuán). Recipientes cerámicos con decoraciones incisas y plásticas hallados en el patio de la tumba QH33". *Boletín de la Asociación Española de Egiptología* 18: 111–135.

Louis, M. and S. Joigneau. 2007. *Rapport de restauration, Ensemble funéraire de Tanetmit.* Unpublished report.

Lucas, A. 1962. *Ancient Egyptian Materials and Industries.* 4th edition, revised by J.R. Harris. London: Edward Arnold.

Lüddeckens, Erich, H.J. Thissen, W. Brunsch, G. Vittmann and K.Th. Zauzich. 1980–2000. *Demotisches Namenbuch.* 18 fascicles. Wiesbaden: Reichert.

Lüscher, Barbara. 1990. *Untersuchungen zu ägyptischen Kanopenkästen: vom Alten Reich bis zum Ende der Zweiten Zwischenzeit* (Hildesheimer Ägyptologische Beiträge B 31). Hildesheim: Gerstenberg Verlag.

Mace, Arthur C. and Herbert E. Winlock. 1916. *The Tomb of Senebtisi at Lisht* (Publications of the Metropolitan Museum of Art Egyptian expedition vol. 1). New York: The Gilliss Press.

Malzbender, T., D. Gelb, and H. Wolters, 2001. "Polynomial Texture Maps". In: *SIGGRAPH '01 Proceedings of the 28th annual conference on computer graphics and interactive techniques*, 519–528. New York: ACM.

Mansi, S., F. Zenucchini, P. Croveri and F. Spagnoli. Forthcoming. "Pulitura laser della cassetta porta-ushabti (Cat.2441) del Museo Egizio di Torino". In: *Aplar 6: Applicazioni Laser nel restauro* (Proceedings of conference held in Firenze 14–16 September 2017). Abstract of paper available at www.apla.eu/pdfs/libro_abstracts_APLAR_6.pdf .

Marini, Paolo. 2012. "I contenitori di *ushabti* dei musei italiani". *Egitto e Vicino Oriente* 35: 83–124.

Martínez de Dios, Jan Luis and Yolanda de la Torre Robles. 2018. "La cámara funeraria principal de la tumba QH33. Campaña 2018". In: Alejandro Jiménez Serrano *et al.* 2018. "La décima campaña (2018) del Proyecto Qubbet el-Hawa: los trabajos arqueológicos de las tumbas QH32, QH33, QH34bb, QH35n, QH35p y QH36". *Boletín de la Asociación Española de Egiptología* 27. (In preparation).

Maspero, Gaston. 1887. "Rapport à l'Institut Égyptien sur les Fouilles et travaux exécutés en Égypte pendant l'hiver de 1885–1886". *Bulletin de l'Institut Égyptien. 2nd Series* 7: 196–251.

——— 1889. *Catalogue du Musée égyptien de Marseille.* Paris, Imprimerie Nationale.

——— 1893. *Guide du Visiteur au Musée de Boulaq.* Boulaq: [Au Musée].

——— 1894. *Guide du Visiteur au Musée de Boulaq.* Paris: [unknown].

Maspero, Gaston and Henri Gauthier. 1939. *Catalogue général des antiquités égyptiennes du Musée du Caire: Sarcophages des époques persane et ptolemaïque (CG 29307–29323).* Le Caire: L'Imprimerie de l'Institut français d'archéologie orientale.

Mazzi, F. and A. Pabst. 1962. "Reexamination of cuprorivaite". *American Mineralogist* 47: 409–411.

Meffre, Raphaële. 2012a. "Cercueil momiforme intérieur d'Ânkhemmaât». In: Perdu 2012, 160–161.

——— 2012b. "Parure de cartonnage d'Ânkhemmaât». In: Perdu 2012, 162–163.

——— 2012c. "Coffret à viscères d'Ânkhemmaât». In: Perdu 2012, 164–165.

——— 2015. *D'Héracléopolis à Hermopolis. La Moyenne Égypte durant la Troisième Période intermédiaire (XXIe-XXIVe dynasties).* Paris: Presses Université Paris-Sorbonne.

Meiggs, Russell. 1982. *Trees and Timber in the Ancient Mediterranean World.* Oxford: Clarendon Press.

Mekis, T. 2015. *Hypocephali.* Dissertation: Budapest, Eötvös Loránd University.

Menegazzi, Alessandra, Nicola Carrara and Susanna Moser. 2013. "Le collezioni egittologiche dei Musei dell'Università degli Studi di Padova". In: *Egittologia a Palazzo Nuovo. Studi e ricerche dell'Università di Torino* (Studi e ricerche storiche (Novi Ligure, Italy)), edited by Paolo Gallo, 219–236. Novi Ligure: Epoké.

Mery, D. (2015). *Computer vision for X-ray testing, imaging, systems, image databases and algorithms.* Springer International Publishing Switzerland. DOI 10.1007/978-3-319-20747-6.

Michel, F. 2011. "Funori and JunFunori: two related consolidants with surprising properties". *Proceedings of the CCI Symposium ICC Adhesives and Consolidants for Conservation: Research and Applications.* Ottawa, Canada. www.cci-ic .gc.ca.

Miniaci, Gianluca and Wolfram Grajetzki (eds). 2015. *The world of Middle Kingdom Egypt (2000–1550 BC)* (Middle Kingdom Studies 1). London: Golden House Publications.

Misihah, Hishmat and Muhammad 'Abd al-Tawwab Hittah. 1979. *Mallawi Antiquities Museum: a brief description.* Cairo: General Organization for G.P.O.s.

Moiso, B. 2008. "Le campagne di scavo di Ernesto Schiaparelli in Egitto dal 1903 al 1920". In: *Ernesto Schiaparelli e la tomba di Kha,* edited by B. Moiso, 199–270. Torino: AdArte.

Möller, Georg. 1901. "Das *Hb-śd* des Osiris nach Sargdarstellungen des neuen Reiches". *Zeitschrift für Ägyptische Sprache und Altertumskunde* 39: 71–74.

Morenz, Siegfried. 1957. "Das Werden zu Osiris. Die Darstellungen auf einem Leinentuch der römischen Kaiserzeit (Berlin 11651) und verwandten Stücken". *Forschungen und Berichte* 1: 52–70.

de Morgan, Jacques. 1894. *Catalogue des monuments et inscriptions de l'Egypte Antique. Series 1. Haute Egypte. Volume 1. De la frontière de Nubie à Kom Ombos.* Vienna: Adolphe Holzhausen.

Moser, Susanna. 2009/2010. *Un sarcofago ligneo del Museo di Antropologia dell'Università di Padova*. Unpublished essay, Università degli Studi di Torino, A.A.

——— 2013. "Sarcofago del sacerdote di Khonsu Padiamon". In: Crevatin and Vidulli Torlo 2013.

Moussa, Ahmed and Hartwig Altenmüller. 1971. *The Tomb of Nefer and Ka-hay* (Ägyptologische Abhandlungen 5). Mainz am Rhein: Verlag Philipp von Zabern.

Müller, H.W. 1940. *Die Felsengräber der Fürsten von Elephantine aus der Zeit des Mittleren Reiches*. Glückstadt: J.J. Augustin.

Müller, Matthias. 2009. "The 'el-Hibeh'-archive: introduction and preliminary information". In: Broekman, Demarée and Kaper 2009, 251–264.

Munro, Irmtraut. 2009. *Der Totenbuch-Papyrus der Ta-schep-en-Chonsu aus der späten 25. Dynastie (pMoskau Puschkin-Museum I, 1b, 121)*. Weisbaden: Harrassowitz Verlag.

Murray, Margaret Alice. 1910. *The Tomb of Two Brothers* (Manchester Museum Handbooks. Publication 68). Manchester/London: Sherratt & Hughes/Dulau & Co.

——— 1949. *The Splendour that was Egypt*. London: Sidgwick and Jackson Limited.

Museum of Fine Arts, Boston. 1982. "Egyptian and Ancient Near Eastern Art". *The Museum Year: Annual Report of the Museum of Fine Arts, Boston* 106, 26–27. Boston: Museum of Fine Arts.

Musso, Simone and Simone Petacchi. 2014. "The inner coffin of Tameramun: a unique masterpiece of Kushite iconography from Thebes". In: Pischikova, Budka and Griffin 2014, 441–452.

Mysliwiec, Karol (ed.) 2008. *Saqqara III, The Upper Necropolis, Part II: Studies and photographic documentation*. Warsaw: Editions Neriton.

Le mythe Cléopâtre. 2014. Paris: Éditions Pinacothèque de Paris: Éditions Gourcuff Gradenigo. Published in conjunction with the exhibition of the same name, shown at the Pinacothèque de Paris, 10 April 2014–7 September 2014.

Nagy, István. 1999. *Guide to the Egyptian Collection (Collections of the Museum of Fine Arts, 2. The Egyptian Collection)*. Budapest: Museum of Fine Arts.

Nervo, M. (ed.). 2013. *Cronache 4: Il Progetto neu_ART. Studi e applicazioni / Neutron and X-ray tomography and imaging for cultural heritage*. Torino: Editris.

Neumann, Katarina, Werner Schoch, Pierre Détienne and Fritz H. Schweingruber. 2001. *Woods of the Sahara and the Sahel. An anatomical atlas*. Bern: Verlag Paul Haupt.

Newman, R. 2015. "Technology". In: *A Companion to Ancient Egyptian Art,* edited by Melinda K. Hartwig, 505–520. Chicester: Wiley-Blackwell.

Nicola, Marco, Maurizio Aceto, Vincenzo Gheroldi, Roberto Gobetto and Giacomo Chiari. 2018. "Egyptian blue in the Castelseprio mural painting cycle. Imaging and evidence of a non-traditional manufacture". *Journal of Archaeological Science: Reports* 19: 465–475.

Nicholson, Paul T. and Ian Shaw. 2000 (eds). *Ancient Egyptian materials and technology*. Cambridge: Cambridge University Press. [Reprinted in 2009].

Niknami, Kamal Aldin and Zahra Mirashe. 2007. "3D Tools for Scientific Visualization and Documentation of Archaeological Heritage Case Study: A Sassanid Shrine of Daregaz, Northeastern Iran". In: *Proceedings of the XXI International CIPA 2007: antiCIPAting the future of the cultural past: Zappeion Megaron, Athens, Greece 01–06 October 2007*, edited by Andreas Georgopoulos. Published online: http://www.isprs.org/proceedings/XXXVI/5-C53/papers/FP106.pdf (accessed 18 May 2018).

Niwiński, Andrzej. 1981. "Untersuchungen zur religiösen Ikonographie der 21. Dynastie (1). Towards the religious iconography of the 21st Dynasty". *Göttinger Miszellen* 49: 47–59.

——— 1984. "Sarg-, NR-SpZt". In: *LÄ* 5, 434–468.

——— 1986 "Cercueil de prêtre égyptien à l'Université Jagellonne". *Bulletin de l'Institut Français d'Archéologie Orientale, Caire* 86: 257–266, pl. XXXVII–XXXVIII.

——— 1988a. *21st Dynasty Coffins from Thebes: Chronological and Typological Studies. Theben 5*. Mainz am Rhein: Verlag Philipp von Zabern.

——— 1988c. "Relativity in iconography. Changes in the shape and value of some Egyptian funerary symbols dependent upon their date and authorship". In: *Funerary symbols and religion. Essays dedicated to Professor M.S.H.G Heerma van Voss*, edited by Jacques H. Kamstra, Hellmuth Milde and Kees Wagtendonk, 96–104. Kampen: Kok.

——— 1989a *Studies on the Illustrated Theban Funerary Papyri of the 11th and 10th Centuries B.C.* (Orbis Biblicus et Orietnalis 86). Freiburg: Universitätsverlag Freiburg.

——— 1989b. "The Solar-Osirian Unity as Principle of the 'State of Amun' in Thebes in the 21st Dynasty". *Jaarbericht van het Vooraziatisch-Egyptisch Genootschap "Ex Oriente Lux"* 30: 89–106.

——— 1989c. "Untersuchungen zur religiösen Ikonographie der 21. Dynastie (3). Mummy in the Coffin as the central element of iconographic reflection on the theology of the 21st Dynasty in Thebes". *Göttinger Miszellen* 109: 53–66.

——— 1990. "The 21st Dynasty religious iconography project: a task for the Egyptology in the Nineties. Exemplified by the Scene with Three Deities Standing on a Serpent". In: *Akten des Vierten Internationalen Ägyptologen-Kongress, München 1985, volume 3,* edited by Sylvia Schoske, 305–314. Hamburg: Helmut Buske.

——— 1995. "Le passage de la XXe à la XXIIe dynastie. Chronologie et histoire politique". *Bulletin de l'Institut Français d'archéologie orientale* 95: 329–360.

——— 1996a. *Sarcophages et cercueils dans le Musée d'Archéologie à Marseille*. Warsaw. Unpublished manuscript.

——— 1996b. *Catalogue général des antiquités égyptiennes du Musée du Caire. La seconde trouvaille de Deir el-Bahari (Sarcophages). (CG 6029–6068).* Le Caire: Supreme Council for Antiquities.

——— 1996c. "Les périodes *whm mswt* dans l'histoire de l'Égypte: un essai comparative". *Bulletin de la Société française d'égyptologie* 136: 5–26.

——— 1996d. "Coffins from the Tomb of Iurudef – A Reconsideration. The Problem of Some Crude Coffins from the Memphite area and the Middle Egypt". *Bibliotheca Orientalis* 53 No. 3/4: 324–363.

——— 1999. *Catalogue général des antiquités égyptiennes du Musée du Caire. The Second Find of Deir el-Bahari (Coffins). (CG 6069–6082)*. Le Caire; Supreme Council for Antiquities.

——— 2000. "Iconography of the 21st dynasty: its main features, levels of attestation, the media and their diffusion". In: *Images as media. Sources for the cultural history of the Near East and the Eastern Mediterranean (1st millennium BCE)* (Orbis Biblicus et Orientalis 175), edited by Christoph Uehlinger, 21–43. Fribourg: University Press Fribourg.

——— 2004. *Sarcofagi della XXI Dinastia (CGT 10101–10122). Catalogo del Museo Egizio di Torino, Serie Seconda, Collezioni, volume 9*. Torino: Ministero per i Beni e le Attività Culturali, soprintendenza al Museo delle Antichità Egizie.

——— 2006a. "The *Book of the Dead* on the Coffins of the 21st Dynasty". In: *Totenbuch-Forschungen.Gesammelte Beiträge des 2. Internationalen Totenbuch-Symposiums, Bonn 25. bis 29. September 2005* (Studien zum Altägyptischen Totenbuch 11), edited by Burkhard Backes, Irmtraut Munro, Simone Stöhr, 245–271. Wiesbaden: Otto Harrassowitz.

——— 2006b. "Fragments of the Early 22nd Dynasty inner Coffin of the Theban Priest of Amun, Nesy-pauty-tauy". In: Sowada and Ockinga 2006, 169–177.

——— 2007. "Coffin for so-called Ankhefenkhonsu". In: *Théby – město bohů a faraonů = Thebes – City of Gods and Pharaohs*, edited by Jana Mynářová and Pavel Onderka, 293–296. Praha: Národní museum.

——— 2008. "Les plus beaux cercueils de l'histoire". *Égypte, Afrique & Orient* 48: 29–38.

——— 2009. "The so-called Chapters BD 141–142 and 148 on the Coffins of the 21st Dynasty from Thebes, with Some Remarks concerning the Funerary Papyri of the Period". In: *Ausgestattet mit den Schriften des Thot. Festschrift für Irmtraut Munro zu ihrem 65. Geburtstag* (Studien zum Altägyptischen Totenbuch 14), edited by Burkhard Backes, Marcus Müller-Roth, Simone Stöhr, 133–162. Wiesbaden: Otto Harrassowitz.

——— 2011. "The Coffin as the Universe: Cosmological Scenes on the Twenty-first Dynasty Coffins". In: *Studies on Religion: Seeking Origins and Manifestations of Religion* (Acta Archaeologica Pultuskiensia III), edited by Joanna Popielska-Grzybowska and Jadwiga Iwaszczuk, 107–110, 187–203. Pułtusk: Pultusk Academy of Humanities.

——— 2014. "The Coffin of a Theban Priest of the Late 10th Century B.C. (early 22nd Dynasty)". In: *Ancient Egypt. The Collection of the Latvian National Museum of Art, Riga*, edited by Baiba Uburĝe and Carolin Johansson, 113–157. Riga: Latvian National Museum of Art.

——— 2017a. "The 21st Dynasty coffins of non-Theban origin. A 'family' for the Vatican coffin of Anet". In: *Proceedings of the First Vatican Coffin Conference, 19–22 June 2013*. Città del Vaticano: Edizioni Musei Vaticani.

——— 2017b".The mystery of the 'high place' from the Abbott papyrus revealed? The results of the works of the Polish Cliff Mission at Deir el-Bahari 1999–2014". In: *Proceedings of the XI International Congress of Egyptologists, Florence Egyptian Museum, Florence, 23–30 August 2015*, edited by Gloria Rosati and Maria Cristina Guidotti, 457–461.

——— 2018. "The decoration of the coffin as theological expression of the idea of the universe". In: *Ancient Egyptian Coffins: craft traditions and functionality, the proceedings of an international colloquium held at the British Museum in 2014*, edited by John H. Taylor and Marie Vandenbeusch. Leuven: Peeters.

——— Forthcoming 1. "History of the *ḏsrw*-area in Western Thebes – the outline of the change of the sacred landscape of Deir el-Bahari throughout the antiquity". To be published in: *Proceedings of the International Conference "At the dawn of Russian Egyptology, 1–3 February 2016, Moscow"*.

——— Forthcoming 2. "Le paysage sacré de Deir el-Bahari – quelques remarques sur une scène bien connue des cercueils de la 21e dynastie". To be published in *Égypte, Afrique & Orient*.

——— Forthcoming 3. "The newly documented treasure of the 21st Dynasty coffins and fragments of these in the basement of the Egyptian Museum, Cairo". To be published in: R. Sousa (ed.), Proceedings of the Conference "Bab el-Gasus in Context. Egyptian Funerary Culture during the 21st Dynasty", Lisbon, 19–20 September 2016,

Odegaard, Nancy, Werner S. Zimmt and Scott Carroll. 2005. *Material characterization tests for objects of art and archaeology*, 2nd edition. London: Archetype Publications.

Oleari, C. 2008. *Misurare il colore*. Florence: Hoepli.

Oppenheim, Adela. 2015. "Temples: Secluded Domains for Kings and Gods". In: *Ancient Egypt Transformed. The Middle Kingdom*, edited by Adela Oppenheim, Dorothea Arnold, Dieter Arnold and Kei Yamamoto, 270–293. New York: The Metropolitan Museum of Art.

Pagès-Camagna, Sandrine and Sylvie Colinart. 2003. "The Egyptian green pigment: its manufacturing process and links to Egyptian Blue". *Archaeometry* 45 (4): 637–658.

Pagès-Camagna, Sandrine and Hélène Guichard. 2010. "Egyptian colours and pigments in French collections: 30 years of physicochemical analyses on 300 objects". In: Dawson, Rozeik and Wright 2010, 25–31.

Pagès-Camagna, Sandrine and J. Langlois. 2007. *Rapport d'étude C2RMF/R 7877b, Cuve du cercueil extérieur de Tanetmit, Bois polychromé, N 2588*. Unpublished report.

Pagès-Camagna, Sandrine and D. Vigears. 2006. *Rapport d'étude C2RMF/R, Couvercle du cercueil extérieur de Tanetmit, bois polychromé, N 2588*. Unpublished report.

Paleological Association of Japan, Inc., Egyptian Committee, Akoris. 1995. *Report of the Excavations at Akoris in Middle Egypt 1981–1992*. Kyoto: Koyo Shobo.

Parkes, Phil and David Watkinson. 2010. "Computed tomography and X-radiography of a coffin from Dynasty 21/22". In: Dawson, Rozeik and Wright 2010, 58–66.

Payraudeau, F. 2003. "La désignation du gouverneur de Thèbes aux époques libyenne et éthiopienne". *Revue d'Egyptologie* 54: 131–153.

——— 2005. "Ioufâa, un gouverneur de Thèbes sous la XXIIe dynastie". *Bulletin de l'Institut Français d'archéologie orientale* 105: 197–210.

——— 2014. *Administration, société et pouvoir à Thèbes sous la XXIIe dynastie, Vol. I* (Bibliothèque d'Etude 160). Cairo: Institut Français d'archéologie orientale.

Perdu, Olivier (ed.) 2012. *Le Crépuscule des Pharaons, Chefs-d'oeuvre des dernières dynasties égyptiennes*. Bruxelles: Fonds Mercator.

Pesi, L. 2008. "Sarcofagi antropoidi a vernice nera nel Museo Egizio di Firenze". In: *Egittologia e giovani studiosi: atti del 2° convegno in onore di Evaristo Breccia, Civiltà Egiziana e Giovani Studiosi", Offagna, Biblioteca Comunale, 12 dicembre 2003*, 41–60. Offagna: Comune di Offagna.

Petrie, W.M.F. 1890. *Kahun, Gurob, and Hawara*. London: K. Paul, Trench, Trübner and Co.

——— 1891. *Illahun, Kahun and Gurob 1889–1890*. London: David Nutt.

Petrie, W.M.F. and Guy Brunton. 1924. *Sedment II* (British School of Archaeology in Egypt 35). London: Bernard Quaritch.

Pischikova, Elena, Julia Budka and Kenneth Griffin (eds). 2014. *Thebes in the First Millennium BC*. Newcastle upon Tyne: Cambridge Scholars Publishing.

Pisani, M. and M. E. Zucco. 2009. "Compact imaging spectrometer combining Fourier-transform spectroscopy with a Fabry-Perot interferometer". *Optics Express* 17: 8319–8331.

Polz, Daniel. 1991. "Die Särge aus Schacht II der Grabanlage". In: Assmann 1991, 244–267.

Polz, Daniel (ed.). 2007. *Für die Ewigkeit geschaffen. Die Särge des Imeni und der Geheset*. Mainz am Rhein: Philipp von Zabern.

Pozza, G., D. Ajò, G. Chiari, F. De Zuane and M. Favaro. 2000. "Photoluminescence of the inorganic pigments Egyptian blue, Han blue and Han purple". *Journal of Cultural Heritage* 1(4): 393–398.

Prestipino, G., U. Santamaria, F. Morresi, A. Amenta and C. Greco. 2015. "Sperimentazione di adesivi e consolidanti per il restauro di manufatti lignei policromi egizi". In: *Atti del XIII Congresso Nazionale IGIIC–Lo Stato dell'Arte (Venaria Reale, 22–24 October 2015)*, 261–270. Fizenza: Nardini Editore.

Quibell, James Edward. 1898. *The Ramesseum* (Egyptian Research Account, 1896 [II]). London: B. Quaritch.

——— 1908. *Catalogue général des antiquités égyptiennes du Musée du Caire: Tomb of Yuaa and Thuiu*. Le Caire: Imprimerie de l'Institut français d'archéologie orientale.

——— 1912. *Excavations of Saqqara (1908–9, 1909–10): The Monastery of Apa Jeremias*. Le Caire: Imprimerie de l'Institut français d'archéologie orientale.

Quirke, Stephen. 2013. *Going out in daylight – prt m ḥrw: The ancient Egyptian Book of the Dead. Translation, sources, meanings* (GHP Egyptology 20). London: Golden House Publications.

Ragai, J. 1986. "Colour: its significance and production in Ancient Egypt". *Endeavour* 10: 74–79.

Rashmi S., S. Addamani and S. Venkat Ravikiran. 2014. "Spectral Angle Mapper Algorithm for Remote Sensing Image Classification". *International Journal of Innovative Science, Engineering & Technology*, 1 (Issue 4): 201–205. www.ijiset.com (accessed 31 October 2018).

Raven, Maarten J. 1978–1979. "Papyrus-Sheaths and Ptah-Sokar-Osiris Statues". *Oudheidkundige Mededelingen uit het Rijksmuseum van Oudheden te Leiden* 59–60: 251–296 and plates.

——— 1981. "On some coffins of the Besenmut Family". *Oudheidkundige Mededelingen uit het Rijksmuseum van Oudheden te Leiden* 62: 7–21 and plates.

——— 2005. "Egyptian Concepts on the Orientation of the Human Body". *Journal of Egyptian Archaeology* 91: 37–53.

Re, A., F. Albertin, C. Bortolin, R, Brancaccio, P. Buscaglia, J. Corsi, G. Cotto *et al.* 2012. "Results of the Italian neu_ART project". In: *Proceedings of XTACH11 Conference, IOP Conference Series: Materials Science and Engineering* 37(1). DOI: 10.1088/1757-899X/37/1/012007.

Re, A., A. Lo Giudice, M. Nervo, P. Buscaglia, P. Luciani, M. Borla and G. Greco. 2016. "The importance of tomography studying wooden artefacts: a comparison with radiography in the case of a coffin lid from ancient Egypt". *International Journal of Conservation Science*, 7 (Special Issue 2), 936–944, www.ijcs.uaic.ro (accessed 31 October 2018).

Reeves, C.N. 2013. "Amenhotep, Overseer of Builders of Amun: An Eighteenth-Dynasty Burial Reassembled". *Metropolitan Museum Journal* 48: 7–36.

Reisner, George A. 1942. *A history of the Giza Necropolis 1*. Cambridge: Harvard University Press.

Riederer, Joseph. 1997. "Egyptian Blue". In: *Artists' Pigments. A Handbook of their History and Characteristics* volume 3, edited by Elisabeth West Fitzhugh, 23–46. Oxford: Oxford University Press.

Rifai, Mai M. and Nesrin M.N. el-Hadidi. 2010. "Investigation and analysis of three gilded wood samples from the tomb of Tutankhamun". In: Dawson, Rozeik and Wright 2010, 16–24.

Riggs, Christina. 2005. *The Beautiful Burial in Roman Egypt, Art, Identity, and Funerary Religion*. Oxford: Oxford University Press.

Rippa Bonati, Maurizio. 1987. "Le mummie egiziane del Museo di Storia Naturale dell'Università di Padova". In: *Padova e l'Egitto*, edited by Alberto Siliotti, 93–99. Firenze: Arte e Natura Libri. Published in conjunction with the exhibition *Viaggiatori veneti alla scoperta dell'Egitto*, shown in Padua, May 1987.

Rippa Bonati, Maurizio and Andrea Giovanni Drusini. 2000. "Il corpo dell'Uomo". In: *La curiosità e l'ingegno. collezionismo scientifico e metodo sperimentale a Padova nel Settecento*, 103–117. Padova: Università degli Studi di Padova, Centro Musei scientifici.

Roeder, Günther. 1924. *Aegyptische Inschriften aus den Staatlichen Museen zu Berlin. Band 2. Inschriften des Neuen Reichs*. Leipzig : J.C. Hinrichs'sche Buchhandlung.

Rogge, E. 1986. *Totenmasken und mumienförmige Särge. Altägyptische Totenhüllen bis zum Ende des Mittleren Reiches*. PhD dissertation, Vienna.

Romano, James F. 1996. "The Armand de Potter collection of Ancient Egyptian art". *Studies in Honor of William Kelly Simpson*, edited by Peter der Manuelian, Volume 2, 697–711. Boston: Museum of Fine Arts.

Royal Ontario Museum. 1964. *Egyptian Mummies*. 2nd edition. Toronto: The Royal Ontario Museum.

Rubensohn, O. and F. Knatz. 1904. "Bericht über die Ausgrabungen bei Abusir el Mäläq im Jahre 1903". *Zeitschrift für Ägyptische Sprache und Altertumskunde* 41: 1–21.

Rusch, Adolf. 1922. *Die Entwicklung der Himmelsgöttin Nut zu einer Totengottheit*. Leipzig: J.C. Hinrichs.

Rydström, K.T. 1994. "*ḥry-sštꜣ* 'In Charge of Secrets': The 3000-year Evolution of a Title". *Discussions in Egyptology* 28: 53–94.

Saczecki, Cl. 2007. "Wachgeküsst: Ein hundertjähriger 'Dornröschenschlaf' endet im Ägyptischen Museum der Universität Leipzig". *aMun* 31: 24–29.

Saleh, Heidi. 2007. *Investigating ethnic and gender identities as expressed on wooden funerary stelae from the Libyan Period (c. 1069–715 B.C.E.) in Egypt* (British Archaeological Reports, International Series 1734). Oxford: John and Erica Hedges.

Sartini, Lisa. 2015. "The black coffins with yellow decoration: a typological and chronological study". *Egitto e Vicino Oriente* 38: 49–66.

Sauneron, Serge. 1952. "Le «Chancelier du dieu» dans son double rôle d'embaumeur et de prêtre d'Abydos". *Bulletin de l'Institut Français d'archéologie orientale* 51: 137–171.

el-Sayed, Ramadan. 1981. "A propos de l'iconographie du cercueil No 2238 au Musée de Turin". *Annales du Service des Antiquités de l'Égypte* 64: 163–173.

Scheurleer, R.L. and Willem Van Haarlem. 2006. *Objecten voor de Eeuwigheid* (Mededelingenblad No. 93). Amsterdam, Allard Pierson Museum.

Schiaparelli, E. 1924. *Relazione sui lavori della Missione Archeologica Italiana in Egitto (1903–1920). Vol. I: Esplorazione della "Valle delle Regine" nella necropoli di Tebe.* Torino: Museo di Antichità/ Giuseppe Gambino.

Schiff Giorgini, Michela. 1971. *Soleb II: Les Nécropoles.* Florence: Sansoni.

Schmidt, V. 1919. *Levende og døde i det gamle Aegypte. Album til ording af sarkofager, mumiekister, mumiehylstre o. lign.* Copenhagen: J. Frimodt.

Schneider, Hans D. and Maarten J. Raven. 1981. *De Egyptische Oudheid.* Den Haag: Staatsuitgeverij.

Schoske, Sylvia , Barbara Kreißl and Renate Germer. 1992. *Anch – Blumen für das Leben: Pflanzen im Alten Ägypten.* Munich: Staatliche Sammlung Ägyptischer Kunst.

Schweingruber, F. H. 1990. *Anatomie europäischer Hölzer: ein Atlas zur Bestimmung europäischer Baum-, Strauch- und Zwergstrauchhölzer.* Bern: Paul Haupt.

Scott, David A. 2016. "A review of ancient Egyptian pigments and cosmetics". *Studies in Conservation* 61: 185–202.

Scott, David, Sebastian Warmlander, Joy Mazurek and Stephen Quirke. 2009. "Examination of some pigments, grounds and media from Egyptian cartonnage fragments in the Petrie Museum, University College London". *Journal of Archaeological Science* 36: 923–932.

Schreiber, Gábor. 2012. "The Burial Ensemble of Tasenet from Gamhud and the Ptolemaic Coffin Style in Northern Middle Egypt". In: Kóthay 2012a, 257–263.

Scott, D.A. 2016. "A review of ancient Egyptian pigments and cosmetics". *Studies in Conservation* 61/4: 185–202.

Seeber, Christine. 1976. *Untersuchungen zur Darstellungen des Totengerichts im alten Ägypten* (Münchner Ägyptologische Studien 35). München and Berlin: Deutscher Kunstverlag.

Seidlmayer, Stephan Johannes. 1990. *Gräberfelder aus dem Übergang vom Alten zum Mittleren Reich: Studien zur Archäologie der Ersten Zwischenzeit* (Studien zur Archäologie und Geschichte Altägyptens 1). Heidelberg: Heidelberger Orientverlag.

——— 2001. "Die Ikonographie des Todes". In: *Social aspects of funerary culture in the Egyptian Old and Middle Kingdoms* (Orientalia Lovaniensia analecta 103), edited by Harco Willems, 205–252. Leuven: Peeters.

Serpico, M. and R. White. 2000. "Resins, amber and bitumen". In: Nicholson and Shaw 2000, 430–474.

——— 2001. "The use and identification of varnish on New Kingdom funerary equipment". In: Davies 2001, 33–42.

Sheikholeslami, Cynthia May. 2002. "A stela of two women from Abydos (Cairo JE 21797)". In: *Egyptian Museum Collections around the World*, edited by Mamdouh Eldamaty and Mai Trad, Volume 2, 1109–1118. Cairo: Supreme Council of Antiquities.

——— Forthcoming. A New Twenty-fifth Dynasty *ḥsyt n ẖnw n ỉmn* (Berkeley, PHMA 5-508).

Sheikholeslami, Cynthia May, and Salima Ikram. 2017. "Twenty-second and Twenty-fifth Dynasty mummies from Thebes: X-ray and CT-scan examination project". *Bulletin of the American Research Center in Egypt* 210: 22–32.

Siano, S., J. Agresti, I. Cacciari, D. Ciofini, M. Mascalchi, I. Osticioli and A.A. Mencaglia. 2012. "Laser cleaning in conservation of stone, metal, and painted artifacts: state of the art and new insights on the use of the Nd:YAG lasers". *Applied Physics A* 106 (2), 419–446.

Skumsnes, R. and Anders Bettum. 2015. "Solar rike – ikkje berre palass og tempel". *Ostrakon, Norsk egyptologisk selskaps bullettin*, 9 and 10: 3–38.

Smith, Mark. 2012. "New references to the deceased as *wsir n NN* from the Third Intermediate Period and the earliest reference to a deceased woman as *H.t-Hr NN*". *Revue d'Egyptologie* 63: 187–196.

——— 2017. *Following Osiris. Perspectives on the Osirian afterlife from four millennia.* Oxford: Oxford University Press.

Smith, Stuart Tyson. 1992. "Intact Tombs of the Seventeenth and Eighteenth Dynasties from Thebes and the New Kingdom Burial System". *Mitteilungen des deutschen archäologisen Instituts, Abteilung Kairo* 48: 193–231.

Sotheby, Wilkinson and Hodge. 1921. *Catalogue of The Amherst Collection of Egyptian & Oriental Antiquities.* London: Sotheby, Wilkinson & Hodge. Catalogue of a sale held on 13–17 June 1921.

Sousa, Rogério (ed.). 2014a. *Body, Cosmos and Eternity. New research trends in the iconography and symbolism of ancient Egyptian coffins* (Archaeopress Egyptology 3). Oxford: Archaeopress.

——— 2014b. "'Spread your wings over me': iconography, symbolism and meaning of the central panel on yellow coffins". In: Sousa 2014a, 91–109.

Sowada, Karin N. and Boyo G. Ockinga (eds). 2006. *Egyptian Art in the Nicholson Museum, Sydney.* Sydney: Mediterranean Archaeology.

Staatliche Sammlung ägyptischer Kunst. 1966. *Die Ägyptische Sammlung des Bayerischen Staates.* München: Studienprogramm des Bayerischen Rundfunks. Published in conjunction with the exhibition of the same name, shown in the Staatliche Graphische Sammlung München, 21 July to 25 October 1966.

——— 1976. *Staatliche Sammlung ägyptischer Kunst.* 2nd revised edition. München: Staatliche Sammlung.

Steckeweh, Hans. 1936. *Die Fürstengräber von Qâw* (Veröffentlichungen der Ernst-von-Sieglin-Expedition in Ägypten, 6). Leipzig: Hinrichs.

di Stefano, Luigi Maria and Robert Fuchs. 2011. "Characterization of the pigments in a Ptolemaic Egyptian Book of the Dead papyrus". *Archaeological and Anthropological Sciences* 3: 229–244.

Stein, Renée and Peter Lacovara. 2010. "Observations on the preparation layers found on ancient Egyptian decorated coffins in the Michael C. Carlos Museum". In: Dawson, Rozeik and Wright 2010, 3–8.

Stövesand, Katharina. 2012. *Anthropomorpher Sarg aus Abusir el-Meleq (Inv. 148.I.1)* (Kataloge der Archäologischen Sammlung und des Münzkabinetts der Universität Rostock 3). Rostock: Institut für Altertumswissenchaften, Klassische Archäologie.

Strudwick, Helen and Julie Dawson (eds). 2016. *Death on the Nile. Uncovering the afterlife of ancient Egypt.* London: D Giles Limited in association with the Fitzwilliam Museum.

Strudwick, H., J. Dawson, J. Marchant, E. Geldhof and C. Hunkeler. Forthcoming. "Complex layered structures on 'bivalve' coffins". *Proceedings of the Second Vatican Conference 6–9 June 2017*. Città del Vaticano: Edizioni Musei Vaticani.

Strudwick, Nigel and John H. Taylor (eds). 2003. *The Theban necropolis: past, present and future.* London, British Museum Press.

Tacke, Nikolaus. 1996. "Die Entwicklung der Mumienmaske im Alten Reich". *Mitteilungen des Deutschen Archäologischen Instituts. Abteilung Kairo* 52: 307–336.

Taylor, John H. 2001a. *Death and the Afterlife in Ancient Egypt.* London: British Museum Press.

——— 2001b. "Patterns of colouring on ancient Egyptian coffins from the New Kingdom to the Twenty-sixth Dynasty: an overview". In: Davies 2001, 164–181.

——— 2003. "Theban coffins from the Twenty-second to the Twenty-sixth Dynasty: Dating and synthesis of development". In: Strudwick and Taylor 2003, 92–121.

——— 2006. "The Coffin of Padiashaikhet". In: Sowada and Ockinga 2006, 263–291.

——— 2009. "Coffins as evidence for a 'north-south divide' in the 22nd–25th Dynasties". In: Broekman, Demarée and Kaper 2009, 375–416.

——— (ed.) 2010. *Journey through the Afterlife: Ancient Egyptian Book of the Dead.* London: British Museum Press.

——— 2016. "The coffins from Shaft I". In: *The Tomb of Pharaoh's Chancellor Senneferi at Thebes (TT99). Part I: The New Kingdom*, edited by Nigel Strudwick, 181–190. Oxford: Oxbow.

——— 2017. "Two lost cartonnage cases of the early Twenty-second Dynasty". In: Jurman, Bader and Aston 2017, 445–490.

Teas, J.P. 1968. "Graphic analysis of resin solubilities". *Journal of Paint Technology* 40 (516): 19–25.

Tiradritti, Francesco. 1999. *Egyptian Treasures from the Egyptian Museum in Cairo.* New York: Harry N. Abrams.

Toda, Eduardo and Georges E. Daressy. 1920. "La découverte et l'inventaire du tombeau de Sen-Nezem». *Annales du service des antiquités de l'Egypte* 20: 151–156.

de la Torre Robles, Yolanda. 2017. "Preliminary report of the works done in tomb QH33. Season 2017". In: A. Jiménez Serrano *et al.* 2017: "La novena campaña (2017) del Proyecto Qubbet el-Hawa: los trabajos arqueológicos de las tumbas QH32, QH33, QH34aa, QH34bb, QH122, QH35p y QH36". *Boletín de la Asociación Española de Egiptología* 26 (in press).

de la Torre Robles, Yolanda and Juan Luis Martínez de Dios. 2015. "C24 y C25: las cámaras de enterramiento principales de la tumba QH33". In: Alejandro Jiménez Serrano *et al.* 2015. "Proyecto Qubbet el-Hawa: las tumbas nº 31, 34cc y 35p". *Boletín de la Asociación Española de Egiptología* 24: 27–34.

——— 2016. "El sector C24 de la tumba QH33". In: Alejandro Jiménez Serrano *et al.* 2016. "Proyecto Qubbet el-Hawa: las tumbas nº31, 33, 34aa, 34bb, 35n, 35p y 122. Octava Campaña". *Boletín de la Asociación Española de Egiptología* 25: 12–15.

el-Toukhy, A. 1993. *Bulletin of the Faculty of Arts (Assiut University Sohag)* 13: 33–35.

Trumpour, M. 2006. "Sheri's Story". *Rotunda* Summer/Fall 2006: 6–7.

Turaieff, Boris. 1899–1903. "Description of the Egyptian Monuments in the Russian Museums and Collections, I–VII". *Zapiski Vostočnogo Otdelenia Imperatorskogo Archeologičeskogo Obščestva* 11: 115–164, pls. I-IX; 12: 179–217; 15: 081–0100. [In Russian]

Uda, M. 2005. "Characterization of Pigments Used in Ancient Egypt". In: *X-rays for Archaeology*, edited by M. Uda, G., Demortier and I. Nakai. 3–26. Dordrecht: Springer Netherlands.

Vandier, Jacques. 1973. *Musée Du Louvre. Le Départment des antiquités égyptiennes: guide sommaire.* Paris: Éditions des musées nationaux.

Vassilika, Eleni. 1995. *Egyptian art* (Fitzwilliam Museum handbooks). Cambridge; New York, NY, USA: Cambridge University Press.

Verhoeven, U. 1998. "The Mortuary Cult". In: *Egypt: The World of the Pharaohs,* edited by Regine Schulz and Matthias Seidel. Köln: Könemann Verlaggesellschaft.

Verner, Miroslav. 1982. *Altägyptische Särge in den Museen und Sammlungen der Tschechoslowakei* (Corpus Antiquitatum Aegyptiacarum: Czechoslovakia 1). Praha: Univerzita Karlova.

Vernier, Émile Séraphin. 1911. "Note sur les boucles d'oreilles égyptiennes". *Bulletin de l'Institut Français d'archéologie orientale* 8: 18, pl. 2.

Verri, G. 2008 "The use and distribution of Egyptian blue: a study by visible-induced luminescence imaging". In: *The Nebamun Wall Paintings*, edited by K. Uprichard and A. Middleton, 41–50. London: Archetype.

Verri, G. 2009. "The spatially resolved characterisation of Egyptian blue, Han blue and Han purple by photo-induced luminescence digital imaging". *Analytical and Bioanalytical Chemistry* 394(4): 1011–1021.

Vittmann, Günter. 1981. "Zu den Raubgrabungen in Abusir el-Meleq". *Göttingen Miszellen* 42: 81–85.

Vittmann, Günter. 1994. "Ein Mumienbrett im Britischen Museum (BM 36502)". In: *Zwischen den beiden Ewigkeiten. Festschrift Gertrud Thausing*, edited by M. Bietak, J. Holaubek, H. Mukarovsky and H. Satzinger, 222–275. Wien: Institut für Ägyptologie der Universität Wien.

Vogelsang-Eastwood, Gillian. 2000. "Textiles". In: Nicholson and Shaw 2000, 268–297.

van Walsem, René. 1997. *The coffin of Djedmonthuiufankh in the National Museum of Antiquities at Leiden I: technical and iconographic/iconological aspects* (Egyptologische uitgaven 10). Leiden: Nederlands Instituut voor het Nabije Oosten.

——— 2000. "Deir el-Medina as the place of origin of the coffin of Anet in the Vatican (Inv.: XIII.2.1, XIII.2.2)". In: *Deir el-Medîna in the Third Millenium A.D. A tribute to Jac J. Jansen*, edited by R.J. Demarée and A. Egberts, 337–349. Leiden: Nederlands Instituut voor het Nabije Oosten.

Walton, Marc Sebastian and Karen Trentelman. 2009. "Romano-Egyptian red lead pigment: A subsidiary commodity of Spanish silver mining and refinement". *Archaeometry* 51, no. 5: 845–860.

Warner, Terence E. 2011. *Synthesis, Properties and Mineralogy of Important Inorganic Materials.* Chichester: Wiley.

Weisser, Christiane. 2012. *Untersuchung altägyptischer Holzobjekte im Hinblick auf die verwendeten Holzarten.* Unpublished Master's thesis, Hochschule für angewandte Wissenschaft und Kunst Hildesheim/Holzminden/Göttingen.

Wheeler, E.A. 2011. "InsideWood – a web resource for hardwood anatomy". *IAWA Journal* 32 (2): 199–211.

Wiedemann, A. 1889. "Some monuments of the prophets of Mont at Thebes". *Proceedings of the Society of Biblical Archaeology* 11: 69–75.

Wiese, André. 2004. "Tutanchamun – Ein ganz normaler 'Grabschatz' der 18. Dynastie? Zur Grabausstattung königlicher und nichtköniglicher Personen im Tal der Könige". In: *Tutanchamun. Das Goldene Jenseits. Grabschätze aus dem Tal der Könige*, edited by André Wiese and Andreas Brodbeck, 83–127. Zürich: Offizin.

Wilkinson, R.H. 2004. *Cómo leer el arte egipcio. Guía de jeroglíficos del Antiguo Egipto.* Barcelona: Crítica.

Willems, Harco. 2014. *Historical and archaeological aspects of Egyptian funerary culture: religious ideas and ritual practice in Middle Kingdom elite cemeteries.* Leiden: Brill.

Wilson, P. 1997. *A Ptolemaic lexicon: A lexicographical study of the texts in the Temple of Edfu* (Orientalia Lovaniensia analecta 78). Leuven: Peeters: Department Oosterse Studies.

Winlock, Herbert E. 1921. "The Egyptian Expedition 1920–1921: III. Excavations at Thebes". *The Metropolitan Museum of Art Bulletin* 16, No. 11, Part 2: 29–53.

——— 1940. "The Mummy of Wah Unwrapped". *The Metropolitan Museum of Art Bulletin* Vol. 35, No. 12: 253–259.

Wodzinska, A. 2010. *A Manual of Egyptian Pottery.* Boston: AERA.

Yaman, B. 2007. "Anatomy of Lebanon Cedar (*Cedrus libani* A. Rich.) wood with indented growth rings". *Acta Biologica Cracoviensia Series Botanica* 49/1: 19–23.

Yoshimura, Sakuji, Ken Yazawa, Jiro Kondo, Masahiro Baba, S. Nishimoto, H. Kashiwagi and Y. Akiyama. 2012. "Preliminary Report on the Waseda University Excavations at Dahshur North: Sixteenth and Seventeenth Seasons". *The Journal of Egyptian Studies* 18: 21–68.

Zanovello, Paola and Emanuele M. Ciampini. 2013. *Egitto in Veneto.* Padova: CLEUP.

Ziegler, Christiane. 2012. *Fouilles du Louvre à Saqqara. II: Les tombes hypogées de Basse Époque F7, F17, H, j1, Q, n1.* Paris/Leuven: Musée du Louvre/Peeters.

——— 2013. *Les Tombes Hypogées de Basse Époque (Fouilles du Louvre à Saqqara).* 2 volumes. Paris/Leuven: Musée du Louvre/Peeters.

Zivie, Alain. 1990. *Découverte à Saqqarah: Le vizir oublié.* Paris: Seuil.

——— 2007. *The lost tombs of Saqqara.* Toulouse: cara.cara ed.

Identifying ancient Egyptian coffin woods from the Fitzwilliam Museum, Cambridge using scanning electron microscopy

Caroline R. Cartwright

There has been much discussion and speculation in the literature on ancient Egypt about the various roles played by indigenous and imported timbers for many different types of artefacts. In every period, and for a number of complex reasons, particular woods have been selected. Selection not only maximized the use of the properties of the woods themselves (which were well understood by the Egyptian craftsman), but also reflected cultural preferences over time. Selection was not merely functional, but aesthetic and economic – and often allied to status. Identification of the woods used for every part of ancient Egyptian coffins vividly exemplifies this selection process in practice. This paper presents the results of a major programme of wood identifications of a large number of Egyptian coffins in the Fitzwilliam Museum collection. It shows the range and use of both local woody resources and the selective import of prestige timbers, fundamental to the development of a distinctive funerary carpentry tradition.

Introduction

A major programme of wood identification of ancient Egyptian coffins and other funerary objects from the Fitzwilliam Museum was established in collaboration with the British Museum as part of a larger research objective by the Fitzwilliam Museum. For this I have taken 770 wood samples from 95 wooden objects in the Fitzwilliam Museum collection of Egyptian artefacts; mostly coffins, but also some models, boxes and figures. Three Roman period mummy portraits from the Fitzwilliam Museum were sampled and identified as part of a separate research project (Cartwright 1997; Cartwright *et al.* 2011).

In order to meet the needs of the *Death on the Nile: Uncovering the Afterlife of Ancient Egypt* exhibition at the Fitzwilliam Museum (23 February–22 May 2016), identification of the woods of the objects to be displayed in the exhibition became the priority, particularly for the catalogue (Strudwick and Dawson 2016). This paper encapsulates the wood identification research undertaken for the *Death on the Nile* exhibition, for the Coffin Workshop (Fitzwilliam Museum 4–6 April 2016), and for the conference *Ancient Egyptian Csoffins: Past • Present • Future* (Cambridge 7–9 April 2016).

Methods and techniques

Following much discussion with Julie Dawson at the outset of the project, I carried out the sampling of the chosen coffins and other funerary objects at the Fitzwilliam Museum, with conservation staff assisting. Care was taken only to sample unobtrusive or already-damaged locations, avoiding areas of paint, decoration, gilding or other surface modifications. No sampling took place in areas with consolidant, adhesive, rot, insect or fungal damage. Sampling was avoided in areas of wood with knots, nail holes, labels or signatures, and adze, saw, or chisel marks. Given the standard wood anatomy requirement for examining three different sections (transverse, radial longitudinal and tangential longitudinal), a small 2 mm cube was extracted, rather than a splinter (which restricts the cutting of an adequate transverse section). Most of the Fitzwilliam Museum coffins are composite objects, and different woods were likely to have been selected for various elements, so wood samples were taken from all the main components and planks as well as from dowels, tenons, pegs, repairs and additions. As it is well known that local wood resources were scarce in ancient Egypt, careful consideration was given to sample possible areas of wood reuse.

The anatomical examination of all wood (reference specimens and ancient) was carried out using scanning electron microscopy (SEM). For desiccated wood and charcoal, the application of SEM rather than light (or optical) microscopy enables illustration of a better depth of field in the preserved cell structure, as well as having the facility to offer high magnification imaging where appropriate (Cartwright 2015). Because of the three-dimensional nature of wood anatomy, each sample, irrespective of size, was fractured manually to show transverse, radial longitudinal and tangential longitudinal sections (TS, RLS and TLS) for examination.

Each TS, RLS and TLS wood sample was then mounted uncoated on an aluminium SEM stub for SEM examination in the Hitachi S-3700N variable pressure (VP) SEM, mostly with an accelerating voltage of 15 kV. For optimal visualisation of diagnostic cellular detail, the working distance varied from 23.5 mm to 11.3 mm, as dictated by the sample being examined. The chamber pressure also varied according to the state of preservation of each sample. Using VP with the back-scattered electron (BSE) detector at 40 Pa (or 30 Pa) chamber pressure, for example, was very successful in eliminating surface charging on non-conducting samples of ancient Egyptian wood. The highly sensitive, five-segment BSE detector on the VP SEM used (Hitachi S-3700N) enabled detailed interrogation and imaging of the topography of the wood samples in TS, RLS and TLS from different orientations and, where necessary, using low accelerating voltages. The 3D mode, rather than Compositional, produced maximum surface topography information.

Samples that were very small, or in poor condition were mounted using Leit-C Plast carbon cement (which is a proprietary brand of conductive material with low outgassing properties suitable for SEM use). After mounting, each stub with its wood sample was sputter-coated with gold to make it conductive in the high vacuum conditions of the Hitachi S4800 field emission (FE) SEM using the secondary electron (SE) detector. Two magnification modes were available: (1) low magnification at x30 to x2000; (2) high magnification at x100 to x800,000. Four objective lens apertures could be selected as required; using aperture 3 or 4 gave the best results. The FE SEM has the flexibility to achieve high resolution imaging with good contrast definition of surface information. In addition, the lower or upper detector signals (on the Hitachi S4800) can be selected to accentuate surface morphology and image contrast according to the detector position, following the same protocols used for the identification of archaeological charcoal (Cartwright 2013). For the ancient Egyptian wood samples, the accelerating voltages of 15 kV or 10kV were used most frequently, and the working distance ranged from 19.7 mm to 7.7 mm, depending on the size, condition and flatness of the sample.

The energy dispersive X-ray spectrometry (EDX) analysis capabilities of both the VP SEM and FE SEM were used to establish whether crystals in cells were calcium oxalate or silica.

Results and discussion

Standard procedures (as outlined above) were followed for the SEM examination and identification of 611 wood samples from 45 objects (although it should be noted that for the purposes of the summary in **Table 1**, each coffin 'set' has been counted as one). Comparisons were made with reference specimens and thin sections of wood in the British Museum's scientific reference collections. Characteristic features of cell anatomy revealed in TS, RLS and TLS were described according to the standards of the International Association of Wood Anatomists (Wheeler 2011). The full anatomical details of these identifications can be found in the Appendix (below).

Table 1 demonstrates that five main woody taxa are present, four of which are indigenous to Egypt and one of which is imported. The indigenous timbers are: *Ficus sycomorus*, sycomore fig; *Ziziphus spina-christi*, sidr, Christ's thorn; *Acacia nilotica (*syn. *Vachellia nilotica)*, Nile acacia / *Acacia* sp., acacia; and *Tamarix aphylla*, tamarisk. *Cedrus libani*, cedar of Lebanon is the imported wood. **Table 1** has been ordered chronologically (where possible), from oldest to youngest, with the intention of revealing if any trends over time exist for particular use of one kind of timber over another. Noting that the numbers in **Table 1** represent samples, three summary groups have been differentiated for each wood species: main, joining and additional. The group designated as "main" includes the principal structural elements of the coffins such as planks and footboards, or the sides of a shabti box, or the central components of a figure or model. The "joining" group includes elements of connective carpentry for all objects, such as tenons, pegs, dowels, and battens. The "additional" group includes separate pieces, wedges, patches, inserts, strips and repairs. There is some overlap of categorisation of the "additional" group with the "main" group, but for the purpose of interrogating the evidence, particularly from the perspective of repair and reuse, it was deemed useful to try to separate it as far as possible.

There has been much discussion and speculation in the published literature on ancient Egypt (e.g. Gale *et al.* 2000) about the various roles played by indigenous and imported timbers for many different types of artefacts. In every period, and for a variety of complex reasons (not least of which is timber availability), a selection of woods has been made. Selection not only maximized the use of the properties of the woods themselves (which were well understood by the Egyptian carpenter), but also reflected cultural preferences over time. Selection was, therefore, not merely functional, but aesthetic and economi For example, an earlier study (Cartwright and Taylor 2008) drew attention to the fact that archery bows, although primarily utilitarian items, were not just used for hunting or warfare but also in ceremonial events and were placed as funerary offerings in tombs to serve the individual in the afterlife. This may have had significant bearing on the choice of woods for the bows, depending on whether they were intended for active use or symbolic representation. Reuse of scarce wood and quality timbers may not simply have been practised for cost-cutting reasons; it may signify a more complex set of cultural preferences that sought to prevent good timber going to waste because its properties were valued, or because there were sacred or cultural justifications for perpetuating the use and reuse of a specific type of wood.

The *Death on the Nile* exhibition catalogue (Strudwick and Dawson 2016) contains a full account of my wood identifications and interpretation, and without replicating that published information (Cartwright 2016), some salient points will be re-examined here. **Table 1** shows just how much use was made of the local fig trees, *Ficus sycomorus*, sycomore fig (**Fig. 1**), particularly for large or long coffin planks, and the model scenes often found in Egyptian tombs such as granaries, bakeries and boats. Its popularity is reflected in all chronological periods. Although fig wood is of medium quality and is susceptible to insect attack, it is light and easy to carve. When objects made from fig wood have been heavily painted and decorated, or protected by internal placement where used as tenons and dowels, the propensity of the wood to suffer insect attack or physical damage can be reduced. Debate continues about the extent of distribution of *Ficus sycomorus* trees in Egypt and East Africa, not least because the species is reliant on a particular type of wasp for pollination (Galil and Eisikowitch 1968; 1974). Cutting a *Ficus sycomorus* tree to achieve the requisite length of coffin planks results in almost inevitable sacrifice of the whole tree, which means that the edible figs and the sacred associations will be sacrificed too. It is interesting to speculate whether, in fact, such a 'sacrifice' might be considered to imbue extra qualities or 'worth' to the fig timber in its used (and reused) form. Either way, given the requirement for wasp pollination for the species, re-establishing *Ficus sycomorus* resources could be a lengthy process, and even if humanly propagated by cuttings, the trees need time to establish themselves and mature. Without isotopic research, it is not possible to evaluate whether, in fact, some *Ficus sycomorus* timber might have been imported from East Africa for use in ancient Egyptian funerary objects.

It is important to insist on correct terminology and spelling of *Ficus sycomorus,* sycomore fig. This type of fig tree, belonging to the Moraceae family is completely unrelated botanically to the true sycamore tree, *Acer pseudoplatanus,* which belongs to the Sapindaceae family and is mainly distributed across central Europe. It is only correct to use the term 'sycamore' when discussing ancient Egyptian timber if the wood has been scientifically identified as *Acer pseudoplatanus,* with the inference being that the wood was imported into Egypt from Europe. It is incorrect to use the term 'sycamore' to describe indigenous *Ficus sycomorus* wood. Using just the word 'sycomore' is insufficient; it must always be accompanied by the word 'fig'.

Table 1 illustrates how important it was when constructing coffins in ancient Egypt for carpenters to choose woods of different properties for the interconnecting elements, such as dowels and tenons, in order to ensure the strength and integrity of the object. By choosing woods for the joining elements that are denser than the planks, such as sidr (*Ziziphus spina-christi*) (**Fig. 2**) and the local acacias (**Fig. 3**), tight joins and connections can be created. Sidr, found in tree and shrub forms, inhabits river-banks, desert wadis and scrubland thickets. Some of these habitats may restrict the straight growth of sidr, resulting in twisted or knotty timber, with wood suitable for coffin planks such as seen in the Nespawershefyt coffin set (E.1.1822) more of a rarity. Whilst some of the larger acacias prefer growing along the Nile river banks, others inhabit more arid locations of Egypt, and extend into the African savannah. African acacias have undergone complex taxonomic reclassification (Kyalangalilwa *et al.* 2013) and adopting the reclassified taxa requires the wood anatomist to identify to species level. For example, *Acacia nilotica* is reclassified as *Vachellia nilotica*, *Acacia laeta* as *Senegalia laeta* and so on (see Appendix below), but many acacias cannot be distinguished one from another on the basis of their wood anatomy. As a consequence, it means that the term *Acacia* sp. (acacia) will have to be retained in such instances. **Table 1** shows that, like sidr, acacia has principally been used for connective carpentry for precisely-fitted dowels and tenons that are integral to the stability and coherence of construction. Short length, twisted or knotty wood is no drawback for this function. Unusually, acacia wood has been used for the coffin main planks, as seen in the *qersu* coffin from tomb 840 at Abydos (E.14.1926).

Table 1 indicates that another indigenous tree, *Tamarix aphylla* (tamarisk) (**Fig.** 4) was used occasionally for coffin plank segments, inserts, tenons and dowels. Tamarisk trees are found in wadi thicket vegetation and on riverbanks. Several tamarisk species indigenous to Egypt occur as shrubs, and these are common in more arid habitats, but are difficult to distinguish from one another on the basis of their wood anatomy. Like fig wood, tamarisk wood is light, of medium to poor quality and is susceptible to insect and fungal damage, but it is comparatively easy to carve (particularly for insert pieces), and was presumably inexpensive to procure.

Although **Table 1** was ordered chronologically to reveal any temporal trends, there seem to be many more factors involved. Certainly when considering one of the most renowned timber imports to Egypt, i.e. cedar of Lebanon (*Cedrus libani*), inevitably the issues of status and money come under consideration. Used for the main planks of the dog coffin (E.47.1902) dating to *c.* 2036–1794 BC (Middle Kingdom; mid-Eleventh to Twelfth Dynasties), *Cedrus libani* next appears on **Table 1** as essential to all elements of the construction of the Coffin of Nakht (E.68.1903) *c.* 1915–1870 BC (Middle Kingdom; mid-Twelfth Dynasty). In the Coffin set of Nespawershefyt (E.1.1822) *c.* 1000 BC (Third Intermediate Period; early to mid-Twenty-first Dynasty) cedar of Lebanon features as good quality offcut wood for joining and additional elements, and as main elements for the head end of a yellow coffin box (E.1.2004) *c.* 955–735 BC (Third Intermediate Period; mid-Twenty-first to end Twenty-second Dynasties). Subsequently it re-emerges as main elements in three Late Period coffins (or coffin fragments).

Cedar of Lebanon (**Fig.** 5) is often regarded as easy to carve, plane and polish, although large knots and ingrowing bark can cause problems, and the wood may be rather brittle. Although many species of *Cedrus* are renowned for being strongly aromatic and resinous (and therefore insect-repellent), there is some debate as to the extent to which *Cedrus libani* trees routinely develop resin canals, or whether they are purely traumatic in origin (Güney *et al.* 2015). In my experience of identifying cedar of Lebanon wood from ancient Egyptian contexts, few specimens show any resin canals (whether traumatic in origin or not), and the resin content of the wood may be considered low. However, the cedar of Lebanon wood used for the Fitzwilliam Museum coffins provides a notable exception; most listed in **Table 1** show one band of (presumed traumatic) resin canals. Might it follow, therefore, that specific selection for highly resinous *Cedrus libani* wood was deliberately ordered for certain coffin sets? Cedar of Lebanon trees are currently under extreme threat as a result of a number of factors, but in the past it is presumed that long-established cedar of Lebanon woodland could offer timber in long lengths with inherently reliable wood properties, well suited for use as coffin planks. Such timber was dispersed through trade in the ancient world bordering the Mediterranean Sea. The popularity of cedar of Lebanon wood for use in high status coffins and for other funerary objects in ancient Egypt has been seen as an integer of the expense and prestige of acquiring this imported resource.

Conclusions

This paper presents some of the highlights of my results of a major programme of wood identifications of a large number of Egyptian coffins in the Fitzwilliam Museum collection. It exemplifies the range, use and limitations of local woody resources, as well as the selective import of prestige timbers, fundamental to the development of a distinctive funerary carpentry tradition. Discussion in the literature on ancient Egypt has speculated about the differing use of indigenous and imported timbers for many types of wooden artefacts. In every period, and for a number of complex reasons, particular woods have

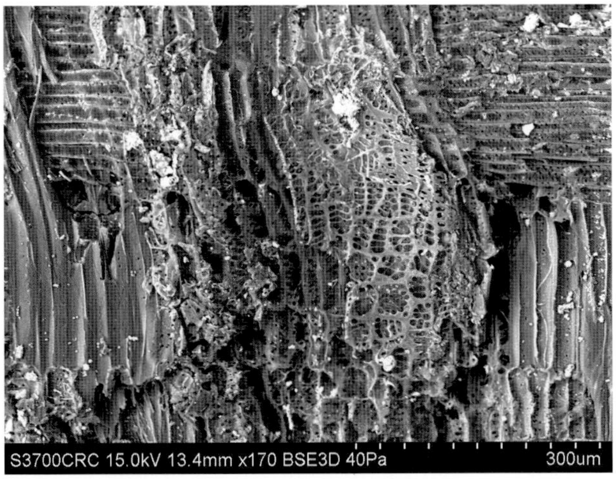

Fig. 1: Variable pressure scanning electron microscope image of a radial longitudinal section of Ficus sycomorus *(sycomore fig) wood. Image: C.R. Cartwright; © The Trustees of the British Museum*

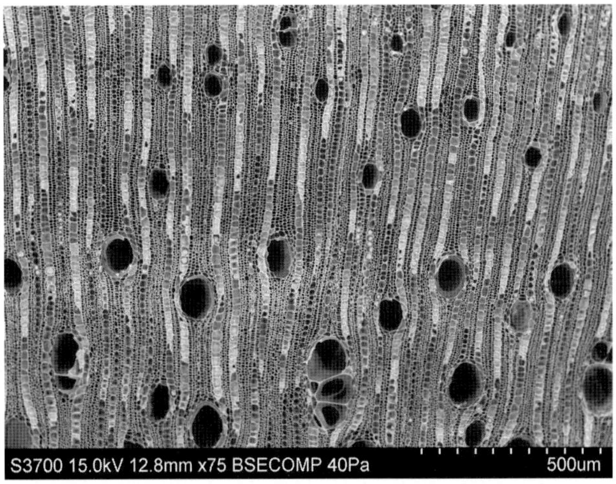

Fig. 2: Variable pressure scanning electron microscope image of a transverse section of Ziziphus spina-christi *(sidr) wood. Image: C.R. Cartwright; © The Trustees of the British Museum*

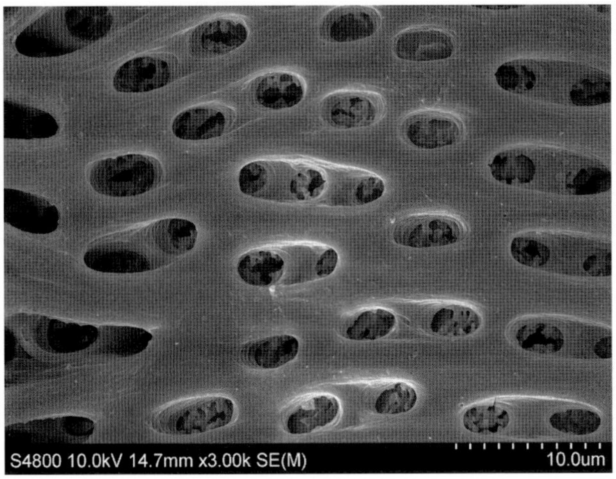

Fig. 3: Field emission scanning electron microscope image of the vestured pits in a radial longitudinal section of Acacia nilotica *(syn.* Vachellia nilotica*), Nile acacia. Image: C.R. Cartwright; © The Trustees of the British Museum*

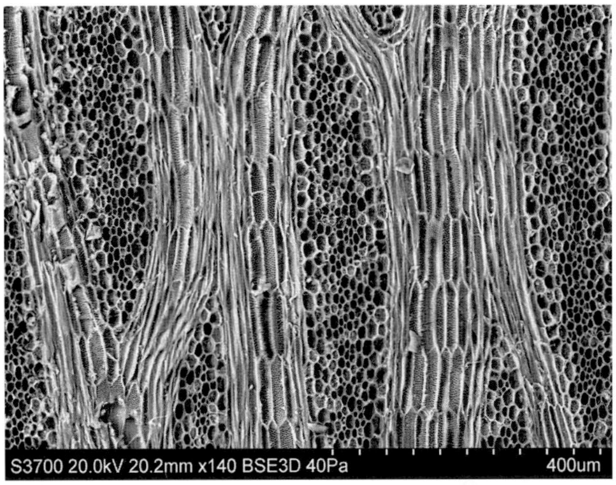

Fig. 4: Variable pressure scanning electron microscope image of a tangential longitudinal section of Tamarix aphylla, *tamarisk. Image: C.R. Cartwright; © The Trustees of the British Museum*

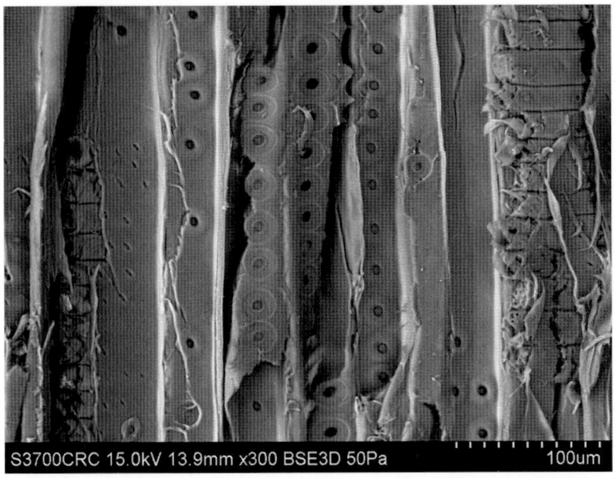

Fig. 5: Variable pressure scanning electron microscope image of a radial longitudinal section of Cedrus libani *(cedar of Lebanon) showing the diagnostic pits with scalloped tori in the tracheids. Image: C.R. Cartwright; © The Trustees of the British Museum*

been selected. Discussion has focused on whether such selection was driven by timber availability, economic forces, cultural choices or a combination of all these (and other) factors. Given the evidence, it seems that selection not only maximized the use of the properties of the woods themselves (which were very familiar to Egyptian woodworkers and carpenters), but may also reflect cultural preferences over time. However, selection was not merely functional, but decorative, economic and apparently status-related in some instances. Identification of the woods used and sometimes reused for every part of ancient Egyptian coffins vividly exemplifies this selection process in practice. Using scanning electron microscopy to reveal the cellular structure has enabled accurate scientific identification of the different timbers, allowed the size of samples required to be kept to a minimum and has permitted the identification of highly degraded specimens, hitherto considered to be unidentifiable.

Acknowledgements

I should like to thank Julie Dawson, not only for allocating some of her conservation team to assist during sampling at the Fitzwilliam Museum, but also for interesting and stimulating discussions throughout the project. I am grateful to Helen Strudwick for providing object and dating information. Thanks are due to Geoffrey Killen and Elsbeth Geldhof for recently-grown samples of cedar of Lebanon wood.

APPENDIX

Principal anatomical characteristics of the woody taxa identified

(also see InsideWood 2004 onwards; Wheeler 2011)

Acacia sp. (acacia) Fabaceae family, Mimosoideae subfamily (Fig. 3)

including *A. mellifera* (syn. *Senegalia mellifera*), *A. laeta* (syn. *Senegalia laeta*), *A. asak* (syn. *Senegalia asak*), *A. tortilis* (syn. *Vachellia tortilis*), *A. tortilis* subsp. *tortilis* (syn. *Vachellia tortilis* subsp. *tortilis*), *A. tortilis* subsp. *raddiana* (syn. *Vachellia tortilis* subsp. *raddiana*), *A. nilotica* (syn. *Vachellia nilotica*), *A. seyal* (syn. *Vachellia seyal*), *A. senegal* (syn. *Senegalia senegal*), *A. ehrenbergiana* (syn. *Vachellia flava*), *A. etbaica* (syn. *Vachellia etbaica*).

Growth ring boundaries mostly indistinct; wood diffuse-porous; vessels in multiples; vessels mostly in short (2–3 vessels) radial rows; vessel outline rounded; sometimes gums and other deposits in heartwood vessels; simple perforation plates; alternate intervessel pits; vestured pits; vessel-ray pits with distinct borders; fibres non-septate; fibres septate in some species; fibres of medium wall thickness or very thick-walled; fibre pits simple to minutely bordered; axial parenchyma present in bands much wider than rays; axial parenchyma bands marginal (or seemingly marginal); axial parenchyma bands may be more than 3 cells wide; diffuse apotracheal parenchyma present; paratracheal axial parenchyma vasicentric, aliform, lozenge-aliform, confluent or unilateral; multiseriate rays 3–5 seriate and 5–10 seriate; homocellular rays with procumbent cells; sheath cells present in some species; fusiform parenchyma cells present in some species; prismatic crystals present, sometimes in chambered axial parenchyma cells; sclerified crystalliferous parenchyma in some species; crystals in enlarged cells in some species.

Cedrus libani (cedar of Lebanon) Pinaceae family (Fig. 5)

Variability in transition from earlywood to latewood: sometimes gradual, sometimes abrupt; growth rings sometimes indented (see Yaman 2007); latewood tracheids thick-walled; noticeable scalloping of the tori of the bordered pits in (earlywood) axial tracheids; piceoid, cupressoid or taxodioid cross-field pitting in rays; trabeculae in tracheids; sparse axial parenchyma; distinct pitting in horizontal walls of ray parenchyma cells; nodular end walls with indentures (of parenchyma cells); rays often bordered by a single row of ray tracheids with smooth thin-walled cells; mostly uniseriate, occasionally biseriate rays; traumatic resin ducts sometimes present; prismatic crystals may be present (also see Cartwright 2001; Crivellaro and Schweingruber 2013).

Ficus sycomorus (sycomore fig) Moraceae family (Fig. 1)

Growth ring boundaries indistinct or absent; wood diffuse-porous; simple perforation plates; alternate intervessel pits; alternate pits polygonal; vessel-ray pits with much reduced borders to apparently simple: pits rounded or angular; vessel-ray pits with much reduced borders to apparently simple: pits horizontal (scalariform, gash-like) to vertical (palisade); tyloses common; fibres with simple to minutely bordered pits; fibres non-septate; fibres thin- to thick-walled; axial parenchyma bands more than three cells wide, sometimes very wide; larger rays commonly 4- to 10-seriate or greater than 10-seriate; sometimes there are rays of two distinct sizes; ray cells procumbent with one row of upright and / or square marginal cells; laticifers present; prismatic crystals present, sometimes in procumbent ray cells; prismatic crystals present in non-chambered axial parenchyma cells.

Tamarix sp. (tamarisk) Tamaricaceae family (Fig. 4)

including *T. aphylla, T. tetragyna, T. nilotica, T. amplexicaulis, T. passerinoides, T. macrocarpa*

Growth ring boundaries sometimes indistinct; wood diffuse-porous; vessel clusters common; vessels in tangential bands in some species; vessel outline rounded; simple perforation plates; alternate intervessel pits; minute intervessel pits; vessel-ray pits with distinct borders similar to intervessel pits; gums and other deposits sometimes present in heartwood vessels; vascular or vasicentric tracheids present in some species; fibres thin- to thick-walled; simple to minutely bordered fibre pits; fibres non-septate; paratracheal axial parenchyma present in vasicentric or confluent distribution; fusiform axial parenchyma; multiseriate rays 5–20 cells in width; heterocellular rays with procumbent, square and upright cells mixed throughout the ray; storied structure present (vessels and axial parenchyma); sheath cells present in some species; prismatic crystals in non-chambered upright and / or square ray cells.

Ziziphus spina-christi (Christ's thorn or sidr) Rhamnaceae family (Fig. 2)

Distinct growth ring boundaries; wood diffuse-porous; vessels mostly in short (2–3 vessels) radial rows; vessel outline rounded; simple perforation plates; alternate intervessel pits; vessel-ray pits with distinct borders similar to intervessel pits; gums and other deposits present in heartwood vessels; fibres of medium wall thickness or very thick-walled; simple to minutely bordered fibre pits; non-septate fibres; banded axial parenchyma; axial parenchyma bands marginal (or seemingly marginal); diffuse apotracheal axial parenchyma present; scanty paratracheal axial parenchyma; vasicentric axial parenchyma; rays exclusively uniseriate; heterocellular rays with procumbent, square and upright cells mixed throughout the ray; prismatic crystals in ray cells, sometimes in non-chambered axial parenchyma cells.

Table 1: Wood identifications of Fitzwilliam Museum funerary artefacts

Fitzwilliam Museum accession number	*Ficus sycomorus*, sycomore fig			*Ziziphus spina-christi*, sidr, Christ's thorn			*Acacia nilotica* (syn. *Vachellia nilotica*), Nile acacia / Acacia sp., acacia			*Tamarix aphylla, tamarisk*			*Cedrus libani*, cedar of Lebanon		
	main	joining	addi-tional	main	joining	addi-tional	main	joining	addi-tional	main	joining	addi-tional	main	joining	addi-tional
Dog coffin (E.47.1902) *c.* 2036–1794 BC; Middle Kingdom; mid-Eleventh to Twelfth Dynasties								3					10		
Coffin fragment with text (E.W.82) *c.* 2119–1794 BC; Eleventh to Twelfth Dynasties	2		2		4			1							
Coffin of Khety (E.71.1903) *c.* 2119–1940 BC; Eleventh to early Twelfth Dynasties	10	4			9			2							
Model sailing boat (E.71a.1903) *c.* 2119–1940 BC; Eleventh to early Twelfth Dynasties	9				1										
Model rowing boat (E.71b.1903) *c.* 2119–1940 BC; Eleventh to early Twelfth Dynasties	8														
Butchery model (E.71*c*.1903) *c.* 2119–1940 BC; Eleventh to early Twelfth Dynasties	6														
Bread and beer-making model (E.71d.1903) *c.* 2119–1940 BC; Eleventh to early Twelfth Dynasties	7														
Granary model (E.71e.1903) *c.* 2119–1940 BC; Eleventh to early Twelfth Dynasties	4				1										
Wepwawetemhat coffin fragments (E.W.66a and b) *c.* 1975–1790 BC; Middle Kingdom; Twelfth Dynasty	2				5			1							
Coffin of Nakht (E.68.1903) *c.* 1915–1870 BC; Middle Kingdom; mid-Twelfth Dynasty		1			20			13					35	22	1

Fitzwilliam Museum accession number	*Ficus sycomorus*, sycomore fig			*Ziziphus spina-christi*, sidr, Christ's thorn			*Acacia nilotica* (syn. *Vachellia nilotica*), Nile acacia / Acacia sp., acacia			*Tamarix aphylla, tamarisk*			*Cedrus libani*, cedar of Lebanon		
	main	joining	addi-tional	main	joining	addi-tional	main	joining	addi-tional	main	joining	addi-tional	main	joining	addi-tional
Anthropoid coffin of Userhet (E.88.1903) *c.* 1855–1790 BC; Middle Kingdom; mid- to late Twelfth Dynasty	3	4	1		3										
Mourning women coffin (E.283.1900) *c.*1680–1510 BC; Second Intermediate Period; mid-Seventeenth Dynasty	6		3		11										
Face from coffin (E.49.1926) *c.*1550–1290 BC; New Kingdom; Eighteenth Dynasty							1								
Face from coffin (E.GA.501.1947) *c.*1550–1070 BC; New Kingdom				1											
Footboard (E.GA.2910.1943); *c.* 1500–1400 BC; early Eighteenth Dynasty	1				3			1							
Face from coffin (E.GA.500.1947) *c.*946–736 BC; Third Intermediate Period; Twenty-second Dynasty							1		1						
Gilded face from coffin (E.GA.505.1947) *c.*946–736 BC; Third Intermediate Period; Twenty-second Dynasty	2														
Lotus flower from coffin (E.GA.5851.1943) *c.*1070 BC–945 BC; Third Intermediate Period; Twenty-first Dynasty	1														
Coffin face (E.GA.507.1947) *c.* 1070–990 BC; Third Intermediate Period; early Twenty-first Dynasty		1			2										
Hand from a yellow coffin (E.GA.2861.1943) *c.* 1070 BC–945 BC; Third Intermediate Period; Twenty-first Dynasty							1								

Fitzwilliam Museum accession number	*Ficus sycomorus*, sycomore fig			*Ziziphus spina-christi*, sidr, Christ's thorn			*Acacia nilotica* (syn. *Vachellia nilotica*), Nile acacia / Acacia sp., acacia			*Tamarix aphylla, tamarisk*			*Cedrus libani*, cedar of Lebanon		
	main	joining	addi-tional	main	joining	addi-tional	main	joining	addi-tional	main	joining	addi-tional	main	joining	addi-tional
Coffin set of Nespawershefyt (E.1.1822) *c.*1000 BC; Third Intermediate Period; early to mid-Twenty-first Dynasty	58	21	18	15	15	1	2	11	1	6		1		2	1
Head end of a yellow coffin box (E.1.2004) *c.* 955 BC–735 BC; Third Intermediate Period; mid-Twenty-first to end Twenty-second Dynasties	6	6			1								6		
Shabti box (E.91.1896) *c.* 925 BC – 890 BC. Third Intermediate Period; mid-Twenty-first to end Twenty-second Dynasties	2			5	10										
Jackal-headed figure buried with Nakhtefmut (E.87.1896) *c.* 925–890 BC; Third Intermediate Period; Twenty-second Dynasty; reign of Osorkon I	2														
Baboon-headed figure buried with Nakhtefmut (E.88.1896) *c.* 925–890 BC; Third Intermediate Period; Twenty-second Dynasty; reign of Osorkon I	1														
Falcon-headed figure buried with Nakhtefmut (E.89.1896) *c.* 925–890 BC; Third Intermediate Period; Twenty-second Dynasty; reign of Osorkon I	2														
Human-headed figure buried with Nakhtefmut (E.90.1896) *c.* 925–890 BC; Third Intermediate Period; Twenty-second Dynasty; reign of Osorkon I	2														

Fitzwilliam Museum accession number	*Ficus sycomorus*, **sycomore fig**			*Ziziphus spina-christi*, **sidr, Christ's thorn**			*Acacia nilotica* **(syn.** *Vachellia nilotica*), **Nile acacia / Acacia sp., acacia**			*Tamarix aphylla, tamarisk*			*Cedrus libani*, **cedar of Lebanon**		
	main	**joining**	**addi-tional**	**main**	**joining**	**addi-tional**	**main**	**joining**	**addi-tional**	**main**	**joining**	**addi-tional**	**main**	**joining**	**addi-tional**
Two coffin pegs associated with Nakhtefmut coffin (E.93a–b.1896) *c.* 925–890 BC; Third Intermediate Period; Twenty-second Dynasty; reign of Osorkon I		2													
Coffin face (E.GA.111.1949) *c.* 945–735 BC; possibly Third Intermediate Period; Twenty-second Dynasty							2								
Footboard from cartonnage coffin (E.GA.2911.1943) *c.* 945–735 BC; Third Intermediate Period; Twenty-second Dynasty	1														
Qersu coffin from tomb 840 at Abydos (E.14.1926) *c.* 745– 650 BC; Late Period; Twenty-fifth Dynasty							29	2							
Fragment of openwork decoration (Osiris) (E.GA.2898.1943) *c.* 700–30 BC; Late Period to Roman Period	1														
Coffin panel (E.GA.120.1949); *c.* 945–655 BC; Third Intermediate to Late Period; Twenty-second to Twenty-fifth Dynasties													1		
Pakepu coffin (E.2.1869) *c.* 680–664 BC; Late Period; late Twenty-fifth Dynasty	55	27	9		8			1							
Miniature coffin (E.43.1907) *c.* 664–525 BC; Late Period; 525 BC; Late Period; Twenty-sixth Dynasty													3		
Coffin panel showing the goddess Nephthys (E.GA.4331.1943) *c.* 790–720 BC; Third Intermediate to Late Period; late Twenty-second to early Twenty-fifth Dynasties													3		

Fitzwilliam Museum accession number	*Ficus sycomorus*, sycomore fig			*Ziziphus spina-christi*, sidr, Christ's thorn			*Acacia nilotica* (syn. *Vachellia nilotica*), Nile acacia / Acacia sp., acacia			*Tamarix aphylla*, *tamarisk*			*Cedrus libani*, cedar of Lebanon		
	main	joining	addi-tional	main	joining	addi-tional	main	joining	addi-tional	main	joining	addi-tional	main	joining	addi-tional
Coffin face (EGA.3011.1943); 306 BC–AD 200; Ptolemaic to Roman period	1				4			1							
Coffin fragment (E.W.89); Late Period; Twenty-fifth to Twenty-sixth Dynasties				1											
Coffin fragment (E.W.90); Late Period; Twenty-fifth to Twenty-sixth Dynasties				1											
Coffin fragment (E.W.92); Late Period; Twenty-fifth to Twenty-sixth Dynasties				1											
Anthropoid coffin (E.W.93); Late Period; Twenty-fifth to Twenty-sixth Dynasties	7		7		12			1							
Jackal figure (head missing) (E.W.94) *c.* 664–525 BC; probably Late Period; Twenty-sixth Dynasty	1														
Coffin plank (E.W.95); possibly Middle Kingdom, Twelfth Dynasty (*c.* 1975–1790 BC)	1				1										
Coffin fragment (E.W.96); possibly Middle Kingdom, Twelfth Dynasty (*c.* 1975–1790 BC)													1		
Coffin fragment (E.W.97); possibly Middle Kingdom, Twelfth Dynasty (*c.* 1975–1790 BC)										1					

numbers = samples main = principal components of artefact joining = connective carpentry elements additional = patches, inserts, wedges, strips

Beyond the Visible

Merging scientific analysis and traditional methods for the documentation of the anthropoid coffin of Amenemhat

Nesrin el-Hadidi, S. Darwish, Mohamed Ragab, Sabah Abd el-Razek and M. Abd el-Rahman

This study focuses on an early example of using the human shape in a third coffin. An ancient Egyptian anthropoid wooden coffin belonging to the Egyptian prince Amenemhat from the Middle Kingdom, Twelfth Dynasty, was found at Deir El Bersha in separate parts and reconstructed 16 years after its excavation in 1900. The goal of this study is to document the structure and materials used in making the coffin. Preliminary investigations confirm that it was made of sidder (or sidr) wood (Ziziphus sp.), the use of which has been relatively rarely documented in making wooden coffins. The feasibility, effectiveness, and overall value of Portable X-Radiography were proven while studying the coffin. It helped identify the structure of the coffin and previous inconsistent conservation, in which a large number of screw nails had been used to join wood. The detached wooden parts that had been joined together were covered with a paste to hide the restoration. On the left side of the head animal glue, which had been used as an adhesive, possibly during earlier restoration of the coffin, and calcium carbonate (CaCO3) could be identified using X-ray diffraction (XRD) analysis and Fourier transform infrared (FTIR) spectroscopy. Digital photography and multispectral imaging (Ultra Violet (UV) and Infrared (IR)) were used in the documentation of the wooden coffin. Samples were studied under both the optical microscope and in the scanning electron microscope (SEM) to obtain a more detailed observation of the condition and physical characteristics of the wood.

Introduction

This study started in 2014 in the basement of the Egyptian Museum, Cairo. An anthropoid inner coffin (box and lid, Egyptian Museum, CG 28093), dated to the Twelfth Dynasty, of a man with a beard and without any inscriptions (Lacau 1906, 64) was chosen for study and conservation. The coffin had been excavated in March 1900 at Deir El-Bersha by Ahmed Bey Kamal, who noted that the condition of wooden objects inside the tomb was very bad. The inner coffin had been broken into many parts, and had been placed into the two large rectangular coffins (Kamal 1902, 30) belonging to Amenemhat  (Egyptian Museum, CG 28091–28092; Lacau 1906, 37–64). The coffin, 200 cm long and 48 cm wide, is composed now of a total of ten irregular wooden pieces, all of which were given the same CG number prior to reconstruction. Years later the coffin pieces were joined together at the Egyptian Museum. No records of the restoration have been found but, from preliminary investigations, it was evident that curved wooden braces had been carved to fit into the interior of the lid and were fixed to the broken parts with the aid of nails and screws. It is difficult to criticise this restoration of the lid, now completed around 100 years ago, because without the added inner structure, the old wood would have warped and deformed many decades ago in the basement of the Museum.

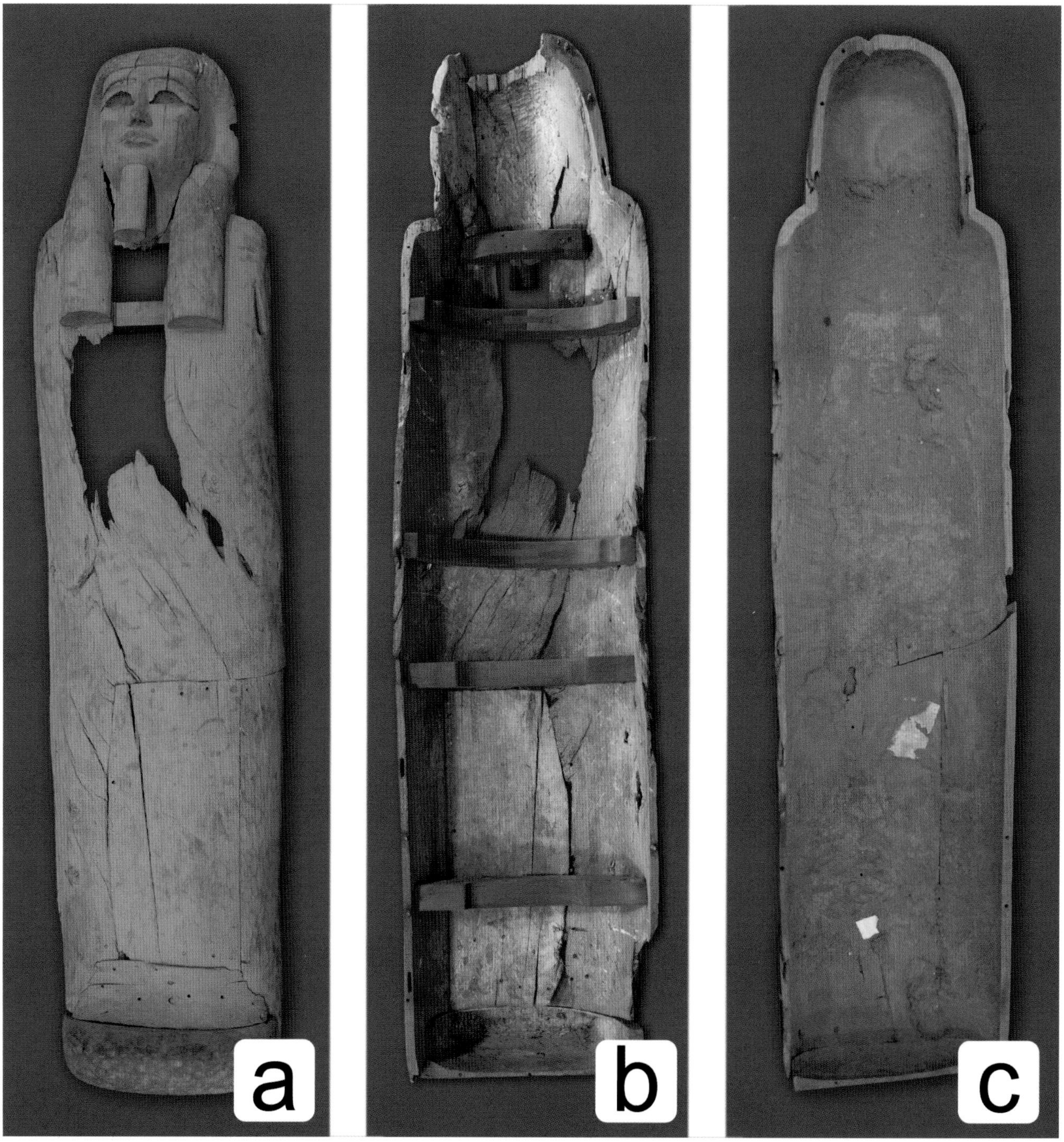

Fig. 6: Coffin lid (1a) exterior, (1b) interior and coffin box (1c), both covered with dust, their colour almost grey. The rim of the box, in which most of the mortises were broken, bears original red paint. Mortises and holes indicate the use of both tenons and dowels to join the lid to the box. The coffin is composed of a total of ten pieces, seven of which formed the lid. In the early restoration all the pieces forming the coffin lid were joined together with five curved wooden braces forming an internal support structure

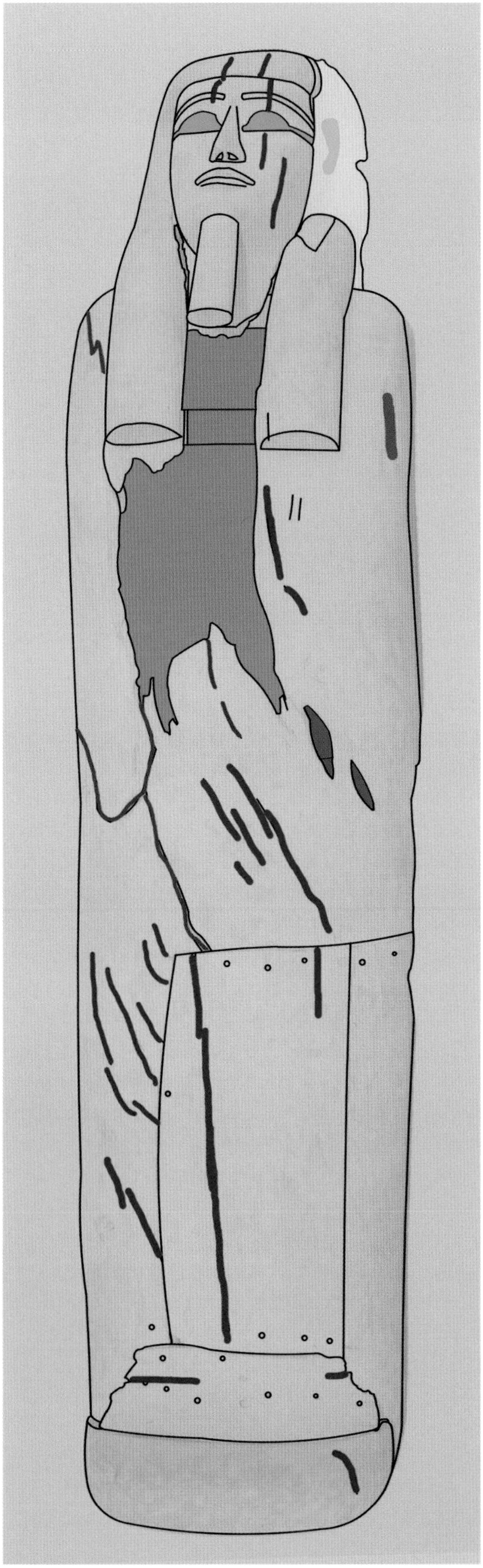

Methods used for examination and analysis

Merging traditional methods of documentation (photography manipulated by 2D and 3D programmes) together with scientific examination and analysis techniques, an investigation was carried out to obtain data from both the original and the restoration materials used in the coffin. The study is divided into three parts:

- Documentation of the coffin using 2D and 3D software programmes (AutoCAD® and Autodesk 3ds Max®)
- Examination of the structure and manufacturing techniques of the coffin
- Identification of coffin materials

Tools used for investigation and analysis included:

Portable digital X-radiography:

This was used in addition to visual examination as an evaluation method of construction and wood condition (Parkes and Watkinson 2010). Coffin box and lid were scanned using a Cuattro Slate, 25 x 30 cm wireless Cesium-I detector system with tablet monitor.

Wood Identification

Wood samples were submerged in water for a few minutes and cut by hand to show the transverse, tangential and radial sections, which were studied at magnifications of x150 and x400 under transmitted light using an OPTKA MICROSCOPY (Italy) B-383PL microscope equipped with an OPTIKA B 9 Digital Camera to determine the anatomical features of the wood and its surface condition (Crivellaro and Schweingruber 2013, 463).

UV optical microscopy

The coffin lid's external surface was studied using UV microscopy. The fluorescence of strange traces of adhesive and a white material on the wood surface were photographed using a Dino-Lite AD4113T^{-1}2v USB digital microscope with 1.3mp sensor and magnification range x20–x220 in ultraviolet mode.

Damage map:

- Cracks
- Splits in wood
- Sharp tool marks
- Fragile part
- Missing inlaid eyes
- Missing part
- Missing ears

Fig. 7: Damage map with colour keys showing the structure of the coffin lid, composed of seven parts, and with various types of damage.

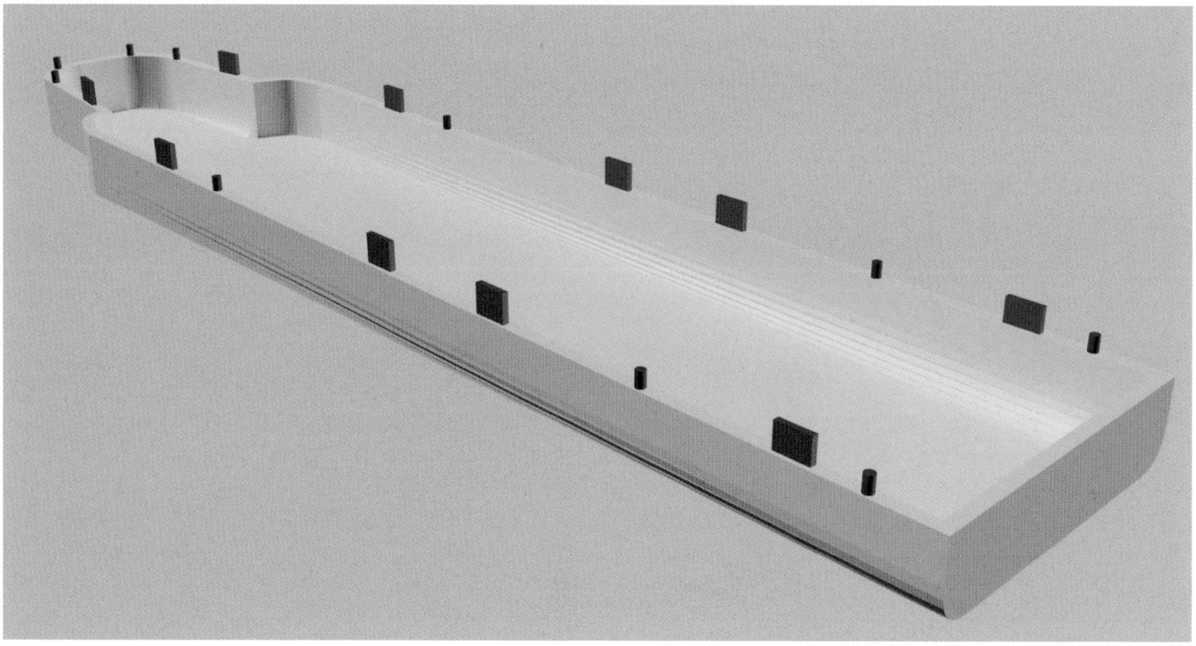

Fig. 8: Visualisation using 3ds Max showing how dowels and tenons were arranged in the coffin box rim.

Scanning electron microscopy (SEM)

A JEOL scanning electron microscope JSM-5400 LV SEM/EDS was used for examining the wood used to make the coffin. The accelerating voltage was 10–15 kV in the magnification range of x200 to x1000. The samples were mounted on aluminium stubs with double-sided cellophane tape for gold coating using a JEOL-JFC^{-1}100E ion sputtering device.

Fourier transform infrared spectroscopy (FTIR)

IRPrestige-21 FTIR spectrophotometer in the 400–4000cm^{-1} range with resolution of 8cm^{-1} and IRsolution software were used for identifying an adhesive material on the inner part of the face. The samples were prepared by mixing with potassium bromide and forming pellets for analysis.

X-ray diffraction (XRD)

A sample of white powdery material from the coffin was studied using X-ray Diffractometer System PANalytical PW3040 pro model, Cu-target tube and Ni filter at 40kV and 30mA, together with X'Pert Highscore software.

Results and Discussion

Documenting damage and deterioration using 2D and 3D software programmes

The coffin box consists of three planks and the lid consists of seven planks that seem to have the same appearance, except for one piece on the proper left side of the head, which is yellow in colour, fragile and has a different texture. Deterioration effects observed on the coffin lid included cracks which occur in different sizes, directions and forms, some of which may date back to when the coffin was buried in the tomb and suffered from variations in burial environment conditions. Cracks that are seen in the direction of the grain are probably due to wood movement (contraction and expansion). However, cracks perpendicular to the wood grain may be due to pressure exerted during attempts to force open the lid whilst the tomb was being plundered, because sharp tool marks are evident on the lid. Missing parts in the chest area could be due to flaws in the original carpentry technique, which depended on joining many planks together, or could be due to attempts to access the chest area of the mummy using heavy tools or force. Fine, cuboidal cracks on the surface may indicate fungal attack. The lid originally had inlaid eyes, now missing. All damage and deterioration features were recorded by photography (**Fig. 6**) and mapping using a computer program (AutoCAD®) which illustrates the shape of the coffin lid and all the damaged parts (**Fig.** 7).

For more than a quarter of a century, 3D modelling has had a special significance in archaeology and has attracted those who are active in archaeological documentation and reconstruction (Niknami and Mirashe 2007). In the case of this coffin, Autodesk 3ds Max® software was used for the virtual reconstruction of the

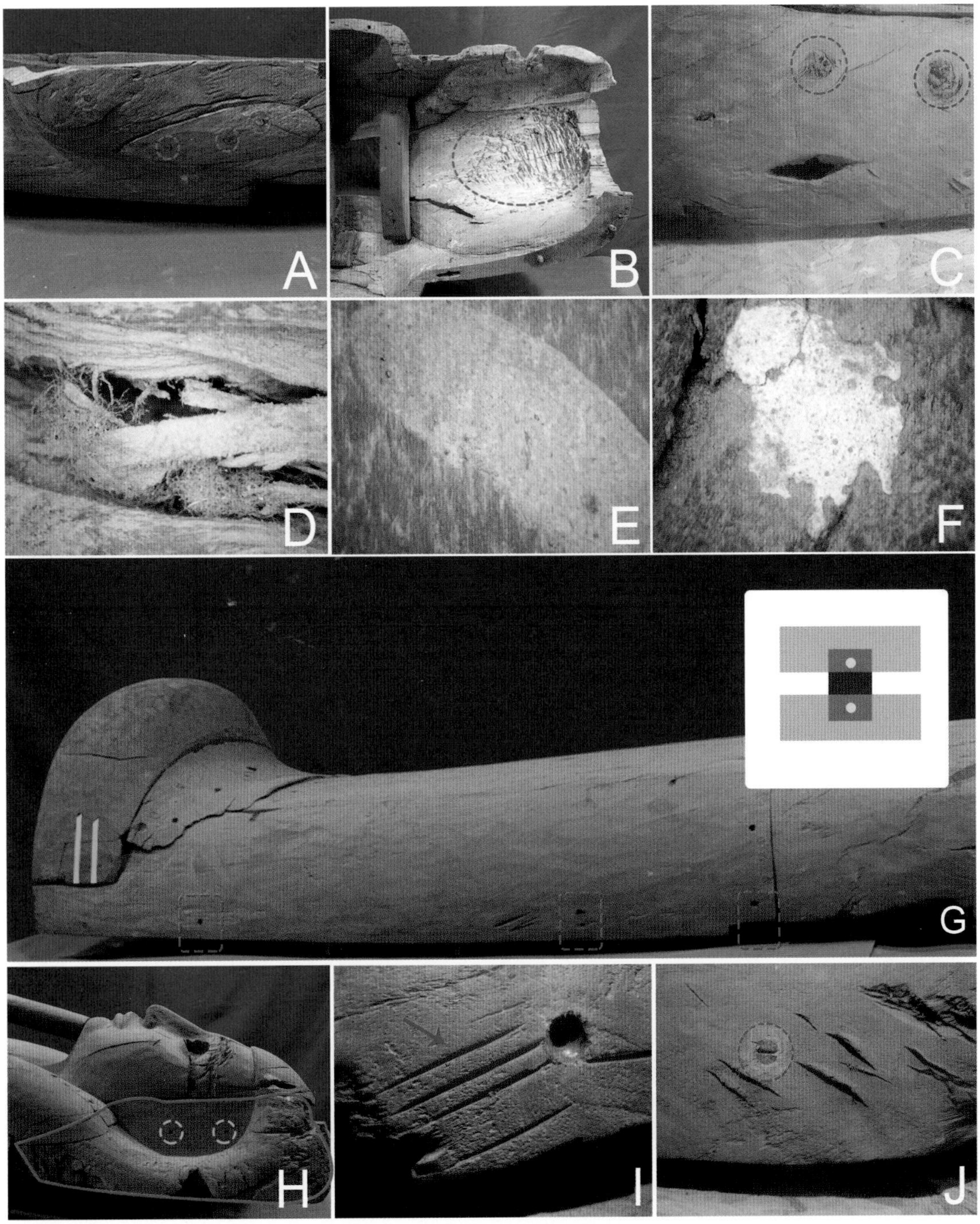

Fig. 9: A) shows how the ancient carpenter repaired wood defects by acquiring another piece of wood and fixing it on with wooden dowels. B) Chisel marks which, together with the various joint types, show the carpentry techniques. In the head part both dowels and tenons were present. C) Wood knots typical for sidr wood. D) Dust, foreign matter, wood defibration and insect galleries. E) and F) Yellow and white colour found on the lid surface. G) Pegged rim tenons (i.e. with crossing dowels to hold them in position) (red squares) used as the closure mechanism for the lid and box. Green lines in the foot mark the position of two dowels. The photograph also shows large amount of dust that had formed a hard crust over the coffin lid surface. H) Deterioration by microbiological attack causing a change in the colour and texture of the wood and cube-shaped cracks as a result of fungal attack. The green dotted circles show the holes for dowels that held on the now-missing left ear. I) Sharp tool marks which may date back to the robbery. J) Screw head that was covered with paste during the reconstruction of the coffin lid.

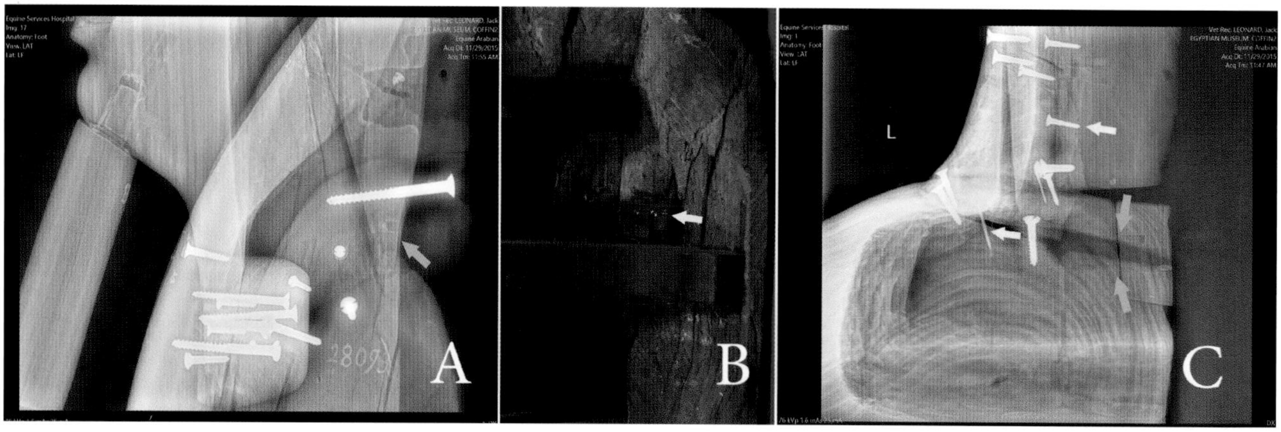

Fig. 10: A) X-radiograph and B) photograph of interior of the head and shoulder area showing wood grain direction, a mortise and tenon joint (pink arrow) used to attach the beard to the chin, a CG number "28093" behind the wig lappet on the shoulder inside the coffin and one on the back side of the beard. There are splits, cracks and a cluster of more than thirteen screws of different lengths from the previous restoration that are embedded inside both the old and the new wood. c) In the foot area the different grain direction can be seen. Also visible are screws and nails, fewer in number and shorter in length, distributed at intervals, in addition to dowels that were used for join two pieces of wood. The two dowels marked in green on **Fig. 9** *G are pointed out here by the pink arrows.*

joinery techniques. It helped with visualisation of the position and use of rim tenons and dowels in the coffin box (**Fig. 8**).

Examination of structure and technique

As noted above, the coffin lid was broken and had been dismantled into several pieces inside the tomb. The coffin was transferred to the Museum 16 years after its discovery, but there are neither known records of the restoration and treatment nor how it was put back together as one piece. The only available data is one old black and white photograph of the reconstructed coffin in the Special Register of the Egyptian Museum Cairo.

The repetition of the Catalogue Général (CG) number on the different parts of the lid confirms that the lid arrived at the Museum in several parts. The wooden braces, a few metal nails and glue in some areas are the only visible evidence of the materials and techniques used in the restoration. According to current conservation standards, some of these materials are considered inappropriate, but their removal would require careful assessment and evaluation. For this reason it was necessary to use non-destructive techniques in order to obtain as much information as possible, without causing additional damage.

It was not possible to move the coffin from the basement of the Museum. The best solution therefore was to study all parts using a portable X-ray unit. The radiographs gave a clear picture of wood grain direction, cracks, fissures, joints, original dowels, metal nails and screws used in the previous restoration (**Fig. 10**). Most of the wood pieces were sawn and cut along the grain in the direction of the long axis of the coffin, with one clear exception, that is in the foot case of the lid. Here the carpenter chose to hollow out part of a tree trunk along the wood grain and lay it on its side (so, with the wood grain perpendicular to the long axis of the coffin) to create the full width of the foot case. The radiograph also shows that it was carved out mainly from the heartwood and that the sapwood had relatively wide annual rings.[1] Straight-grained pieces of wood were chosen to create the separately attached face and beard. This shows that the ancient carpenter had a good knowledge of how to choose suitable wood for the important parts of his work.

Various types of metal nails and screws were observed in the X-ray images. They were of a range of sizes and diameters and were well hidden under a black and brown paste. More than seventy-eight screws and two metal nails were recorded in the coffin lid; most of them were used for attaching the wooden restoration supports. It is interesting to note that in the shoulder area the restorers used an astonishingly large number

[1] The years for which the annual rings are relatively wide were relatively wetter and therefore the tree grew faster. This feature could assist in an understanding of the dendrochronology of native Egyptian trees.

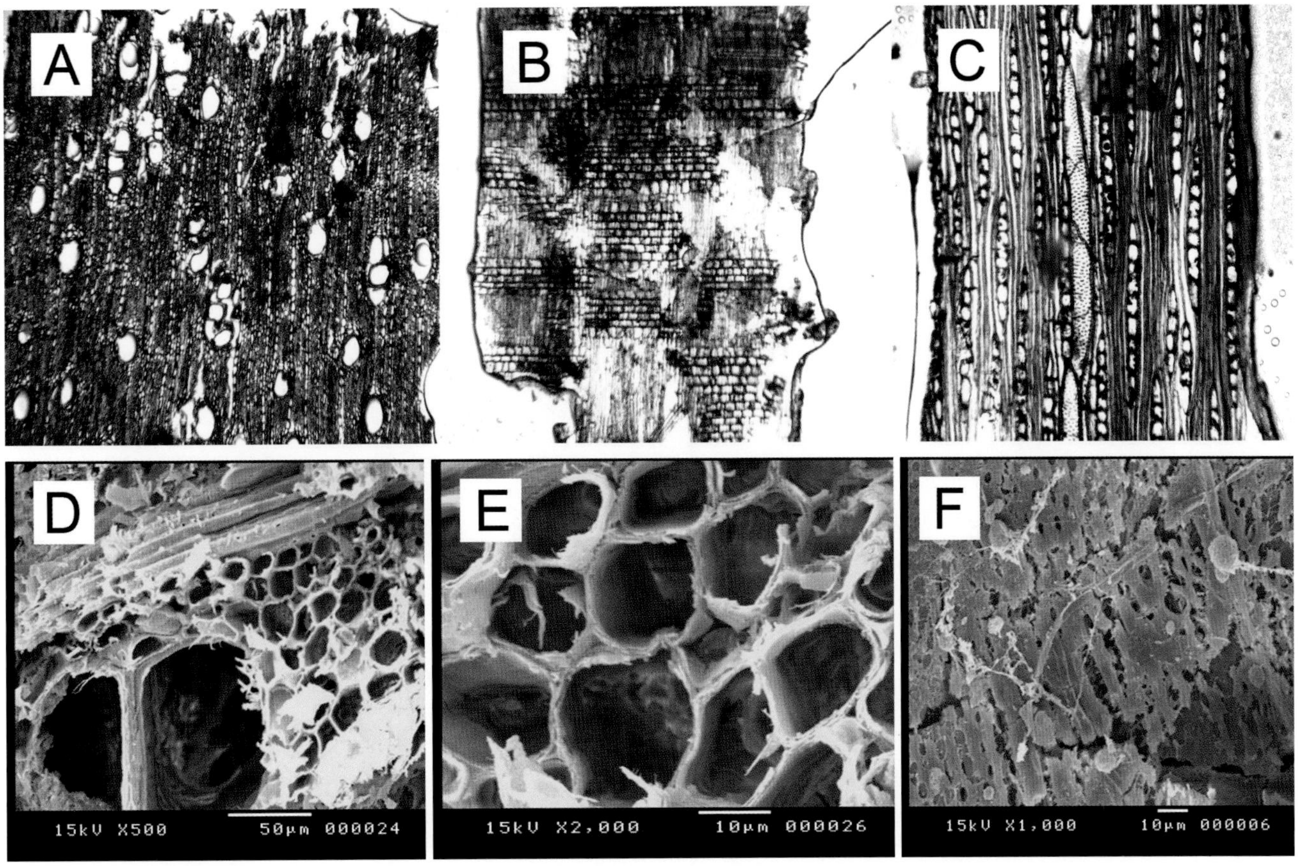

Fig. 11: A) Transverse section of Ziziphus spina-christi *L. (sidr) with growth ring boundaries distinguished by zones with fibres of variable cell wall thickness, and by a lack of vessels in terminal latewood. B) Vessel solitary and in radial multiples of 2 to 4, common fibres thick to very thick-walled. Radial section rays with procumbent, square and upright cells mixed throughout the ray. C) Tangential section rays uniseriate to 3 cells wide (Crivellaro and Schweingruber 2013, 463). D) SEM micrograph of* Ziziphus spina-christi *L., showing two vessels and tracheids in transverse section (bar: 50µm). E) At a higher magnification separation of secondary cell wall layers (S_1,S_2, S_3 and middle lamella) can be seen (bar: 10µm). F) In longitudinal section deterioration of pits and cells due to fungal attack is noticeable (bar: 10µm).*

of screws perpendicular to the wood grain, which will be challenging when the time comes to remove them in future conservation processes. In the foot part the choice of nails and screws was slightly different. Screws were shorter and distributed farther apart from each other and in different directions to join the old wood parts together.

Identifying original coffin parts and added material

Wood

After preparing wood sections in all three directions from two different parts of the original wood from the coffin and examining them under the microscope, the wood species was identified as *Ziziphus spina-christi* (L.) Willd. (Sidr) (Nabk). Sidr was commonly used in much of the joinery in ancient Egypt, ranging from dowels in small objects to tenons in objects as big as the Cheops boat (Lipke and Moustafa 1984), yet it has been recorded infrequently as structural elements in coffin construction (Lucas 1962 and Gale *et al.* 2000, 347, give examples from the Old and Middle Kingdoms, while Strudwick and Dawson 2017, 117 and 184 give an example from the New Kingdom and one from the Twenty-first Dynasty). Scanning electron microscopy (SEM) was used to assess the condition of the wood, which shows evidence of fungal attack (**Fig. 11 F**).

Adhesive

Small pieces of wood forming the face had been adhered together using an adhesive material in the past restoration. The appearance of this material ranges from transparent to opaque and brown in visible light, but

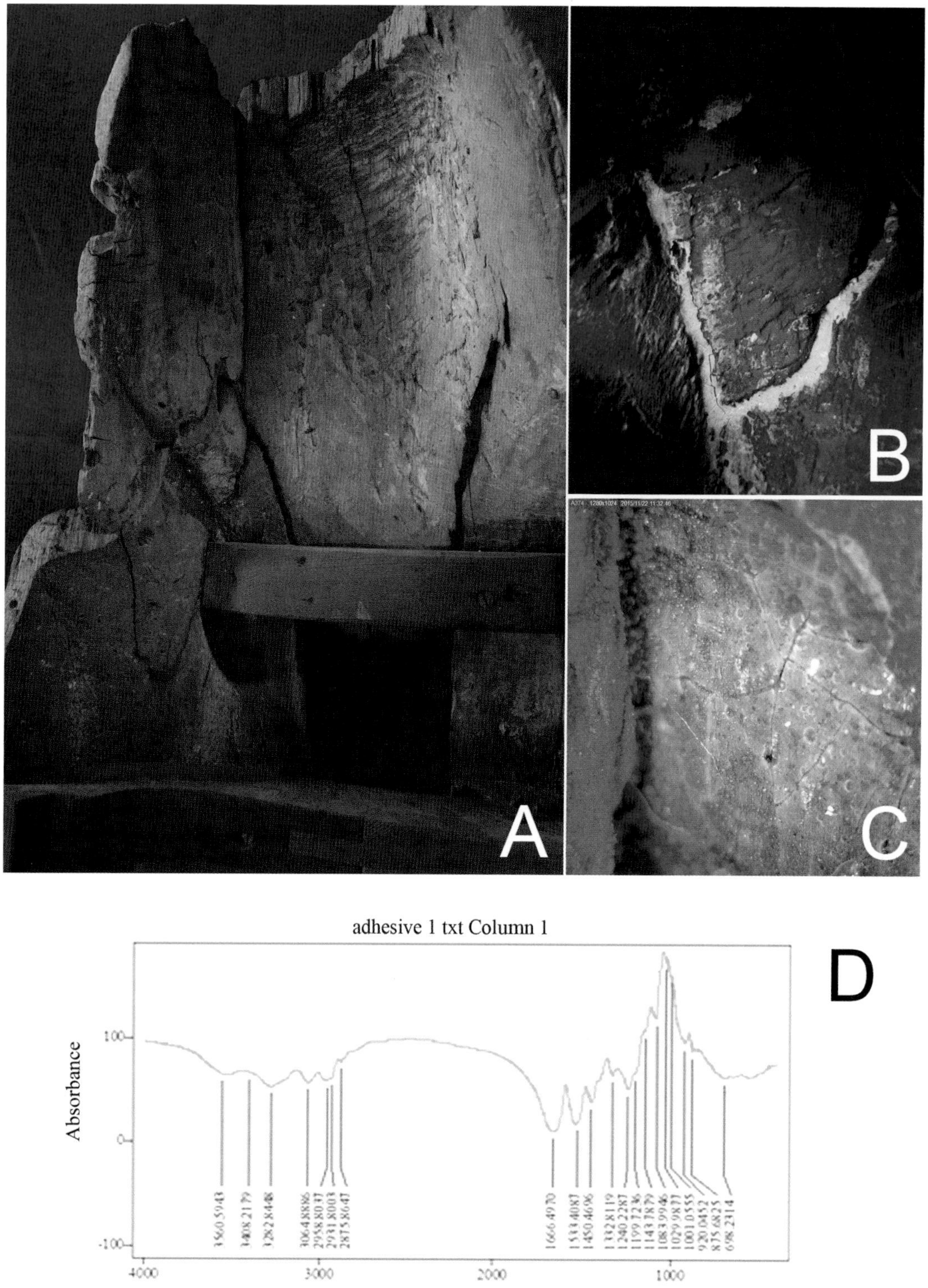

Fig. 12: Image of adhered inner part of coffin head, photographed under white light. B) Ultraviolet fluorescence image. This shows fluorescence of the adhesive which was applied irregularly all over the sides of the wood. C) UV fluorescence (Dino-Lite microscope image, ×100) showing the surface of the adhesive full of pits and cracks. D) FTIR spectrum of the adhesive sample, showing that it is proteinaceous, probably animal glue.

under a UV light source it shows a yellowish-green fluorescence. Fourier transform infrared spectroscopy (FTIR) was used to identify this adhesive, showing it to be proteinaceous, probably animal glue. In the FTIR spectrum (**Fig. 12 D**), there are the following diagnostic features: a band at ≈1667 cm^{-1}, assignable to C=O stretching (amide I); a band at ≈1533 cm^{-1} associated with C–N stretching and the deformation vibration of the N–H (amide II) and a band at ≈1240 cm^{-1} assignable to C–N stretching and N–H bending (amide III). In addition to these characteristic bands of protein there are other bands at ≈3561 and ≈3283 cm^{-1} due to O–H and N–H stretching. C–H stretching bands appeared at ≈3065 and ≈ 2959 cm^{-1}, while C–H bending appeared at ≈1451 and ≈1333 cm^{-1} (Derrick *et al.* 1991 97–98; Kong and Yu 2007 and Dallongeville *et al.* 2016).

Traces of white colour

A white powder sample from the coffin was analysed by X-ray diffraction (XRD). The results showed the presence of calcite ($CaCO_3$), indicating that this may be from a painting ground on the wood or from a white paint. Calcite was common, both as a painting ground, and as pigment used for the final paintings themselves (Scott 2016, 189).

Conclusion

Wooden artefacts, especially coffins, are very important for developing our understanding of ancient Egyptian technologies. Analytical methods were applied to study the composition of this interesting ancient Egyptian anthropoid coffin (CG 28093), which belonged to Amenemhat and is dated to the Twelfth Dynasty. It had been stored in the Egyptian Museum basement and was registered by mistake with the belongings of a person called "Sipi" who was a military general. Sidr (*Ziziphus spina-christi* (L.) Willd.) was used by the ancient Egyptian craftsman to make the coffin planks. The white traces on the coffin are calcite (CaCO3), which was most likely used as a ground or a painting material. Materials and techniques from the old restoration were identified.

This study has helped in assessment of the state of preservation of the coffin, and will assist in the conservation, a challenge that conservators may take up now that we have all the data and images available. The X-radiographs in particular should help minimise the sorts of surprises with which conservators are familiar when they are asked to treat an object that has been conserved in the past according to a totally different approach.

Acknowledgements

The authors would like to thank Mr Moamen Othman, Head of the Conservation Center, Egyptian Museum, Dr Ohyama Monitary for his help in identifying the wood species, Dr Karim Attia for his generous help with the X-radiography and Dr Hanaa el-Gaoudi and the rest of the team for their help during work in the Egyptian Museum basement.

Middle Kingdom mummy-shaped coffins

Investigating meaning and function

Uta Siffert

Middle Kingdom coffins appear in great numbers in burials, yet only in rare cases have so-called anthropoid or mummy-shaped coffins been found. The genesis, function and iconography of these coffins have never been studied systematically. This paper highlights several stages in their development and interpretation, in order to show their conceptual complexity and relevance within the mythological conception of the afterlife. As a matter of course this development was closely connected with evolving burial customs and the changing perception of the afterlife. New religious beliefs emerged and the encroachment of the Osiris cult caused a fundamental modification of the conception of death and afterlife, which in turn affected the configuration of the funerary equipment.

Introduction[1]

General terms like "coffin" or "mummy" are used to convey specific notions. However, if these phrases are not adequately qualified they can often lead to misunderstandings and confusion. For example, the phrase "Old Kingdom coffins" conveys significantly different thoughts to the phrase "Middle Kingdom coffins", in terms of changes in coffin composition and coffin-shape, as well as interpretations of burial customs and prevalent ideas regarding the afterlife. This situation highlights the importance of establishing a precise nomenclature and definitions. However, modern designations are sometimes misleading and need to be reviewed.

Due to their original purpose, coffins are closely connected with dead bodies (i. e. mummies). Although originally devised in order to protect the dead body, in the course of time they formed a symbiosis. In particular, the so-called Middle Kingdom mummy-shaped coffins cannot be studied without consideration of the bodies they contained and the two must be given equal status in any studies of them. Especially when it comes to study so called Middle Kingdom mummy-shaped coffins they cannot be isolated from each other and must therefore be studied equally. In fact, mummies form the basis for my investigation of these coffins to help reveal their meaning.

In general, an Egyptian mummy is the body of a human being or animal embalmed and mummified according to specific methods or techniques as a preparation for burial in order to try and halt decomposition. With the aid of linen wrappings it acquired a special and particular body shape. Sometimes the mummy was also provided with additional attributes like mummy masks or jewellery. However, during all epochs, mummies were created with the objective of ensuring the durability and imperishability of the body which was needed for the

[1] The present paper was compiled as part of the project 'From Object to Icon' funded by the Austrian Science Fund (FWF, Project No. P 25958) and conducted at the Department of Egyptology, in cooperation with the research group Multimedia Information Systems, at the University of Vienna (http://meketre.org/). I am thankful to Helen Strudwick and Julie Dawson for the great organisation of the conference "Ancient Egyptian Coffins: Past • Present • Future" and for the opportunity to publish my paper. I would also like to express my thanks to the editors for their helpful comments and revision of my English writing.

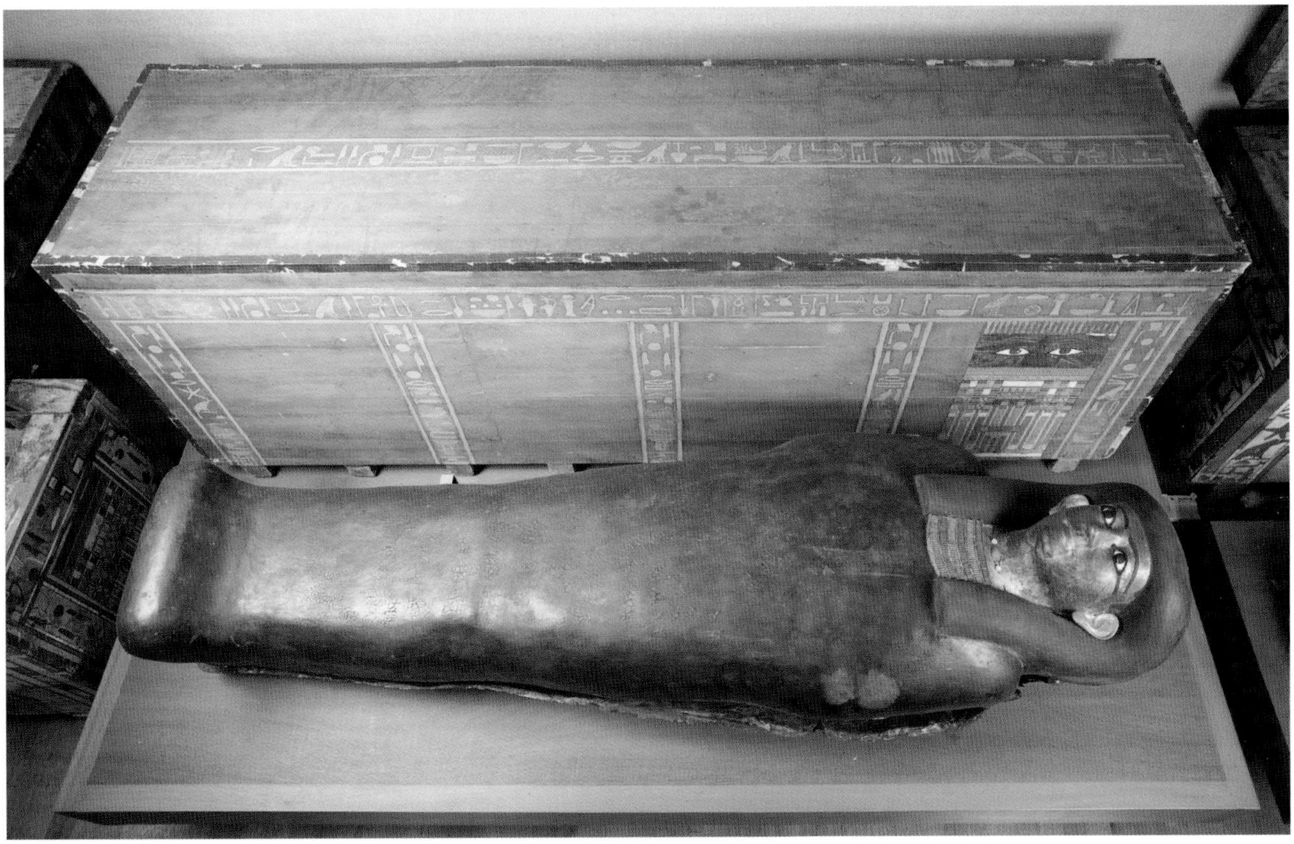

Fig. 13: Box-shaped coffin, mummy cover and mummy of the Lady Nephthys from Meir, Twelfth Dynasty. © MMA, 11.150.15a–c, Rogers Fund, 1911, http://www.metmuseum.org/art/collection/search/590947

Fig. 14: Canopic chest of Hapiankhtifi from Meir, Twelfth Dynasty. © MMA, 12.183.14a–c, Gift of J. Pierpont Morgan, 1912; http://www.metmuseum.org/art/collection/search/544327

afterlife. Coffins were, in addition, meant to guarantee the body's continued existence.

The way of preparing and equipping the mummy varied significantly with epoch, location and social status of the deceased person. It mainly depended on the evolution of the mummification technique, as well as on the changing beliefs in the afterlife. The afterlife was imagined in many different ways depending on a multiplicity of traditions. But the main motive for conserving the body was the belief in some form of existence after death, for which an intact and entire body was necessary. Thus the mummification method and its product – the mummy itself – reflected contemporary religious beliefs. Coffins went through a similar progression as regards the development of decoration with protective themes and spells.

Fig. 15: Box-shaped coffin and mummy of Ukhhotep, son of Hedjpu, from Meir, Twelfth Dynasty. © MMA, 12.182.132a, b, Rogers Fund, 1912, http://www.metmuseum.org/art/collection/search/546303

Once established (not later than the Old Kingdom;[2] Lüscher 1990, 1), mummification was used continuously in Egypt until the early Coptic Period. However, over this long period of time, the quality of treatment, as well as the technique, varied considerably. In particular, comparing mummies from the Old Kingdom with mummies from the First Intermediate Period or the Middle Kingdom demonstrates significant differences. They differ in appearance and arrangement, but especially the treatment of the mummy changed significantly (see below).

Old Kingdom mummies and coffins

The majority of bodies from Pre- and Early Dynastic times were found skeletonised, although they might have been mummified naturally (and artificially?)[3] before. Indeed, by the late Predynastic Period, some bodies were already being enclosed in small, undecorated coffins of clay, reed or several other materials, but it was not until the Old Kingdom that coffins became a standard form of burial. During the Old Kingdom, wooden coffins and stone sarcophagi of the non-royal dead were regularly full-length and box-shaped, and they continued in use until at least the end of the Middle Kingdom (e.g. Donadoni Roveri 1969, *passim*). Their decoration developed over time and depended on the status of the owner. However, an essential feature, which can be found on almost every coffin of this kind, is the presence of *wedjat* eyes (**Fig. 13**). They allowed the deceased inside to have a view right through them. However, it was also the very introduction of coffins that led to the rapid decomposition of the dead body, since

[2] Jones *et al.* 2014 published the results of a chemical investigation of linen funerary wrappings from bodies in Badarian and Predynastic period tombs. They identified some ingredients with antibacterial properties as well as resin. However, we do not know the reason for the impregnation. There could have been plenty of good reasons other than mummification for impregnating wrappings (e.g. to avoid a strong smell; the reuse of wrappings used during lifetime etc.). Textual evidences for a belief in some form of existence after death first started to appear in the Old Kingdom (e.g. Coffin Texts, but also non-royal funerary texts).

[3] Jones *et al.* 2014, *passim*. Compare footnote 2.

it excluded the dry sand, which had previously aided the natural preservation of bodies. This most probably contributed to the development of mummification, since belief in the integrity of the body presupposed the continued existence after death. The body was protected physically by mummification and magically by funerary equipment, such as coffins, as well as rituals and magical spells.

Even though no royal mummies from the Old Kingdom are preserved (Germer 2004, 18), intentional mummification was practised from at least the Fourth Dynasty, judging from the remains of upper class people. After applying techniques of dehydration and embalming in order to conserve the body, it was wrapped in copious amounts of linen. However, only a small percentage of people were mummified during this time and even fewer have been preserved.[4] Moreover, they often show a poor state of preservation since during the Old Kingdom the methods of preserving the dead body were experimental and innovative, and carried out by inexperienced practitioners. Many different methods of mummification were used in parallel or tried as a 'one off' – such as covering the wrappings around the mummy with mud or plaster (Tacke 1996, 307–336; Dulíková *et al.* 2011, 11, fig. 5). Nevertheless, the development of artificial mummification had just begun.

Irrespective of the mode of body treatment, however, the corpse was almost always wrapped in linen. The conservation of the corporal shape was of utmost importance. The aim was to retain the original shape of the corpse, to model a lifelike appearance, and consequently to make the final product – the mummy – look like a living image of the deceased. So the non-royal dead were not transformed into another form of being, but preserved as themselves.[5] All limbs and extremities were individually wrapped, and the outmost layer was worked to indicate the face and even sometimes the male genitals or the female breasts (Germer 2004, 19). In some cases, facial details such as the eyes, mouth, nose, beard, and even nipples, were painted to give a more naturalistic appearance. Moreover, the mummies could be dressed in clothing, wear wigs or be adorned with jewellery, similar to those they wore during their lifetimes.[6] Such detailed modelling and adornment became the norm for mummies of upper class people during the Old Kingdom and were aimed at making the mummy as lifelike as possible. Therefore, one might name this type of mummy as "anthropomorphic".

Since the Fifth Dynasty onwards mummies were usually laid, slightly flexed, on their left side, or supine in the box-shaped coffin. According to Stephan Seidlmayer this position might be interpreted as being asleep (Seidlmayer 2001, 205–252). This might suggest that death was understood as some form of sleep and that corpses were prepared and positioned in the tomb according to this conception. This assumption might be confirmed by the use of headrests, which were used to cushion the heads of mummies (for example, in an anonymous burial from Gebelein/Fifth Dynasty (Suppl. 15701) (Donadoni Roveri 1989, 39, fig. 3); also the burials Hag.89.C2, C3, C5, C6 in tomb D11/Eighth Dynasty or First Intermediate Period from El-Hagarsa contained headrests (Kanawati 1989, 38–39, pl. 30, 31, 34)). Furthermore, most Old Kingdom tombs contained only a few funerary objects. The objects found were probably used during the lifetime of their owner, since they show signs of wear (Seidlmayer 2001, 226–240). The afterlife seemed to be understood as some kind of continuation of life.

First Intermediate Period and Middle Kingdom mummy-shaped objects

During the First Intermediate Period and the Middle Kingdom new religious beliefs emerged that resulted in a striking modification of the funerary inventory. The concept of death and the perception of the deceased changed significantly. In addition to the objects from everyday life, new objects, which seem to have had a primarily ritual and symbolic function, were made explicitly to be used in a funerary context (Seidlmayer 1990, 425–430; Willems 2014, 135–136; Grajetzki 2014, 141–146). Mummy-shaped objects were also introduced. Their appearance was geared to typical Middle Kingdom mummies, which were totally distinct from Old Kingdom mummies.

4 There seem to be fewer than ten known extant mummies from the Old Kingdom. See: Lacovara *et al.* 2015, 65.

5 In Old Kingdom private monuments the earliest textual references to Osiris can be found in offering formulas. However, Osiris and the deceased were never identified with each other (Smith 2017, 133–135). It also appears that the royal dead were distinct from Osiris and subordinated to him (Smith 2017, 136–165). The dead hoped to associate themselves with Osiris and wished to enjoy a beneficial relationship with him.

6 A good example is the anthropomorphic female mummy from tomb G 2220 in Giza, Fourth Dynasty. The body, including breasts, were modelled from linen and she was dressed in linen clothing. See: Reisner 1942, pl. 42b, d.

The preparation of Middle Kingdom mummies changed in many respects: the limbs were first separately wrapped and then the mummy was additionally bound in numerous layers of linen bandaging. Finally, the mummy was entirely wrapped in linen, without the separation of individual limbs.[7] The emphasis was, therefore, on giving the final product a non-anthropomorphic shape, which was quite contrary to Old Kingdom mummies. Different kinds of amulets were also placed among the wrappings in order to protect the deceased (Grajetzki 2014, *passim*, esp. 114–134).

Moreover, several new attributes formed the mummy's appearance. During the First Intermediate Period mummy masks emerged sporadically in Middle and Upper Egypt in a range of burials of non-royal people (Rogge 1986; Seidlmayer 1990, 426–427; Tacke 1996, 307–336). From the Eleventh Dynasty onwards, they became an inherent part of the funerary equipment both for private and royal people (Rogge 1986, 204–6; Seidlmayer 1990, 426). Most masks show a general similarity, with some stylistic differences that can be attributed to regional or chronological impacts. Often the face was framed by a wig, usually with a broad collar, which lay over the chest (Rogge 1986, 204–207). The masks represented a substitute face for the deceased. However, it is hard to decide whether they are intended to represent the face in an idealised, individual or standardised way. Certainly they became an intrinsic part of the mummy inasmuch as they were bound into the linen wrappings as well. Above all, the mummy mask became integrated in the layout of mummy-shaped coffins during the Twelfth Dynasty.

A similar and comparable development can be recognised in canopic jars. In the Old Kingdom, they were equipped with a flat or curved lid (see, for example, Germer 1998, 51, fig. 40, inv. no. 3106 and 3251, Pelizaeus-Museum Hildesheim). Jars with human heads appeared sporadically from the Eleventh Dynasty and became a characteristic funerary feature at the end of the Twelfth Dynasty (for example, the canopic jars of Nakht-Ankh from the so-called tomb of the two brothers in Deir Rifeh (Murray 1910, pl. 20, 21; David 2007, fig. 35); inv. no. Manchester 4727–4730, Manchester Museum). They certainly demonstrate a close relationship between the organs and the rest of the body. In addition, there are also examples of small mummy masks which covered the canopic jar or the visceral package (Dodson 1994, 17; Garstang 1907, 92–93, fig. 83a/b). Consequently, the lid should probably be interpreted as a mask rather than as a head. It indicates that the viscera and canopic jars were regarded as being of equal importance as the mummies themselves (Lüscher 1990, 9). Sometimes canopic jars even had human arms hanging down their sides or stood on short legs and feet (Raven 2005, 44; Dobrowolska 1970, 76). We also know of canopic containers in the form of a mummy-shaped coffin.[8] Moreover, the jars were placed into a canopic chest, whose design and decoration broadly followed that of contemporary box-shaped coffins (**Fig. 14**), suggesting they were looked upon as coffins for the mummified viscera (see, for example, the canopic chest of Nakht-Ankh from the so-called tomb of the two brothers in Deir Rifeh (Murray 1910, pl. 1); inv. no. Manchester 4726, Manchester Museum).

Middle Kingdom mummy-shaped coffins

It is interesting that jars with lids in the form of masks appeared at around the same time as the so-called mummy-shaped coffins came into use. Quite often these coffins are called "anthropoid" or "anthropomorphic". However, this designation is somewhat misleading since the shape resembles a classic Middle Kingdom mummy much more than a human form – as discussed above. Therefore, it is more appropriate to describe their form as "mummy-shape" or "mummy-form".

Only a few examples of mummy-shaped coffins stood the test of time, since they were often made of very thin wood or cartonnage. Sometimes even only small metal parts have been preserved (Mace and Winlock 1916, 36–42). Furthermore, it was only the elite who could afford such an object. Therefore, very few examples from the Middle Kingdom are known.[9] The earliest example seems to be the mummy case of Ashayet (museum

[7] All stages of wrapping can be seen in the mummy of Wah, which was unwrapped in the 1940s. Mummy of Wah, Thebes/Asasif, tomb of Wah (MMA 1102), Twelfth Dynasty, Winlock 1940, 253–259, fig. 1.

[8] For example the canopic container inscribed with the name of Duamutef from Meir/Twelfth Dynasty (The Metropolitan Museum of Art, MMA 12.182.61a, b, Rogers Fund, 1912, https://www.metmuseum.org/art/collection/search/546311).

[9] Garstang 1907, 171–176; Hayes 1978, 305, 308–312; Mace and Winlock 1916, 36–56; Rogge 1986, 207–227; Schmidt 1919, 40–88; coffin sets from The Metropolitan Museum of Art: Hapianhktifi from Meir, MMA 12.183.11b, 12.183.11c.1–.2, Gift of J. Pierpont Morgan, 1912; Nephthys from Meir, MMA 11.150.15a–c Rogers Fund, 1911; coffin sets from the Manchester Museum, University of Manchester: Khnum-Nahkt and Nahkt-Ankh from Rifeh, Murray 1910; David 2007.

Fig. 16: Mummy cover and inner box-shaped coffin of Hapiankhtifi from Meir, Twelfth Dynasty. © MMA, 12.183.11b, 12.183.11c.1–.2, Gift of J. Pierpont Morgan, 1912, http://www.metmuseum.org/art/collection/search/546301

number unknown; presumably stored in the Cairo Museum) dating to the reign of Nebhepetra Mentuhotep II (Winlock 1921, 50; Hayes, 1978, 310). It is regarded as an intermediate form between the mask and coffin, since the mummy was fully enveloped in a cartonnage mummy-shaped coffin.

Middle Kingdom mummy-shaped coffins may be interpreted as a variation of a typical mummy mask. In effect, they appear to be an imitation of the wrapped mummy wearing a mask (compare **Fig. 13 and Fig. 15**). Characteristically, only the head – clearly representing the mask, often with a gilded face – protruded from the wrappings, which covered the whole body, and sometimes a collar or necklace was shown. As with contemporaneous mummies, they were formed as an almost featureless body with no further anatomical details. They were manufactured as two parts (a lid and a box), which were roughly similar in size. The box was plain and formed the back of the mummy.

Two major types of mummy-shaped coffin are known. The earlier examples showed the deceased with a wig and collar, and the body was painted white to represent the linen wrappings around it or black as the colour of fertility (**Fig. 13 and Fig. 16**). Like the mummies themselves, the earliest examples of this type of coffin did not bear any inscriptions or further decoration on the body (van Walsem 1997, 27). As time passed, however, the decoration became more elaborate. Instead of merely imitating mummy features it evolved independent characteristics. The later examples – from the reign of Sesostris II onwards (Rogge 1986, 227) – showed in addition the mummy wearing a nemes headdress, a broad collar, and the body was decorated in a multi-coloured pattern. Some had a single, vertical column of text running from below the mask down to the foot, which gave the name and title of the deceased, and funerary formulae (van Walsem 1997, 27–28).

The use and treatment of these objects are particularly interesting, since they reveal their function and the concept underlying them. All known examples of mummy-shaped coffins were part of a coffin set, consisting of at least one additional outer box-shaped coffin (**Fig. 13 and Fig. 16**). Just like mummies, they were laid on their left side within the box-shaped coffin, with the

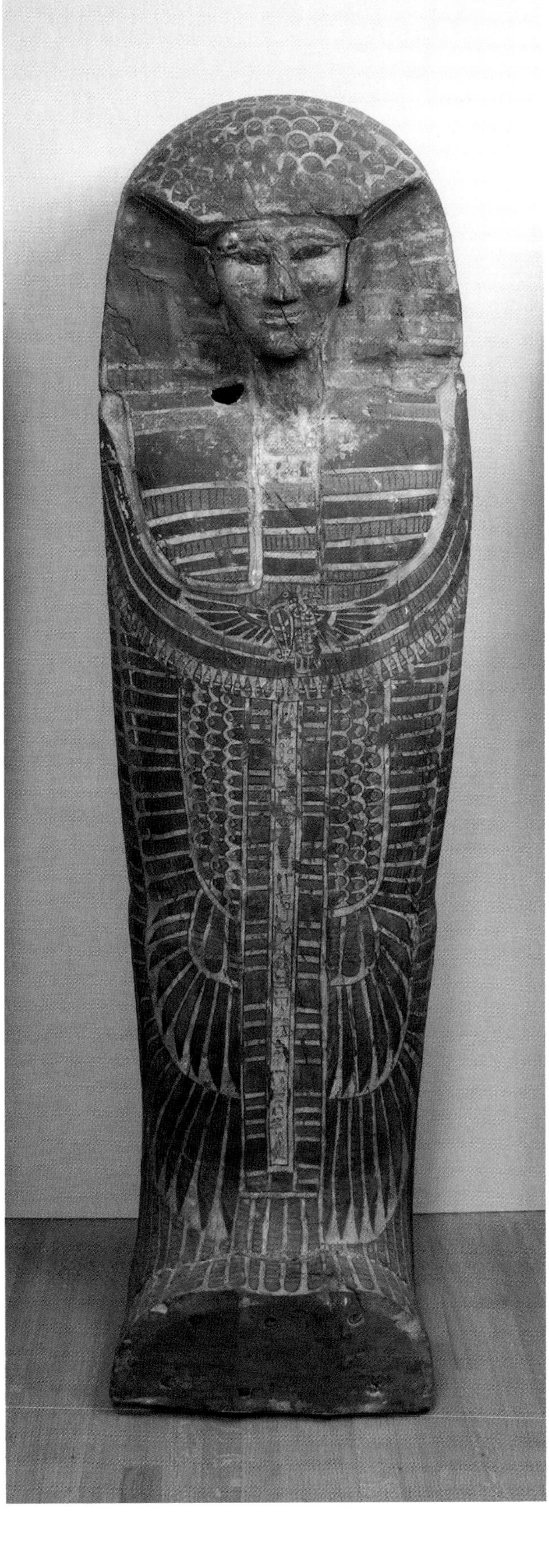

Fig. 17: Rishi coffin from Thebes, Asasif, Seventeenth Dynasty. © MMA, 12.181.299a, b, Rogers Fund, 1912, http://www.metmuseum.org/art/collection/search/544788

clear intention that the eyes of the mummy should see through the *wedjat* eyes painted on the outside of the box-shaped coffin. In some cases they were also found in a supine position or were placed on top of a bier and covered with a shroud (for example, the mummy-shaped coffin of Sobekhat, Dashur, shaft 106, late Twelfth to early Thirteenth Dynasties (Baba and Yazawa 2015, 3–9, pl. XIII)).

It becomes apparent that the mummy-shaped coffin afforded more than just protection for the deceased. It was a solid, protective cover, which imitated the mummy. Moreover, it represented the deceased in his new, post-mortal form, as a mummy. Therefore, perhaps no functional distinction is to be made between the mummy-shaped coffin and the mummy itself, since they were essentially the same. The enclosed mummy and the surrounding coffin became united eternally. The cover even functioned as a substitute and became one with the mummy. It identified absolutely with the mummy it contained and had no independent role in terms of function or rituals.

In this context the locking mechanism of these coffins is a meaningful feature. Once the lid was closed, it could be separated from the bottom only by force (Mace and Winlock 1916, 40–41). It was meant to be an everlasting protection. Hence, the so-called mummy-shaped coffin served as a cover and became the mummy itself rather than being a "coffin" in the classic sense. In other words, the box-shaped coffin containing the cover and the mummy was the only true coffin and its decoration and inscriptions formed a magical environment of protection for the deceased.

Therefore, it is necessary to rethink the designation "mummy-shaped coffin" for these particular objects, since the term "coffin" has associations that do not apply to these objects from the Middle Kingdom. The term "mummy cover" might thus be more appropriate.

Osiris in the Middle Kingdom

This development described herein was closely connected with evolving burial customs and the changing perception of the afterlife. New religious beliefs emerged and caused a fundamental modification to the concept of death and the afterlife, which in turn affected the configuration of funerary equipment. As mentioned above, mummies were a reflection of contemporary religious beliefs. During the First Intermediate Period the encroachment of the Osiris cult caused changes in the mythological conception of the afterlife, since Osiris became the superior god of death. However, these changes are firstly attested only in textual evidence (Smith 2017, 264–270). Finally, during the late Middle Kingdom the mummy shape and so-called royal insignia (such as flagellum, crook, crown, etc.) evolved as the typical iconographical attributes of Osiris. The earliest proof of this iconography seems to be the stela of Wahka I (Ägyptisches Museum Berlin, inv. no. 21823; Steckeweh 1936, pl. 17a).[10] Subsequently, the mummy-shape as an iconographical feature became accessible to, and adopted by, non-royal people. They believed in becoming one (form of) Osiris after death (Morenz 1957, 52–70) and aspired to interact, not identify, with him (Smith 2017, 266–268). Therefore, the meaning and interpretation of the mummy changed. While during the Old Kingdom the mummy reflected an image of the person during lifetime, in the late Middle Kingdom the mummy with all its attributes became a "ritual object" as Harco Willems has shown (Willems 2014, 136). Furthermore, at the very end of the Middle Kingdom the mummy became a stereotypical representation of the deceased as a god (Osiris).[11]

Further conclusions

Even though only a few mummies and mummy covers from the Middle Kingdom have been preserved, the almost featureless form of the mummy, which developed during that time, became the standard shape of mummies afterwards. It is arguably, nowadays, seen as the classic mummy-form.

After a short break, mummy-shaped coffins came into use again in the Seventeenth Dynasty (in the form of the so-called *rishi* coffins, **Fig. 17**). However, they took on new characteristics of their own and stood alone within the funerary ritual due to the fact that they were no longer placed in a box-shaped coffin. Their decoration and inscriptions changed significantly, so presumably the meaning and function attached to them also changed. They became the sole container for the mummy and consequently "true coffins" – in the sense of a funerary box intended to keep the deceased in a magical and regenerative environment. At this time they became the typical coffin form and are therefore correctly termed "mummy-shaped coffins".

[10] There are just a few depictions of Osiris known from the Middle Kingdom (compare the list given by Oppenheim 2015, 284, footnote 3). However, all these references must be viewed with caution. None of the depictions can be identified with Osiris without doubt. They are either fragmentary, without inscriptions or a syncretic form of Osiris is depicted (e.g. Khentiamentiu). So the evidence is equivocal.

[11] It is part of my ongoing research to investigate if the theological interpretations concerning the Osiris cult were attendant on the mummification technique, which developed significantly at that time, or vice versa.

Black coffins with yellow decoration of the New Kingdom

An original iconographic study

Lisa Sartini

The paper shows several results of my Master's dissertation I sarcofagi a vernice nera della XVIII – XIX dinastia: uno studio tipologico e cronologico, *written under the supervision of Professor Marilina Betrò and defended at the University of Pisa. In this paper I present the details of my iconographic study and its results, relating my investigations to other studies in this research area. In addition, I show some new black coffins I recently added to my catalogue, especially some specimens from Dahshur, which might confirm that the tradition of the black coffins with yellow decoration continued after the reign of Ramesses II.*

Black coffins with yellow decoration were first used in the reign of Hatshepsut/Tuthmosis III, replacing the previous white coffins, and apparently fell out of use around the reign of Ramesses II, when yellow coffins started to replace them. However, as I will discuss below, two coffins found by the Waseda University Egyptian Expedition in Dahshur North may disprove this second date. With regard to their geographical distribution, most of the examples come from the necropolis of Thebes, which was probably the epicentre of production. All the oldest coffins were discovered in this area, but a few examples are known from Saqqara (Zivie 2007; Bragg 1914, 51), Dahshur (Baba and Yoshimura 2010, 12; Yoshimura *et al.* 2012, 39–47), Gurob (Petrie 1890, 38), Sidmant (Petrie and Brunton 1924, 49), Akoris (Paleological Association of Japan 1955, 59–60), Amarna (Bettum and Skinner 2015) and Soleb (Schiff Giorgini 1971, 253 and 305).

Since in-depth chronological and typological studies on black coffins with yellow decoration have never been carried out,[1] I have tried to fill this gap in my Master's dissertation.[2] Construction techniques, decoration techniques, funerary texts, but most particularly iconographic themes have been considered in my research. This investigation has led to new results, which have both confirmed and refuted several different hypotheses suggested so far about black coffins with yellow decoration.

In an article (Sartini 2015), I have concisely reported the key results from my iconographic analysis of black coffins with yellow decoration and my proposals for new chronological and classification methods. In this paper I present other results of my iconographic investigation and I will discuss some new black coffins recently added to my catalogue.

Box decoration and the representation of the four Sons of Horus

The investigation of black coffin boxes shows how the iconographic elements are repeated and formulated in

[1] For general discussion of the black coffin with yellow decoration, see Dodson 1998; Taylor 2001b; Niwiński 1984; Niwiński 1988, 11–12.

[2] Master's dissertation with the title "I sarcofagi a vernice nera della XVIII-XIX dinastia: uno studio tipologico e cronologico" written under the supervision of Marilina Betrò at the University of Pisa, 2014. I am continuing my study of black coffins with yellow decoration as part of my PhD at the University of Pisa.

Table 1: Combinations of deities on four coffins

Coffin	*Dating*	*Gods*	*References*
Coffin of Hetempet	Tuthmosis III – Amenhotep II	Geb and Shu	Egyptian Museum, Cairo, JE 61017: Daressy 1909, 24–26
Outer coffin of Maiherpri	Amenhotep II	Geb and Horus	Egyptian Museum, Cairo, CG 24001: Daressy 1902, 2
Middle coffin of Yuya	Amenhotep III	Geb and a mummy figure	Egyptian Museum, Cairo, CG51002: Quibell 1908, 4–5
Coffin of Tutankhamen's daughter	Tutankhamen	Geb and Horus	Egyptian Museum, Cairo, JE60695: Griffith Institute, Carter Archives, no. 317°, http://www.griffith.ox.ac.uk/gri/carter/317a(1).html (accessed 1 June 2018)

Table 2: Black coffins by date phase

Before The Amarna Period		*After The Amarna Period*	
Phase 1		*Phase 3*	
Coffin of Tamyt	Tuthmosis III – Amenhotep II	Coffin of Ipuy	End Eighteenth/Nineteenth Dynasty
Coffin of Maiherpri	Amenhotep II	Coffin of Anen-tursha	Ramesses II
Coffin of Kenamun	Amenhotep II	Coffin of Hanura	Ramesses II
Phase 2		Anonymous coffin	Ramesses II
Two coffins of Yuya	Amenhotep III		
Anonymous coffin	Amenhotep III		

Table 3: Summary of dating criteria identified

Features	*Dating*
Nut depicted as a woman on the breast	Hatshepsut/Tuthmosis III–Amenhotep II
Nut depicted as a vulture on the breast	Amenhotep II–Amenhotep III
Nut depicted as a winged woman on the breast	Amenhotep III–End Eighteenth Dynasty/Ramesses II
Hands depicted under the *wesekh* collar	Hatshepsut/Tuthmosis III–Amenhotep III
Hands depicted slightly overlying the *wesekh* collar	Amenhotep II–Tutankhamen
Hands depicted completely overlying the wesekh collar	Amenhotep III–End Eighteenth Dynasty /Ramesses II
wesekh collar with polychrome bands and tear-shaped drops hanging from the outer edge	Hatshepsut/Tuthmosis III–Amenhotep III
wesekh collar decorated with a series of petals	Amenhotep III–End Eighteenth Dynasty/Ramesses II
Terminals of the collar represented in the shape of lotus flowers on the shoulders	Amenhotep III–Tutankhamen
The goddesses Nephthys and Isis represented sitting on a *nb* sign	Hatshepsut/Tuthmosis III–Amenhotep II

various versions and combinations. One can find: the *wedjat* eye on a shrine, the god Anubis in anthropomorphic form with jackal head or in jackal form on a shrine, the four Sons of Horus with human or animal heads, and the god Thoth, with an ibis head, opening a gate in the sky with a rod.

In my Master's dissertation, I identified three phases of decoration, each one with a diagnostic iconographic scheme on the box.[3]

Phase 1: From the reign of Hatshepsut/Tuthmosis III to the reign of Amenhotep III, the preferred scheme shows one or two *wedjat* eyes on a shrine and the god Anubis between two Sons of Horus (which is the iconographic scheme of Chapter 151 of the Book of the Dead).

Phase 2: From the reign of Amenhotep III to the end of the Amarna Period, the predominant iconographic scheme is the vignette from Chapter 161 of the Book of the Dead (BD 161): mirrored figures of Thoth opening a gate in the sky with a rod at either end of the side of the box, and Anubis between two Sons of Horus in the centre. This appears in the decorative programme from the reign of Tuthmosis III, but it is only under Amenhotep III that it becomes predominant, especially in Thebes. With very few exceptions, coffins from the time of Amenhotep III have BD 161 decoration.

Phase 3: From the reign of Tutankhamen to the reign of Ramesses II, the *wedjat* eyes on the shrine return to being represented on the panel at the shoulders, but with more prominence, sometimes without Thoth being depicted in the panel near the foot-end of the coffin.

In addition, a few examples show other iconographic elements represented on the panel near the foot-end of the coffin. Two examples, dating to the reign of Ramesses II, namely a coffin from TT41 and the coffin found in tomb 605 at Gurob (Assmann 1991, 254–259 (Sarg 3); Bell 1985, 64–65), respectively show the *tjt* sign and the *djed* pillar, while four other examples show figures of gods, in these combinations (**Table 1**).

The representation of the four Sons of Horus deserves particular consideration. In the past it has been their iconography that has been discussed, since Niwiński first suggested that their depiction with animal heads could be connected to the post-Amarna period, in an attempt to define a chronological evolution of black coffins with yellow decoration (Niwiński 1988, 12). My own study, however, shows that the four Sons of Horus with animal heads first appear from the reign of Amenhotep II, but it is noteworthy that the iconography of this feature is not standardised. This information is summarised in **Table 2**.

Six coffins with this feature are dated before the Amarna period and four after it. Other than the coffin of Anen-tursha, which is from Gurob, these coffins come from Thebes. Three may be placed in my Phase 1, three in Phase 2 and four in Phase 3.

Coffin of Tamyt (British Museum, EA6661: Strudwick and Dawson 2016, 176–177)

This is an atypical decoration. The right side of the box shows two human figures and one anthropomorphic figure with a baboon head, although the inscriptions refer once to Hapi and twice to Qebehsenuef. On the left side Hapi and Duamutef have human heads instead.

Outer coffin of Maiherpri (Egyptian Museum in Cairo, CG 24001: Daressy 1902, 2)

It shows only two Sons of Horus with animal heads (Hapi and Qebehsenuef) on the left side of the box.

Coffin of Kenamun (Museo Archeologico Nazionale di Firenze, 9477)

This coffin has recently been attributed to Kenamun, the god's father who lived under Amenhotep II (Betrò 2013). On the box two Sons of Horus are represented with animal heads: Qebehsenuef with a jackal head and Duamutef with a hawk head.

Coffins of Yuya (Egyptian Museum in Cairo, CG51001 and CG51002: Quibell 1908, 1–5)

The two famous black coffins of Yuya both show all four Sons of Horus with animal heads on the sides of the box.

Anonymous coffin (Egyptian Museum in Cairo, JE 49549: Bruyère 1925)

Despite the bad condition of the decoration, Bruyère in his publication says that the four Sons of Horus have animal heads on the sides of the box (Bruyère 1925, 152).

Coffin of Ipuy (Museo Archeologico Nazionale di Firenze, 2175A: Pesi 2008)

This coffin has the four Sons of Horus with animal heads on the lid.[4]

Coffin of Anen-tursha (Ashmolean Museum, 1889.1035: Petrie 1890, 38)

On the sides of the box, the Sons of Horus are shown with

[3] For an in-depth description see Sartini 2015, 55–61

[4] Although Niwiński has stated that the practice of placing depictions among the inscribed bands on the lid was related to the appearance of later yellow coffins (Niwiński 1988, 12), sometimes other decorative elements are present on the lid of black coffins. For an in-depth examination of this, see Sartini 2015, 52.

animal heads, except for Qebehsenuef who has a human head. Duamutef is shown with a hawk head.

Coffin of Hanura (found in the tomb of Amenope (TT41): Assmann 1991, 245–249 (Sarg 1))

On the sides of the box, all four Sons of Horus have animal heads: Duamutef is shown with a hawk head and Qebehsenuef with a jackal head.

Anonymous coffin (found in the tomb of Amenope (TT41): Assmann 1991, 249–254 (Sarg 2))

The representation of the four Sons of Horus on this coffin is unconventional. On the right side of the box, Anubis, Imsety and Duamutef have human heads while, on the left side, Anubis is represented with a human head, Hapy with a baboon head and Qebehsenuef with a jackal head.

Curiously another atypical coffin found in TT41 (Assmann 1991, 254-–259 (Sarg 3)) shows, on both sides of the box, a human figure that replaces the four Sons of Horus. The latter are referred to in the inscriptions, however.

Normally, the four Sons of Horus are represented simply standing facing the head of the coffin, but there are some exceptions. For example, on the two black coffins found in the KV 62, which belonged to two foetuses, daughters of Tutankhamen, they are depicted seated (Egyptian Museum in Cairo, JE 60692 and 60695: Griffith Institute, Carter Archives, n° 317a (http://www.griffith.ox.ac.uk/gri/carter/317a(1).html, accessed 1 June 2018)). In addition, on the right-hand side of the box of JE60695, each figure holds an ankh sign in his hand, as does Anubis.

Three other coffins have an unusual feature: some of the Sons of Horus are shown facing the foot-end of the coffin:

Coffin of Amenhotep (Uppsala, Victoria Museum, VM 151 (box): Reeves 2013, 11–13)

Reign of Amenhotep II; from Thebes

On both sides of the box, Anubis and one of the two Sons of Horus are turned to face the foot-end of the coffin.

Anonymous coffin (found in the tomb of Amenope (TT41): Assmann 1991, 254–259 (Sarg 3))

Reign of Ramesses II; from Thebes

The anthropomorphic figure replacing the Sons of Horus (already discussed above) is turned towards the foot-end of the coffin on the right side of the box.

Coffin of Wiay (Baba and Yoshimura 2010, 12)

Late Eighteenth Dynasty; from Dahshur North

I have recently added to my catalogue the black coffins found in the necropolis of Dahshur North by the Egyptian Expedition of Waseda University. The coffin of Wiay shows the Sons of Horus and Anubis all facing toward the foot-end of the coffin.[5] It is noteworthy that another black coffin, found in the same area and belonging to Tjay, has an unusual element in its decoration: a pyramid is represented on the foot-end, like the coffin of Setau from Deir el-Medina dated to the post-Amarna period (Muzeum Narodowe w Warszawie, 138983 NMW: Bruyère 1937, 102–103).

Coffins recently added to my corpus of black coffins with yellow decoration[6]

The coffins discussed below were not included in the research I carried out for my Master's dissertation. I begin by presenting the dating criteria I established on the basis of the investigation of their decoration. For several iconographic characteristics it was possible to identify the particular period to which their use was limited (see **Table 3**).

The coffin of Takhat (Royal Ontario Museum ROM 910.9.1&2)[7]

Late Eighteenth Dynasty; from Thebes (?)

This shows typical decoration. Despite much of the paint and gilding having been lost on the lid, one can see the *wesekh* collar and a winged being (probably Nekhbet). On the box, a *wedjat* eye on a shrine and the god Anubis are represented between two Sons of Horus (with human heads), while, at the foot-end of the coffin, Isis is represented on a *nb* sign.[8] This coffin has been linked to the coffin of Sennefer dated in the reign of Tutankhamen (Louvre Museum E 14026: Andreu 2002, 25). Unfortunately, the coffin of Takhat does not have any obvious iconographic dating elements, but the likeness with the coffin of Sennefer, especially in the rendering of the decoration on the box, is unquestionable.

[5] Unfortunately, I was unable to obtain information about the decoration on the other side of the box. Ken Yazawa, chief of excavation in Dahshur, told me that they will publish more details on these coffins soon (15 February 2016, personal communication).

[6] I wish to thank Anders Bettum for his suggestions and support.

[7] I am grateful to Gale Gibson of the Royal Ontario Museum for providing me with images and information.

[8] Traces of paint suggest that Nephthys may once have been represented on the head end of the coffin.

Anonymous coffin (University Museum of Bergen BMU E3882: Skumsnes and Bettum 2015, 19–22)

Reign of Amenhotep II (?): from Thebes

This coffin also presents typical decoration. The iconography on the lid and box sides is like that on the coffin of Takhat but, on this example, one can see a significant iconographic element: the collar with petals on the outer edge. In addition, the goddess Nut at the foot end is depicted standing on a *djed* pillar.[9] In light of these considerations, although a dating in the reign of Amenhotep II is proposed for this coffin, I would date it later, to at least the reign of Amenhotep III.

Two further coffins found by the team of Waseda University (Yoshimura *et al.* 2012, 39–47)

Nineteenth to Twentieth Dynasty (?); from Dahshur North

In closing, I wish to briefly discuss the black coffins found by the Egyptian Expedition of Waseda University.

In addition to the two black coffins mentioned above, a pair of nested black coffins were found in Shaft 110 at Dahshur North. In the preliminary report, it is noted that the flat lids and the decorative programme of their upper side bears a resemblance to coffins of the late New Kingdom or Twenty-first Dynasty. In addition, an amphora found in the tomb may be dated approximately to the Twentieth Dynasty, according to David Aston (Aston 2014). This lends weight to the suggestion by John Taylor, in his report about coffins found in the tomb of Iurudef in Saqqara, that black type coffins had a longer tradition in the Memphite area (Yoshimura *et al.* 2012, 39–47).

On the basis of this information I would like to consider some iconographic details. It is clear that these coffins must be dated to the last phase of use of black coffins. The lid decoration is typical of some coffins of the Nineteenth Dynasty; the offering scenes, in particular, suggest such a dating. The shape of the wig, with the tiara of petals and the lotus on the forehead, is present on some coffins of the Nineteenth Dynasty, and even on the black coffins of Ipuy in my corpus, which date to the end of Eighteenth to beginning of the Nineteenth Dynasty. In addition, the decoration of the box, with Thoth opening a gate in the sky with Anubis between two Sons of Horus, was common on black coffins and other coffins of the Nineteenth Dynasty at Thebes. Bettum states that, by the late Nineteenth/early Twentieth Dynasty, the four Sons of Horus appear twice on coffins, four on each side (Bettum 2013, 186–187). It is this latter version of the New Kingdom decoration that seems to be revoked in the Twenty-First Dynasty. After this initial change, the number of deities lining the walls gradually increased, and their identities changed until the full Great Litany of Re appears on some coffins from the Twenty-First Dynasty (Bettum 2013, 208–14).

In the same tomb, the black and yellow colouring appears on two shabti boxes and a series of shabtis. Paolo Marini, a PhD candidate at the University of Pisa who is working on a typology of shabti boxes, has informed me that the shape of these examples from Dahshur is attested in the Nineteenth Dynasty. In addition, the prevalence of representations of the Sons of Horus suggested a 'high' dating, but the offering scene on one box is typical of the first half of the reign of Ramesses II. Therefore, he believes that there is nothing to suggest a dating after the Nineteenth Dynasty for the shabti boxes in question (Marini, 29 March 2016, personal communication). Nevertheless, it seems that there are some 'overseers' among the shabtis wearing daily life costume. If so, a date in the Twentieth Dynasty has to be proposed since this type of overseer shabti first appeared in the reign of Ramesses IV (Marini 2012).

In conclusion, although I would date the black coffins no later than the Nineteenth Dynasty, on the basis of iconographic considerations, I cannot refute the dating proposed by the team of Waseda University.

[9] On the majority of the black coffins the goddess Nephthys (or Isis) is depicted standing or sitting on a *nb* sign. However, by the reign of Amenhotep III, the latter goddess came to be generally depicted standing on a *djed* pillar (Sartini 2016, 53).

The outer coffin of Pa-seba-khai-en-ipet

New insights on manufacture, history and treatment

Anna Serotta, Lisa Bruno and Yekaterina Barbash

Several coffins in the collection of the Brooklyn Museum were examined and treated for the traveling exhibition "To Live Forever" (2008). The outer sarcophagus of the Royal Prince, Count of Thebes, Pa-seba-khai-en-ipet (c. 1075–945 BC) is the focus of this paper. The treatment of this outer coffin provided the first opportunity since it was acquired in 1908 to perform an in-depth examination of its structure, components, history of restorations and relationship to its inhabitant. This paper presents the results of collaborative research carried out by conservation and curatorial staff, highlighting instances where previous assumptions about the coffin were challenged by new observations and scientific analysis, and how previous museum practices affected its current state of preservation.

Introduction[1]

In 2008, the Brooklyn Museum mounted a travelling exhibition titled "To Live Forever", which focused on beliefs in the afterlife and burial rituals from the Predynastic period through the Roman period in Egypt. The exhibition presented over 120 objects from the Brooklyn Museum's collection. For the great majority of the objects, it was the first time they had been examined in the Museum's conservation laboratory, and it allowed conservators to bring modern treatments and philosophies to the conservation and presentation of these objects.

Highlights of this campaign of examination and treatment included re-joining the mummy of Demetrius (Brooklyn Museum 11.600) with his mummy portrait and surface cleaning the reused and re-inscribed Coffin of the Lady of the House (Brooklyn Museum 37.47Ea–e) (Kariya *et al.* 2010). Demetrius was excavated in 1910 and accessioned by the Museum in 1911. His face mask had been removed in 1939 for conservation and display. The Coffin of the Lady of the House, collected by Henry Abbott in the 19th century, was black with centuries worth of soot from coal furnaces.

In addition to conservation, the exhibition afforded the opportunity for technical study. Carbon-14 (C-14) analysis was undertaken on the linens of most of the complete mummies[2] and gas chromatography-mass spectrometry (GC-MS) was carried out on resin samples from the human and animal mummy remains.[3] The characterisation and source of the red lead pigment from the shroud of Demetrius were published by Walton and Trentelman (2009). Infrared reflectography was used by conservators to aid in the cleaning of this mummy. The exhibition also generated a project to scan all six mummies in the Museum's collection by computed tomography (CT), which provided information

[1] Anna Serotta was a Project Conservator at the Brooklyn Museum from Fall 2015 through Summer 2016, during which time the most recent campaign of examination and treatment of this object was carried out.

[2] The analysis was done at the NSF-Arizona AMS Laboratory, Physics Building, 1118 East Fourth St, PO Box 210081, University of Arizona Tucson, AZ 85721-0081, USA.

[3] Dr Lucy Cramp and Dr Richard Evershed at University of Bristol, Organic Geochemistry Unit, School of Chemistry.

Fig. 18: Outer coffin of the Royal Prince, Count of Thebes, Pa-seba-kai-en-ipet (Brooklyn Museum, 08.480.1a-b), c. 1075–945 BC

regarding the physiognomy of the individuals as well as insights into the mummification and wrapping processes.

This project additionally served to fill out records for objects that had a less than ideal history of care and treatment at the Museum. Unfortunately, the Roman-era mummy of an anonymous man (Brooklyn Museum, 52.128a-e) had been unwrapped in the summer of 1956. The renewed focus on the mummies in the collection led curators to wonder if he could be re-wrapped and, in the summer of 2010, the mummy was re-wrapped using his original linens, all of which had been retained. Each layer was documented with photography and a written description, noting the thread count and structure (Bruno 2014).

Another object which underwent significant treatment and study was the anthropoid outer coffin of Pa-seba-khai-en-ipet, the Royal Prince, Count of Thebes (Brooklyn Museum, 08.480.1a–b; **Fig. 18**). The inner coffin, mummy board and mummy of Pa-seba-khai-en-ipet are also in the Museum's collection (Brooklyn Museum, 08.480.2a–c), and the ensemble has been dated stylistically to the Third Intermediate Period, Twenty-first Dynasty; this was corroborated by C-14 dating of linen from the mummy. The outer coffin returned to the Conservation Laboratory in 2015 in preparation for another travelling exhibition and to address a perplexing condition issue, the investigation of which precipitated a renewed campaign of analysis. The results of these two campaigns of technical study and treatment are the focus of this paper.

History of acquisition

The coffin of Pa-seba-khai-en-ipet and the associated inner coffin and mummy were discovered in 1893, supposedly near Deir el-Bahari, and were acquired by Armand de Potter. The coffin set was obtained by de Potter from Emile Brugsch the year after he discovered them "150 mètres au n-e du temple de DeB". (Romano 1996, 703). De Potter was a Frenchman who emigrated to the United States and established a successful tourist agency which led tours to the archaeological sites of Egypt amongst numerous other destinations. It was during these tours that de Potter acquired antiquities in shops in Cairo and Upper Egypt.

In 1893, de Potter exhibited a part of his collection in the Anthropology Building of the World's Columbian Exposition in Chicago. Rather than selling his collection following the exposition, de Potter lent it to the University Museum in Philadelphia (Romano 1996, 697, n. 2). He continued to purchase antiquities and ship them to the University Museum afterwards. After de Potter's death, the coffins and mummy of Pa-seba-khai-en-ipet, along with other objects from his collection, were purchased by the Brooklyn Museum in 1908 from his widow, Aimee S. de Potter.

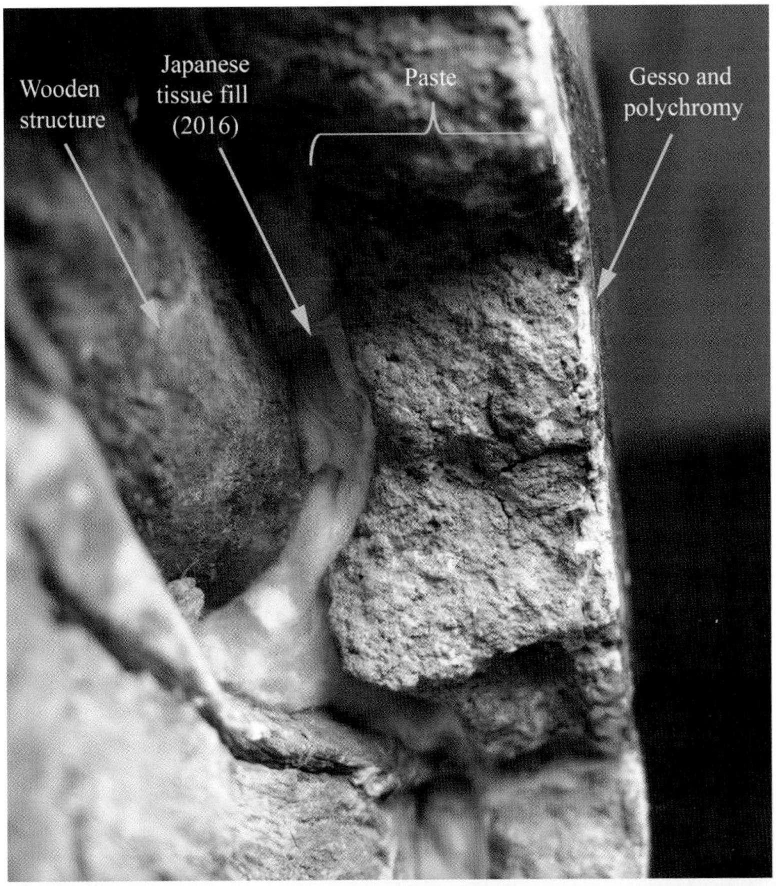

Fig. 19: Cross-section of preparatory layers visible along the edge of a large loss in the head area on the coffin lid

Fig. 20: Detail of the black coating on the interior of the coffin box

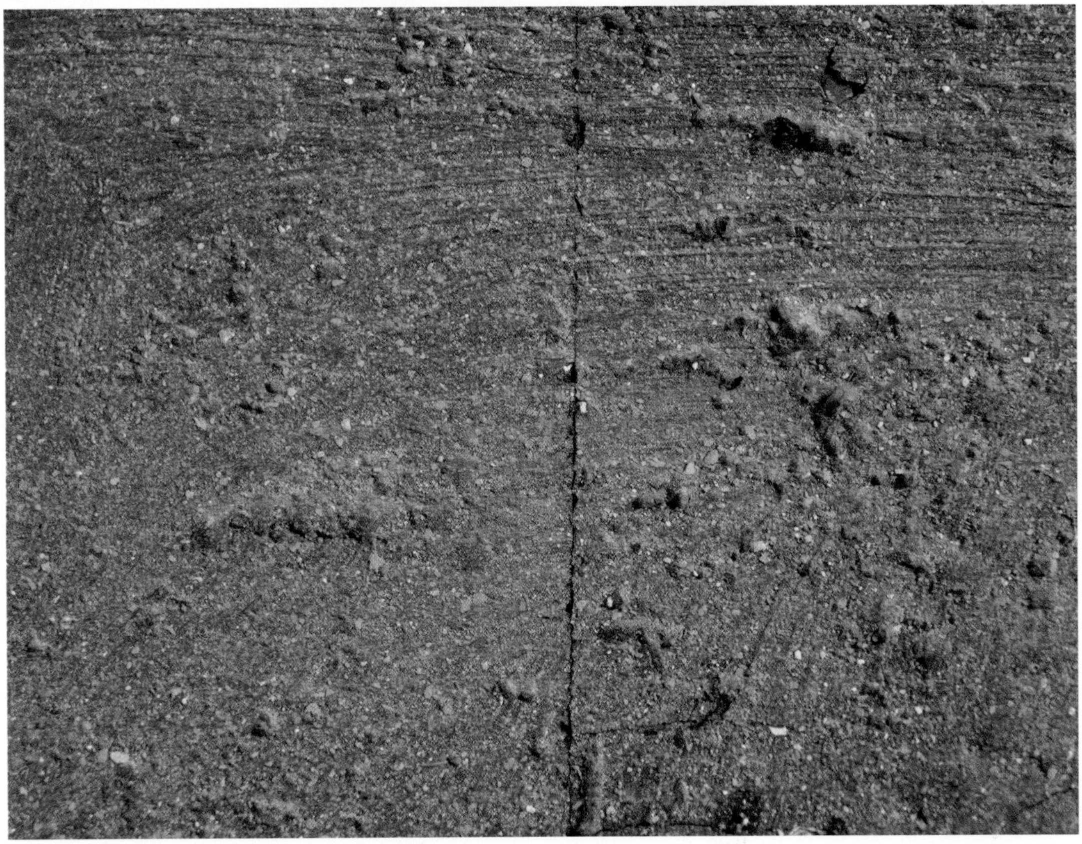

Description

The head, feet and crossed arms depicted on the lid of the outer coffin represent the deceased as a partially wrapped mummy with a collar painted on the breast and jewellery and amulets on the hands and arms. The bands of inscriptions evoke linen bandages that bound the mummy. The deceased is shown wearing a striated tripartite wig, and appears to have an attachment for a divine (long, braided and curved) beard, which is now missing. Below the striated wig at the head end of the coffin is an image of an Isis knot with arms spread in protection and two hieroglyphs representing the West on either side. The top of the foot end is decorated with an image of the goddess Nephthys with arms raised in a protective gesture, surrounded by mummiform figures of the Four Sons of Horus. A multi-coloured Isis knot remains on the lower portion of the foot end. According to Niwiński, the coffins of Pa-seba-khai-en-ipet belong to Type II-b (Niwiński 1988, 71–74), which dates to the middle of the Twenty-first Dynasty. The yellow background of the painting, symbolic of the gold skin of the gods, is characteristic of the late New Kingdom and Third Intermediate Period. The interior of the coffin and the exterior surface of the bottom of the coffin box are coated with a black substance.

Construction

Both the coffin lid and box are constructed from multiple pieces of wood,[4] which have been mechanically joined with dowels and mortise and tenon joints. The lid is constructed of several long pieces of wood, and the head, wig, hands and foot case are separately attached. Likewise, the box is composed of boards of varying sizes; the shoulder areas have been widened by attaching a thinner veneer of wood to the underlying board with small wooden dowels. Similar wooden dowels are visible throughout the coffin, some of which are clearly used to secure elements whilst the function of others is not immediately evident. Both the lid and the box have stepped lips; there are eight mortise holes in the lip of the box and the lid originally had eight wooden tenons, four of which are now extant. The lid was most likely further secured to the box with small wooden dowels through these tenons, remnants of which are visible on the sides of each mortise hole.

The coffin exterior is surfaced with gesso, polychromy, and varnish; the latter was identified as a natural tree resin.[5] A textile layer adhered to the wooden substrate is visible in many areas below the surface layers and some areas of the wooden substrate appear to be surfaced with a tan-coloured paste identified as a mixture of kaolin, calcite, gypsum and quartz.[6] These preparatory materials would have served to even out the surface of the wooden structure and cover up gaps and joints prior to the application of decoration (**Fig. 19**).

The interior of both the coffin lid and box are covered with a brittle black coating. The black coating appears to be a mixture of bituminous materials, as well as (possibly) some natural resin or oil and wax;[7] some of the oil and/or resin appears to have penetrated the underlying tan-coloured preparatory layer. A similar black coating is also present on the underside of the coffin box, directly on the wood (**Fig. 20**).

During the 2007 treatment campaign infrared reflectography was used to address questions about the painting on the coffin's foot. Differences in the drawing styles of the decoration on the head end and foot end of the coffin were noted, and the disparity in styles between the Isis knot on the head end and the Isis knot on the foot end was of particular concern. When examined with a shortwave infrared camera, the Isis knot on the foot end, in contrast to that on the head end, appeared to have a sketchy under-drawing, particularly

4 In 1971 the bottom surface of the coffin box was sampled and tentatively identified as cedar and acacia by Dr. N.H. Michaels of the Department of Physics, University of Pennsylvania. The same samples were used for C-14 analysis.

5 Samples were analysed with Fourier transform infrared microspectroscopy (FTIR) by Orion Analytical LLC.

6 A sample of the paste material was analysed in 2008 with FTIR by Orion Analytical LLC and found to consist of a mixture of kaolin, calcite, gypsum and quartz. For the project described in this paper, a sample of the same paste material from the head area on the coffin lid was analysed with scanning electron microscopy (SEM) and energy dispersive spectroscopy (EDS) performed using a Bruker TM3000 tabletop SEM and the Quantax 70 EDS system and associated software at the Conservation Center, Institute of Fine Arts, New York University. The sample was found to contain predominantly silica, oxygen, calcium, carbon and aluminium, with some potassium, sulphur, chlorine, magnesium and iron. These constituents are consistent with the compounds found in 2008. Those results were confirmed in 2016 when cross-sections containing the tan-coloured paste were analysed with FTIR in the Department of Scientific Research at the Metropolitan Museum of Art.

7 Samples of the black interior coating were analysed with FTIR and pyrolysis-gas chromatography/ mass spectrometry (Py-GC/MS) in the Department of Scientific Research at the Metropolitan Museum of Art.

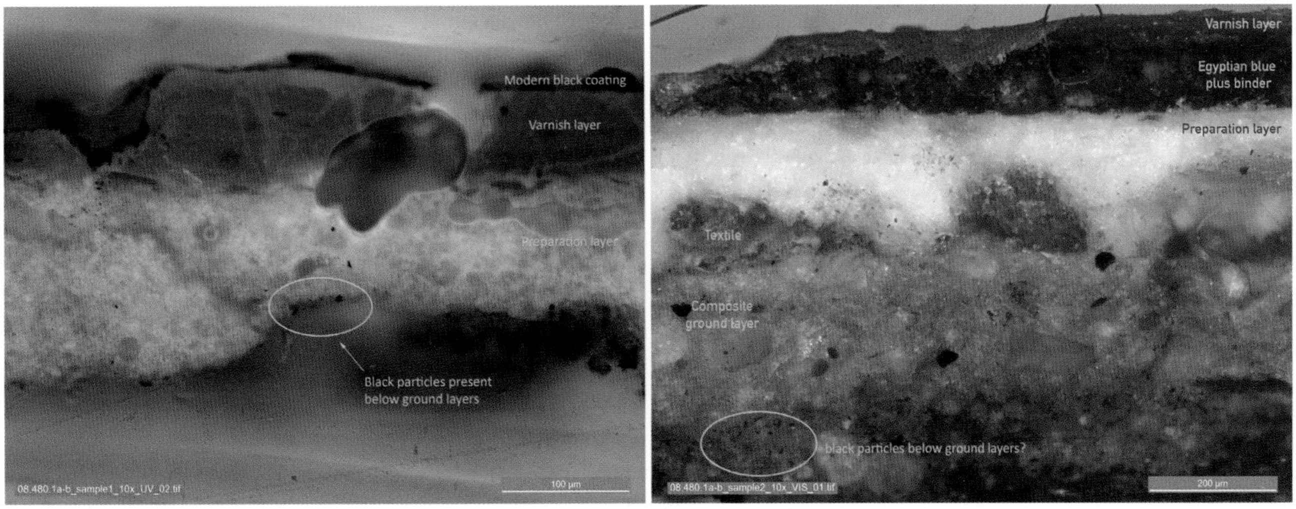

Fig. 21: Left: cross-section from the lip of the coffin box, where black restoration material is applied over original varnish, viewed under ultraviolet radiation. Right: cross section including varnish, polychromy and preparation layers from along a crack in the coffin lid

visible around the hands and the top loop of the knot.[8] This observation, in combination with visual analysis of the materials present on the surface, led conservators to conclude that this area was a modern restoration of unknown date, corroborating a previous comment in the curatorial records.[9]

Many elements of the surface decoration have subtle relief. Although it has been suggested that such raised surfaces were created by moulding gesso (Bianchi 1983, 13), in the case of this coffin the relief seems to have been created by building up Egyptian blue. Low relief created with Egyptian blue has been noted on objects from the Third Intermediate Period (Strudwick and Dawson 2016, 106 and 187).

Evidence for reuse

Coffins constructed from previously used wooden elements were not uncommon in the Third Intermediate Period when access to imported wood was limited (Cooney 2012). There is evidence to suggest that the outer coffin of Pa-seba-khai-en-ipet is constructed from previously used wood. C-14 dating carried out in 2016 indicates that at least some of the wood dates to approximately 500 years before the Twenty-first Dynasty.[10] Also, there are traces of red pigment along the top edge of one of the boards on the foot end and traces of black pigment along the top edges of one of the bottom boards, both of which are probably the remains of decoration from previous use of these boards (Taylor 2001b, 176); these edges are now exposed by losses in the adjacent boards, but would not have been visible in the Twenty-first Dynasty configuration. Additionally, there are some dowels and dowel holes that do not appear to be related to the current coffin construction. And lastly, the black coating on the interior is inconsistent with Twenty-first Dynasty coffin decoration; rather, black coffins are typical of the later Eighteenth Dynasty (Lakomy 2016, 122–124). No evidence of a similar black coating is visible on the exterior of the coffin (except on the underside of the box). However, cross-sections taken from the box and lid reveal black particles present below the ground layers. Although this evidence is by no means conclusive, it could be that these black particles are traces of a black bitumen-containing coating that was

[8] Examination was carried out with a shortwave infrared (SWIR) camera made by Sensors Unlimited using an InGaAs (indium gallium arsenide) crystal sensor.

[9] This modern restoration was carefully removed during the 2007–2008 conservation treatment campaign.

[10] A sample of wood from the coffin base (less than 50mg) was sent to University of Arizona AMS Laboratory. The sample dates from approximately 1616 BC to 1507 BC (Calendar Age Range 95%). Prior to this, in 1971, Dr. N.H. Michaels of the Department of Physics, University of Pennsylvania, took samples (approximately 20 grams each) of wood from the coffin by boring holes (approximately 14) in to bottom of coffin. All samples were used for C-14 testing, which dated the coffin to 1000 years before the Twenty-first Dynasty. C-14 analysis was repeated in 2016 because a) the 1971 analysis was not adequately documented and b) significant advancements have been made in the accuracy of C-14 over the past several decades.

scraped down prior to the application of the Twenty-first Dynasty surface decoration (**Fig. 21**).

Given these observations, it is possible that Pa-seba-khai-en-ipet's outer coffin is actually a modified Eighteenth Dynasty coffin, and at least some of the elements may have had a third (pre-Eighteenth Dynasty?) use, either as part of another coffin or as a different type of wooden object. X-radiography or CT-scanning may be able to provide additional data about both the coffin's current configuration and the history of its materials. A comprehensive campaign of multiband imaging might show evidence of the previous surface treatment.[11]

Treatment history

There are numerous old repairs to the coffin recorded in unpublished treatment reports. These include: iron nails securing the bottom boards to the coffin sides and the application of a plaster-like fill material in gaps and losses (between 1932 and the 1970s); stabilisation of cracks with a polyvinyl acetate emulsion (1978). The plaster-like fill material has been identified as a mixture of gypsum, a protein binder and natural pigments.[12] In addition to the recorded treatments, areas of modern over-paint, a waxy fill material and an area of polyvinyl acetate restoration varnish[13] have been noted, and much of the exterior of the coffin is covered with a restoration varnish identified as a natural tree resin,[14] which is distinguishable under UV radiation. Losses in the interior surface which have been filled with the plaster-like fill material are surfaced with a matte black coating which absorbs more strongly under UV radiation than the original black coating material; particulate matter (which is slightly sandy in appearance) is lodged in both this restoration coating and in the original black coating. It is likely that this campaign of restoration included widespread consolidation of the interior surface with an animal glue, in which particulate material subsequently became lodged.[15]

In 2007 the lid was determined to be structurally unstable due to significant cracking and distortion, and both the coffin box and lid exhibited significant delamination of the paint and the paste layer. The 2007 treatment included the following: surface cleaning, reduction of the plaster-like fill material, adhesion of loose fragments and stabilisation of cracks,[16] consolidation of surface layers[17] and filling of losses.[18]

Investigation of fill efflorescence

While the coffin was travelling with "To Live Forever" it was noted that the fills appeared to be efflorescing. At the time, the efflorescence was photographed and removed with cotton swabs and water, but when the object was re-examined in 2015 the efflorescence was again noted (**Fig. 22**). Approximately two-thirds of the fills from

[11] In 2015 the Brooklyn Museum Conservation Laboratory adopted a protocol for multiband imaging based on the guidelines provided by the British Museum Technical Imaging Project, CHARISMA. One section of the coffin's proper left side was selected for multiband imaging (including visible-reflected imaging, visible-induced infrared luminescence imaging, infra-red-reflected imaging, UV-reflected imaging and UV-induced luminescence imaging). Although this suite of low-tech imaging methods allowed conservators to map globally the visual characteristics of materials present on the coffin's surface, it did not provide any information about previous surface decoration.

[12] Cross sections containing the plaster-like fill material were analysed in the Department of Scientific Research at the Metropolitan Museum of Art with FTIR and Py-GC/MS.

[13] A sample of restoration varnish from the area of fill material on the lid was analysed in 2008 with FTIR by Orion Analytical LLC and was found to consist of polyvinyl acetate.

[14] This varnish is over the whole coffin (including over fills) and overlies the original varnish. A sample of restoration varnish from over a conservation fill on the main body of the lid was analysed in 2008 with FTIR by Orion Analytical LLC and was found to consist of natural tree resin. As the underlying original varnish is also tree resin (see footnote 5), no attempt was made to reduce the restoration varnish overall.

[15] Cross sections of the modern black layer, containing the black coating material and particulate matter, were analysed in the Department of Scientific Research at the Metropolitan Museum of Art with FTIR and Py-GC/MS. On one sample, this layer was found to consist of a proteinaceous binder, gypsum, earth pigments and natural resin/oil; from a second sample this layer was found to consist of calcium carbonate, earth pigments and a proteinaceous binder.

[16] with Paraloid B-72 (methyl acrylate/ethyl methacrylate co-polymer) in acetone.

[17] with 20% Aquazol 200 (poly(2-ethyl-2-oxazoline) in water or 2.5% sturgeon glue in water; interior surface of lid was consolidated with warm sturgeon glue or 3% Paraloid B-72 in acetone

[18] Japanese tissue was adhered to areas of loss. In areas with ancient textile and possible original fill material, this was coated with 20% Paraloid B-72 in acetone and heat set. Elsewhere, Japanese tissue was adhered with 20% Aquazol in ethanol. Losses were then filled with 30%-40% Paraloid B-72 in acetone (bulked with glass microballoons and/or cellulose powder and surfaced with a layer of 7% Klucel™ G (hydroxypropyl cellulose) in ethanol bulked with microballoons and cellulose powder. Areas of loss not in need of structural support were filled just with the Klucel™ G mixture. Fills were inpainted with gouache.

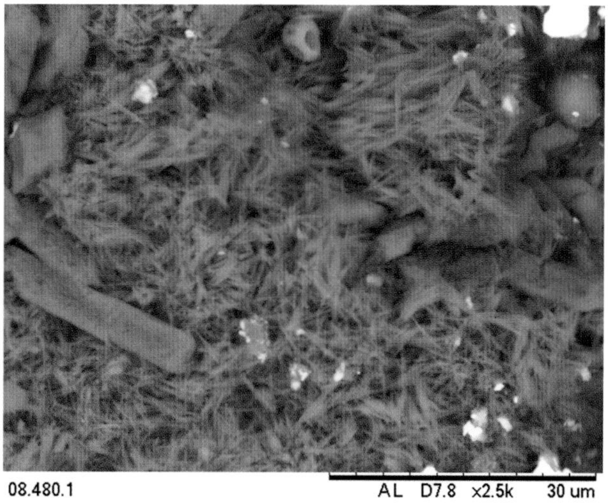

Fig. 22: Left: white efflorescence on the surface of a fill from the 2007 treatment campaign. Right: scanning electron microscope (SEM) image of the white efflorescence of a sample of the 2007 fill material

the 2007 treatment exhibited some efflorescence. It was particularly concentrated around the edges of fills; some had only a small area exhibiting efflorescence, while others were completely covered. There does not appear to be any correlation between the location of a fill and appearance of efflorescence. No efflorescence was observed anywhere on the object itself. Samples of the efflorescence were examined under magnification and appear to consist of tiny white spherical particles sitting on the surface of the object. Samples were analysed with micro-chemical spot testing with negative results produced from all tests.[19] X-ray diffraction analysis also produced inconclusive results.[20] However, SEM-EDS analysis found the spherical efflorescence to be composed of shard-like crystals which appear to consist almost entirely of sodium, oxygen and carbon.[21] These results suggest that the needle-like crystals may be natron, a naturally occurring mixture of sodium carbonate decahydrate (Na2CO3.10H2O) and sodium bicarbonate (NaHCO3). Similar results were obtained with FTIR and Raman spectroscopy, which found the samples analysed to consist of sodium bicarbonate, sodium carbonate and sodium acetate (CH3COONa).[22] The origin of the sodium acetate is not clear.

Natron was used in mummification, glass and faience making, and other manufacturing processes, but its presence in the coffin matrix is still unexplained. These salts are highly soluble, and it is possible that they were solubilised inadvertently when the old plaster fills were removed during the 2007 treatment, as this was done by first softening the plaster with water poultices. If any moisture remained in the wood when the new fill material was applied, it would have been pulled into that material along with the solubilised salts. Additionally, fluctuating relative humidity whilst the object was in transit could have caused the salts to deliquesce, move through the wood up to the surface of the coffin and then re-crystallise on the surface of the fills. It is notable that the efflorescence only appears on the surface of the fills, never on the original object. Possibly the presence of the thick layer of varnish(s) on the original surface decoration sealed the surface sufficiently so that the water carrying the natron chose the path of least resistance.[23]

[19] Micro-chemical spot tests for sulphates, chlorides, nitrates, cellulose and protein were undertaken to attempt to characterise the efflorescence on the coffin fills. Tests were carried out using procedures outlined in Odegaard *et al.* 2005 All tests were run with positive and negative control samples.

[20] X-ray diffraction analysis was carried out by George Wheeler at Columbia University.

[21] Scanning electron microscopy (SEM) and energy dispersive spectroscopy (EDS) were performed using a Bruker TM3000 tabletop SEM and the Quantax 70 EDS system and associated software at the Conservation Center, Institute of Fine Arts, New York University with George Wheeler. Samples were adhered to graphite stubs using graphite-infused tape. Once introduced into the SEM, the chamber was evacuated to a low vacuum and the viewing and analyses performed. For EDS, collection of elemental data was carried out at 15 keV for approximately 100 seconds. All samples were uncoated.

[22] Analysis by FTIR and Raman spectroscopy was carried out in the Department of Scientific Research, Metropolitan Museum of Art, New York.

[23] It should be noted that a small sample of the coffin wood

2015–2016 treatment campaign

Due to the recurrence of the efflorescence, it was decided that all of the 2007 fills should be removed and replaced with new light-weight fill materials. The location of all the 2007 fills was documented, differentiating the ones which had efflorescence. The location of the iron nails was determined using a rare earth magnet.

The 2007 fills were then mechanically removed; care was taken to use minimal solvent to minimise risk to adjacent original material. Fills in relatively inaccessible areas were left in place.

It was decided that, as much as possible, old plaster fills should be removed. These fills added significant weight to the object, were often friable or cracking, and in some places they obscured evidence of ancient joins, such as dowels and tenons. Although the plaster softens slightly with water, fills were removed mechanically to avoid the introduction of moisture to the wooden substrate. As with the 2007 material, plaster fills that were not safely accessible for mechanical removal were left in place, and most of the plaster fills on the interior of the coffin were left in place owing to time constraints. In many cases, the removal of the plaster fills from the exterior of the coffin revealed interesting construction details, such as the mortise and tenon joint in the proper right head area of the coffin box.

It was decided that losses would be re-filled only where structurally necessary, and that weaker more reversible fill materials would be selected. Even though they were executed with standard conservation materials, the 2007 Paraloid B-72 fills were actually very difficult to remove without introducing a significant amount of solvent. So, we decided to use what we felt was a slightly less invasive filling method. Deep losses were filled with dry Japanese tissue, tacked down in several spots with Klucel™ G (hydroxypropyl cellulose), and then surfaced with Klucel™ G bulked with 3M™ glass microballoons. The adhesive was delivered in ethanol, rather than water, in an attempt to avoid mobilizing more of the strange efflorescence. In two areas (along the bottom of the proper left side of the coffin box in the head area and on the proper right side of the foot area on the lid) losses were first filled with a balsa wood core and then bulked out with tissue and surfaced with Klucel™ G and microballoons.

Fills were toned using Japanese tissue tinted with washes of Golden™ acrylic emulsion paints. Tissue was adhered with 5% Klucel™ G in ethanol and, if necessary, were further toned with Golden™ acrylic emulsion paints. It was decided not to match lost decoration with the exception of the following areas: the lines in the wig, the dark lines throughout the inscription, and the green feathers on the chest of the figure.

The removal of the restoration plaster, particularly along the bottom edge of the coffin, often left a visually distracting surface with unstable wood and gesso along the edges of the losses. Rather than fully filling these losses to replicate the form of missing parts, tinted Japanese tissue was applied over the losses, both to stabilise these areas and to reintegrate them visually with the surrounding surfaces.

Conclusion

The process of examining an object and determining its history from manufacture to present day is often slow and multi-layered. This is especially true for objects such as the coffin of Pa-seba-khai-en-ipet, which have a complex construction and which incorporated reused materials at the time of manufacture. As new scientific techniques of examination are added to the way in which objects are studied, new information will inevitably be discovered adding to the richness of what we can know about an object. More importantly, as we share new discoveries, it allows all of us in this field to be more informed and to bring a more nuanced way of looking at these complex and fascinating objects.

(~2mm square) was submitted to destructive analysis (soaking in deionised water) in an attempt to extract any salts that might be related to this phenomenon, but the only materials that could be extracted from this sample were the water-based consolidants used in the 2007–2008 treatment campaign. However, the absence of soluble salts in this sample does not discount their presence elsewhere in the coffin; this sample was taken from an area near the surface, which means that, theoretically, any salts in this area would have been pulled into the fill material by evaporating water introduced by consolidation.

Multi and hyperspectral imaging and 3D techniques for understanding Egyptian coffins

T. Cavaleri, P. Buscaglia, A. Lo Giudice, M. Nervo, M. Pisani, A. Re and M. Zucco

Just before the reopening of the Museo Egizio (April 2015), a large number of Egyptian coffins of different types came to the Centro Conservazione e Restauro (CCR) "La Venaria Reale" for conservation. For evaluating the uniqueness of each piece, we combined classic and modern imaging techniques to get the best results in a non-invasive manner. Here we present some outcomes about coffins of 'yellow' type, looking at the way they were created: from the wood to the finishing. Construction was investigated through digital X-radiographs, focussing on the condition of the dowels used to join the wooden panels. A complete CT scan was performed on each coffin, highlighting the ancient means of assembly, modern interventions and traces of probable reuse of part of the coffin.

Drawings on these coffins were made of red ochre-based pigment: the absence of a possible underlying black carbon-based layout, present in other coffin types, was confirmed by infrared reflectography. The palette was found to contain yellow and red ochres, green copper-based pigments and Egyptian blue: false-colour techniques allowed a preliminary overview of pictorial materials, better characterised through hyperspectral imaging. Visible light induced infrared luminescence (VIL) revealed small, invisible traces of Egyptian blue on some incomplete surfaces. On black areas, where the presence of carbon-based pigment was suspected, it often revealed instead the presence of Egyptian blue, indicating a poor state of preservation.

Introduction

The Centre for Conservation and Restoration La Venaria Reale (CCR) was involved recently in the study and conservation of a large number of coffins belonging to the Museo Egizio in Turin and destined for its new displays (from April 2015). These coffins are of the yellow coffin type, dating from the Twenty-first and Twenty-second Dynasties, and a group of late Third Intermediate Period and Late Period coffins from Schiaparelli's excavations in the Valley of the Queens (for a full listing see Buscaglia *et al.* in this volume).

The work was carried out within the framework of the Vatican Coffin Project, a large international and interdisciplinary study, launched by the Vatican Museums and directed by Alessia Amenta, which focuses on polychrome Egyptian coffins and, in particular, the yellow coffin type (Amenta 2013). Close observation of the artefacts presented a good opportunity for the conservators and conservation scientists at CCR to collect a great deal of data about Egyptian funerary art materials and techniques. Data from previous research was gathered and integrated into this research.

Diagnostic techniques based on both classical and innovative technologies were employed for examining the materials used for painting the coffins, the techniques

Fig. 23: Coffin of Hor (Inv. Nr. Cat. 05228) during a hyperspectral video acquisition.

of assembly and the state of preservation of both the structures and the surfaces. The aim of this paper is to highlight the importance of combining traditional and new non-invasive techniques in order to get as much data as possible whilst respecting the unique and precious nature of each piece: this process allows us to reduce to a minimum the amount of sampling required.

Materials and methods

Investigation of the wooden support: technique of assembly and state of preservation

X-radiography and CT scanning were carried out with an innovative apparatus installed at CCR and specifically designed for examining large size artworks (up to 4 m wide and 3 m high). It was developed by the National Institute of Nuclear Physics (INFN) and the Department of Physics of the University of Turin in collaboration with CCR and within the neu_ART research project (Re *et al.* 2012, Nervo 2013). The X-ray source and linear detector can both move vertically, the linear detector can also move horizontally. In this way, different radiographs can be obtained sequentially by varying the height of the X-ray source and the position of the detector accordingly. The radiographs can then be stitched with an appropriate software.

The X-raying of a complete coffin (acquisition and processing with a resolution of 0.2 mm per pixel) takes less than 15 minutes. For obtaining the CT scan, a number of X-rays have to be acquired whilst the object rotates on a motorised rotary stage: even if the acquisition procedure is synchronised, this requires much more time for acquisition and post-production. The CT scan of a coffin can require more than 90 hours of acquisition (Nervo 2013). More details about the instrument and other applications can be found in Re *et al.* 2016.

One coffin was selected for a complete CT scan and study of the technique of assembly, by examining the main wooden elements, the smaller pieces and the joints.

Investigation of the coffin surfaces: execution technique and state of preservation

The entire surface of each artefact (36 pieces, belonging to 20 coffin sets) was examined. In addition to X-radiography, the following multispectral imaging methods were applied:

Two types of infrared reflectography (IRR1 and IRR2). The aim here was to reveal possible underdrawing and improve the readability of the decoration. The IRR1 (750–950 nm) was acquired with an X-Nite Nikon D810 IRUV camera equipped with a R72 Hoya IR filter. The IRR2 (950–1150 nm) was acquired with an Art

Innovation Artist Camera. The coffins were illuminated with Ianiro Varibeam Halogen 800W lamps.

Ultraviolet fluorescence (UVF) was recorded in order to visualise the distribution of original finishing materials over the coffin surfaces and the presence of modern intervention materials. We used an X-Nite Nikon D810 camera equipped with a Hoya IR/UV-cut filter, illuminating the coffins with Labino® UV lamps floodlight (emission peak at 365 nm). Both IRR and UVF acquisitions required an XRITE Classic ColorChecker® of 24 colours and a 99% reflective white ceramic tab as references.

False-colour (FC) images were generated by following the British Museum's recommendations on survey methods, post-production and diagnostic applicability (Dyer *et al.* 2013), in order to emphasise the major chemical differences of the surfaces.

Visible-light induced luminescence (VIL) was adopted for revealing and mapping the presence of Egyptian blue on the coffins because the pigment emits a characteristic fluorescence in the near infrared spectrum (with an emission peak at about 916 nm) when stimulated by visible light (Verri 2008). Images were recorded with an X-Nite Nikon D810 IRUV camera equipped with a Hoya R72 IR filter, illuminating the coffins with visible (400–700 nm) LED sources equipped with a Hoya IR/UV cut filter. An XRITE 24 colours ColorChecker® Classic, an Egyptian blue tab and a 99% reflective white ceramic tab were used as references.

All images were post-produced in Adobe Lightroom and Adobe Photoshop.

Investigation of selected areas: materials, pictorial technique and state of preservation

Hyperspectral imaging (HSI) and reflectance transformation imaging (RTI) were used for investigation of pigment distribution on selected areas and to highlight particular features of the pictorial technique and the superficial state of preservation. Non-invasive point analysis techniques were used for improving the material characterisation.

A prototype instrument developed by the National Institute of Metrological Research (INRiM) was employed for the hyperspectral imaging (HSI) (Pisani and Zucco 2009). It exploits the use of a Fabry-Perot interferometer inserted in the optical set-up between the object and a monochromatic camera (a low noise CMOS Hamamatsu Orca Flash 4.0). As with other devices, the system provides a hyperspectral cube combining the artwork's image with the spectral information at each pixel, which is useful as a diagnostic tool for pigment identification. The imager works in the 400–720 nm range with a spectral resolution of about 5 nm at 500 nm; the wavelength range is extendible by changing filters and detector; the spatial resolution depends on the optical system and on the number of pixels of the camera sensor used. In contrast to other HS technologies, this set-up allows a rapid spectra acquisition of the entire area because it does not need any mechanical scanning system. The system acquires a video that is the sequence of the interference images produced while the optical path between the interferometer's mirrors is changed. From the video, it is possible to extract the interferogram for each pixel and, ultimately, calculate the reflectance spectrum by applying a Fourier transform-based algorithm. From a video of 3 minutes spectral information on 1 million pixels can be collected; the time could decrease to a few seconds at the expense of spectral resolution (Cavaleri *et al.* 2015, Biondi *et al.* 2015). See **Fig. 23.**

RTI was applied to areas of about 20 x 30 cm. This technique requires the shooting of several digital images of the object surface from a stationary camera position. In each photograph, light is projected from a different known direction, with a small spherical and high reflective reference inserted within the scene. This information is used to generate a mathematical model of the surface and the software enables the interactive re-lighting of the surface from every direction (Earl *et al.* 2011, Malzbender *et al.* 2001).

Point analyses with fibre optic reflectance spectroscopy (FORS) were carried out in the 350–1000 nm range with 0.5 nm resolution by means of an Ocean Optics HR2000+ES spectrophotometer and an Ocean Optics HL2000 halogen lamp connected by optical fibres of 400 µm diameter. Using a probe, we worked in a 45°x/0° geometry following the CIE standard illuminating/viewing geometry (Oleari 2008, 53–60) and measuring areas of fixed dimension (approximately 3 mm in diameter). A 99% reflective Spectralon © was used as the white reference.

Discussion and results

Investigation of the wooden support: technique of assembly and state of preservation

Digital X-radiography on all the coffins has increased information about the techniques of assembly and the state of preservation by visualizing the distribution of

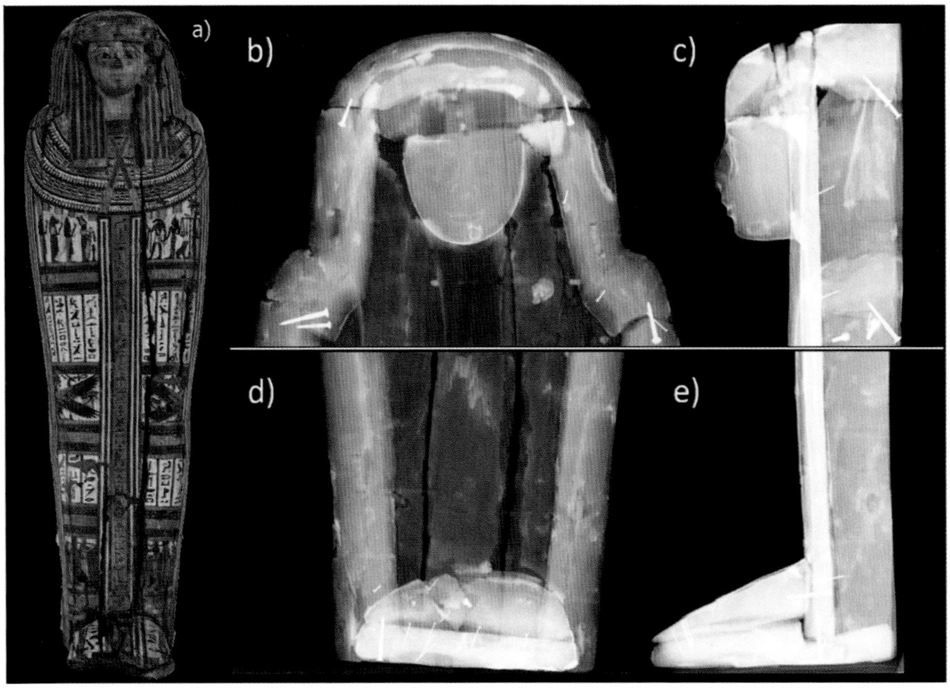

Fig. 24: Coffin lid of Tadiaset (Inv. Nr. S. 05244). a) in visible light; b) frontal and c) lateral X-radiographs of the upper part; d) frontal and e) lateral X-radiographs of the lower part.

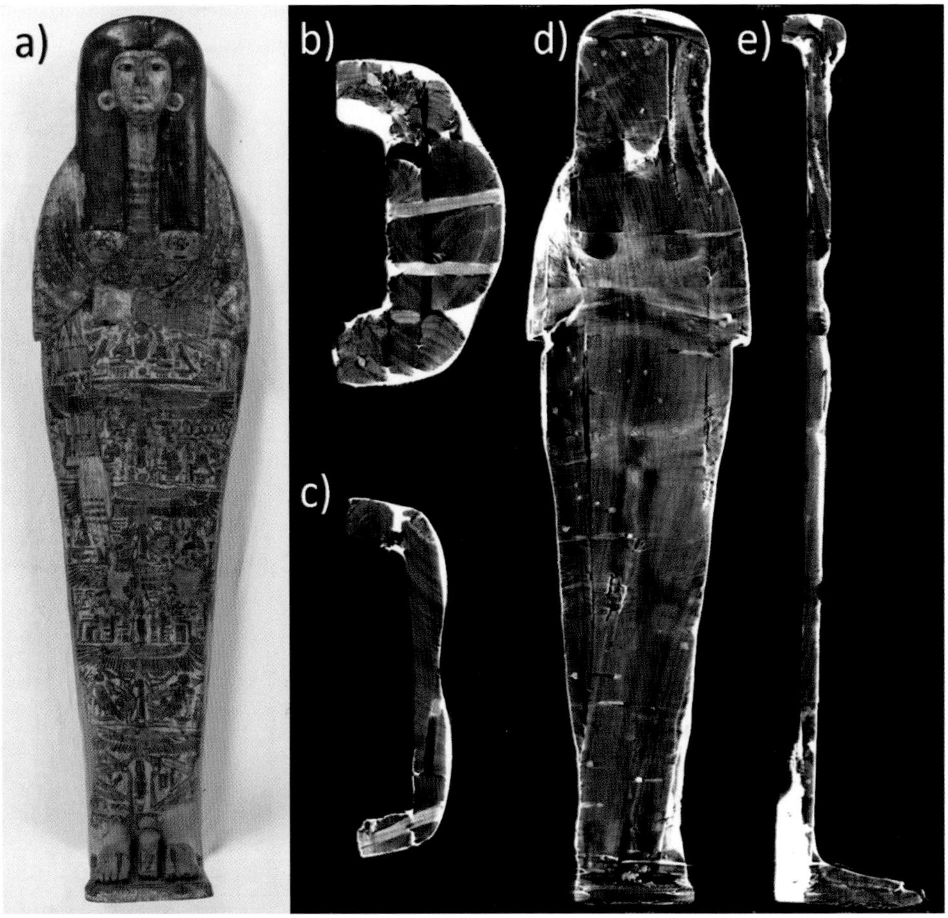

Fig. 25: Coffin lid of Taiefmutmut (Inv. Nr. Cat. 2228). a) In visible light, b) horizontal sections of the CT scan at the head level and c) at the legs level; d) vertical section and e) lateral section of the coffin.

different materials, the presence of previous restorations and other internal features invisible to the naked eye.

Although a radiograph projects all the coffin volume onto a single plane, radiographs at different angles can provide information that clarifies the features. In **Fig. 24**, radiographs are shown alongside an image of the coffin lid of Tadiaset-Tahekat (Inv. Nr. S. 05244): two of the X-ray images have been acquired frontally (**Fig.** 24b, **Fig.** 24d) and two laterally (**Fig.** 24c, **Fig.** 24e). Previous structural interventions were detected through the presence of metal nails and screws, which appear white in the radiographs. The combination of two radiographs of the same part of the coffin, acquired at different angles, was useful for understanding both the length and the orientation of the nails.

The complete CT scan performed on the coffin lid of lady Taiefmutmut (Inv. Nr. Cat. 2228), chantress of Amun, has highlighted the ancient means of assembly, modern interventions and also traces of probable reuse of part of the coffin. A CT scan was required to provide the complete internal three-dimensional view of the wooden blocks that form the coffin and for measuring their dimensions. It was then possible to navigate the 3D reconstructed volume, virtually cutting the coffin in any direction.

Fig. 25 shows two horizontal, one vertical and one lateral section from the CT scan slices. These highlight information about the technique of assembly. Three main longitudinal wooden planks form the flat part of the lid (**Fig.** 25d), whilst other, smaller wooden blocks form the lateral parts and are fixed to the main flat part with wooden dowels (**Fig.** 25b, **Fig.** 25c). A fill material can be easily detected because of its higher radiopacity: it has been used to help build and model projecting parts, such as the wig, breasts, arms and feet. Thanks to the CT scan sections, the thickness of this material can be measured at each point. Some features revealed by the scan images may suggest a reuse of materials. For example, the area below the chin appears to have been rebuilt with an assembly of wood pieces over a similarly radiopaque fill (Re *et al.* 2016, **Fig. 26**) and there is an empty cylindrical hole (**Fig.** 25c) which was probably made to hold a dowel in a previous use of that particular wooden block.

CT scanning provided information about previous interventions, as shown for example in the lower part of the coffin lid (**Fig.** 25d, **Fig.** 25e). In this case, the missing parts of ankles and heels were filled with a material of a dark-ochre colour, which appears more radiopaque than the wood in the CT section images: this feature is clearly distinguishable and the extent of the intervention can be evaluated. Furthermore, CT reconstruction has allowed us to assess the presence and extent of some degradation phenomena: cracking of the wood (distribution and direction), lack of adhesion of the preparation layers and evidence of a previous infestation by wood-eating insects. Finally, by comparing the direction of fibres and density of each wooden plank as shown in the scan images, we can speculate about the use of different wood species in the lid. Further information about the CT scanning of the Taiefmutmut coffin lid can be found in Re *et al.* 2016.

Direct observation, coupled with X-radiography, has made it possible to see common features between the construction of the groups of coffins examined in this work, but also to note differences such as the greater thickness and irregularity of shape of the wooden pieces used in the Valley of the Queens' coffins than those used in the yellow type coffins (Buscaglia *et al.*, this volume). Moreover, the yellow type coffins examined were generally constructed with circular section dowels, whereas in the group of late Third Intermediate Period coffins from the Valley of the Queens, the planks were often joined with loose tenons whilst the other parts were joined with dowels.

Investigation of the entire coffin surface: techniques of execution and state of preservation

By combining close visual observation of a coffin's entire surface with the application of multispectral imaging techniques, we have obtained information about the execution technique and the state of preservation of both the internal and external surfaces of the coffins.

Returning to the coffin of Taiefmutmut (Inv. Nr. Cat. 2228), here, as on other coffins of the yellow type, it was difficult to distinguish between green and blue details painted above the yellow background, and to visualise the original chromatic intention. In this case, the UVF enabled detection of a thick organic layer on the surface, with some gaps and lacunae that resulted in dark patches in the UVF image (**Fig.** 26c). On the same detail, the VIL image has clearly shown the position of the details made of Egyptian blue pigment (**Fig.** 26b). So, from the two analyses we can presume a significant yellowing of the surface coating finishing that has affected the original colours.

The coffin of Nesimenjem (Inv. Nr. S. 05227), one of the coffins of the late Third Intermediate Period

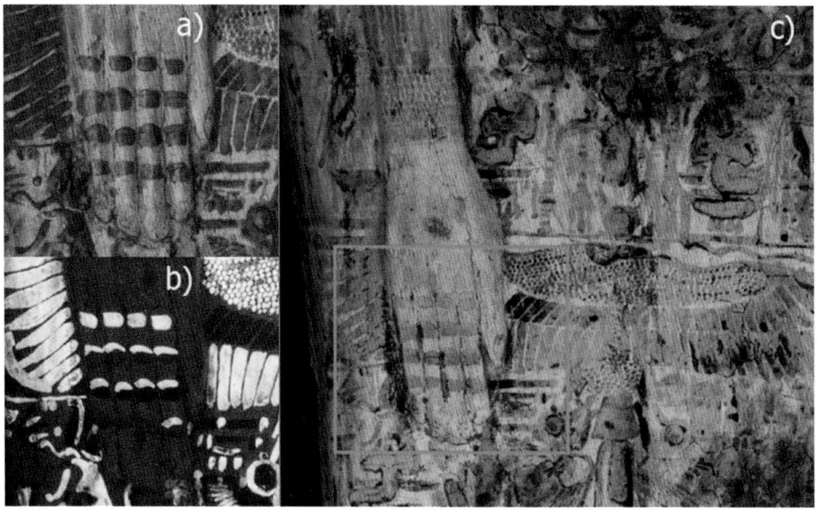

Fig. 26: Detail of the coffin of Taiefmutmut (Inv. Nr. Cat. 2228). a) in visible light; b) VIL; c) UVF.

Fig. 27: Detail of the coffin lid of Nesimenjem (Inv. Nr. S. 05227). In visible light (a); IRR1 (b); VIL (c).

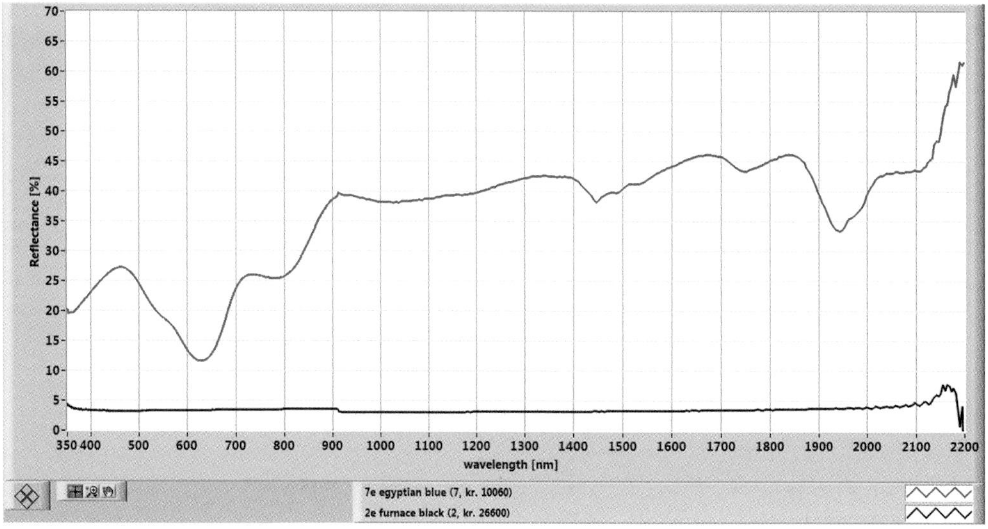

Fig. 28: FORS spectrum of an Egyptian blue-based mock-up (blue line) compared to the one of a carbon black-based mock-up (black line).

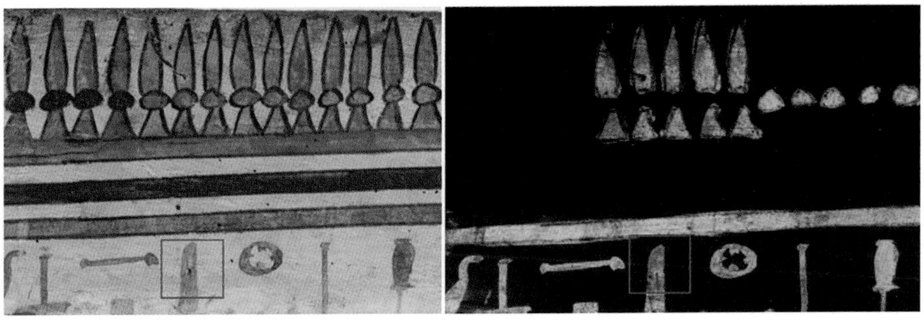

Fig. 29: Detail of the outer coffin box of Padiamenemipet (Nr. Inv. Cat. 2235/2). In visible light and VIL.

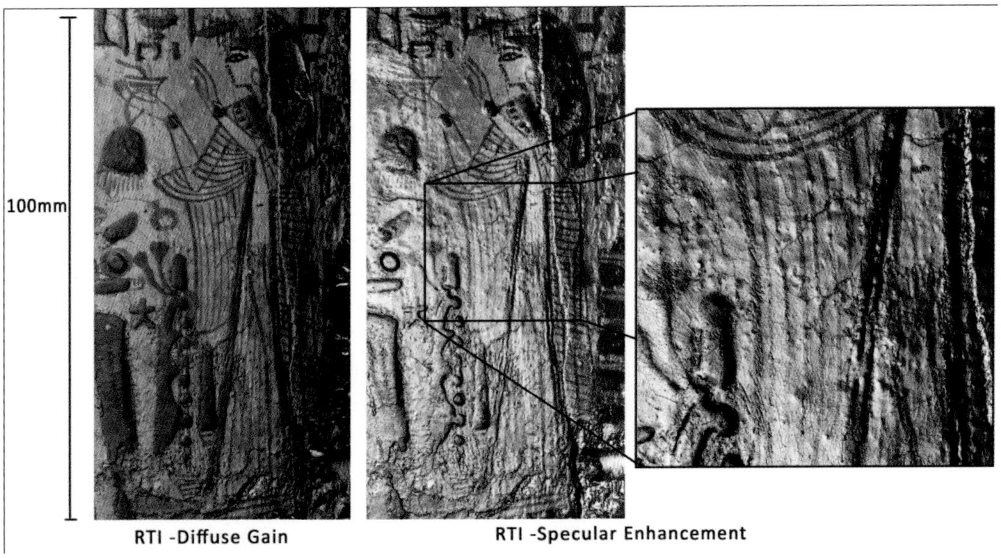

Fig. 30: Detail of the coffin of Khonsumose, mummy board (Nr. Inv. Cat. 2238/3). RTI visualisation in diffuse gain and specular enhancement modes.

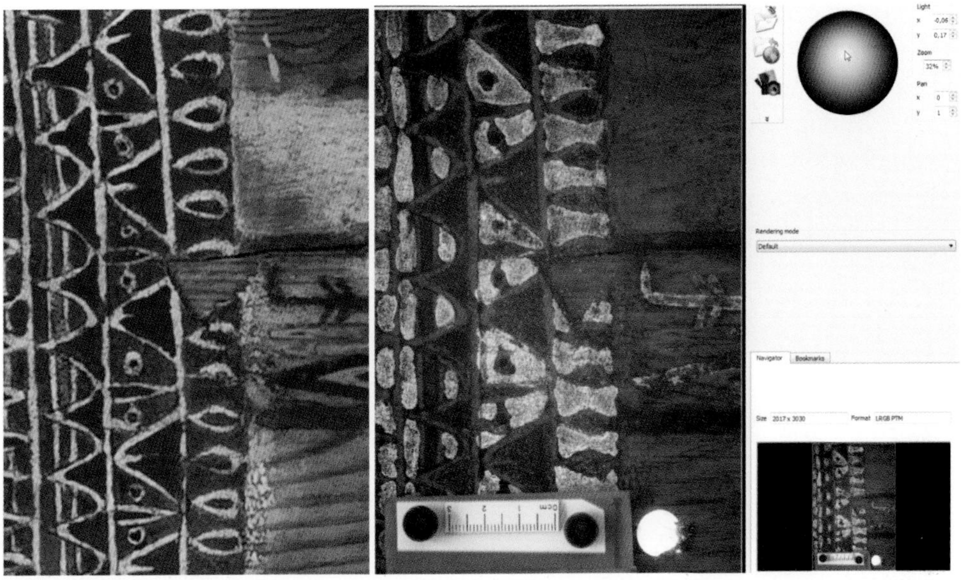

Fig. 31: Detail of the intermediate coffin of Meinturdis (Nr. Inv. S. 5220/2). Picture in visible light and RTI-VIL.

coming from the Valley of the Queens, presented a different problem: in visible light the hieroglyphs looked very dark and in some areas were difficult to read. This darkness could be due to dust deposited over time or simply to the use of a black pigment.

In IRR1 also the hieroglyphs appeared dark, which would be compatible with the presence of a carbon-based pigment (**Fig. 27**b). Thanks to VIL however, it has been possible to detect the presence of Egyptian blue (**Fig. 27**c). **Fig. 28** shows the FORS spectrum of an Egyptian blue-based mock-up compared to the one of a carbon-based black mock-up. The combination of the three techniques (IRR, VIL, FORS) has provided a non-invasive way of arriving at a fairly reliable interpretation: the blue pigment was probably applied over a first, black draft of the text. In general, on many dark areas, where the presence of carbon-based pigment might have been suspected, the VIL technique has revealed instead the presence of Egyptian blue, but in a poor state of preservation.

Moreover, thanks to the VIL technique, it has been possible to map the original distribution of the blue areas of paint even where the pigment seemed lost. As an example, **Fig. 29** shows the outer coffin box of Padiamenemipet (Nr. Inv. Cat. 2235/2) where some details in blue seem to have almost entirely disappeared. Not only the VIL, but also the FORS spectra acquired in areas corresponding to this loss of material are clearly diagnostic, revealing all the absorption bands typical of the pigment.

Investigation of selected areas: materials, pictorial technique and state of preservation

Another case study is the mummy board of Khonsumose (Nr. Inv. Cat. 2238/3) belonging to a yellow type coffin. Here the morphology of the surface decoration was highlighted with the RTI technique. The RTI software allows different tools of surface visualisation, one of which is the specular enhancement mode. This tool was decisive in studying the Khonsumose coffin (**Fig. 30**) and could be exploited for other coffins of the yellow type that present to the naked eye a very "flat" drawing. With RTI, we have observed, in a totally non-invasive way, the thickness of the red drawing, the superimposition of the different colours and the techniques of painting. The decoration layers have a three-dimensional aspect and their morphology indicates a specific sequence of application of the different colours, from the red and yellow, to the green, to the blue.

In order to highlight specifically the thickness and extent of the Egyptian blue areas, we tested the combination of the VIL technique with RTI (**Fig. 31**). Even though the VIL is not a strictly superficial analysis (as it makes use of infrared radiation that goes a little beyond the surface), the RTI-VIL combination can be extremely useful for evaluating the state of preservation and the distribution of the blue layer.

For identification of the painting materials, we report the example of an anthropoid coffin (Nr. Inv. S. 05239), where we applied the FORS technique in combination with HSI. As noted above, HSI was undertaken with prototype equipment by INRiM, that makes use of an innovative Fabry-Perot interferometer-based technology.

The palette contains yellow and red ochre and earths, green copper-based pigments and Egyptian blue, whose absorption bands all recorded first with the spectrophotometer. In addition, the hyperspectral cubes acquired on different portions of surface allowed reconstruction of the colour of the surface and mapping of the pigment distribution. To reconstruct the colour, spectra from the HS cubes were normalised to the lighting source (that means to the spectrum of the reference white added

Fig. 32: Colour image calculated from 2 hyperspectral cubes acquired on an anthropoid coffin lid (Nr. Inv. S. 05239).

Fig. 33: False-colours hyperspectral image detail of an anthropoid coffin lid (Nr. Inv. S. 05239).

into the scene) and were then weighted to the CIE1964 colour matching functions and to the CIE standard illuminant D65 (daylight 6500 K). **Fig. 32** is the result of two hyperspectral cubes combined together with such calculated colours. See **Fig. 33** for the false-colour image showing the pigment mapping for part of the same detail.

To calculate the false-colour image we used an algorithm to recognise similar reflectance spectra and therefore similar pigments: each spectrum is represented by a vector in the vector space of the spectral components. Since a different lightness would have changed the length of the vector but not its direction, we have trained the software to assign different false colours to the pixels by using the Spectral Angle Mapper (SAM) algorithm (Rashmi 2014). This measures spectral similarity by calculating the angle between the two spectra. In this first version, we have used 4 false colours: blue for the black and the Egyptian blue pixels, yellow for the white and yellow ochre, red for the red ochre and green for the green copper based pigment. This tool could be helpful also for mapping the distribution of specific pigments if used in mixture.

Conclusions

The opportunity to study a large number of artworks or artefacts of similar period, style or provenance is a productive way for developing suitable methods of investigation and tailoring *ad hoc* combinations of complementary techniques.

In this paper we progress through different case studies with the aim of highlighting the application of non-invasive, imaging or point analysis techniques, with each one designed for a specific target. The multi-technique approach has been shown to be efficient for many purposes during the study of the Egyptian coffins belonging to the Museo Egizio and analysed at CCR.

Information about the methods of assembly and execution of the coffins, and about the state of preservation has been collected by means of classical multispectral imaging techniques, such as UV fluorescence and IR reflectography. These have been combined with techniques used only recently in the field of heritage science or innovative technologies, such as the hyperspectral imager prototype by INRiM or the shielded, locally designed CT scanner for large-size artworks.

Noble burials?

Notes on the use of black coffins in KV40

Hans-Hubertus Münch

The paper introduces and discusses the unpublished fragments of black coffins of the Eighteenth Dynasty from KV40 that have been excavated by the University of Basel Kings' Valley Project between 2011 and 2014. The analysis of the material offers several suggestions for the reconstruction of the original types and sizes of coffins used for the burial of mostly female members of the royal family during the second half of the Eighteenth Dynasty (c. 1400–1350 BC). In addition, they also illustrate the choice and style of coffins used at the royal court, which in turn raises the question of conformity and difference in burial practice among the elite at that time.

Around eighty wooden coffin fragments of the so-called "black type" were discovered by the University of Basel's Kings' Valley Project (UBKVP) in KV40.[1] Although the majority of these fragments are small and therefore do not allow a reconstruction of individual coffins, their presence nonetheless gives important information about the burial practices of members of the royal court during the reign of Amenhotep III, as this paper aims to show.

The archaeological context

KV40 is located in the southern part of the Valley of the Kings – close to the tombs of Thutmose III (KV34) and Maihirpri (KV36). It is the largest non-royal tomb of the Eighteenth Dynasty in the Valley and its ground plan (**Fig. 34**) is like that of KV30, which is a short distance from KV40 on the other side of the wadi. As suggested by the discovery of Amenhotep III's name on a selection of objects and two inscriptions mentioning the year 25, the tomb must have been used as a burial place over a considerable space of time during this king's reign. Unfortunately, the tomb was ransacked on several occasions between the end of the New Kingdom and modern times. In addition, it was reused as a burial place for the priestly families of Thebes during the Third Intermediate Period. As a result of these incidents, the interior of KV40 was found in a heavily plundered and the contents mostly in a fragmentary state of preservation (**Fig. 35**).

According to nearly one hundred inscriptions, consisting of names and often additional titles, found on pottery sherds, wooden tags and other objects, KV40 was used as a burial place for around thirty members of Amenhotep III's extended royal family (Bickel and Paulin-Grothe 2014). This group of people was comprised of daughters, sons, and granddaughters of the king as well as some close servants or confidantes, like women, whose names are of foreign origin. The latter individuals may be associated with the diplomatic marriages of the time and the sizeable entourages that accompanied the "wives-to-be" to Egypt.

Although it is not possible to attribute any of the fragments of the "black coffins" recovered from KV40 to particular owners, there can be little doubt that they actually represent the remains of coffins that were used for the burials of members of the royal court during the reign of

[1] For general discussions of "black coffins", see Dodson 1998; Polz 1991, 264–267; Sartini 2015; Taylor 2016. I owe a special debt of gratitude to Lisa Sartini and Jonathan Elias for their support and most helpful advice.

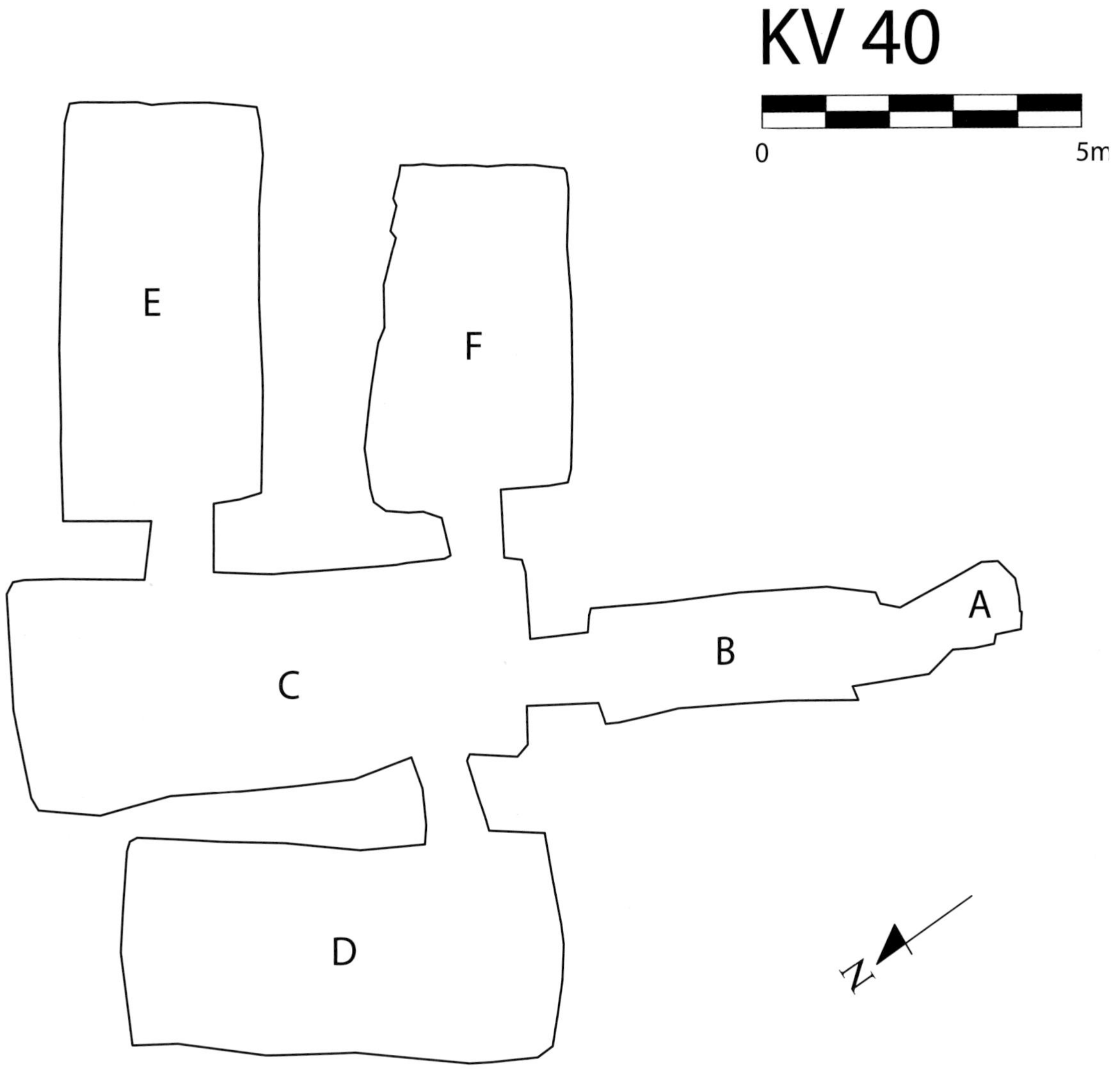

Fig. 34: Plan of KV40. © UBKVP, Tanja Alsheimer & Faried Adrom

Amenhotep III. This is because the decoration on all of the surviving fragments is consistent with the outer decoration of other black-type coffins attested for the second half of the Eighteenth Dynasty. In addition, most of the wooden fragments were discovered just in front of the back walls of various rooms at the lowest stratigraphic level. Hence, a displacement of these fragments from burials other than those interred into KV40 seems rather unlikely.

The use of "black coffins" among the elite

"Black coffins" are usually anthropoid and characterised by a lustrous black bitumen background.[2] Their decoration features texts and divine figures that are either painted in yellow or made of gilded plaster. They were fashionable in the period between the middle of the Eighteenth Dynasty and the reign of Ramesses II, and were commonly used among all levels of the elite by the time of Amenhotep III. "Black coffins" of this date often show highly complex designs, with multiple columns of texts and figures on the lid and the box, whereas earlier examples are less decorated. For example, they might leave the space between columns undecorated and the figures mostly unaccompanied by texts.

High-status individuals were often buried in multiple coffins, nested within each other, which were made with the highest quality craftsmanship and materials (Berman 1992; Smith 1992, 198; Wiese 2004). Some of these multi-layered burials consisted of two or three outer coffins enclosing an entirely or partly gilded inner coffin with the mummy of the deceased. These nests of "black

2 For a detailed overview, see Taylor 2016, 181–183.

Fig. 35: Side room E as found. © UBKVP, Matjaz Kacicnik

coffins" were regularly contained within huge box-like outer coffins, which were coated once again with black bitumen and often decorated with bands of inscriptions and figures of the gods in gold leaf over gesso.

Individuals who were very close to the king had even more elaborate and expensive coffin sets. For example, while Amenhotep III's father-in-law Iuya was buried in a nest of three anthropoid "black coffins" featuring a silver-covered middle coffin and an inner gilded coffin, the king's mother-in-law Tuya had an entirely gilded outer and inner coffin (Quibell 1908, pls. II–IV, IX–X). Just as precious as Iuya and Tuya's coffin sets are the extravagant ones of Amenhotep III's northern vizier Aperel, his wife, and his son. These coffins display inscriptions and figures in multi-coloured inlaid glass paste, as a substitute for the moulded and gilded gesso (Zivie 1990, pls. 45, 52, 60–69, 95–96).

The high status associated with coffin sets of this type can also be observed among members of the extended royal family, even if their examples are not as splendid as those of Iuya, Tuya, and Aperel. For example, although Maihirpri's life (KV 36) certainly pre-dated the reign of Amenhotep III, he was also buried in an elaborate style. He was laid in an inner gilded coffin that was enclosed in a "black coffin", both of which rested within a huge black style rectangular outer coffin decorated with gilded inscriptions and figures (Lakomy 2016, pls. 23–25, 27–32, 55–60).

Burial wealth among this courtly group can also be observed via a "black coffin" of a presumably royal infant boy, which might be dated to somewhere in or around the lifetime of Amenhotep III.[3] Although it did not feature a gilded inner coffin, on the basis of the published data, its decoration originally showed bands of inscriptions and figures of the gods in gold leaf over gesso. It also seems to have had inlays of glass paste in the areas of the face and collar. In this context, one might be reminded of the miniature coffin nests of two royal foetuses from the tomb of Tutankhamun, which also featured an outer "black coffin" enclosing an entirely gilded inner box.[4]

[3] Egyptian Museum Cairo, JE 49549, see Bruyère 1925 ; Dodson 1998, 338.

[4] Coffins of foetus A: Egyptian Museum Cairo, JE 60692–3;

Fig. 36: Parts of a deity from the side of a coffin. © UBKVP, Matjaz Kacicnik

Fig. 37: Part of an inscription from the side of a coffin lid. © UBKVP, Matjaz Kacicnik

Examples of coffins of the black type used for the burials of individuals from somewhat lower in the elite hierarchy were frequently far less costly than those just described.[5] For example, the outer decoration of the coffins was neither executed in gesso nor in sunk relief, but was simply painted directly onto the wooden surface. In addition, the gilded parts of the decoration were replaced by yellow, which frequently included orpiment (arsenic trisulphide). Furthermore, the bitumen was replaced by either a mixture made out of bitumen, charcoal, and tree gum, or simply by black paint. Finally, the mummy of the deceased was only surrounded by a single coffin rather than multiple layers of coffins.[6]

coffins of foetus B: Egyptian Museum Cairo, JE 60695–6).

[5] Cf. the coffin of Tamyt (British Museum, EA6661), see Strudwick and Dawson 2016, Cat. 24.

[6] cf Smith 1992, 218.

The remains of "black coffins" from KV40

The coffins from the first phase of use of KV40 during the reign of Amenhotep III appear to have been systematically dismantled and smashed during the intense period of plundering at the end of the New Kingdom. As a result of these violent actions, larger wooden elements, such as the side boards and back panels, are entirely missing from the archaeological record; most of the recovered fragments that date to this timespan are splinters that do not exceed 15 cm in length.

The few traces of decoration that survived on the fragments, such as the bits and pieces of inscriptions and figures of gods in yellow on a black background, are consistent with the exterior designs typical for Eighteenth Dynasty coffins of the black type. There were also fragments showing the figures of deities outlined in bold red (**Fig. 36**); this stylistic feature was fashionable between the last quarter of Amenhotep III's reign and the reign of Ramesses II (Polz 1991, 245–264, 266–267).

The method of applying the black coating varied among the corpus of fragments; on some it was applied directly onto the wood, while on others it was put over a white plaster-like material. Visual inspection suggests that the coating on nearly half of the coffins was made out of charcoal and tree gum.

Hardly any of the content of the inscriptions can be identified. Besides single isolated hieroglyphic signs, only a larger determinative of a seated god has survived (**Fig. 37**). It seems to have been part of a Nut-utterance running along the right side of a coffin lid.[7] When compared to similar examples, both the position of the fragment and the size of the hieroglyphs suggest that the coffin was made for an adult. It probably featured a central inscription on its lid, an inscription on each of its sides, and four inscriptions running across the lid lateral to the box, dividing the its sides into sections that contained figures of gods or other divine emblems.

Because of the small size of the other fragments recovered from KV40, it is not possible to attempt further reconstructions of individual coffins. However, due to the method of applying the black coating on the wood and the variation in scale of decorative elements, it seems plausible to assume that KV40 contained coffins in a number of different sizes, meant for adults as well as children or infants. Nevertheless, there is no evidence that would confirm the existence of any larger outer coffin or nests of coffins, as is the case with the high elite burials mentioned above.

Absent coffins

According to the number of names attested at the site, KV40 must have hosted around 30 coffins of different sizes by the final years of Amenhotep III's reign. By this reasoning, the surviving corpus of wooden fragments represents, without doubt, only a tiny sample of those "black coffins" which must have once existed. It is, however, impossible to determine whether this lack of material evidence results from the common practice of reusing coffins or is rather due to the possibility that the coffins were dismantled outside KV40.

There is, however, evidence that tentatively points to the existence of at least one other coffin, which is otherwise unattested by any kind of fragment within in the

Fig. 38: Fragment of a canopic chest. © *UBKVP, Matjaz Kacicnik*

archaeological record of KV40: a wooden fragment has been found that presumably belonged to a canopic chest that differed in both style and quality from the coffins represented by the aforementioned wooden fragments (**Fig. 38**).[8] Although assemblages comprising coffins and canopic chests that date to the Eighteenth Dynasty are not always identical in their exterior designs, it would not be entirely surprising to assume that KV40 might have contained such a corresponding assemblage.

As is clear from the limited number of coffin fragments dating to the Eighteenth Dynasty, the plundering of tombs in search of whole coffins or even single wooden elements must have been very intense, leaving only the clearly unwanted and luckily overlooked items behind.

Unfortunately, due to the intensely looted nature of the archaeological context, it is impossible to determine whether or not KV40 contained "black coffins" of the type commonly associated with high class court burials, such as those introduced above. However, there have been no observations of any kind of gilded gesso in the

[7] I am very grateful to Lisa Sartini and Jonathan Elias for bringing this to my attention.

[8] Cf. the canopic chest of Amenemhat (British Museum, EA 35809).

course of excavation of KV40 that would point to the former existence of such burials.

Conclusion

The key point about KV40 is that it preserved the remains of the burial equipment of various members of Amenhotep III's extended royal family. This was a social group within court society of the Eighteenth Dynasty and, to date, very little information on their burial practices is available, especially when compared to other elite groups of that time.

One essential observation that can be made on the basis of the archaeological finds from the context is that the coffins used for the burials of this courtly group were significantly less rich and luxurious than those of other courtiers. This becomes especially clear when the material is compared to the famous burial equipment of Iuja and Tuja, and also to those of other high officials like Aperel or Kha. In the latter case, even their wives were buried in lavish coffin sets, which were quite similar to those of their husbands.

A second important observation is, that some of the wooden fragments from KV40 seem to have even more in common in regard to their quality and style with "black coffins" owned by individuals outside the inner circles of the court, such as those whose status was dependent on their relationship to Amenemope (TT 41) at the very end of the Eighteenth Dynasty (Polz 1991, 266–267).

Finally, although it is impossible to determine which objects from the various burial assemblages are absent from the archaeological context of KV40, it is clear from the existing fragments of "black coffins" that there was great variation in regard to their style and quality.

Following on from the premise that all those individuals who were interred together in KV40 belonged in one way or the other to the extended royal family of Amenhotep III, these three observations have a significant impact on our understanding of the burial practices of members of the royal court during the second half of the Eighteenth Dynasty.

On the one hand, they vividly illustrate that the fact that being a member of the court did not mean a person automatically had access to considerable resources in putting together a noble burial assemblage. On the other hand, they do not support the idea of a standardised burial among specific groups of the elite like the extended royal family.[9]

However, it is equally possible to assume that the fact of having a tomb in the Valley of Kings, an area that was considered by the ancient Egyptians to be a very special place for burial upon death, was of much more significant weight in the internal set of rules applying to elite status display than a splendid and expensive burial somewhere else in or outside the Theban necropolis.

In any case, the wooden fragments of "black coffins" from KV40 indicate clearly that the link between social status and both burial practice and mortuary investment at the Eighteenth Dynasty royal court represents a rather more complicated issue than is at first sight apparent.

---

9 This conclusion stands in opposition to Smith 1992, 217.

Coffins of the Twenty-first and Twenty-second Dynasties: the sacred landscape of Western Thebes

Andrzej Niwiński

The beautiful yellow-ground coffins, alongside the funerary papyri of the Twenty-first to Twenty-second Dynasties, belong to the rare sources of information about the period. The very rich iconography shows thousands of symbolic motifs as a reflection of the religious beliefs of the late New Kingdom. However, behind this formal façade, numerous iconographic details make it possible to discover important information about historical events, the economic situation, a picture of the Theban society, the work of the craftsmen, etc. The analysis of some scenes and motifs (among others, the 'scene with the Hathor cow emerging from the mountain', and 'the scene with the sycamore'), usually understood as the vignettes to the 'chapters' of the Book of the Dead, also manifests the reality of the sacred landscape of the central part of the Theban Necropolis in that period. This paper offers an explanation of these scenes, and the historical situation in which this subject appeared in the iconographic repertoire on the coffins.

An investigation into the development of the iconographic repertoire of the Twenty-first and the early Twenty-second Dynasty "yellow" coffins seems to be one of the most serious research challenges.[1] Several distinct phases of this development can be distinguished within the span of about 180 years, between the end of the Ramessides and the end of the production of the yellow grounded coffins, and the question arises: why did these changes taken place? From my studies of the coffin decoration, an observation emerges, that every clear qualitative change of the iconographic repertoire was related to an important event, sometimes of a political nature, like the change in the office of the Theban high priest of Amun. This can be relatively easily exemplified by the situation in the early Twenty-second Dynasty.

Scenes of ritual ceremonies performed during the burial, together with some motifs from the royal Amduat,[2]

[1] The following publications present the most complete descriptions of the coffins of Twenty-first and Twenty-second Dynasties, or the results of research into the iconography of this period: Abbas 2014a, 2014b; Boeser 1916, 1917; Bogoslovsky 1973; Budge 1893; Chassinat 1909; Cooney 2007, 2011, 2014; Dąbrowska-Smektała 1966; Daressy 1909; Dautant *et al.* 2011; Devéria 1855; Duarte 2014; Egner and Haslauer 1994; Englund 1974; Falck 1987; Gasse 1996; Grothe-Paulin 1988; Guilhou and Perraud 2010; Haslauer and Egner 2009; Heyne 1998; Hornung 1984; Jamen 2016; Kitchen 1990; Koefoed-Petersen 1951; Küffer and Renfer 1996; Küffer and Siegmann 2007; Leemans 1867; Lavrentyeva 2015; Liptay 1992, 2000, 2002, 2003, 2008, 2011; Möller 1901; Moser 2013; Niwiński 1981, 1986, 1988a, 1988c, 1989b, 1989c, 1990, 1991b, 1999, 2000, 2004, 2006a, 2006b, 2007, 2009, 2011, 2014, 2017a, 2018, forthcoming 2, forthcoming 3; el-Sayed 1981; Sousa 2014b; Turaieff 1899–1903; Verner 1982: 57–93; Walsem 1997.

[2] Distinct burial ceremonies (including the burial procession and the ritual of the Opening of the Mouth) are represented on Twenty-second Dynasty coffins: Ägyptisches Museum Berlin, 58; National Museum of Finland, Helsinki, KM/Vk/14560:660; Egyptian Museum Cairo, 5.12.25.4; Rijksmuseum van Oudheden, Leiden, AMM 18 (M3; cf. Walsem 1997); British Museum, London, 22941, 36211; Museu de Arqueología e Etnologia, São Paulo, 1679; Museo Gregoriano Egizio, Vatican, 25008.2.2. Motifs from the royal Amduat are represented on Twenty-second Dynasty coffins: Ägyptisches Museum, Berlin, 58; Muzeum Archeologiczne, Cracow, AS 2442; Collection of the Jagiellonian University, Cracow (cf. Niwiński 1986); National Museum of Finland, Helsinki, KM/Vk/14560:660; Rijksmuseum van

Fig. 39: The motif derived from the Book of the Celestial Cow on the coffin of Ankhesenmut, The Egyptian Museum, Cairo, inv. 29675 (drawing A. Niwiński)

were typical for the latest phase of the development of the yellow-type coffins, some of which were well dated to the reign of Osorkon I.[3] Suddenly in the same reign the burial equipment changed completely, with the introduction of the richly painted cartonnages combined with a set of sparingly decorated coffins. This new type of burial equipment can be illustrated with the mummy ensemble of Nakhtefmut, of which the cartonnage is exhibited in the Fitzwilliam Museum, Cambridge.[4] On the mummy inside the cartonnage a large piece of linen was found, inscribed with "Year 33" (Quibell 1898, 10). The position of this inscription strongly suggests that it was written during the bandaging process, which offers the exact date of that burial, corresponding to about 893 BC.[5] Just one year before this burial the new high priest Iuwelot came to office (Kitchen 1973, 480) and it is feasible to suppose that the whole revolutionary change of the burial equipment may have been authorised by him.

Another example of the real influence of political events on the iconographic repertoire of the coffins of the Twenty-first Dynasty is furnished by the appearance, first on funerary papyri, and afterwards in coffin decoration, of the motifs of the royal Books of the Underworld, scenes of some royal ceremonies, and motifs of royal iconography towards the end of the long pontificate of Menkheperre, when this high priest in the 48th regnal year of his brother Psusennes I adopted royal titles, and the function of the Theban pontiff was probably taken over by one of his sons.

From the Bab el-Gusus tomb a number of coffin-sets originate that can be securely dated to these years, first of all through the presence of mummy-braces stamped with the name of Menkheperre (twice written in the a cartouche), or with the name of the king Amenemope. It is most interesting to observe that some elements of royal iconography appear in the decoration of these coffins. For example, the rituals of the run of pharaoh and of the offering of the crowns are represented on the coffin-sets A.24 (The Egyptian Museum, Cairo, 29623: Niwiński 1996b, fig. 58),[6] A.64 (The Egyptian Museum, Cairo, 29656), and A.135 (The Egyptian Museum, Cairo, no inventory number). The final scene of the Book of Caverns appears on the coffins A.38, A.109 and A.113 (The Egyptian Museum, Cairo, 29675, 29660 and 29659: Niwiński 1999, fig. 41, 76, pl. XV.1). On coffin A.38 (Egyptian Museum, Cairo, 29675) yet another motif from a royal funerary composition is illustrated, namely a representation of the theme of the Book of the Celestial Cow, with the image of Re sitting on the back of the cow (Hornung 1982, 42: the line 141, 99 n. 21) (**Fig. 39**). Some individual royal motifs appear, too, for the first time in the decoration, such as the motif of the vulture in coffin A.113 (Egyptian Museum Cairo, 29659; cf. Niwiński 1999, 62, fig. 92). Finally, several coffins belonging to the same well-dated group feature atypical decoration made partly on a white (and not yellow) ground (the coffins A.11, Egyptian Museum Cairo, 29698; A.14, Museo Arqueológico Nacional, Madrid, 18254; A.81 (Egyptian Museum, Cairo, 29649). It seems feasible that this atypical ground colour may have resulted from the idea of imitating the decoration of some royal tombs of kings (for example, some scenes in the tombs of Seti I, Seti II, Ramesses VI) or queens (for example, the tomb of Nefertari).

Imitations of the contents of the last four hours of

Oudheden, Leiden, AMM 18 (M.10) and Amm 18 (M.3); British Museum, London, 22900, 22941, 22942; Musée du Louvre, Paris, N.2612; Museo Gregoriano Egizio, Vatican 25012.2.2. For the occurrence of both kinds of motifs on the coffins, see Duarte 2014.

3 The coffins in the Museum of Art, Cleveland, CMA 14.714 and Rijksmuseum van Oudheden, Leiden, AMM 18 (M.3) (Niwiński 1988a, 81).

4 Fitzwilliam Museum Cambridge, E. 64.1896: Dawson and Strudwick 2016, 198–200.

5 Kitchen 1972, 308. On the mummy of Khonsu-maakhru, buried in a cartonnage case, a bandage has been found with the date "Year 23" (Altenmüller 1976, 57), and the mummy-braces of Osorkon I lying on the mummy indicate the date of the production of this bandage in the year 902.

6 According to Daressy's list (Daressy 1900, 141–148; Daressy 1907, 3–38).

Fig. 40: The solar scene represented on the coffin of Panebmontu, The Louvre, Paris, inv. E. 13029 (photo A. Niwiński)

the royal Amduat were reproduced on funerary papyri at the same time (Niwiński 1989a, 174ff). On the coffins, these motifs appear only some 30 years later, under the pontificate of Psusennes. They can be best exemplified in the coffin-sets A.132, A.133 and A.148 from the Bab el-Gusus (Egyptian Museum, Cairo, 29612, 29738 and 29611).

The first important change in the iconography on coffins, within the period in discussion, took place together with the inception of the Renaissance Era, and are thus probably related to Herihor's pontificate (Niwiński 1995, 340ff; 1996c). This novelty consisted in the introduction of a second funerary papyrus (Niwiński 1989a, 42), and the addition of some new motifs to the traditional Ramesside repertoire of coffin decoration.

The number of coffins datable to the Twentieth Dynasty is very low,[7] and this absence provokes discussion. We cannot exclude the possibility that most of the coffins of that period may have been reused in the following Twenty-first Dynasty, when the original

[7] In the study by K. Cooney (Cooney 2007, 397ff), a list of sixty-one Ramesside coffins and fragments of these was suggested, of which a date of the Twentieth Dynasty was proposed for fifteen pieces (the catalogue numbers D.2–7, E.1–6, F.2, F.5–6).

However, the first group of these objects, originating from the tomb of Iurudef in Saqqara, represents most probably post-Twenty-first Dynasty provincial coffins (Niwiński 1996d, *passim*), and the objects Ägyptisches Museum, Berlin 8505, National Museum, Copenhagen, AEIN 62, and Museo Gregoriano Egizio, Vatican, XIII.2.1–2, belong to a group of mid-Twenty-first Dynasty coffins produced in Akhmim (Niwiński 2017). Also belonging to the same group is a coffin in the Kunsthistorisches Museum, Vienna, ÄS 6066, for which K. Cooney has recently suggested a dating of the "Twentieth – Twenty First Dynasty" (Cooney 2014, 48). In no way can the coffins mentioned in the same table, i.e. those of Nodjmet (Egyptian Museum Cairo, 26215), of Sutymes (Louvre, Paris, N. 2609–2611), and of Butehamon (Museo Egizio, Turin, 2237), be dated to the Twentieth Dynasty (Cooney 2014, 48): these people were living at the turn of the Twentieth to Twenty-first Dynasty, but their coffins were produced in the early Twenty-first Dynasty, most probably early in the reign of Psusennes I.

Fig. 41: The scene of the Judgment of the Dead on the coffin of Sutymes, The Louvre, Paris, inv. N. 2610 (Photo A. Niwiński)

decoration may have been removed or covered with a new one.[8]

On the basis of the decoration covering the coffin cases found on the few objects possibly produced in the Twentieth Dynasty (of which I would suggest adding two coffins in the Metropolitan Museum of Art, New York, MMA 26.3.1 and MMA 26.3.4 to the list), one can observe the following features which were most typical towards the end of the Ramesside period:

- The upper edge of the wall (outside) was at this time not yet topped with one long decorative element (a frieze, a line of hieroglyphic inscription);
- At the height of the head, horizontal parallel stripes are painted;
- The decorative panels are usually narrow, containing single figures.
- The inside of the coffin case was not yet decorated.

It seems that on the eve of the Twenty-first Dynasty some decorative panels painted on the exterior of the walls became larger, and scenes with two or more figures appeared (for example, Thoth making a gesture of presentation towards an enthroned figure of Osiris, accompanied by a female personification), and the sides of the head receive figurative and textual decoration. Such a scheme is represented on the coffin of Nesamon (City Museum, Leeds, D.426–426a.1960). The leather braces found on the mummy of Nesamon were stamped with the name of Ramesses XI, which probably refers to the last years of his reign, which coincides with the Renaissance Era. The process of innovation that had begun at that time, enriched very soon the iconographic repertoire of the coffins by the additions of inner decoration of the case, and new scenes painted on the outside, first of all the solar scene with Apopis (**Fig. 40**), as well as cosmological compositions.[9]

In the early Twenty-first Dynasty the repertoire of

[8] This is probably the case for the following coffins: British Museum, 29579, Museo Archeologico, Florence, 7450, National Museum Copenhagen, 3912, and Ägyptische Sammlung, Munich, ÄS 12.

[9] Exemplified by the coffins of Masaharti (Egyptian Museum, Cairo, 26195: Daressy 1909, pl. XXXVII, Niwiński 1988a, pl.

Fig. 42: The pavement slab, intentionally destroyed and reconstructed in antiquity, lying in the western part of the temple of Thutmosis III at Deir el-Bahari (photo A. Niwiński)

motifs expanded, reaching, quantitatively, its peak, with a great number of iconographic variants of old and new scenes, which – besides the above-mentioned compositions – represented the motifs only occasionally met up to this time, mainly on papyri and Theban tombs, and which are traditionally regarded as vignettes from some so-called chapters of the Book of the Dead. The coffin-set of Sutymes in the Louvre, Paris, N.2609–2611, represents the most characteristic example of this phase of the development of coffin decoration (**Fig. 41**) (Champollion and Guichard 2013, 238–239; Niwiński 2008, 35 fig. 9–10; Niwiński 2014, 118 fig. 8; Cooney 2014, 53, fig.6). It seems feasible that this new stage of the development may be linked to the induction of the high priest Menkheperre, since the coffin of his predecessor, Masaharti, stylistically preceded this new phase. It is possible, however, that not only the change in the office of the high priest, but also two significant events in the early years of Menkheperre's pontificate, played the most influential role at this time, because these events were undoubtedly very important for Theban society and may well have exerted influence on the whole of coffin decoration in the next half-a-century.

First of these, which presumably took place in the fifth year of Psusennes I's reign, was the burial of the king Neferkare Amenemensu, the Theban co-regent of the Tanite pharaoh (Niwiński 1988a, 43, 49–50). King Neferkare was probably the son of Herihor and he may have been buried in the same tomb, in which his father had reposed for some 34 years. Herihor, who had been promised by the oracle of Khonsu and Amon to have a pontificate of twenty years' length, died unexpectedly early, probably in his sixth year in the office (Niwiński 1995, 347), while his original tomb, which had only just been started, was in the course of being excavated in the so-called Gebel Ragab (Niwiński forthcoming 1).

According to numerous traces furnished by the cleaning works done by the Polish Cliff Mission between 1999 and 2015 at Deir el-Bahari, the burial

XVI) and Panebmontu (The Louvre, Paris, E.13029, see Fig. 2 of this paper), probably made in the reign of Smendes.

Fig. 43: The scene showing the sacred landscape of Deir el-Bahari on the coffin of Tanethereret, The Louvre, Paris, inv. E. 13034 (photo A. Niwiński)

place adapted, in this situation, for Herihor was the old tomb of Amenhotep I, which can probably be expected to have been located in the western part of the temple of Thutmosis III at Deir el-Bahari (Niwiński 2017b). In the corner of the cliff, on the top of the slope above this temple, the Cliff Mission has detected an artificial platform, on which a structure was certainly once built. I strongly suggest that this might have been the tomb chapel of Amenhotep I, which in the period of the New Kingdom came to be the major landmark of the necropolis, crowning the area and being known as "The Holy Horizon". This was the much discussed point of reference for the tomb of Amenhotep I in the Abbott Papyrus. This structure is probably known from the vignettes in some papyri and tombs of the New Kingdom (Davies 1938, Faulkner and Andrews 1972, 187). By the time of Herihor's burial, the temple of Thutmosis III was already ruined, and the tomb of Amenhotep I had also shared the fate of all the royal tombs in the Valley of the Kings, having been robbed during the revolt of the Kushite corps of the army in the 18th year of Ramesses XI (Niwiński 1995, 336ff). It is possible that the mouth of the shaft of this tomb had originally been covered with an exceptionally large slab of the pavement still lying in the western part of the temple of Thutmosis III, excavated by Lipińska in 1965. This slab had been broken into several pieces, probably by the robbers, but was afterwards carefully reconstructed, as has recently been observed by the Polish Cliff Mission (**Fig. 42**). This slab has been laid as an integral part of a most strange and secondarily arranged group of pavement stones there. Be that as it may, this place at the time of the excavations by Lipińska was covered with an accumulation of stones and debris reaching 24 m in height (Lipińska 1977, 10), which under could definitely not have been formed naturally.

I propose the following reconstruction of the history of this area. Probably soon after the burial of Herihor's son, a decision was taken (certainly with the agreement of the high priest Menkheperre) to apply a very special means of protection of the tomb where the last two Theban kings reposed: Herihor and Neferkare Amenemensu.

In light of this decision a gigantic technical operation, probably supervised by Butehamon, took place: the whole southern part of the *ḏsrw* area (today known as Deir el-Bahari), including the ruins of the temple of Thutmosis III and the temple of Mentuhotep, was covered with an artificial accumulation of stones, debris and dust, imitating a natural slope of the mountain. Every architectural element higher than about 1.5 m, for example the columns of both temples and the pyramid of the temple of Mentuhotep, were then removed. The same procedure was applied to the old chapel of Amenhotep I in the corner of the cliff. The last mentioned structure was, however, rebuilt nearby, and its remnants can be seen on some old photographs of the time of Naville's works at Deir el-Bahari (Niwiński 2017b, fig. 7). Almost certainly this chapel is an ever-present element on the coffins of the Twenty-first Dynasty (Niwiński forthcoming 2) (**Fig. 43**).

The second important event in the early years of Menkheperre's pontificate was the burial of Pinodjem I – yet another person of the highest importance in the eyes of the Thebans, bearing the honorific title of king, the father both of the reigning pharaoh Psusennes I and the Theban high priest Menkheperre (Kitchen 1973, 262). One can easily imagine how much pomp and circumstance must have been conferred on the burial ceremony of Pinodjem I. The burial procession may have proceeded slowly, visiting all the Theban sanctuaries with the very probable climax in *ḏsr ḏsrw* – the most sacred temple originally built by Hatshepsut, which – after the modification of the southern part of Deir el-Bahari area into the imitation slope, discussed above – was the only temple visible there. Every element of the funeral procession of Pinodjem I, passing through the sacred landscape of the Theban Necropolis, may have been then commemorated in a symbolic way on the coffins of the Theban priests of Amon. It seems that in this way the numerous scenes, in which the deceased is presented in front of the chapels of many divine forms, on the lids and the cases of the coffins from the early Twenty-first Dynasty onwards may be interpreted as representing the symbolic visits made by the funeral procession to various sanctuaries, most of them situated in Karnak. Similar motifs were, to be sure, also shown on coffins from the preceding phase; however, now the accent is put on ritual ceremonies, probably performed during the final stage of the burial, when the procession reached its final destination, at Deir el-Bahari.

It should be stressed again that the sacred landscape of *ḏsrw* underwent an abrupt change after the creation, in place of two temples, of an artificial imitation slope of the mountain. Previously, in the New Kingdom, one would have been able to see an ensemble of three temples, which – to a much lesser degree – is also possible today. At the beginning of the fourth decade of the Twenty-first Dynasty, only one temple remained there, with the sanctuaries of Hathor and Anubis, which are symbolically rendered in the well-known scene to be found on practically every coffin of that period (Niwiński forthcoming 2) (cf **Fig. 43**). Beyond the chapel of Hathor, one would at that time have been able to see only the artificially created slopes of the mountain, topped with the reconstructed chapel of the tomb of Amenhotep I, which had been for centuries the most characteristic landmark of the Theban Necropolis. It is likely that all the so-called solar scenes on the coffins of that time allude to the visit of the funeral procession to the solar sanctuary of the temple of Hatshepsut, where the solar hymns – probably some so-called chapters of the Book of the Dead, for example Chapter 15, were certainly recited. What is less certain is the location in which was celebrated the theatrical ceremony (observed one thousand years later by Diodorus) of the Judgment of the Dead (cf **Fig. 41**); however the placement of this frequently included scene, near the composition showing the sacred landscape of Deir el-Bahari, as well as the role of Anubis usually operating the balance, seem to indicate that this ritual may have taken place inside or in front of the chapel of Anubis within the Hatshepsut temple. The so-called "sycamore" scene (Billing 2002, 407–419) seems to be one more symbolic rendering of the sacred landscape. The role of the Nut-dryad sanctuary may have been played by one of the sycomore fig trees planted along the processional way leading to the temple of Mentuhotep. In some examples of this scene the base of the tree is encircled by a round border, which probably represents the planter cut in the rock (Niwiński 1999, pl. XIX,2; XXVIII,2).

It is significant that exactly those scenes that reflect the most characteristic landmarks of the sacred landscape of Deir el-Bahari – the scene with the Hathor-cow, the slope of the mountain with the chapel of Amenhotep I and the "sycamore" – not only were already known before the Twenty-first Dynasty (Heyne 1998, 59–60; Billing 2002, 358–390, 407), but also survived to the very end of the timespan for the production of yellow coffins, even if they were sometimes much transformed, having been imagined even in some very poor workshops

(Niwiński 2014, 129–132). Therefore, even these late variants of the scene, being sometimes no more than a distant echo of the original design, continue to inform us about the sacred landscape of the Western Thebes, which did not change at least until the final phase of the Third Intermediate Period, when the area of the Hatshepsut temple became the burial place for some of the families of the priests of Montu.

The coffin of Somtus from Abusir el-Meleq

(Cairo, Egyptian Museum JE 36806): Egyptological Study

Raphaële Meffre

The coffin of Somtus (Cairo, Egyptian Museum JE 36806) was found by Otto Rubensohn during his excavations in Abusir el-Meleq, near Herakleopolis. Rubensohn's diary tells us that it was found in a tomb where three generations of a single family were buried. If we compare the decorative programme and funerary texts of Somtus's coffin to other coffins from Abusir el-Meleq, or most probably from this site, we can highlight regional characteristics from Middle Egypt and local distinctive features from Abusir el-Meleq. Moreover, some specific details, such as the shape of hieroglyphic signs and errors in the funerary texts, are clues showing that some of these pieces were made in the same workshop as the one where Somtus's coffin was crafted during the mid-Ptolemaic period.

Provenance and context

The coffin of Somtus (*smꜣ-tꜣwy*) was found during the German excavations in Abusir el-Meleq and was allocated to the group of objects that entered the Egyptian Museum after the objects discovered in 1904 were shared between the Berlin and Cairo museums.[1] Abusir el-Meleq is a necropolis located in northern Middle Egypt, near the entrance of the Fayum, some 20 km north of Herakleopolis. During the First Millennium BC, it was the main necropolis of the inhabitants of Herakleopolis and it was the location of the tombs of most of the local elites. Otto Rubensohn excavated the site on behalf of the Egyptian Museum of Berlin over four main campaigns at the beginning of the 20th century. His digging diary for 29th February 1904 gives details concerning the Ptolemaic period tomb in which the coffin of Somtus was discovered:[2] it was located just below the surface and contained the bodies of five persons from three generations of a single family. One photograph (**Fig. 44**), taken during the excavations, and a sketch from Rubensohn's diary (**Fig. 45**) show how this tomb group was organised. Somtus's coffin bears the number 3 on Rubensohn's sketch; being one of the best-preserved coffins of this tomb, it was photographed after its discovery (**Fig. 46**).[3]

Four inhumations (no. 1, 2, 3 and 5), including

[1] The ensemble, comprising the lid, the box and the mummy decorated with pieces of cartonnage, bears the number JE 36806. The Journal d'Entrée gives this description of the ensemble: "Cercueil anthropoïde de Somtous fils d'Ahmès. Caisse en bois stuqué et peint. Momie couverte de découpages". After entering the Museum, its elements were quickly separated and their provenance, lost: the lid received a Special Register number (SR 6101) and the box with its mummy were registered in the Temporary Register (TR 25/8/19/3).

[2] See Germer, Kischkewitz and Lüning 2009, 185.

[3] I would like to thank Fr. Seyfried and R. Germer who gave me access to Otto Rubensohn's digging journal and authorised me to use it in my research. I must also thank S. Abd el-Raziq, who was always of great help in my work at the Cairo Museum. The pictures of the coffin JE 36806 published here were kindly supplied by the Egyptian Museum, Cairo. I would also like to thank Chr. Kunicki for the pictures of Djedhor's coffin, D. Wannagat and J. Fischer for the picture of the Ptah-Sokar-Osiris statuette kept in Rostock and H. W. Fischer-Elfert, D. Raue and K. Seidel for the pictures of the coffin of Tadiusir in Leipzig.

Fig. 44: The tomb of Somtus's family during Otto Rubensohn's excavations on the 29th of February 1904 (© Ägyptisches Museum und Papyrussammlung, Staatliche Museen zu Berlin, Ph. 5808, Photo: Otto Rubensohn).

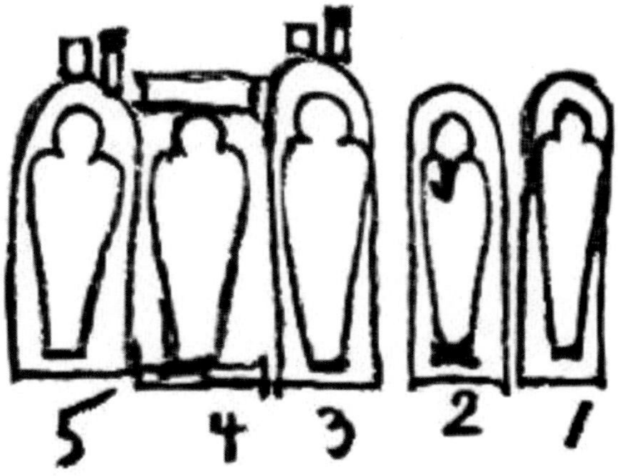

Fig. 45: Sketch from Rubensohn's diary showing the organisation of the burials in Somtus's family tomb. Somtus's coffin is no. 3 (© SMPK Ägyptisches Museum, Archiv).

that of Somtus, had the common Ptolemaic period rude limestone sarcophagi with rounded heads, each containing one wooden coffin; no. 4 had only a wooden coffin. According to Rubensohn, coffins 4 and 5 were of the same type as coffin 3, but they were too damaged to be removed. No. 2 was described as a black mummiform coffin bearing texts written in white and yellow.[4] Coffin no. 1 was made for a woman named Ibet, who was Somtus's spouse. Its decoration is of much higher quality than that of Somtus's coffin. It was found in a good state of preservation and was taken by Rubensohn for the Berlin Museum.[5] Thanks to the genealogies inscribed on the five coffins found in this tomb, it is possible

[4] The location of this coffin is not known at present.

[5] Berlin Ägyptisches Museum, 17104 (coffin) and 17105 (mummy with cartonnage ornaments, lost during World War II). See Germer, Kischkewitz and Lüning 2009, 185–188 and fig. 297–299.

Fig. 46: Photography of Somtus's coffin after its discovery (© Ägyptisches Museum und Papyrussammlung, Staatliche Museen zu Berlin, Ph. 5823, Photo: Georg Möller).

to reconstruct the genealogy of this family (**Fig. 47**). Somtus and Ibet are the senior generation buried in this tomb. Other occupants were their son and their daughter, and also the latter's son.[6]

A few funerary goods were found in this tomb, located near the head of the coffins of Somtus and of his son Horwedja, the two men buried in this tomb; in this family, women do not seem to have had the benefit of funerary objects. At the head of Somtus's coffin were only two objects: an empty canopic chest with a falcon statuette crowned with two feathers on the top[7] and a wooden figure of Ptah-Sokar-Osiris (**Fig. 55**).[8]

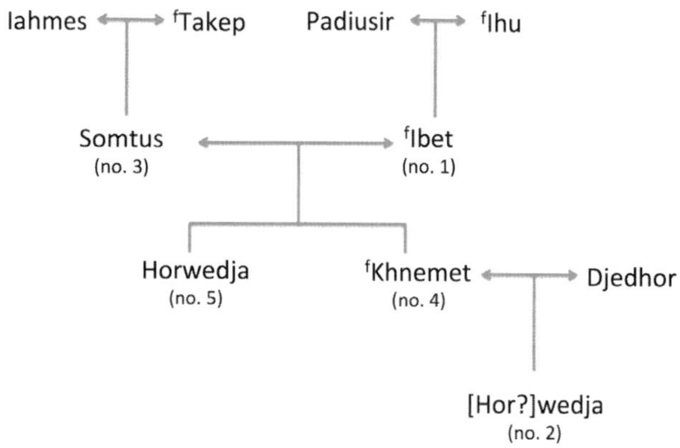

Fig. 47: Genealogy of Somtus's family, according to the texts copied by G. Möller.

The owner of the coffin and his family (Fig. 50)

The axial text of the lid, written in retrograde script, presents Somtus in columns 2–3 as:

wsir sš-nṯr smꜣ-tꜣwy sꜣ iʿḥ-ms ir(w n) nbt-pr tꜣ-kp

The Osiris, scribe of the god[9] Somtus, son of Iahmes, conceived by the lady of the house Takep.

The texts of the other coffins from the tomb, copied by G. Möller at the time of the discovery,[10] give these labels for their owners:

No. 1:[11] Text of the lid, col. 4:

wsir ibt sꜣt pꜣ-di-wsir ms nbt-pr iḥw

[6] As far as we can see on the picture taken by Rubensohn, all the coffins belong to adults; the mummy of Ibet was that of a woman aged about 35, according to Germer, Kischkewitz and Lüning 2009, 186.

[7] The location of this item is not known at present.

[8] Rostock, Archäologische Sammlung Schliemann Institut, Inv.-Nr. 148.I.11. See the Addendum.

[9] The title *sš-nṯr*, scribe of the god, is unusual. It could be a miswriting for *sš mḏꜣt nṯr*, scribe of the documents of the god, but this hypothesis is unlikely since the title is consistently written with this spelling on the coffin of Somtus, on his Ptah-Sokar-Osiris statuette and on the coffin of his son (see below, copy of text no. 5 after G. Möller). The title *sš-nṯr* could be compared to other titles combining the title of scribe with the name of a deity, such as *sš n ḥr-š.f*, scribe of Herishef, held by a Pasherienaset son of Ankhpakhered on an unpublished set of canopic jars dating to the Twenty-sixth Dynasty sold at Sotheby's New York, sale 6642–"Granita", the 14/12/1994, lot 7, or the titles *sš n ḥkꜣ*, scribe of Heka, and *sš sšꜣt*, scribe of Seshat, attested during the Old Kingdom (Jones 2000, II, 863, no. 3158, and 873, no. 3195).

[10] Unpublished notebook of G. Möller, p. 27–30.

[11] See Germer, Kischkewitz and Lüning 2009, 187, fig. 297–298.

Fig. 48: The coffin and mummy of Somtus (Cairo JE 36806) (© Egyptian Museum Cairo).

Osiris Ibet, daughter of Padiusir, born of the lady of the house Ihu.

Text of the box, col. 1:

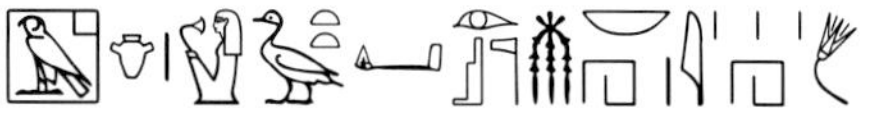

ḥwt-ḥr ỉbt sꜣt (pꜣ)-di-wsỉr ms nbt-pr ỉhw

Hathor[12] Ibet, daughter of (Pa)diusir born of the lady of the house Ihu.

No. 2:

wsỉr [ḥr?]-wḏꜣ sꜣ ḏd-ḥr ỉr(w n) nbt-pr ẖnmt

Osiris [Hor?]wedja son of Djedhor, conceived by the lady of the house Khnemet.

No. 4:

wsỉr n ẖnmt sꜣt n smꜣ-tꜣwy ỉr(w n) nbt-pr ỉ[b]t mꜣꜥ ḫrw

Osiris of Khnemet, daughter of Somtus, conceived by the lady of the house I[be]t, true of voice.

No. 5:

ḥr-wḏꜣ sꜣ sš-nṯr smꜣ-tꜣwy ỉr(w n) nbt-pr ỉbt

Horwedja, son of the scribe of the god Somtus, conceived by the lady of the house Ibet.

With these labels, it is possible to rebuild the genealogy of the family on four generations, some members of the three last generations having been interred with Somtus in his family tomb (**Fig. 47**).

Description and texts of Somtus's coffin

The coffin of Somtus[13] (**Fig. 48**) belongs to a small ensemble of coffins with a background painted pink, a colour not often used in funerary contexts before the Roman period.[14] The colours used in its decoration are two shades of blue, green, red and yellow.

The decorative programme of the lid is quite simple. The torso bears a very wide *wesekh* collar with floral motives. The belly area shows a double motif consisting of a winged scarab with a solar disc and a kneeling goddess with a solar disc spreading her wings over the body below. Both of them are set between images of the four Sons of Horus, mummiform and standing. On the legs, the central part is occupied by a text disposed in 3 columns. On each side, two goddesses are depicted in compartments displayed in two registers, each one being associated with a small column of text; the upper register shows two standing goddesses holding a papyrus sceptre and the lower one shows Isis and Nephthys standing, holding one hand before their face in lamentation. The plinth is decorated on the front with two recumbent jackals.

On the box, the dorsal pillar is covered with depictions displayed in two registers; the first one is occupied by an anthropomorphic *djed* pillar and the second one by a Nut-goddess standing, with a *nu* pot on her head. The side parts show on each shoulder a praying monkey facing to the exterior of the coffin. Below, four registers are divided into compartments, containing four standing deities looking in the same direction, each one associated

[12] The reference to a feminine deceased as a Hathor, and not as an Osiris, became more widely used after the 4th century BC, during the Ptolemaic period, even if it appears on a few examples before. See lastly Smith 2012, 193–196 and references cited in note 31 (p. 193). We can note that in Somtus's family tomb, the expression "Hathor NN" referring to a female deceased is used only once for Ibet, in the text of the box of her coffin; the other occurrences of her name, on the lid, are preceded by "Osiris NN", as on the coffin of the other woman buried in the tomb, Khnemet (no. 4). This could suggest that the use of "Hathor NN" was not generalised when Ibet's coffin was produced. The decoration of its box is very different from that of its lid; this could suggest that the two parts were decorated by two different painters, one using the phrase "Hathor NN" on the box and the other one preferring "Osiris NN" on the lid.

[13] H. 196.5 cm.

[14] The pink coloured background is found on at least two other Ptolemaic Period coffins from Abusir el-Meleq: the coffin of Usirnakht (Adelaide, South Australia Museum, A.40014; see Petrie 1891, pl. XXVIII, middle) and the coffin of Tadiusir (Leipzig, ÄMUL, 1496; **Fig. 53**, see Saczecki 2007, 24–29). Another, unpublished, example (Cairo GEM, 66096) belonging to an Imhotep son of Ptahemakhet comes from the neighbourhood of Beni Suef (probably from Abusir el-Meleq). The pink background is also found on some other examples coming from the nearby necropolis of Gamhud (unpublished coffin kept in the basement of the Egyptian Museum, Cairo, unknown no.; Cracow, MAK/AS/2441 (see Kóthay 2012, pl. 51, 4); Burgdorf, Museum für Völkerkunde, 7634, see Küffer 2007, 179, fig. 3; Budapest, Museum of Fine Arts 51.1989, see Győry 2006, 23, fig. 3; two others in Budapest, Museum of Fine Arts (illustrated by Nagy 1999, 115, fig. 95); Vienna, Kunsthistorisches Museum, ÄS 6689). A darker pink background is known on some coffins coming Saqqara. Another coffin bearing the name of Tawennefer and coming from Tuna el-Gebel (Mallawi Museum, no. 120; see Misihah and Hittah 1979, 12 and pl. X) also shows a pink background; it has some of the distinctive features of Ptolemaic period coffins from Middle Egypt such as the simple decorative programme combining the winged scarab and the kneeling goddess (for which see the conclusion of this article).

Axial text of the lid, in retrograde script

Text inscribed above the winged scarab

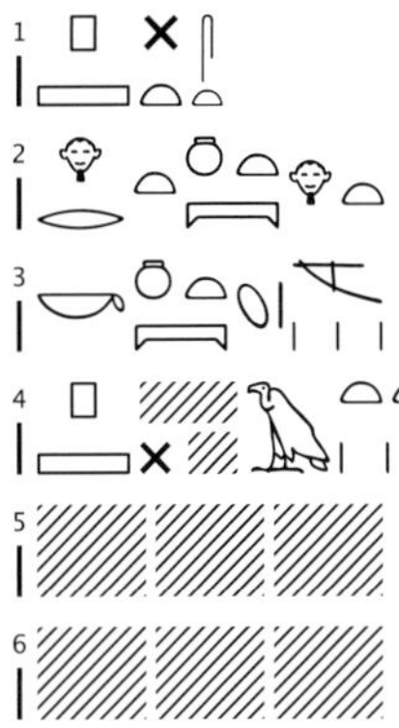

Text of the winged goddess

Left side 

Right side 

Texts above the winged goddess and relating to the Sons of Horus

Left side 

Right side 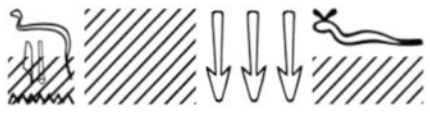

Texts relating to the deities on the right side of the legs, from top to bottom

Texts relating to the deities on the left side of the legs, from top to bottom

Fig. 49: Texts on the lid of the coffin.

with a small column of text. The first two registers show male deities whereas the two lower ones show goddesses.

The mummy is adorned with an ensemble of eleven cartonnage ornaments painted in blue, green, red and yellow. A funerary mask covers the head and the upper part of the torso. Its face is gilded, and the eyebrows, eyes, nostrils, mouth and beard are painted; the area below the wig lappets is decorated with a winged scarab pushing a solar disc. The torso and belly are covered by three cartonnage elements: a *wesekh* collar with falcon-headed clasps, an image of a winged scarab with a solar disc and a kneeling winged goddess holding two ostrich feathers and wearing a solar disc on her head. The area of the legs is decorated with a thin axial band inscribed with a column of text and six rectangles, in "playing card style", in openwork depicting the four Sons of Horus, mummiform and standing, and Isis and Nephthys, kneeling and mourning. The feet do not seem to have had any cartonnage overlay, neither a foot-case nor a sole.

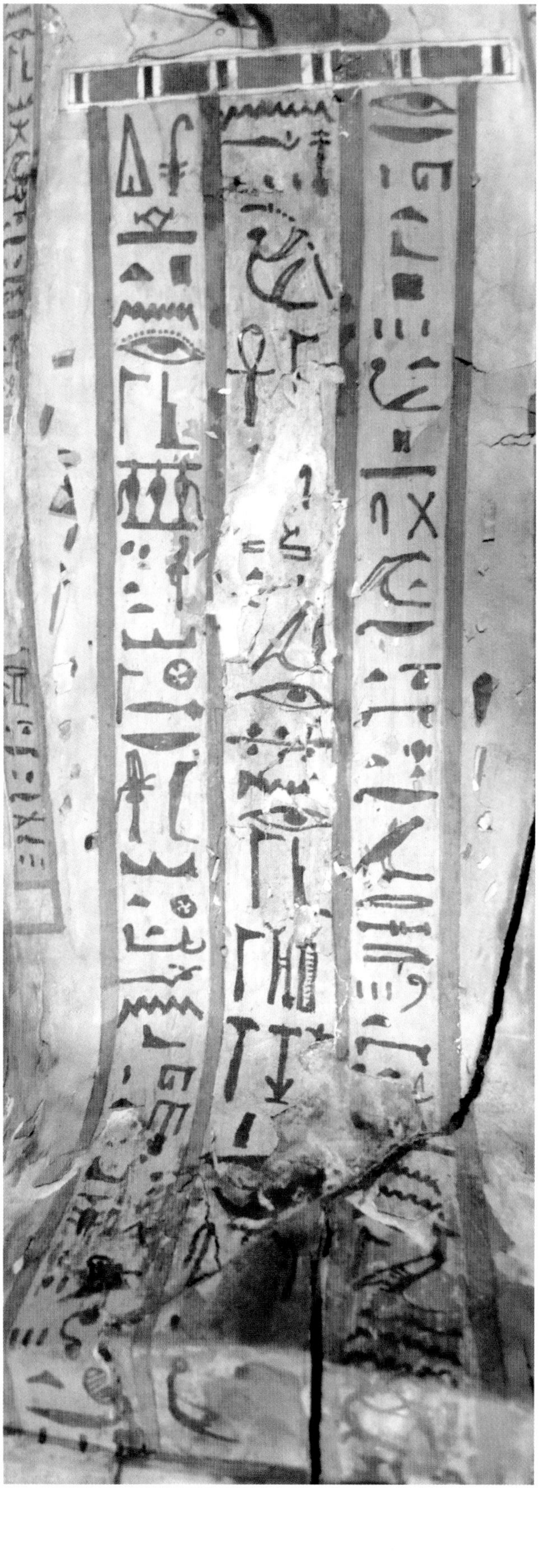

Fig. 50: Axial text of the lid, conservation work in process (© Egyptian Museum Cairo).

Fig. 51: Detail of the winged scarab and the winged goddess on Cairo JE 36806, during conservation (© Egyptian Museum Cairo).

Texts written on the lid (Fig. 49 and Fig. 50)

Axial text of the lid (Fig. 50), in retrograde script:[15]

(1) ḥtp dỉ nswt n wsỉr ḫnty ỉmntt nṯr ꜥꜣ nb ꜣbḏw dỉ·f (…?) prt-ḫrw t ḥnqt ỉḥw ꜣpdw ḫt nbt (2) nfrt wꜥbt ꜥnḫ nṯr ỉm ḥtp nṯr ỉm ỉr sꜣ n wsỉr sš-nṯr smꜣ-tꜣwy sꜣ ỉꜥḥ-ms (3) ỉr(w n) nbt-pr tꜣ-kp psš·t mwt·k nwt m r(n)·s m (št)-pt dỉ·t wnn·k m nṯr nn ḫfty

(1) A boon the king gives to Osiris who presides in the West, the great god lord of Abydos, may he give (…?)[16] an invocation offering consisting of bread, beer, meat and poultry, all (2) good and pure things a god lives on and a god is satisfied with; may he make the protection of the Osiris, scribe of the god Somtus son of Iahmes, (3) conceived by the lady of the house Takep. Your mother Nut spreads over you in her name of (Shet)-pet; she allows you exist as a god without enemy.

Text inscribed above the winged scarab, consisting of two versions of the Nut formula:

(1) psš·t (2) <ḫrt> (mwt·k) nwt ḥr·k (3) <nwt> ỉnk sꜣ·(k) mr·(k)
(4) psš·t mwt (5) […] *(6)* […]

(1) (Your mother) Nut spreads (2) over (3) you. I am (your) beloved son.
(4) [Your] mother [Nut] spreads (5) [over you …] (6) […].

Text of the winged goddess:

(1) ḏd mdw ỉn nwt wrt ms (nṯrw)
(2) ḏd mdw ỉn nwt wrt ms (nṯrw)

(1) Words spoken by Nut the great who gave birth (to the gods).
(2) Words spoken by Nut the great who gave birth (to the gods).

Texts above the winged goddess and relating to the Sons of Horus:

Right side:

ḏd mdw ỉn dwꜣ-mwt·f
Words spoken by Duamutef.[17]

Left side:
ḏd mdw ỉn [qbḥ]-snw·f
Words spoken by [Qebeh]senuef.

Texts relating to the deities on the right side of the legs, from top to bottom:

a) ḏd mdw ỉn wsỉr dwꜣ-mwt·f ỉnk sꜣ·k mr·k nwt ḫrt
b) [ḏd mdw ỉn …] nbt-ḥwt ỉnk sꜣ·k mr·k

a) Words spoken by Osiris Duamutef:[18] I am your beloved son, Nut the far-off.
b) [Words spoken by …] Nephthys: I am your beloved son.

Texts relating to the deities on the left side of the legs, from top to bottom:

a) ḏd mdw ỉn wsỉr ꜣst nbt-ḥwt nwt ỉnk sꜣ·k mr·k
b) ḏd mdw ỉn nbt-ḥwt ỉnk sꜣ·k mr·k wnn·k

a) Words spoken by Osiris, Isis, Nephthys and Nut: I am your beloved son.
b) Words spoken by Nephthys: I am your beloved son whom you created.

Texts written on the box (Fig. 48 and Fig. 52a)

The texts accompanying the deities depicted on the right and left sides of the box are borrowed from chapter 42 of the Book of the Dead.

Texts on the right side, from top to bottom:

a) ḏd mdw ỉn rꜥ ḥr ỉnk ỉwf·k wsỉr smꜣ-tꜣwy sꜣ ỉꜥḥ-ms
b) ỉw <n> rdwy wsỉr smꜣ-tꜣwy sꜣ ỉꜥḥ-ms
c) ỉw ẖt·k nwt ỉnk sꜣ·k mr·k wnn·k m mꜣꜥ ḫrw
d) ỉw ỉbḥw·(k) ḥwt-ḥr ỉnk sꜣ·k mr·k wnn·(k) wsỉr smꜣ-tꜣwy

a) Words spoken by Ra Horus: I am your flesh, Osiris Somtus son of Iahmes.[19]
b) The legs of Osiris Somtus son of Iahmes.[20]
c) Your stomach is Nut. I am your beloved son whom you created as true of voice.

[15] The use of retrograde script is not common for this kind of text (offering formula and Nut text) on coffins and does not correspond to the regular uses of retrograde script as listed by Fischer 1977. It is attested on several other coffins coming from Abusir el-Meleq or attributed to this site: the coffin of Tadiusir (Leipzig ÄMUL, 1496; **Fig. 53**), the coffin of Usirnakht (Adelaide, South Australian Museum, A.40014; Petrie 1891, pl. XXVIII) and the coffin of Djedhor (private collection; **Fig. 54**). The retrograde writing of axial texts consisting of offering formulae could be a distinctive feature of a workshop associated with the necropolis of Abusir el-Meleq.

[16] At this point, the copy of G. Möller indicates a lacuna. One could suggest to read *nk(t) (n)* "a little bit of" (Wb II, 347, 10–11), but this reading does not take account of 𓉐 and of the stroke.

[17] Curiously, the name of Duamutef is written using 𓈋 at the beginning, maybe with the value *ḏw* > *d* to assure the reading of 𓇼 (N14) as *dwꜣ*. This writing occurs two other times on the same ensemble. It also occurs on the right side of the coffin Leipzig ÄMUL, 1496 (**Fig. 53**) and on the right side of the coffin of Djedhor (**Fig. 54**).

[18] See previous footnote.

[19] In chapter 42 of the Book of the Dead, the flesh is usually linked to the lords of Kheraha (*nbw ḫr-ꜥḥꜣ*). See e.g. Quirke 2013, 119.

[20] In chapter 42 of the Book of the Dead, the legs are usually linked to Ptah. See e.g. Quirke 2013, 119.

d) (Your) teeth are Hathor.[21] I am your beloved son whom (you) created, Osiris Somtus.

Texts on the left side, from top to bottom:

a) [...]
b) iw ḏrwyt n wsir [smꜣ]-tꜣwy sꜣ iꜥḥ-ms
c) iw ibḥw m srqt ink sꜣ·k mr·k wnn·k m mꜣꜥ (ḫrw)
d) iw ꜥnḫwy [n wsir] smꜣ-tꜣwy sꜣ [iꜥḥ]-ms ink [sꜣ·k] mr·k
a) [...]
b) The hands of Osiris [Som]tus son of Iahmes.
c) The teeth are those of Serqet. I am your beloved son whom you created as true (of voice).
d) The ears [of Osiris] Somtus son of [Iah]mes. I am [your] beloved [son].

The text accompanying the goddess Nut depicted at the bottom of the central part is a version of the Nut formula:

(1) ... psšt mwt·k ḥr·k m rn·s m (št)-pt ḫt wrt [...] (2) nn ḫftyw·k m rn·<s> m nṯr ḫnm [...] twt wr [...] šp [...]
(1) ...[22]. Your mother Nut spreads over you in her name of (Shet)-pet [...] (2) your enemies do not exist in <her> (your) name of god, enclose [...] you are the eldest [...].[23]

Texts on the cartonnage pieces (the parts covered by mummy bandages are indicated between brackets) (Fig. 52b)

Above the winged scarab:

(1) ḏd mdw in rꜥ nb (2) [ ] nṯr ꜥꜣ nb
(1) Words spoken by Ra lord (2) [ ] the great god lord (sic).

Above the winged goddess:

(1) ḏd mdw in nwt (2) wrt ms nṯrw
(1) Words spoken by Nut (2) the great who gave birth to the gods.

The axial piece bears a version of the hymn to the Western (or Libyan) goddess known from many other examples, more or less developed and corrupted, on cartonnage pieces.[24] This version is very corrupted, but some parts, when compared with other versions, are still intelligible:

[inḏ ḥr·t] wrt <ḥrt> wrt n pt (irt) rꜥ ḫsf nšny ... [ ] ... ṯḥn iwn <m> ꜥšꜣ ḫkrw m [ ] ir sꜣ n wsir smꜣ-tꜣwy sꜣ iꜥḥ-ms
[Hail to you] the great, the great in the sky,[25] the (eye) of Ra, who repels fury,[26] ...[27] [ ] ... the one with brilliant colours,[28] lavishly ornamented[29] in [ ],[30] who provides protection to Osiris Somtus son of Iahmes.

Cartonnage pieces located on the right side, from top to bottom:

ḏd mdw in wsir [ ]
Words spoken by Osiris [Imsety].

ḏd mdw in wsir [ ]
Words spoken by Osiris [Duamutef].[31]

ḏd mdw in ꜣst [ ]
Words spoken by Isis [ ].

Cartonnage pieces located on the left side, from top to bottom:

ḏd mdw in ḥp ink sꜣ[·k]

[21] In chapter 42 of the Book of the Dead, Hathor is usually linked to the eyes, the teeth being linked to Serqet (as here on the left side of the box). See e.g. Quirke 2013, 119.

[22] This passage seems corrupted, but its original meaning may be: "Her arms are raised up to receive you". Compare this version to the text related to the goddess of the West on the sarcophagus of Horemheb son of Tjeru (Cairo, Egyptian Museum, JE 8390): "The Western goddess places her arms to receive you and she makes your place within herself" (*di imntt ꜥwy·s r ššp·k ir·s st·k m-ẖnw·s*). See Leitz 2011, 447, l. 5 and, for another example Rusch 1922, 55–56. Somtus's reading shows a confusion between the signs [illegible] and [illegible], the first one being written instead of the last one.

[23] For another, more developed and less corrupted, version of this text from chapter 178 of the Book of the Dead on a coffin from Abusir el-Meleq, see Petrie 1891, pl. XXVIII (coffin of Usirnakht, Adelaide, South Australian Museum, A.40014).

[24] The more complete and best-preserved versions of this hymn date to the Twenty-sixth Dynasty (e.g. the cartonnage of Tjaennahebu, Bresciani *et al.* 1977, pl. XXXI). Many other later versions are known on cartonnage leg pieces, including a variable number of epithets, sometimes so corrupted that they are not easily understandable unless they are compared with other versions. For other later versions, see e.g. Mysliwiec 2008, pl. CCXLVIII, c; Meffre 2012b, 162–163; Ziegler 2012, II, pl. 26, 111–113; pl. 144, 619; Schreiber 2012, 261 and pl. 56 (coming from Gamhud and close to Somtus's example).

[25] Leitz 2002, II, 486, b.

[26] Leitz 2002, V, 956, c.

[27] This is a corrupted section; other versions place the epithet *ḥnwt n ḏw-mꜣnw ṯmḥt n ḫꜣst imntt*, "the mistress of Dju-manu, the Libyan of the Western desert" (see e.g. the cartonnage of Tjaennahebu (Bresciani *et al.* 1977, pl. XXXI)).

[28] Leitz 2002, VII, 479, c.

[29] Leitz 2002, II, 221, b.

[30] The reading of the cartonnage piece found in Gamhud is quite close in this part, but allows a different translation (Schreiber 2012, 261 and pl. 56).

[31] This is the third time on this coffin that Duamutef is written with the desert-sign at the beginning of his name. See *supra* n. 17.

Words spoken by Hapy: I am [your] son [ ].

ḏd mdw in wsir qbḥ-snw·f [ ]
Words spoken by Osiris Qebehsenuef [ ].

ḏd mdw in sꜣ·k mr·k sꜣ·k [ ]
Words spoken by your beloved son, your son [ ].

A group of coffins from the necropolis of Abusir el-Meleq

Somtus's coffin is representative of a group of coffins found in the necropolis of Abusir el-Meleq. It shares with them a few features that are distinctive of coffins from Middle Egypt, such as the simple decorative programme of its lid, combining a winged scarab and a kneeling goddess on the torso (**Fig. 51**) with an axial text in columns and the depiction of several deities on the sides. Several other characteristics found on Somtus's coffin, and on coffins belonging to the same group, are distinctive of local workshops and are good clues to link several other coffins of unknown provenance to the necropolis of Abusir el-Meleq.

Coffins discovered in Abusir el-Meleq

The coffin of Tadiusir (Leipzig, ÄMUL, 1496)

The coffin of Tadiusir (**Fig. 53**)[32] is more crudely made than Somtus's coffin, as is particularly clear on the angular shoulders, on the feet and on their junction to the plinth, but their decoration shows many similarities. Like Somtus's coffin, the coffin of Tadiusir is decorated on a pink background, the axial text being written in columns with an alternating yellow and blue background. Tadiusir's coffin has the same decorative layout as Somtus's coffin but includes, between the winged goddess and the axial text, a depiction of the mummy on a funerary bed with four canopic jars; on both sides, there are five registers of deities depicted, accompanied by a label in one column, just as on Somtus's coffin. On the front of the plinth, two jackals are shown lying on chests painted in the same colours as on Somtus's coffin. The decorative programme of the boxes of these two coffins is also very closely comparable. Under the wig on Tadiusir's box, we find in three registers the depictions of a falcon spreading its wings, an anthropomorphic *djed* pillar and a standing figure of the goddess Nut with a *nu* pot on her head; on both sides, deities are depicted in five registers, accompanied by texts borrowed from chapter 42 of the Book of the Dead.

The similarities between Tadiusir's and Somtus's coffins are not limited to the general decorative programme but are also found in the decorative motifs and in the way the texts are written. The decorative bands, made of coloured rectangles, on which the winged goddesses are kneeling on the lid, and also used to separate the registers on the central part of the back, are very similar on both coffins. The beads of the *wesekh* collars on both coffins are depicted in the same way and using the same colours, but they are arranged in a different order. The winged scarabs and the winged goddesses are also very similar on the two coffins: they show the same motif in the wings (being in three parts for the scarabs and four parts for the goddesses) and the goddesses are depicted with the same shawls over their arms; furthermore, the elbows, wrists and ankles are rendered in the same way. Even the texts and the shape of the hieroglyphs are very similar on both coffins: both axial texts use retrograde script, the texts of the Nut formulae are very close parallels, as if they were taken from the same model, both coffins show the same misspelling of the name of Duamutef (beginning with) and the way of drawing specific signs (**Table 1**), such as the introductory formula *ḏd-mdw in*, , , or , is very similar on both coffins. All these similarities suggest that these two coffins were decorated in the same workshop at almost the same time.

Another coffin discovered by Rubensohn in 1903

The decorative programme of Somtus's coffin is also comparable with that on another female coffin found during Rubensohn's excavations in 1903.[33] Here again, we can recognise the simple decorative programme showing a winged scarab and a kneeling goddess below the *wesekh* collar, this being completed by a scene just above the axial main text. Unfortunately, the location of this coffin is not known at present, and no further similarities can be seen from the picture.

The coffin of Usirnakht (Adelaide, South Australian Museum, A.40014)

The coffin of Usirnakht,[34] which according to Petrie comes from Abusir el-Meleq, shows also some similarities

[32] Saczecki 2007, 24–29; see also, but dealing more specifically with the mummy found in the coffin (Leipzig, ÄMUL, 1497), Germer *et al.* 1995, 139–141.

[33] Rubensohn and Knatz 1904, 15, fig. 12.

[34] Petrie 1891, pl. XXVIII, middle.

a. Texts on the right side, from top to bottom

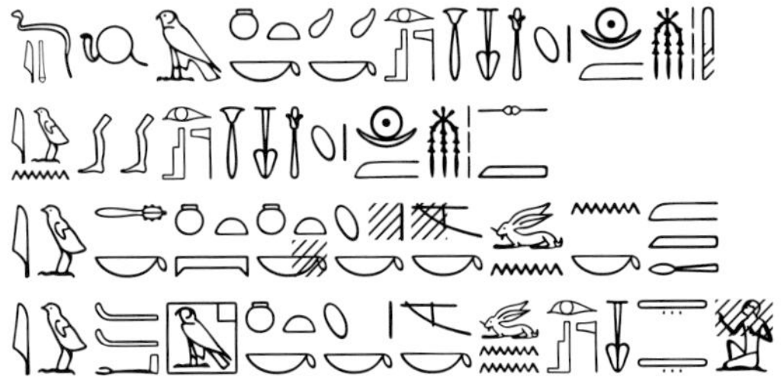

Texts on the left side, from top to bottom

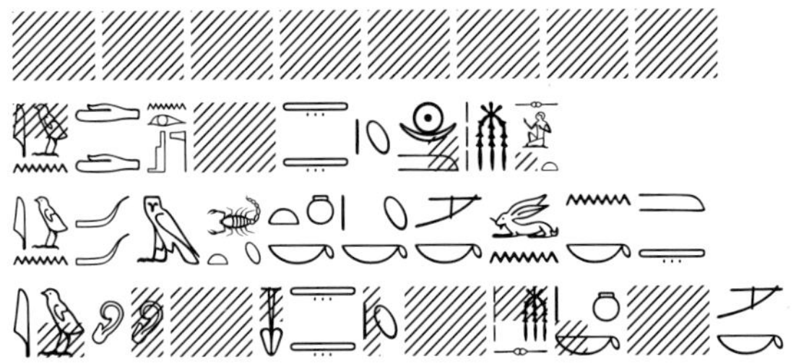

Text accompanying the goddess Nut depicted at the bottom of the central part

b. Above the winged scarab

Above the winged goddess

Cartonnage, axial text

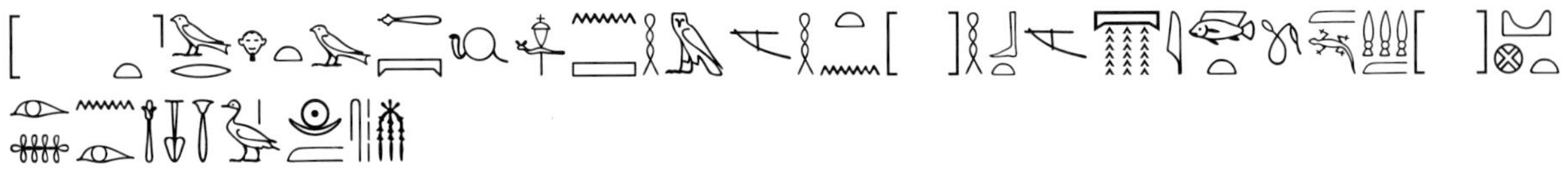

Cartonnage pieces located on the right side, from top to bottom

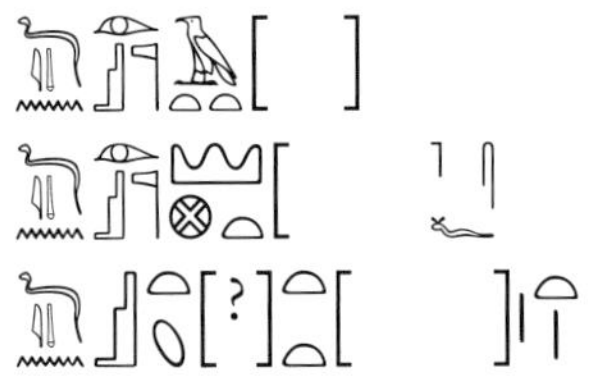

Cartonnage pieces located on the left side, from top to bottom

Fig. 52: Texts on the box (a) and on the cartonnage pieces (b).

with that of Somtus, even though the decoration of its upper part is totally destroyed and the remaining decoration seems of higher quality: they are decorated on the same pink background and decorative bands made of coloured rectangles are used to separate the kneeling goddess from the axial text and as ground lines under the depictions of deities.

Coffins of unknown provenance, but coming most probably from Abusir el-Meleq

Coffin of Djedhor (private collection)

A coffin belonging to a man named Djedhor (**Fig. 54**)[35] is very close to Somtus's coffin. In addition to their general shape, which is very similar, their decorative programmes are the same, including both the winged scarab and the kneeling goddess, a three-column axial text and deities depicted on each side. Looking at details, they also show great similarities: the beads painted on the collars are of the same design, but arranged in a different order; the drawings of the scarab and of the goddess are very similar, even in small details, such as the eyes of the scarab or the design of the feathers of the wings. The texts are arranged in the same way: they are written in retrograde script, using the same offering, protection and Nut formulae, with the same distinctive writing of her name of Shet-pet and of Duamutef, suggesting that the same model was used for both coffins. Moreover, their hieroglyphic signs are drawn in a similar way (**Table 1**), this being particularly clear in the phrase *ḏd-mdw in*, the signs 𓊵, 𓃀, 𓏠, 𓄿 and 𓁐. There are also great similarities on the boxes of both coffins. The same decorative programme with, on the dorsal pillar, an Osirian symbol above the text of a Nut formula (much destroyed but recognisable thanks to a few signs) and on both sides rows of divinities facing to the exterior. Moreover, the decorative features, such as the lines of coloured rectangles under the wig and under the *djed* pillar, are also very similar and small details such as the shawl on the goddesses' arms are depicted on the two coffins. All of these similarities support the proposition that the coffin of Djedhor was decorated in the same workshop which produced the coffins of Somtus and of Tadiusir (Leipzig, ÄMUL 1496) and that Djedhor was also buried in the necropolis of Abusir el-Meleq.

Coffin of Imhotep (Cairo, GEM 66096)[36]

A second coffin, made for a child named Imhotep son of Ptahemakhet, shares with Somtus's coffin both the pink background and the simple decorative programme: below the *wesekh* collar, its decoration consists of a winged scarab surmounting a kneeling winged goddess, both of them with a solar disc over their heads, and a three-column axial text consisting of an offering formula (this time not written in a retrograde script); on both sides are depictions of the four Sons of Horus, mummiform and standing, and Isis and Nephthys, standing and mourning. On the plinth, there are two facing jackals, recumbent on a large chest. The drawing of some hieroglyphic signs, such as 𓊵 or 𓃀, is very similar on both coffins and the same colours are used for the background of the axial texts and the jackals' chests. The general shape of these two coffins is quite different, Imhotep's having a rather long neck, but this may be due to the fact that it is the coffin of a child, only 120 cm in height. The close similarity of the decoration of the coffins of Somtus and Imhotep suggests that the latter could come from Abusir el-Meleq necropolis, from the workshop which produced Somtus's coffin.

Coffin of Djedhor (private collection)

Another coffin, belonging to another Djedhor, son of Nakhtkhonsu,[37] shows affinities with Somtus's coffin, even if it is of higher quality and has a more elaborate decorative programme. Nevertheless, it has the same general characteristics: a winged scarab and a kneeling goddess on the torso, surmounting a text in five columns and, on each side, five registers depicting deities converging toward the axial text. Some differences are noticeable in the general organisation of the decoration: several more deities are represented and on each side of the axial text, the legs and feet of the deceased are depicted. The arrangement of the back is somewhat different from the coffin of Somtus, since a text in five columns occupies the central part; however, the decoration of the side parts is very similar: the depictions of several deities, most of them facing to the left, are arranged in seven registers. Thanks to its texts which mention Osiris Naref, Nâret-khentet and Northern Abydos, it is clear that this coffin comes from the Herakleopolis region. Its affinities with coffins found in Abusir el-Meleq suggest that it also comes from this necropolis.

[35] The coffin was most recently sold by Paris, Drouot Richelieu, PBA, on 01/12/2007, lot 452.

[36] This coffin was kept for a long time in Beni Suef Museum.

[37] See Dils 1991, 253, no. 337.

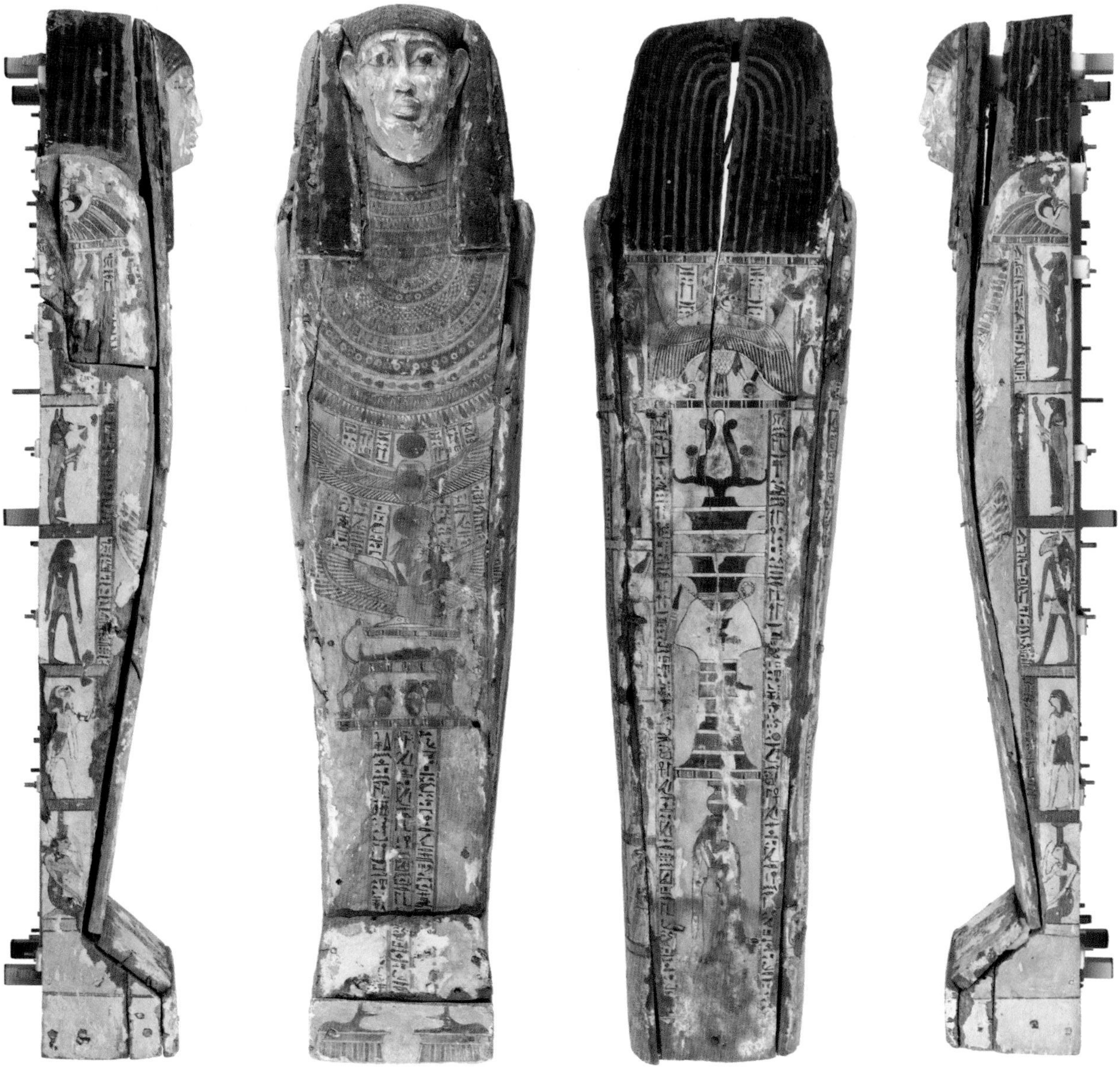

Fig. 53: Coffin of Tadiusir Leipzig, ÄMUL 1496 (© Ägyptisches Museum Universität Leipzig).

Coffin of Meretites (Kansas City, Nelson Atkins Museum, 2007.12.2.A-B)

The combination of winged scarab and kneeling goddess exists also on coffins with a much more elaborated decorative programme, such as that of Meretites. Her father's title, *sameref* priest, suggests the family was established in Herakleopolis and that her funerary ensemble comes from Abusir el-Meleq.

Conclusion: Regional and local features

In conclusion, these coffins show several distinctive features, which, when combined together, distinguish them as a coherent ensemble coming from the same area (the necropolis of Abusir el-Meleq) and dating to almost the same period.

Some of their characteristics are recognisable on coffins from various sites in Middle Egypt and seem to be distinctive features related to the production of this area. The first of these Middle Egypt features is the use of a simple decorative programme on the lids, including, on the face, a winged scarab and kneeling goddess above an axial text and rows of divinities on both sides. On the boxes, beneath the traditional Osirian symbol, the depictions of the standing goddess Nut and of the deities associated with chapter 42 of the

Fig. 54: Coffin of Djedhor (© Pierre Bergé Auctions).

Book of the Dead are particularly favoured. This quite simple decorative programme is not specific to Abusir el-Meleq, but to the area of Middle Egypt: it is for example attested in the nearby necropolis of Gamhud, but with some differences, principally in the choice of decorative elements. For example, the Gamhud coffins regularly place depictions of the kneeling goddess and the mummy on a funerary bed[38] on the torso, the winged scarab being scarcely represented.[39] Moreover, the general shape of the coffins coming from Gamhud is very different from those from Abusir el-Meleq. The pink background, which is quite rare in a funerary context before the Roman period, is also a distinctive feature of the coffins coming from Middle Egypt.[40] The repeated use of decorative bands made of coloured rectangles as ground lines and the depiction of the legs and feet of the deceased along the axial text seem also to be particularly well attested in Middle Egypt.[41]

The group of coffins listed here also have features that are distinctive of material from Abusir el-Meleq. Among these, we can cite the retrograde script used for the offering and Nut formulae of the axial texts, the misspelt name of Duamutef including the desert-sign N25 at the beginning, the distinctive writing of some funerary texts (specially some parts of the Nut formula) and the special way several hieroglyphic signs or groups of signs are drawn (**Table 1**). The presence of a shawl on the shoulders of the goddesses may also be a peculiarity of the material produced in Abusir el-Meleq.

The great similarities in the decoration and writings of the coffins of Somtus, Tadiusir and Djedhor suggest that these three items were made in the same workshop, which also produced Somtus's Ptah-Sokar-Osiris statuette (see the Addendum). The coffins of Djedhor son of Nakhtkhonsu and of Meretites have the same decorative programme but their decoration and texts are of much higher quality, an indication that the choice of a simple decorative programme is a regional tradition rather than an economic question.

The main problem concerning the group of coffins discussed here remains their date within the Ptolemaic period. The general shape, the big face with thick lips and the depictions of the goddesses wearing shawls with fringes on Somtus's, Tadiusir's and Djedhor's coffins suggest the mid-Ptolemaic period, i.e. between the 3rd and 2nd centuries BC. This is in accordance with the fact that Somtus's spouse Ibet is sometimes referred to as a Hathor, instead of an Osiris, on her coffin (Berlin, ÄM 17104), as is the box of Tadiusir on her coffin (Leipzig, ÄMUL, 1496), this designation becoming widely used after the 4th century BC.[42]

Addendum

Another piece has been located from Somtus's funerary ensemble: the Ptah-Sokar-Osiris statuette Rostock, Archäologische Sammlung Schliemann Institut, Inv.-Nr. 148.I.11 (**Fig. 55**).

From the two funerary items buried with Somtus, only the location of the Ptah-Sokar-Osiris statuette is known at present, being kept in Rostock. It is not certain whether the statuette and the base belong together because their style and proportions differ; they may have been assembled afterwards.

The base bears in col. 2–3 a genealogy identical to the ones found on the coffin of Somtus, but without his title:

wsỉr smꜣ-tꜣwy sꜣ ỉʿḥ-ms ỉr(w n) nbt-pr tꜣ-kp
Osiris Somtus, son of Iahmes, conceived by the lady of the house Takep.

Many similarities can be found between the texts on the base of the Ptah-Sokar-Osiris statue, those on Somtus's coffin and those on the mummy cartonnage (**Table 1**): the hieroglyphic signs (V16), (O1),

[38] See e.g. the coffin of Tasenet (Cairo, Egyptian Museum, Serial no. 275) (Schreiber 2012, pl. 53, 1); the anonymous coffin Burgdorf, Museum für Völkerkunde, 7634 (Küffer 2007, 179, fig. 3); the anonymous coffin Budapest, Museum of Fine Arts, 51.1998/1–2 (Kóthay and Liptay 2010, 128–129, no. 60); the coffin Milwaukee, Art Museum Wisconsin, M1967.20, coming in all likelihood from Gamhud (see the article of J. P. Elias in this volume).

[39] See Budapest 51.2011 (Kóthay 2012, pl. 49, 3); Vienna, Kunsthistorisches Museum, ÄS 6688 (Haslauer 2013, 136, fig. 4).

[40] See *supra* n. 14.

[41] See for example the coffin from Tuna el-Gebel kept in the museum of Mallawi cited *supra* n. 14 and the coffin lid sold by Christie's London, 11/07/1973, sale Kapkap, lot 133. This last piece joins the depiction of the winged scarab and kneeling goddess to a scene showing the mummy on its funerary bed flanked by Isis and Nephthys as mourners; on the lower part, the legs and feet of the deceased are depicted along the central axis, between the columns of text (such an arrangement is also attested e.g. on the coffin Vienna, Kunsthistorisches Museum, ÄS 6688 from Gamhud (see Haslauer 2013, 136, fig. 4)).

[42] See *supra* n. 12.

(N29) and the determinative (A1) are formed in a very similar manner on the three monuments. Moreover, the writing of the name of Somtus's father, Iahmes, is very particular and is similar on the three items: after the lunar sign, there is an unnecessary and the group *ms* is written with the three plural strokes between and the phonetic complement . These similarities seem to indicate the three objects were made, or at least inscribed, in the same workshop, perhaps by a single hand.

Fig. 55: Ptah-Sokar-Osiris statuette Rostock, Archäologische Sammlung Schliemann Institut Inv.-Nr. 148.I.11 (© Schliemann Institut, Rostock).

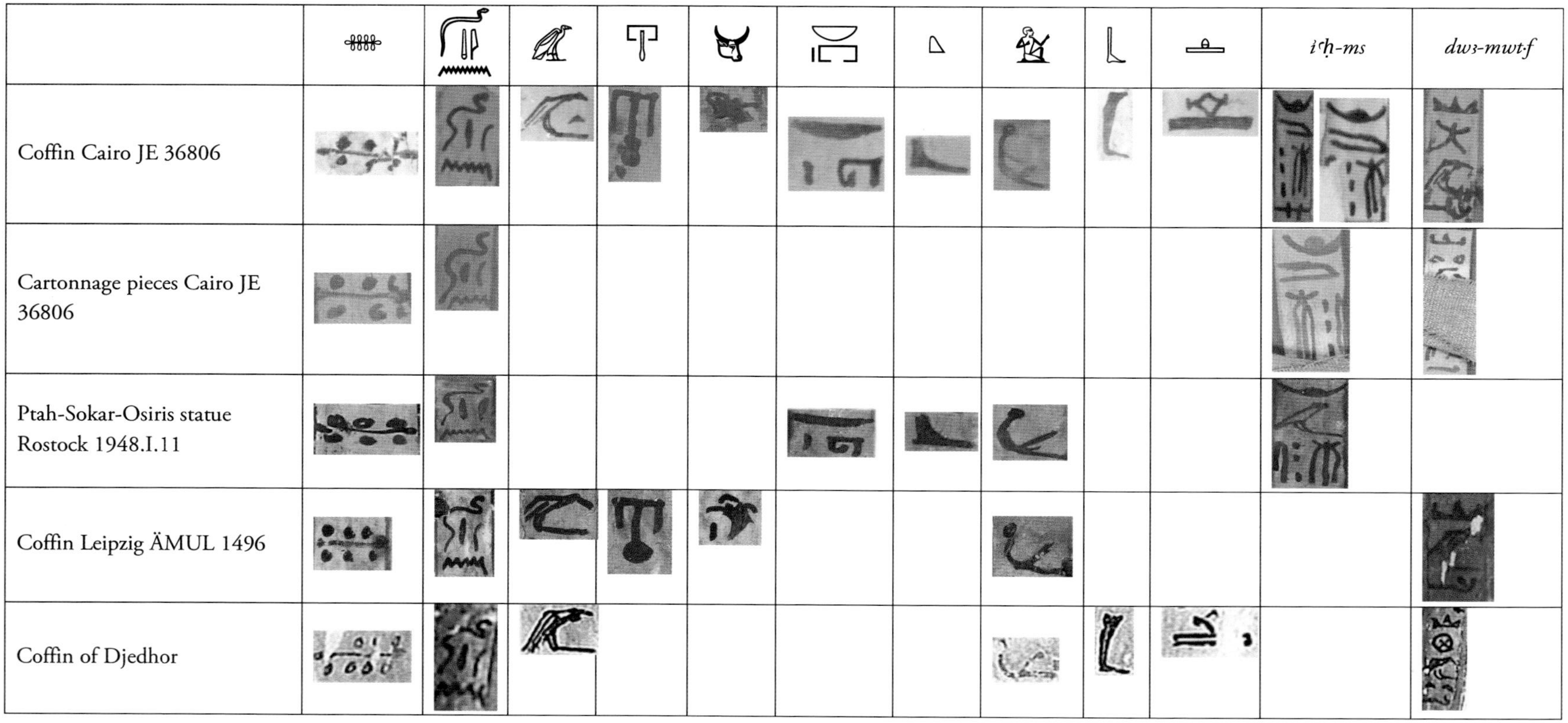

Table 1. Comparison of the hieroglyphs inscribed on Somtus's coffin, cartonnage pieces and Ptah-Sokar-Osiris figure with those inscribed on the coffin of Tadiusir (Leipzig ÄMUL 1496) and of Djedhor (private collection).

Nesimenjem and the Valley of the Queens' Coffins

P. Buscaglia, M. Cardinali, T. Cavaleri, P. Croveri, G. Ferraris di Celle, A. Piccirillo and F. Zenucchini

During the recent redevelopment of the Museo Egizio, the Centro Conservazione e Restauro (CCR) "La Venaria Reale" studied and stabilised a group of polychrome wooden coffins of different typologies. Here we present some findings from the Valley of the Queens' coffins, chronologically later than yellow coffins. Common technical features were identified in several examples through observation and scientific analyses. We identified different approaches to the selection and use of wooden materials, with evidence of irregular and diffuse assemblies, and volumes obtained by connecting numerous elements of small size and irregular shape. We also noted the use of mixtures of plant fibres and glue to fill cracks and to conceal irregularities on the wooden supports; also the frequent use of mixtures made of clay and coarse-grained sand was observed.

While cleaning the lid of the coffin of Nesimenjem, a combination of scientific analyses and laser technology allowed the authors to identify the presence of a protective resin-based layer on the whole surface. This study highlighted similarities with other coffins of unknown origin, in materials and iconographic and technical aspects, such as the use of Egyptian blue for hieroglyphs and of a yellow orpiment-based pigment for the background of decoration.

Introduction

During the recent refurbishment of displays in the Museo Egizio di Torino, the Centro Conservazione e Restauro (CCR) La Venaria Reale had the opportunity to study and conserve several wooden polychrome coffins. These objects were attributed, on the basis of iconographic features and technique of execution, to two different typologies: five coffins and four mummy covers to the yellow coffin type, belonging to the Twenty-first and Twenty-second Dynasties, and thirteen coffins, chronologically more recent (late Third Intermediate Period and Late Period), coming from the Valley of the Queens excavations. See Appendix for full list of coffins.

The study was divided into several phases, in order to define conservation priorities for the individual finds. Specific projects were drawn up on the basis of assessments made during technical profiling and from the results of image analysis processing, both of which were conducted initially to assist in the determination of conservation materials and methods.

The research activities were carried out within an international project promoted and coordinated by the Vatican Museums (Vatican Coffin Project). That project focuses on the scientific and technological study and the conservation of polychrome coffins, in particular yellow coffins dating from the Twenty-first Dynasty (1076–944 BC) to the beginning of the Twenty-second Dynasty (*c.* 943–870 BC).[1] The diagnostics campaign

[1] Project partnership: Musei Vaticani, Le Louvre, Centre de recherche et de restauracion des musées de France, Rijksmuseum van Oudheden, Museo Egizio di Torino and Centro Conservazione

and analyses were carried out according to the protocol defined by the research group of the Vatican Coffin Project (Amenta 2013). This prioritises a non-invasive approach, leaving the invasive techniques exclusively for the study of very complex cases.

Different imaging techniques have been applied and each has revealed important details that increase understanding of the coffins (see also Cavaleri *et. al.*, this volume). In particular:

X-radiography and computed tomography carried out at CCR highlighted the assembly techniques, revealing probable reuse of some wooden parts.[2]

Infrared reflectography identified under-drawing. It also helped discriminate between carbon black-based sketches (hypothesised due to the strong absorption in infrared, wavelength at 950 nm) and ochre or earth pigment-based sketches (transparent in infrared reflectography).

VIL (visible-light induced luminescence) photography clarified the presence of Egyptian blue, even in very damaged areas, thus contributing to reconstruction of the original decorative scheme. For example, this technique highlighted Egyptian blue on hieroglyphs that today appear to be black due to degradation processes or the presence of dust (Daniels *et al.* 2004).

UV fluorescence allowed observation and location on the surfaces of inorganic and organic substance layers attributed to past conservation interventions.

Reflectance transformation imaging (RTI) provided detailed information on the preservation state of the objects (i.e. depth of cracks and lacunae) and notable features of original production techniques.[3]

Finally, non-invasive point analyses and invasive analysis (on samples) were carried out:

X-ray fluorescence (XRF) and Vis-NIR (visible-near infrared) fibre optic reflectance spectroscopy (FORS), coupled with IR false colour reflectography permitted reconstruction of the colour palette.

On micro samples, embedded and prepared as cross sections, scanning electron microscopy coupled with energy-dispersive X-ray spectroscopy (SEM-EDX) and micro-Fourier transform infrared spectroscopy (FTIR) analyses clarified layering sequences and degradation phenomena.

Organic components have been studied by FTIR microscopy and gas chromatography–mass spectrometry (GC-MS).

Through direct and microscopic observation, scientific analysis and evidence emerging during conservation, it was possible to identify both common features and technical differences in technique of execution between the two typologies of coffin. By the end of the study, it was possible to trace an evolution in the manufacture of coffins that seemed to show a loss of quality in both carpentry and decoration in Late Period coffins.

Valley of the Queens' coffins: Technical features and conservation treatments

Through the diagnostic protocol, an overview has been gained of the composition of original materials, together with the distribution and location of interventions. In addition, increased knowledge has been acquired about carpentry and possible reuse, both of wooden elements and entire coffins. This overview provided a basis for defining objectives for the conservation work. Moreover, scientific analyses allowed continuous monitoring to check that treatments were not interfering with the original material.

The group of coffins from the Valley of the Queens is well known from photography made during Schiaparelli's archaeological excavations, on the tomb of Setherkhepeshef (QV43) and the tomb of Khaemuaset (QV44,) (Schiaparelli 1924, 187–188 and 192).[4] However, the exact composition of the corpus is not yet known; a complete list of all the finds discovered does not exist (Guzzon 2017, 193). The finds are generally dated between the end of the Third Intermediate Period and the beginning of the Late Period, with recent studies suggesting dates from 720 to 600 BC (Twenty-fifth and Twenty-sixth Dynasties) (Aston 2009, 258–260).

Overall, quite consistent technical features have been observed in these coffins, even though stylistic differences have been noted.

As is common, the structures are made from wooden

e Restauro 'La Venaria Reale'. Coordinator Dr. Alessia Amenta. See Amenta 2014.

[2] The equipment, available at CCR, and set up within the neuART project in collaboration with INFN Torino section and the Physics Department of the University of Torino, enables X-radiography and tomography (CT, computerised axial tomography) on works of art of large dimensions (up to 2.5 x 3.0 m long).

[3] RTI is a computational photography technique that uses a specific photographic set-up with the object lit from different angles. The lighting information is then synthesised to generate a series of raking visualisations of the surface micromorphology of the artefact. These tools and methods were published in a landmark paper (Malzbender *et al.* 2001). See also Earl *et al.* 2011.

[4] For a detailed description of Schiaparelli's excavation activity see also D'amicone 2008 and Moiso 2008, 199–270.

elements connected by dowels and tenons. But, compared with the yellow coffin group analysed in parallel, the wooden elements here are less regular in thickness and morphology and the construction of the assemblages is less accurate.

The ground layers generally consist of two different bands: the first, directly in contact with the wooden surface, has a greater thickness and a high granularity. It is a brownish-yellow or pink colour and was used to help define the anatomical features and to decrease the roughness of the wooden support. Where it has been used to cover joints it is mixed with vegetable fibres. The second ground layer (white, thinner and calcium carbonate based) was used to level the surfaces and to receive the painting.

In most of the objects, large areas of *incamottatura*[5] have been detected to a much greater extent than on the yellow coffin type. In some cases, such as the Mentuirdis inner coffin (S. 5219), this layer was present over the entire surface of the lid and of the box, including across the lid-box junction, which means that the application of the textile was carried out after the final closure of the coffin, with the body already inside. Presumably, the *incamottatura* was cut when the coffin was opened after excavation. The current level of study of this specific aspect allows us only to speculate on the fact that all the subsequent decoration was therefore realised after the body was placed inside the coffin.[6]

The decorative layers of these coffins have common characteristics: the absence of a red sketch and embossed decoration, a flat chromatic ground, imprecise pictorial layouts and generally, in macroscopic observation, an absence of a natural resin layer on the surface (although, during conservation, some traces of a resinous finish were observed on several objects).[7]

The palette is characterised by the use of pigments such as carbon black, which defines the outline in all decorative elements, yellow and red ochres/earth pigments, orpiment, Egyptian blue and copper-based green.

The scientific analyses enabled also recognition of past conservation interventions and the materials used. X-radiography highlighted structural reinforcement by insertion of metallic elements (screws holding modern supports in place and nails). Previous application of adhesives and materials for consolidation of paint layers was detected by their chromatic response to UV irradiation (mainly a light blue fluorescence that corresponds to synthetic materials) and later confirmed by FTIR analyses. 'Witness areas' (small areas, rectangular in shape, where the complete stratigraphy including the layers of dirt, has been preserved), considered to be evidence of previous cleaning intervention, were noted. Direct observation also allowed identification of pale tone fills, some of which had a structural function, retouches and, in one instance (reported below in the case study), the presence of cleaning tests, meaning that a cleaning intervention was not finished.

Taking into account the experience acquired by the Vatican Coffin Project, conservation treatments complied, where possible and appropriate, to the guidelines developed by the conservators of the Vatican Museums, with a special focus on adhesives.[8] However, the state of preservation of the coffins we have examined and some technical differences from the yellow coffin type, have led us to reflect on the desirability of developing alternative and specific materials and intervention methods.

Soft paint brushes and a micro-vacuum cleaner were used to remove incoherent deposits from surfaces; dry cleaning procedures were applied to remove coherent dust. PVC-free and vulcanised rubber erasers were tested. The PVC-free erasers were suitable for cleaning those surfaces that do not have any resinous finish. The vulcanised-rubber eraser was more appropriate on coated areas.[9]

The different technical features of the two groups of

[5] *Incamottatura*: a layer of textile overlying the wood and beneath the ground layers.

[6] This phenomenon, on a coffin in the Fitzwilliam Museum, Cambridge, was discussed in a paper given by Strudwick, Dawson, Marchant, Geldhof and Hunkeler at the Second Vatican Coffin Conference, Rome, 6–9 June 2017. (Strudwick *et al.* forthcoming).

[7] As reported later in this paper, the coffins studied were treated in the past and it is possible that the varnish layers were accidentally removed. To date, without a full characterisation of the resin layers, is not possible to clarify whether the coating was original or was applied after excavation, even if, as explained in the case study below, there is some evidence that this layer should be considered original.

[8] The defining of the conservation guidelines is still a work in progress. Recommendations from the research group took account of the first experimental results and the individual experience of the conservators involved. First results on adhesives have been published (Prestipino *et al.* 2015).

[9] Interesting insights into dry cleaning emerged through a research project carried out by the Rijksdienst voor het Cultureel Ergoed in 2006–2009. Investigation considered a broad range of dry cleaning materials (latex sponges, make-up sponges, PVC erasers, Factis™ erasers, gum powders, microfibre cloths, mouldable materials) with results ranging from efficient and safe cleaning to abrasion and hazards from residues. For an approach to dry cleaning see Daudin-Schotte *et al.* 2013.

coffins, such as the presence of a resinous finish on some (mainly yellow coffins) and the complete absence on others, led to the use of different types of consolidating solution based on the susceptibility to water of the surface. Water-based adhesive solutions were chosen if varnish was present, hydro-alcoholic solutions if not.

Choice of adhesive within each of these categories was based on the compatibility and reversibility of the treatments with respect to original materials and stratigraphy. Generally, a low content solution of non-ionic hydroxy propyl cellulose (Klucel G®) gave good results in the case of slight and moderate problems of adhesion, even when a partial decohesion of materials was detected. In the case of larger scale detachment, an acrylic dispersion in water (Acril E411®), was used as this had greater adhesive power even in low percentages (Prestipino *et al*, 2015). Where it was necessary to limit the amount of water in contact with the object, the dispersion was diluted with up to 10% ethanol.

Treatments were developed to resolve specific problems identified during condition reporting. On many coffins, areas affected by cracks in the wood were observed, sometimes impairing the readability of the object. Gaps in the ground and pictorial layers were considered particularly risky in case of handling, especially where these layers were thick. In some cases, deformation of both ground and pictorial layers was combined with defects of adhesion to the wooden support.

Materials used in previous interventions, such as gap-fills with nitrocellulose-based substances, were too compact, highly rigid, difficult to remove, chromatically discordant with the original colours and had a disturbingly irregular surface. It was necessary to identify alternative solutions. Looking at the state of preservation of these fills (cracking and breaking, especially at the edges in contact with original wooden materials, probably due to mechanical stress related to temperature and relative humidity changes), different methodologies were applied. Where structural repair was needed, an adhesion to contact points was carried out by application of an acid free acrylic emulsion adhesive (Bindan RS®).[10] For gaps, a new filler was developed. The aim was to give a better match to the surface, compatible with the original materials and with the ones proposed by the Vatican Coffin Project's intervention guidelines. The requirement was for the mixture to have enough elasticity to be mouldable, to have appropriate adhesive properties and to be compatible chromatically.

The need to achieve reproducible colour mixtures led us to consider dyeing materials with synthetic and natural dyes. Cellulose pulp-based paste was proposed: cellulosic materials are lightweight and can be dyed.[11] The intrinsic technical characteristics of this material meant that the choice of adhesive for making the paste was limited to water-soluble products. We undertook an experiment to measure mechanical responses of the chosen mixtures, to assess their colour saturation and to verify the durability of the dyes to light exposure.[12]

At the end of this experiment, a mixture of 2% Klucel G® (w/v), in an aqueous solution of (1.5%) JunFunori®[13] was selected: this solution presented the best mechanical and working properties when mixed with the cellulose (proportions: 20ml. binder to 6–8g. dyed cellulose). Cellulose pulp dyed with both natural and synthetic

[10] Bindan RS® is free from harmful substances, fillers and fillers, without solvents and without addition of formaldehyde. No discolouration of the woods containing tannin; no release of acetic acid with aging. The average tensile strength according to DIN 68 602 / EN 204 is > 11.0 N/mm². See technical sheet on www.collmon.it.

[11] Cellulose pulp: Arbocel BWW40®, average fibre length 200 microns. Tests were conducted on pre-metallised dyes (Indosol series, Clariant®, usually used for the dyeing of cellulose textile fibres such as cotton) and natural dyes fixed on fibre with innovative stains following a dyeing method developed by CRITT-Couleurs des Plantes and already tested on textile fibres at the CCR La Venaria Reale in a previous research project (INNOCOLORS Project) (Croveri *et al.* 2014).

[12] The tests of stability to light were made with a chamber SUNTEST CPS+ (Atlas 300–800 nm with Xenon lamp (1500W) and a standard UV filter that cuts out the wavelength below 320nm). Tests were conducted on samples of the binder+charge mixture (Funori 1.5% w/w + Klucel 4% w/w + dyed cellulose) and only dyed cellulose (tablet in tablet, diameter 1 cm.) following international regulations ISO105 BO2 for the evaluation of the light fastness of textile dyes, evaluating the fading by measuring the alteration kinetics by colorimetric controls (by instrument: Konica Minolta CM700d with geometry d/8°, 400–700 nm, source D65,10nm resolution). Colour differences (ΔE00) have been calculated using the formula CIEDE2000 (Buscaglia *x* 2015).

[13] Funori is made from three types of Japanese red algae (Rhodophyta): Gloiopeltis Tenax (ma-funori), Gloiopeltis Complanata (hara-funori), and Gloiopeltis Furcata (fukuro-funori). They differ from each other by their adhesive capacity, viscosity and water solubility. A dispersion based on ma-funori is denser, the one based on fukuro-funori less viscous. The hana-funori presents strong surfactant qualities. The purified Funori homologue from fukuro-funori is JunFunori®, developed by the Empa laboratory. The qualities that have made JunFunori particularly interesting are the excellent cohesive power, high permeability, high elasticity, low index of refraction ensuring no interference with opaque optical surfaces, good stability to light. For insights, see Geiger and Michel 2005; Michel 2011.

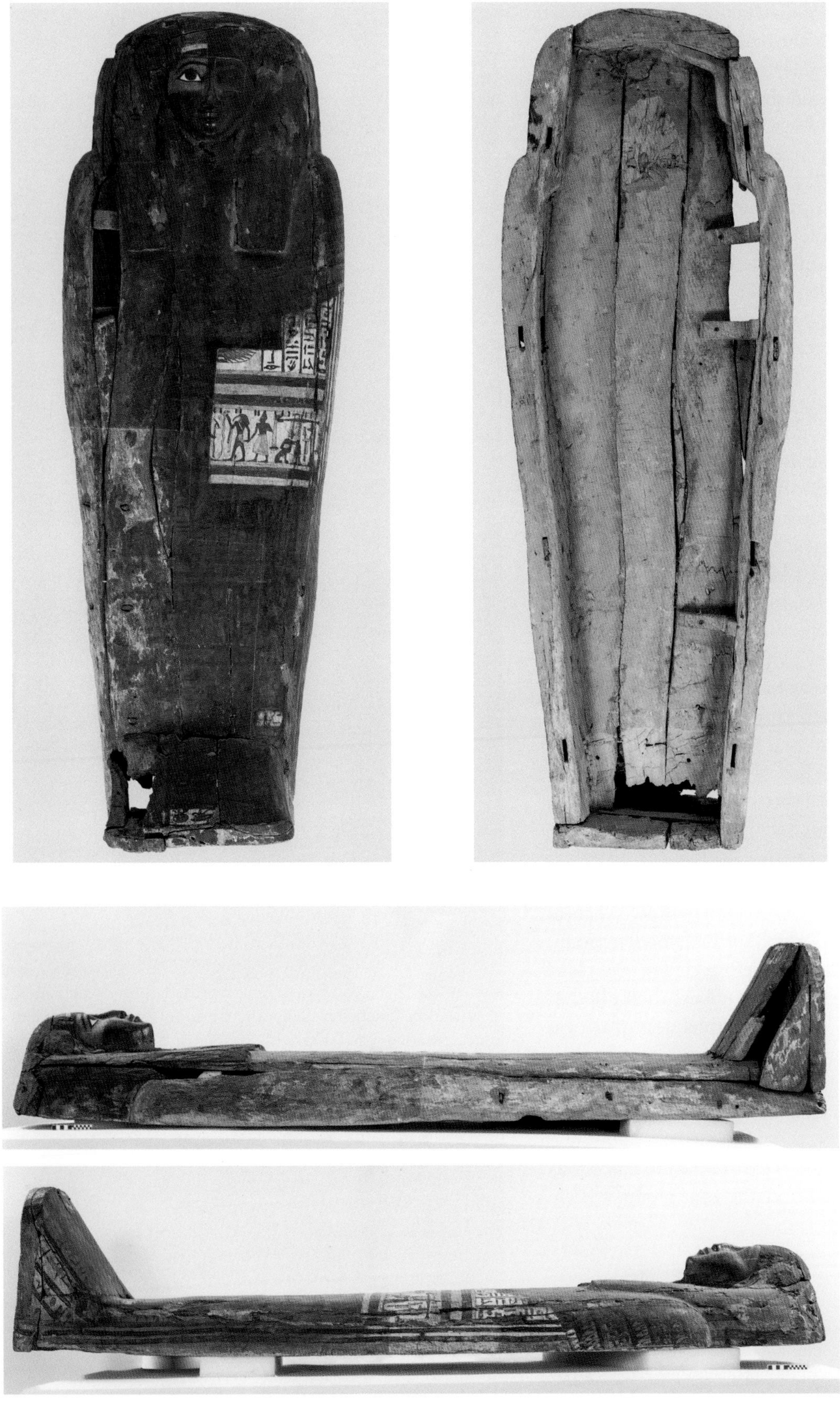

Fig. 56: The Nesimenjem coffin lid (S. 05227) before the intervention. See ***Fig. 60*** *detail A.*

dyes showed no loss of colour due to wetting. The colorimetric measurements showed variations in colour after exposure: these were negligible for synthetic dyes, more significant for natural dyes.

Case Study: The coffin of Nesimenjem

Within the conservation programme a case study was identified, which is significant in terms of style, manufacturing techniques and state of preservation: the Nesimenjem coffin lid (S. 5227) (**Fig. 56**).[14] A thick layer of black deposits on the painted surface completely hid the coloured decoration, which was visible only in two areas cleaned during a previous conservation campaign. The opportunity to work on a partially treated artefact meant that it was possible to undertake a more in depth diagnostic phase and, after the conservation, compare the results with other artefacts that showed similar technical characteristics.

The carpentry contains further aspects of interest and, in general, presents technical affinities with other Valley of the Queens' coffins. The main body consists of five shaped boards: radiographic analysis showed four loose tenon joints for each of the two central joins, positioned in a staggered manner so as to distribute the assembly support over the entire structure and ensure the flatness of the three boards. The two long, shaped pieces of wood that make up the sides of the lid show evidence of internal wooden dowels attaching them to the top boards; the face is a single carved wooden element. The ears are made of modelled paste. The lappets of the wig are attached to the chest with perpendicular dowels. The shape of the foot-case was created with two vertical planks as the footboard to which further wooden pieces, inclined by about 30 degrees were added at the front creating side triangular cavities that were then filled in with additional pieces. Within the thickness of the lid rim, there are eight rectangular section mortises, part of the assembly for closing the lid and the box together. Fragments of tenons have been detected inside these mortises (**Fig. 57**).

The stratigraphy of the surface decoration layers was comparable to other coffins from the same group.[15] There

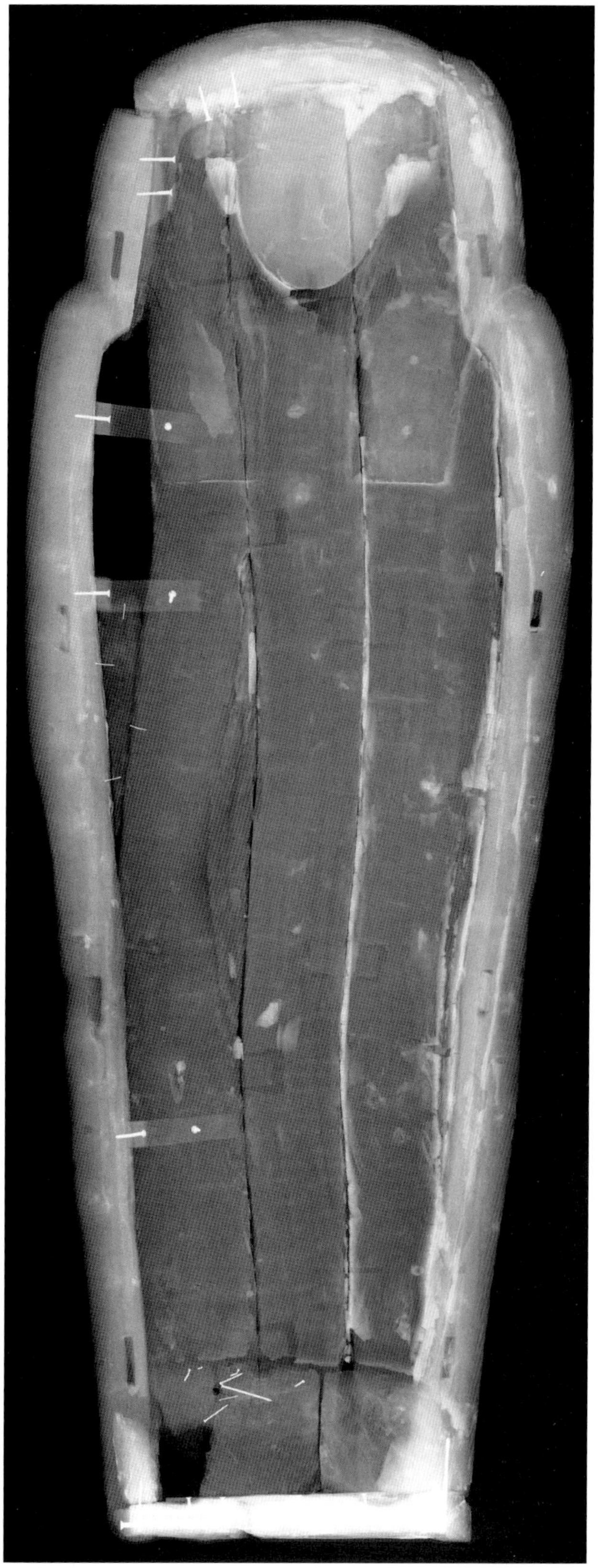

Fig. 57: X-radiograph of the Nesimenjem coffin lid. Voltage: 90 kVp; Current: 10 mA.

[14] See Appendix for details. Measurements: H. 44 x W. 212 x D. 65 cm.

[15] Two different groups can be distinguished on the basis of the characteristics of the preparatory layers among the Valley of the Queens' coffins: Group 1: coffins which have *incamottatura* over almost the entire surface among the preparatory layers (S. 5239 anthropoid coffin; S. 5226 Harwa I coffin lid; S. 5220 Mentuirdis

was an interesting use of a coarse-grained, coloured material, applied thickly to refine the rendering of anatomical features and thinly to correct carving inaccuracies and wood defects; it was frequently combined with plant fibre and glue mixtures to fill cracks and irregular joints. It is made up of earth pigments with black from iron and titanium minerals (iron-titanates) and small amounts of calcium carbonate (with a little gypsum/anhydrite that could be intentional or the result of sulphation). It is noteworthy that there are similarities in the colour, morphology and, when sampled, composition of this layer in coffins that do not have *incamottatura*. In particular, close analogies of composition in this layer have been noticed between the case study, Nesimenjem, and the coffin of Harwa II (S. 5229).[16] Over this layer, there is a whitish preparation layer across the entire surface and composed mainly of calcium carbonate (as limestone), used also as a background for the decoration.

The lid has decoration only on the exterior, applied with a brush on the carefully polished preparation layer. The thick layer of black accretion on almost the entire surface did not initially allow an evaluation of the decoration and of its material composition and preservation state. These became evident only after the cleaning intervention. Only the already exposed areas were analysed before the intervention.

The decoration was characterised by geometric elements alternating with hieroglyphs and figurative scenes, distributed on six horizontal registers separated by coloured bands (yellow, red, blue) and divided by a yellow vertical band with hieroglyphic inscriptions. A black under-drawing was visible. Its high NIR absorbence suggested that it was executed in a carbon black-based paint. The other pigments used in the decoration are Egyptian blue, a copper-based green (copper acetate or Egyptian green), yellow and red ochres/earths and orpiment (results obtained by NIR1-FC, FORS, XRF analyses). The GC-MS analysis conducted on a detached fragment to characterise the binder used led us to hypothesise the use of egg, perhaps combined with another protein binder.[17]

The Egyptian blue areas are the most prominent: it was used not only for the coloured bands alternating with the red and yellow ochre/earths pigments, but also for the hieroglyphs and to define some figures. The background is a bright yellow colour in two figurative scenes, created with a veiling of orpiment. At the edges of the already cleaned areas, residues of a natural resin (detected by FTIR analysis) were found.

In addition to embrittlement of the wood due to previous infestation of wood-eating insects, the original joints on the lid had become loose, causing mobility in the structure (especially the footboard) during handling. Inspection showed that structural reinforcement had been applied in a previous intervention. The pictorial stratigraphy showed detachment of the ground and paint layers from the support, with deformations and contractions, especially in the areas modelled with sandy material, which is more hygroscopic and responsive in terms of dimensional changes.

A synthetic organic acrylic substance Paraloid B72® applied during the previous intervention was detected, acting as a consolidant also for the superficial black layer; its presence made the development of a controlled cleaning procedure more complex, especially considering the probable presence of original varnish underneath. We proceeded carefully, securing the surface using materials and methodologies specifically tested within the framework of the Vatican Coffin Project, using water/ethanol solutions to dilute the consolidants as appropriate (see p. 85).

After securing the ground and paint layers, cleaning tests were undertaken, firstly with various solvent mixtures to assess their efficacy in removing both the Paraloid and the black deposit without interfering with the original resinous surface.

Given the intrinsic characteristics of the materials to be removed (with particular reference to the non-homogeneous, coherent black surface deposit) and considering the original stratigraphy (wooden support, ground

middle coffin lid; S. 5219 Mentuirdis inner coffin; cat 2234 Padiamenemipet middle coffin lid; cat 2233 Padiamenemipet inner coffin). Group 2: coffins with the decoration on a preparation composed of two different layers but without the presence of *incamottatura* (S. 5253 anthropoid coffin; S. 5244 Tadiaset-Tahekat coffin; S. 5229 Harwa II coffin; S. 5221 Mentuirdis outer coffin box; cat 2235 Padiamenemipet outer coffin; S. 5227 Nesimenjem).

[16] Calcium carbonate and red earth with black particles from iron and titanium minerals (iron-titanates).

[17] This is a highly unusual feature. We were able to analyse only a detached fragment from this coffin lid and did not have the chance to undertake GC-MS analysis on other coffins of similar provenance to make comparisons with apparently technically similar materials. Therefore, further evidence is required to confirm this unexpected choice of binder. Moreover, we do not have a clear idea of the materials that were used on site at the moment of the discovery; this too indicates that further investigation is necessary.

and paint layers, natural resin) a comparison of the effectiveness and non-interference of both traditional cleaning methods (organic solvents) and LASER (Light Amplification by Stimulated Emission of Radiation) technology was considered appropriate. The LASER physical method has been widely used in the conservation of cultural heritage in recent years, and offers a non-contact tool of great precision.[18]

It was necessary to consider the risks that a physical cleaning method may entail. The availability of mock-ups reproducing the pictorial stratigraphy of Egyptian paintings (and artificially aged in a solar box), made specifically to test the tool at different operating conditions, helped establish an operating range of relative safety. The results of the tests have been scientifically evaluated through colorimetric tests and stratigraphic sampling.[19]

Organic solvent[20] tests considered binary and ternary mixtures of low polarity and high volatility (fd (dispersion force) with a value between 60 and 70, selected to avoid overlap with the area of solubility of natural resins).[21] Preliminary LASER tests were undertaken with a Nd:YAG ThunderArt QS and a Nd:Yag Eos Vario LQS made by El.En group.[22]

The cleaning methodology, aimed at removal of black deposits and old restoration materials with the simultaneous preservation of natural resin finishes, was defined taking into account the positive results obtained with laser cleaning, and observing a lesser efficacy and control capability with the traditional methods. It was considered appropriate to adopt as a maximum fluence threshold the value considered optimal during tests:[23] the disruptive and ablative action of the Q-switch beam at these operating conditions provided a first step of cleaning that left residues and did not affect the substrate.

The next step, refining the cleaning, was carried out with a different type of laser instrument and tuning of the pulse and the consistency of the beam (Nd:Yag Eos Vario Long Q-Switch mode λ 1064 nm, fluence 0,64 J/cm^2). Alternatively, a localised application of a mixture of organic solvents which did not interfere with the resin layer was used, or in some other cases, dry cleaning with PVC-free rubbers.

The efficacy and non-interference of the cleaning methods were confirmed by trials on each colour, defining the proper operational conditions by following the response of the substrate. Moreover, the intervention was adjusted also as a function of the presence/absence of the conservation acrylic resin on the surface.[24]

[18] The principle behind laser cleaning relies on the emission of a precisely focused narrow beam of pure light in very short pulses, directed onto the object's surface. The dirt that overlies that surface will absorb heat from this beam much more rapidly than the substrate and, as it heats up and expands, it will be ejected from the surface as a vapour. The first application in conservation, the removal of black encrustations from stone, was extensively investigated for side effects, such as laser-induced yellowing of white stone (Siano *et al.* 2012). There are different types of lasers, characterised mainly by the wavelength at which the radiation is emitted and the energy and duration of the pulse of the beam. For further information on the development of laser cleaning in conservation see Koss and Marczak 2015; Fotakis *et al.*,2007; Brunetto 2004; Cooper 1998.

[19] The mock-ups were created by Serena Mansi and Bianca Ferrarato as part of two Master's theses (Degree Course in Conservation and Restoration of Cultural Heritage of the University of Turin, in agreement with the CCR La Venaria Reale), focusing on the effects of laser cleaning on ancient Egyptian materials. At the time of the cleaning of the coffins, the tests were underway and were subsequently presented at the conference Aplar 6 in 2017 (Mansi *et al.* 2017; Ferrarato *et al.* 2017).

[20] Different solvent mixtures tested. Solvents: ethanol, isopropanol, Ligroin (100–140, apolar mixture of aliphatic hydrocarbons with an aromatic content of less than 0.5%) and acetone. For the use of organic solvents in cleaning of polychrome surfaces see Cremonesi and Signorini 2004.

[21] The solubility of natural and synthetic organic materials have been extrapolated from Horie 1987. For resin solubility see also Teas 1968.

[22] Eos Vario LQS with near-infrared emission (Nd: Yag λ 1064nm) has a particular pulse duration of 100 ns with linear energy growth (50 to 380 mJ). The laser beam transmission takes place in optical fibre which produces a homogeneous beam profile. There is an adjustable handpiece and a guide beam emitting at 632.8 nm. This laser system is optimised for use where particularly accurate interventions are required and is suitable for a range of applications. Thunder Art works in QS mode (Nd: Yag λ 1064 nm) configuration and delivers a maximum energy of about 1J. It provides optional wavelengths (λ 532 nm and 355 nm), the pulse duration is 8 ns. The beam is transmitted by a seven-mirror articulated arm with a fixed, interchangeable focal length. This tool is technologically advanced and is applicable on a wide range of materials.

[23] The best results were obtained by Nd:YAG ThunderArt QS, fluence 0,65 J/cm2, frequency at 10 Hz, which allowed a partial removal of the black material, leaving some residues. It was possible to observe the underlying presence of a layer of natural varnish (UV investigation) that had been maintained. Other good results were obtained with Nd:Yag Eos Vario LQS, fluence 0,64 J/cm2 frequency 3 Hz to refine the first step with Nd:YAG ThunderArt QS.

[24] In summary: **White backgrounds, yellow ochre and yellow orpiment**: Without Paraloid: laser λ 1064nm, QS mode, fluences between 0,20 and 0,35 J/cm^2, frequency 5Hz. Primary ablation gradual thinning of the material. With Paraloid: I step: Laser λ 1064nm, QS mode fluence 0,30 J/cm^2, frequency 5

The tests performed on Egyptian blue mock-ups did not provide good results: during the preliminary tests a slight discolouration in the green tones was observed with the fluence required for complete ablation of dirt. In addition to this, the porosity of the paint had encouraged the dirt to penetrate. In these areas it was decided to thin the layer by traditional chemical methods.[25] Thus the readability of the blue colours was partially recovered. Given the porosity of this paint, it was thought appropriate to avoid going deeper for complete removal of the black layer, thus avoiding the risk of loss of original material.

As the cleaning procedures progressed, they were monitored with the aid of UV radiation examination to check the correct removal of the layer without any interference with the resinous finish (**Fig. 58**). The possibility of working mainly with LASER has ensured the consistency of the intervention through using the same operating conditions, even these were calibrated to suit the specific colour substrate treated.

In-depth study of the previously invisible pictorial decoration became possible. Evidence from VIL imaging, showed the use of Egyptian blue for hieroglyphic inscriptions, whilst XRF analysis confirmed the use of orpiment in coloured backgrounds of figurative scenes but not in inscriptions. This technical feature suggests an intention to differentiate specific areas of the decorative scheme.

After cleaning, the presence of a yellowish, transparent layer (almost completely removed in the area of the previous restoration cleaning test) was evident. This resinous layer appeared patchy in its application to the surface, with very large quantities evident in the areas with hieroglyphs (**Fig. 59** and **Fig. 60**). FTIR analysis of samples from this layer confirmed that it is a natural resin (see note 7).

The presence of a resinous finish on the Nesimenjem coffin lid allowed us to hypothesise its presence on other coffins of the same context and historical period. It was not initially noticed through visual inspection and its absence was assumed at first to be a distinct characteristic of Late Period coffins.[26] The wish to investigate this aspect in greater depth and the presence of witness areas on artefacts similar in chronology and provenance encouraged us (with permission) to carry out laser cleaning tests on limited portions of these areas (keeping one part untreated). Stratigraphic micro-sampling was undertaken to confirm the hypothesised presence of the natural resin. On this occasion, laser technology proved to be a powerful tool, not only allowing a correct reading of material in situ (and fully respecting the original morphology) but also, through controlled operating conditions, guaranteeing the preservation of the resinous layer on the surfaces.

Laser cleaning tests revealed resin underneath the witness areas of the coffins of Harwa, in particular on the lids of the Harwa I coffin (S. 05226/1) and the Harwa II coffin (S. 05229). Resin was detected also on the inner coffin of Mentuirdis (S. 05219) where it had already been noticed through UV fluorescence, and on the Padiamenemipet intermediate coffin lid (Cat. 2234) thanks to a cross section of a micro-fragment sampled from the witness area. It is worth noting, in these last two cases, the additional similarity to Nesimenjem in the use of orpiment as a coloured background and, for

Hz. II step: finishing touch with Laser λ 1064nm, LQS mode, fluence 1,13 J/cm^2, frequency 5Hz. Primary and secondary ablation. Finishing touch by dry cleaning with PVC-free erasers. **Black lines**: laser, λ 1064nm, QS mode, fluence 0,30 J/cm^2, frequency 1Hz. The identification of a different way of working was dictated by the extreme sensitivity of the black pigment to the laser spallation. Non-interference. **Red ochre colour bands**: Without Paraloid: laser λ 1064nm, QS mode, fluence 0,65 J/cm^2, frequency 10Hz with filter overlay (Japanese paper) applied to the laser handpiece output window. Good level of removal by thinning the dirt. With Paraloid: laser λ 1064nm, QS mode, fluence 0,30 J/cm^2, frequency 10Hz, inhomogeneous results; extra step: finishing with organic solvent. The action of the solvent is more effective thanks to a first pass of the laser. **Copper-based green**: Without Paraloid: laser λ 532 nm, QS mode, fluence 0,37 J/cm^2, frequency 4 Hz; With Paraloid: laser λ 1064 nm, LQS mode, fluence 0,41 J/cm^2. respectful of the green pigment at the wavelength of 532 nm. Localised extra cleaning with organic solvent. Finishing touch by dry cleaning with PVC-free erasers. **Red ochre face**: I step: Laser λ 1064nm, QS mode, fluence 0,47 J/cm^2, frequency 10Hz ; II step: Laser λ 1064nm, LQS mode, fluences between 0,59 and 0,92 J/cm^2, frequency 7/9 Hz. Secondary ablation, with swelling of the material and subsequent removal by means of organic solvent. Finishing touch by dry cleaning with PVC-free erasers.

[25] Areas where the Egyptian blue had not been treated previously with acrylic resin proved to be more reactive to the aqueous mixtures necessary for the removal of the dirt layer. Therefore, a Ligroin solvent gel was used in which a small part of surfactant aqueous solution (Ethomeen C12) had been dispersed. This guaranteed completely apolar rinsing, a gradual action and limited penetration of the material into the stratigraphy. In areas previously treated with the acrylic resin, a high viscosity gel based on xanthan gum was used to thicken a mixture of water and acetone, which allowed a superficial action without spreading in the lower layers.

[26] On the nature and use of resins in ancient Egypt see Serpico and White 2006.

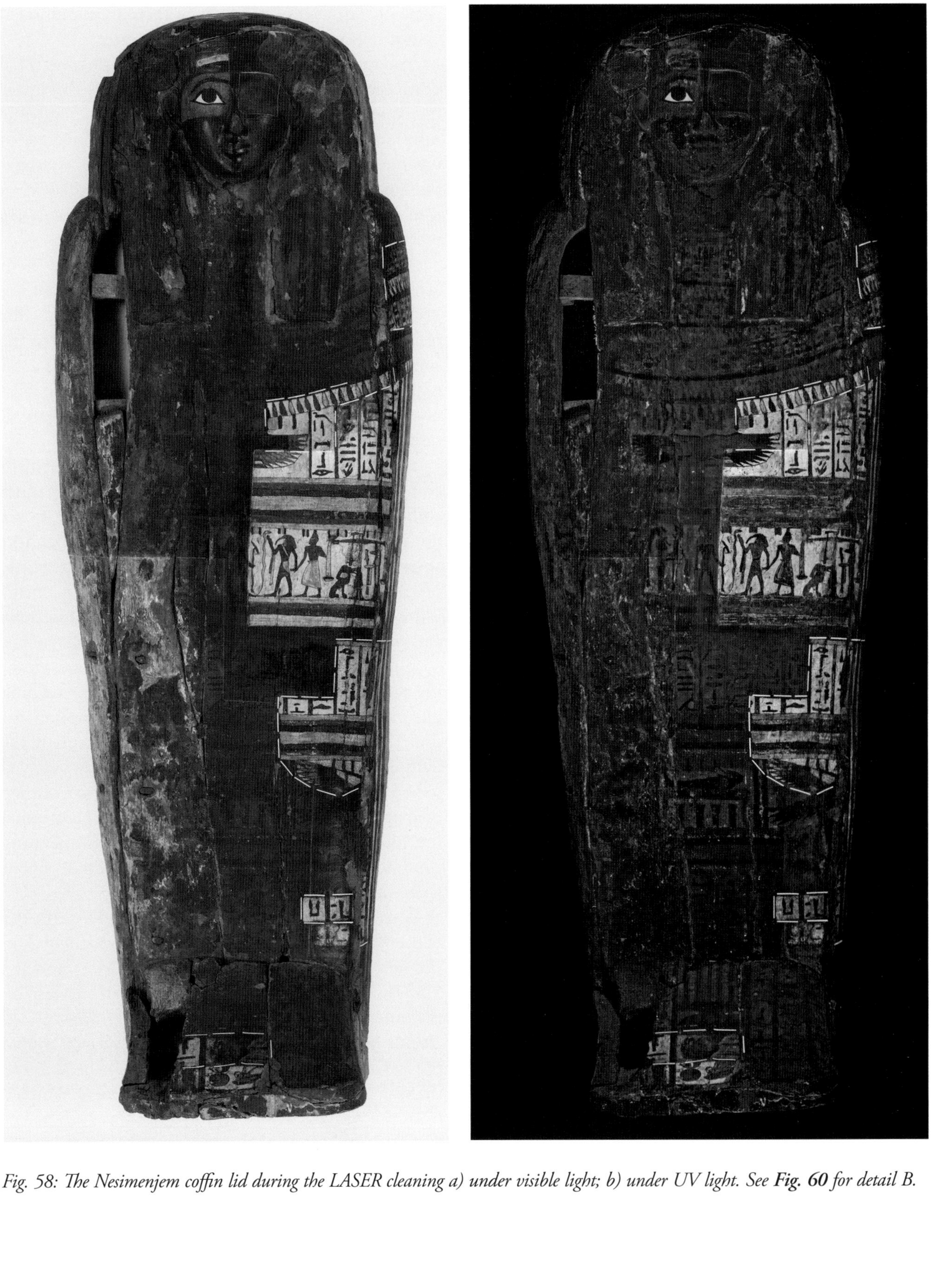

*Fig. 58: The Nesimenjem coffin lid during the LASER cleaning a) under visible light; b) under UV light. See **Fig. 60** for detail B.*

*Fig. 59: The Nesimenjem coffin lid: a) during conservation; b) after conservation. See **Fig. 60** for detail C.*

Padiamenemipet, the use of Egyptian blue for the hieroglyphs on the outer, middle and inner coffins. Amongst the coffins that share the presence of a resinous layer, technical and formal similarities were also observed.

Conclusions

The results of conservation work on the Nesimenjem coffin lid highlight the practice of using resinous materials on polychrome wooden coffins also in the late Third Intermediate Period and in the Late Period. The presence of the resin, not always detected, was perhaps more widespread than visible evidence on the coffin surfaces today would suggest.

The role of conservation treatment must not be underestimated: intervention must always be considered

Fig. 60: Detail A showing a previously cleaned area (in visible light in the image on the left, under UV light in the image on the right). In the upper right area there is a brownish-yellow material that fluoresces under UV light in a way that could indicate a resinous finish on the painting

Detail B showing a previously cleaned test area (below) and a LASER cleaned test area (above). The patchy distribution of the resin and its brownish-yellow colour are notable.

Detail C showing the distribution of the resin on the surface. The difference between the previously cleaned area (on the right) and the result of the LASER cleaning is pronounced.

as a critical act that can be carried out safely only when coupled with a deep knowledge of original techniques and the conservation history of the objects. The correct interpretation of a pictorial surface minimises the possibility of unintentional removal of original materials or the alteration of substrates. Only in recent decades has a gradual and controllable approach, using minimally interfering materials and methods and supported by scientific and technological innovation and by the improved potential for diagnosis, become a matter of primary importance.[27]

Appendix

Yellow Coffins

Coffin set of Tabakenkhonsu (Cat. 2226/1, /2, /3) Third Intermediate Period, Twenty-first Dynasty (Tanis) (1070–946 BC).

Coffin set of Teifmutmut (Cat. 2228/1,2,3) Third Intermediate Period (Thebes), Twenty-first/Twenty-second Dynasty (1070–736 BC).

Anthropoid coffin box (Cat. 2227) Third Intermediate Period, Twenty-first/Twenty-second Dynasty (950–930 BC).

Coffin set of Khonsumose (Cat. 2238/1,2,3) Third Intermediate Period, Twenty-first Dynasty (990/970 BC).

Anthropoid coffin lid and coffin box (S. 07715), Third Intermediate Period, Twenty-first/Twenty-second Dynasty (950–930 BC) and mummy board of Mutemperimen (S. 07715/02).

Valley of the Queens' coffins

Coffin set of Padiamenemipet, Third Intermediate Period, Twenty-second/Twenty third Dynasty (946–712 BC):
• Outer (lid, Cat. 2235/1; box, Cat. 2235/2), Theban necropolis (?)
• Intermediate coffin (Cat. 2234/1, Cat. 2234/2)
• Inner coffin (Cat. 2233/2, Cat. 2233/3), Theban necropolis (?)

Coffin set of Mentuirdis, Third Intermediate Period–Late Period, Twenty-fourth/Twenty-fifth Dynasty (740–655 BC):
• Outer coffin (S. 05221), unknown provenance
• Intermediate coffin (S. 05220), Valley of the Queens/Tomb of Khaemuaset (QV 44) and tomb of Sethherkhepeshef (QV 43)
• Inner coffin (S. 05219, S. 05219), unknown provenance.

Coffin of Harwa I (S. 05226/1 A, S 05226/1 B) unknown provenance, Third Intermediate Period–Late Period, Twenty-fourth/Twenty-fifth Dynasty (740–655 BC).

Coffin of Nesimendjem (S. 05227) Valley of the Queens/Tomb of Khaemuaset (QV 44) and tomb of Sethherkhepeshef (QV 43) Third Intermediate Period-Late Period, Twenty-first/Twenty-fifth Dynasty (1070–655 BC).

Coffin of Hor (S. 05228/1, S. 05228/2) Valley of the Queens/Tomb of Khaemuaset (QV 44) and tomb of Sethherkhepeshef (QV 43) Third Intermediate Period–Late Period, Twenty-fourth/Twenty-fifth Dynasty (740–655 BC).

Coffin of Harwa II (S. 05229/A, S. 05229/B) Third Intermediate Period–Late Period, Twenty-fourth/Twenty-fifth Dynasty (740–655 BC).

Coffin lid of Tadiaset-Tahekat (S. 05244) Third Intermediate Period–Late Period, Twenty-fifth /Twenty sixth Dynasty (740–525 BC).

Anthropoid coffin (S. 05253), unknown provenance, Third Intermediate Period-Late Period, Twenty-fourth/Twenty-fifth Dynasty (740–655 BC).

Anthropoid coffin (S. 05239) Valley of the Queens/Tomb of Khaemuaset (QV 44) and tomb of Sethherkhepeshef (QV 43), Late Period, Twenty-fifth Dynasty (740–655 BC).

[27] I would like to thank Julie Dawson for her helpful comments and careful editing of this paper.

Patterns of coffin reuse from Dynasties 19 to 22

Kathlyn M. Cooney

Twenty-first Dynasty coffins are important social documents, but they are difficult to record, photograph, and analyse. Robust scholarship has advanced our understanding of these objects and their social contexts, including studies by Andrzej Niwiński, John H. Taylor, Nicholas Reeves and Karl Jansen-Winkeln. For the past seven years, I have been examining human reactions to social crises, specifically focusing on material adaptations evident within an ideological context, but also documenting the Twenty-first Dynasty coffin corpus. I am now able to see patterns of reuse in different groups of coffins, including 1) Twentieth Dynasty, 2) early Twenty-first Dynasty, 3) coffins from the Bab el-Gasus cache, 4) Twenty-first Dynasty coffins from the Royal Cache, and 5) Stola coffins of the early Twenty-second Dynasty. In this paper, I examine some of the patterns I have found.

When we think of funerary arts we usually think of forever ownership – immortality, eternity, perpetuity. In fact some of the most successful Egyptian funerary art exhibitions are so named in museums around the world; I worked on two such exhibitions, one called *Quest for Immortality*,[1] the other *To Live Forever*,[2] each one fetishising the notion that the Egyptians prized single, uncomplicated, and non-competitive ownership of priceless body containers, tombs, and other funerary equipment. Such an understanding automatically assumes that ancient Egyptian mortuary art was intended by its commissioners and makers to be owned once and forever, never to be used or even touched by another, unless, of course, an archaeologist is lucky enough to discovery such materiality and place it into a museum space for our consumption – also forever and uncomplicated.

However, there exist multiple times during Egyptian history when short term use of funerary materials was demanded by economic and political conditions, in particular during the Bronze Age collapse, a process of social upheaval and turmoil that began in Egypt around the Twentieth Dynasty and continued until the early Twenty-second Dynasty, at the least. During this time of trade route disruption, mass migration, elite replacement and government collapse, a different pattern of funerary ownership emerged that demanded short term use by wealthy Egyptians who could spend disposable income on their burials. Throughout this turmoil, the evidence indicates that wealthy Egyptians still considered funerary materiality essential to create ritual transformation of the dead, not to mention essential for manufacturing social prestige for the bereaved family.[3] Just because economic scarcity had set in, does not mean there was an interest in shutting down the materiality of death. Instead, Egyptian elites (who had not been replaced, at least) adapted with a defensive negotiation of burial materiality (Cooney 2011). Funerary reuse thus became the only moral alternative in the face of economic scarcity. This article tracks the larger patterns of coffin reuse diachronically,

[1] This exhibition opened at the National Gallery of Art in Washington, D.C. in 2002. Hornung and Bryan 2002.

[2] This exhibition opened at the Brooklyn Museum of Art in Brooklyn, N.Y. in 2008. Bleiberg 2008.

[3] See the idea of "functional materiality" in Cooney 2007, 259–282.

from the Nineteenth Dynasty to early Twenty-second Dynasty, as well as synchronically, according to different find-spots, including caches.

A few caveats on our data. Archaeological preservation is a tricky thing. Sometimes objects are preserved from the past; sometimes they are not. We cannot expect the surviving archaeological data to be representative through time or space. We lack northern coffins in general, not just during the Bronze Age Collapse, but throughout the entirety of the New Kingdom. Most of our coffins come not only from Upper Egypt, but more specifically from the stronghold of the High Priesthood of Amen at Thebes. We also lack the coffins of lower elites; if a piece was not considered attractive to the antiquities market or museum world, it was often destroyed as firewood or discarded by archaeologists. We also lack coffins from older time periods. Indeed, we lack Nineteenth and Twentieth Dynasty coffins in comparison to Twenty-first Dynasty coffins, on a ratio of about 1 to 10, probably because there was so much reuse. In other words, there are so few Nineteenth and Twentieth Dynasty coffins precisely because they were so often reused – as entire coffins or as broken down lumber – and made into Third Intermediate Period coffins. The nature of the data is, in itself, evocative of the practice of reuse. My current data set, that is, the coffins I have personally examined, includes 58 Nineteenth Dynasty coffins, 41 Twentieth Dynasty coffins, 188 early Twenty-first Dynasty coffins, and 45 late Twenty-first/early Twenty-second Dynasty coffins.

Because there are so few surviving Ramesside coffins, we tend to concentrate on these examples more in our scholarship. There are reasons for this. First, such Nineteenth and Twentieth Dynasty coffins are rare. Second, they are frozen in time, never having been reused. A Nineteenth Dynasty coffin set, like that of Henutmehyt in the British Museum, is a remarkable thing: found intact, ostensibly by treasure hunters, who put it on the antiquities market, and a miracle for not having been reused, as nowhere on this woman's set is there evidence that later generations made further use of it. In comparison, some Twenty-first Dynasty coffins can show three or four visible reuses, an untidy jumble of lumber, construction methods, plaster layers, and painting styles. Indeed, my current research has proven to me, at least, that Twenty-first Dynasty coffins were cycled in and out of ownership far more than we ever imagined.

Nonetheless, we may continue to have a hard time unravelling our own assumptions. First, regular seriation is more attractive to us archaeologists and Egyptologists, because it implies a clear use of object creation, style change, and then new object creation, which makes sense in our constructed typologies of fashion change. When one and the same object goes through multiple updates in construction and decoration, sometimes in a circular fashion in which old styles are retained, however, it is difficult for us to see where one time period begins and another ends, an untidy conflation of form, image and techniques, not to mention of commissioners and craftsmen. Second, reuse is difficult for many Egyptologists to accept for the simple reason that most Egyptian commissioners and artisans were trying to hide what they were doing, veiling old decoration with a new plastered layer that is only visible if some of the new layer has fallen away, or making wood modifications that are invisible underneath iconographically complex polychrome layers. With such attention to covering the tracks of their reuse, how do we identify it at all? Finally, many Egyptologists might be flummoxed by the simple fact that the Egyptians themselves never openly recorded or discussed funerary reuse. They did not make explicit receipts for this kind of work, ordering the redecoration of an older coffin.[4] Indeed, the notion that coffin reuse was a regularised and accepted practice in Egypt during the Twentieth and Twenty-first Dynasties is very hard for many specialists to accept, so much so that I was once complemented by another Egyptologist for my "imaginative" analysis of these coffins, with the obvious takeaway being that all of this reuse was a fanciful and manufactured product of my own devices.

Patterns of coffin reuse

Over the past ten years, I have examined over 300 coffins in museums around the world for craftsmanship,

[4] However, a careful look at west Theban coffin receipts from the Twentieth Dynasty shows that almost all commissions were for painting, rather than carpentry. While I previously assumed this was because the Deir el-Medina artisans had a niche specialisation in painting, I am now of the opinion that there was little wood to craft and that most coffins were created from already existing coffins, either legally pulled out of family burial chambers or purchased on the black market after theft. The fact that Deir el-Medina artisans were engaging in this kind of work makes sense; they lived and breathed in the necropolis. They were the ones who knew where the burial chambers were. The evidence of their private industry in coffin production is testament to their ability to find the raw materials from which to make new coffins, especially if the only raw materials were older coffins. For discussion of the cost components for coffins see Cooney 2007, 111–113.

Table 1: Rate of reuse for 20th–22nd Dynasty coffins analysed thus far

Museum/Institution	**Coffins**	**0**	**1**	**2**	**3**	**TBD**	**Reuse %**
Berlin, Germany, Ägyptisches Museum	15	8	3	1	3	1	46.67%
Bodrhyddan, UK	2				2		100%
Bristol, UK, City Museum and Art Gallery	4	2			2		50.0%
Brussels, Belgium, Musée Royaux d'Art et d'Histoire	12	3	1	1	6	1	66.66%
Cairo, Egypt, Egyptian Museum	31		3	3	25		100%
Copenhagen, Denmark, Copenhagen Nationalmuseet	11	5	3	1	2		54.54%
Copenhagen, Denmark, Ny Carlsberg Glyptotek	1				1		100.0%
Cortona, Italy, Museo dell'Accademia	2					2	TBD
Edinburgh, UK, National Museums of Scotland	5	2	1		2		60.0%
Exeter, UK, Royal Albert Memorial Museum	1	1					0%
Florence, Italy, Museo Archeologico	17	4	2	1	10		76.46%
Houston, TX, USA, Houston Museum of Natural Science	1	1					0%
Leeds, UK, City Museum	2	2					0%
Leiden, Netherlands, Rijksmuseum van Oudheden	14	5	3	1	4	1	57.14%
Liverpool, UK, World Museum, National Museums Liverpool	4		3		1		100%
London, UK, British Museum	33	15	11	1	6		54.54%
London, UK, Petrie Museum	1				1		100%
Manchester, UK	1		1				100%
New York, NY, USA, Metropolitan Museum of Art	26	8	2		12	4	68.2%
Paris, France, Musée du Louvre	31	10	7	8	6		68.24%
Perth, Scotland, UK	2				2		100%
Stockholm, Sweden, Stockholm Medelhavsmuseet	4	1	1		1	1	50.0%
Swansea, UK, The Wellcome Museum	1		1				100%
Turin, Italy, Museo Egizio	20	6	4	4	5	1	65.0%
Vatican City State, Museo Gregoriano Egizio	17	9	1	1	5	1	41.17%
Vienna, Austria, Kunsthistorisches Museum	15	1	7		7		93.34%
Warrington, UK, Warrington Museum & Art Gallery	2				2		100%
Totals	**275**	**83**	**54**	**22**	**105**	**12**	**65.82%**
Totals for reuse with high confidence				**22**	**105**		**46.18%**

style and reuse. This work began with my first book on Ramesside coffins and social agency, in which I analysed about 80 coffins of Dynasties 19 and 20.

The work continued with analysis of almost 300 Twenty-first and some early Twenty-second Dynasty examples, and those that I have visited in person are listed in the second chart below. Each museum is accompanied by a reuse percentage and by a reuse score, a number between 0 and 3, 0 being no visible evidence of reuse, 1 being circumstantial evidence, 2 being stronger, and 3 being incontrovertible evidence of coffin reuse. This score allows me to rate my own confidence in the reuse under analysis, a necessity given that much of the time my analysis is hampered by my ability to see a coffin without a glass vitrine blocking my access, or by a coffin which I cannot examine fully, by opening a given body container and peering inside, for example. The ability to see all surfaces of a coffin, inside and out, top to bottom, is essential to ruling out coffin reuse. And even if there is no visual proof of coffin reuse, in some cases Carbon 14 analysis has shown reuse of older wood, if not also older coffins.[5] This is why the chart below shows some collections with a 100% reuse rate, while others only have a 20% reuse rate, a frustrating reality based on access to the material. The uncomfortable reality is: the more time and access I have to the coffin, the more I can prove definitively that it is either reused or not, and when a Twenty-first Dynasty coffin is under scrutiny, that access usually proves reuse rather than not.

The reuse rate for the entire corpus of Twenty-first and early Twenty-second Dynasty coffins is almost 70%, and, lest one believe that my imagination has run away from me, we can focus instead on the rate of reuse in which I am confident, i.e. those receiving a score of 2 or 3, and that nears 50% (**Table 1**). The more I examine coffins from this time period of social

[5] In 2013 nine wood samples were taken from different pieces of wood from the Houston Stola coffin for C-14 dating at the University of California Irvine. Calibrated age dates for these pieces of wood were as follows: 926–832 BC, 901–822 BC, 972–844 BC, 998–897 BC, 877–811 BC, 1393–1262 BC, 1373–1357 BC, 1298–1212 BC, 1109–936 BC, and 1047–931 BC.

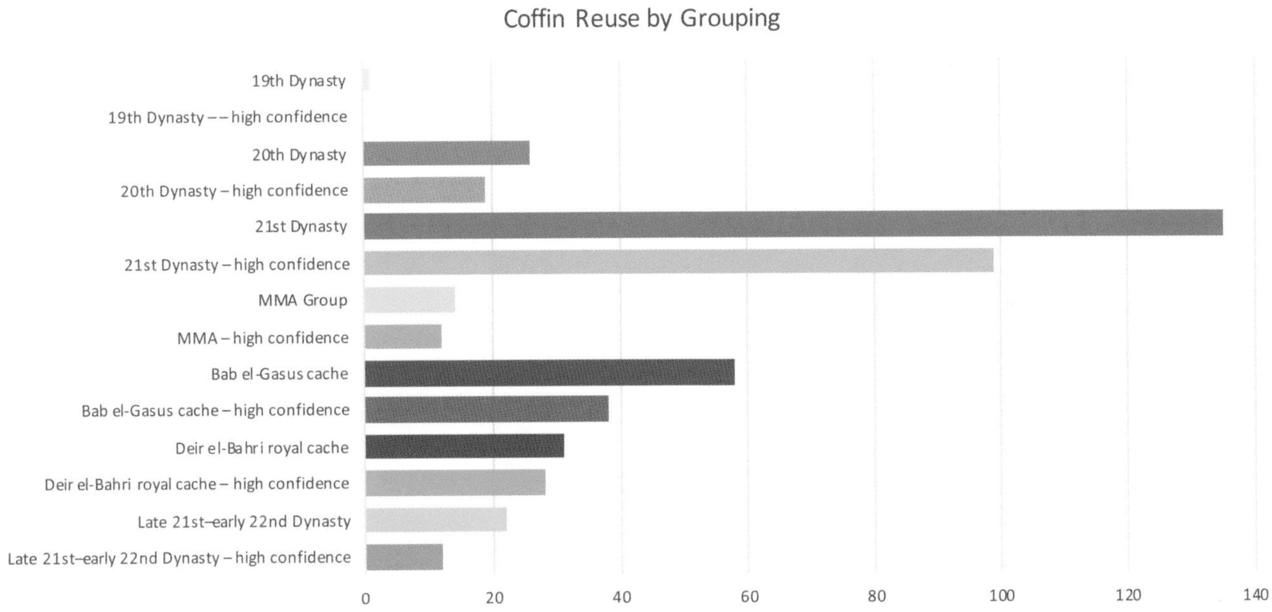

Fig. 61: Diachronic coffin reuse by grouping

instability, the more I believe that most of them are the product of some kind of reuse, whether I can identify it or not. Nespawershefyt's coffin set in Cambridge, for example, only gave up the secrets of its reuse when CT scans showed an older mortise in a reused piece of wood (Strudwick and Dawson 2016, 182–189). Indeed, access to all parts of a coffin has been so instrumental to proving reuse that I suspect that if I had access to CT scanning and Carbon 14 sampling for each coffin, most coffins dated to the Twenty-first Dynasty would prove themselves reused in some way or fashion. In lieu of such expensive analysis, suffice it to say that the reuse rate of over 65% was found despite incomplete access and non-sophisticated technology (my own eyes and a variety of flashlights), indicating that most Egyptians at this time period were engaged in coffin reuse and that this practice was socially accepted by those who could afford and commission coffins. Indeed, most elite Egyptians with disposable income were now actively participating in an activity traditionally seen as immoral – not because they wanted to but because there was no other choice.

Let us start examining patterns of coffin reuse diachronically (**Fig. 61**). If we assume that we can still organise coffins according to certain construction and style parameters, even taking into account the complications of reuse, we can assign a given coffin's decoration to a final use date, though certainly without the precision that has been previously been assumed (Cooney 2014, relying on van Walsem's comments on Niwiński's typology). According to my current thinking, coffins from this time period of heavy reuse should only be roughly dated to date ranges using key features such as arm position and modelling, wig shape, and collar length, allowing us to make some very broad date assignments and to track reuse according to those dates. This admittedly imprecise method is preferred to fitting particular coffins exactly into the reigns of specific High Priests or kings. Imprecise though this dating is, we still see a bell curve pattern: few if any reuse examples from the Nineteenth Dynasty, an explosion of reuse in the Twentieth Dynasty, even among very few coffin examples, a maintenance of the reuse percentage over 50% throughout the Twenty-first Dynasty, and then a tapering off of reuse through the early Twenty-second Dynasty. The fact remains that, in many instances, reuse can only be established with full access to a given coffin, like examining the coffin seams or looking inside the case, but despite such research inconsistencies, the trend remains statistically significant, because the Twentieth and Twenty-first Dynasties both show more than 50% reuse, while the Nineteenth Dynasty shows less than 10%, if that.

Indeed, the one documented case of coffin reuse, that of Katebet in the British Museum (Cooney 2007, 404; Budge 1924, 58, pl. VII; Edwards 1938, 35, pl. XII; Murray 1949, pl. XXVII; Dawson and Gray 1968, 28–29, pl. 146; Niwiński 1984, 462, n. 25; Niwiński 1988a, 150), may have happened after its original

Fig. 62: Coffin of Katebet (British Museum, EA 6665) shows gender modification from male to female, with repainting of the wig to create rectangular lappets rather than a tiered tripartite wig. Earrings and breasts were added in paint only. © Trustees of the British Museum

creation in the Nineteenth Dynasty (**Fig. 62**). The coffin shows an alteration from male to female, with repainting of the wig to create rectangular lappets rather than a tiered tripartite wig. Earrings and breasts were added in paint only. The coffin's central text column was probably altered during these updates as well. However, the hands remain fisted, as would be expected for a male; the tripartite wig is still clearly visible because the wood modelling was never changed. The mummy mask found inside the coffin does not match the coffin in style (it seems later in date), materials (including gilding and glass inlay), gender (it is female with flat hands wearing jewellery), but the mask nonetheless seems Ramesside in style. Thus perhaps with Katebet's coffin set we are dealing with a Twentieth Dynasty reuse of a Nineteenth Dynasty coffin, in which only a minimum of style adjustments were performed to the coffin in terms of remodelling and repainting.

One thing the Katebet coffin reuse establishes is that the Egyptians were ill-prepared for the demands that extensive and repeated coffin reuse would make on them, and we see many examples showing they did not understand how best to hide the reuse they were performing. For example, the coffin lid of Muthotep (Budge 1924, 57; Niwiński 1988a, 153; Cooney 2007, 464–466; Strudwick and Dawson 2014, 180–181), probably Twentieth Dynasty in date, reveals another, earlier layer of Nineteenth Dynasty decoration clearly visible underneath because the uppermost decoration layer has fallen away along the edges as the craftsman

Fig. 63: The inner coffin of Khnumensanapehsu (Ägyptisches Museum, Berlin ÄM 8505) shows evidence of gender modification from female to male, indicative of reuse. Here one can see male ears painted onto a female wig made into a man's wig. Photo by Neil Crawford

did not (care to) remove the varnished decoration layer before reworking and updating the coffin. For whatever reason and probably out of inexperience doing such reuse, the craftsman took a shortcut and applied new plastered decoration over a linen base, applied directly to the varnished surface, a tactic which was likely successful in the short term, maybe making it through the funeral and into the tomb, but which was unsuccessful in the longer term as the reuse is highly visible to museum visitors and researchers.

Other Twentieth Dynasty coffins show clear gender modification, much like the coffin of Katebet. The coffin **of** Nakht in Toronto, **for example, retains pierced ear** lobes, while the rest of the ear was added in plaster, a modification to change a female coffin, on which only pierced ear lobes are traditionally visible, into a male coffin, on which the entire ear is meant to show. The coffin of Nakht also shows unnaturally small fisted hands, probably because they were cut down from a different style, likely a flat female hand. Similarly the coffin of Khnumensanapehsu (PM V, 24; Barta 1968, 172; Erman 1894, 176; Roeder 1924, 444–454; Seeber 1976, 214, pl. 6; Niwiński 1988a, 109; van Walsem 2000; Cooney 2007, 462–464), also Twentieth Dynasty in date, currently in Berlin, shows another gender modification from male to female (**Fig. 63**). The ears were painted on the sides of the head, not even modified by plaster modelling, and like the Nakht coffin, tiny fisted masculine hands were carved out of the available wood, likely once female flat hands. It is interesting that the earliest examples of coffin reuse in the New Kingdom – Katebet, Nakht, and Khnumensanapehsu – show gender modification as it suggests that coffin reuse was happening in a legal context, within the family unit. Indeed, if the main means of acquiring reused coffins was through theft and the concomitant black market, then people would have purchased coffins of males or females as need drove them; but, if they were reusing

Fig. 64: The coffin of Sutymes (Louvre, N2609, N2610, N2611) is an example of a coffin set put together from multiple sources and shows last minute adjustments that cut through polychrome decoration. Photo by Kathlyn M. Cooney

the limited funerary materiality available to their own family group, then they were forced to change the gender of the body container depending on which relative died next, male or female.

Reuse of coffins of the early Twenty-first Dynasty shows a similar learning curve for the craftsmen forced into this new way of coffin creation for their clients. The coffin of Butehamun in Turin, for example, was clearly assembled opportunistically from a variety of sources – an outer coffin much larger in scale than the inner coffin and mummy board. Some of the pieces even seem to have been decorated at different points of time, with different styles, ostensibly by different craftsmen: the outer coffin betrays its own white background style, while the inner coffin and mummy board are decorated with a more complicated and dense scheme and varnished a darker yellow. We can assume that no fresh wood was available for Butehamun's outer coffin as it was crafted from an earlier Eighteenth Dynasty coffin, probably originally an Eighteenth Dynasty inner coffin (New Kingdom sets were much larger in scale), as evidenced by the remnants of thick black varnish underneath the Twenty-first Dynasty plastered decoration layer.[6] Much smaller coffins seem to have been commandeered for the inner coffin and mummy board, but the craftsmen had to fit them to one another nonetheless. Nested coffin walls are ideally meant to fit within centimetres of each other, but the coffin of Butehamun shows a massive gap between outer and inner coffins, but gaps too small between the mummified body, mummy board and inner coffin. Presumably, when the body was placed into the inner coffin and covered with the mummy board, the inner coffin lid would not close, demanding last minute wood modifications to the inner coffin. The deep scars left by this chiselling are clearly visible in

[6] This visual conclusion of mine was scientifically confirmed by Giovanna Prestipino and Alessia Amenta in their examination of this coffin. For more on Butehamun's coffin, see Cavillier 2017, 97–100; 576–577.

Fig. 65: This outer coffin of an anonymous woman (Museo Archeologico, Florence, Inv. 8524) shows a double reuse in which the previous decoration was removed except for one small fragment of the old striped headdress preserved at the back of the lid's head. Photo by Neil Crawford

the inner coffin, as it cut through the carefully applied polychrome decoration. Craftsmen and commissioners alike were obviously still learning how to adjust to using reused coffins in their commissions.

A similar coffin set is that of Sutymes in Paris (Niwiński 1988a, 166; Seeber 1976, 215; Vandier 1973, 102). Like Butehamun, it shows mismatched pieces, forced by craftsmen to fit together (**Fig. 64**). Like Butehamun, we see last minute adjustments that cut through polychrome decoration. It seems craftsmen were pulling coffins together from multiple sources but not fitting them carefully to each other before decorating each piece. It seems stunning that craftsmen capable of producing the decoration on the set of Sutymes were not able to check the fit of the set before beginning their decoration, but it likely indicates that many of the craftsmen responsible for coffin reuse were specialised draughtsmen with little understanding of carpentry. Indeed both the coffin sets of Butehamun and Sutymes suggest reuse by men specialised in plaster and painting, not in wood crafting.

As we move into the mid-Twentieth Dynasty, thus incorporating various coffin groups and caches, such as Bab el-Gasus and the Metropolitan Museum of Art Group, we see craftsmen becoming better able to deal with the demands that old coffins and old wood be used and redecorated, sometimes multiple times. In fact, wood modifications were now clearly done before most reuse decoration, avoiding last minute chiselling actions into decorated surfaces. For example, the anonymous coffin Florence 8524 (Niwiński 1988a, 139) shows a double reuse in which most of the previous decoration was removed except for one small fragment of the old striped headdress preserved at the back of the lid's head, visible underneath an added 1 cm plaster added when the piece was updated (**Fig. 65**). In other words, craftsmen had now learned to removed the old decoration. They had also learned to use plaster to fill gaps if they were opportunistically sourcing wood, as in taking a lid from one place, and a case from another and then crafting the wood of each piece to create a reasonable fit. In fact, the anonymous inner coffin in Florence (2155) was crafted from a case and lid that did not previously belong to one another. The lid was once a much larger piece, maybe an outer coffin. This lid was cut down on the sides so that it could fit the much smaller case. This very technique is probably why one starts to see another marker of coffin reuse during the mid-Twenty-first Dynasty, namely the lack of matching seams. Indeed if one was using an old case, then the stepped ledge of the case would ostensibly be retained, but if a new lid was cut down, then it seems the craftsmen were not interested in creating a new stepped ledge that would fit the box, instead making do with flat seams that simply sat upon the stepped case. These mismatched ledges are a key indicator of reuse, and they increase in frequency from the Twentieth Dynasty and into the Twenty-first Dynasty. By the time we reach the late Twenty-first Dynasty and early Twenty-second Dynasty, craftsmen are producing coffins with flat, matching seams, particularly for the stola group.

By the mid-Twenty-first Dynasty another key pattern becomes clear, especially in the Bab el-Gasus cache, but not restricted to it: varnished blank spaces for personal names (**Fig. 66**). To varnish over a blank text column is to imply that the area was never meant to be filled in with a new name, at least not permanently, even after careful wood, plaster and paint modifications may have been undertaken to update a given coffin's style. This feature, more than anything else, suggests a very short term use of these body containers, so short term that it might have been preferred to paint a name over the varnish, a slick surface from which it was quite easy to remove the name later with a damp cloth when the coffin was needed again. How long such a turn around would be is unknown, but by the mid-Twenty-first Dynasty, ancient Egyptians seem to have been happy to be buried in coffins that had no long term, permanently inscribed (i.e. under the varnish), painted name at all. Indeed, this is why so many coffins in the dataset are categorised as "anonymous."

In other instances, the craftsmen were reusing a coffin that demanded more wood modification than he had time or payment to do, causing him to retain old Ramesside wood modelling in a newly decorated Twenty-first Dynasty piece. For example, the anonymous coffin Turin 2228 used to be seen as an archaising style coffin (Niwiński 1988a, 139), when it is actually a reused coffin repainted and updated with mid-Twenty-first Dynasty decoration. No old decoration layers are visible, suggesting that the craftsmen did indeed know by this point to chisel and scrub this layer away, but they did not modify the body undulations or the unusual arm position, both of which were typical of a much older Nineteenth Dynasty style, as seen in the coffin lid of Iset in Cairo, for example (Maspero 1887, 204; Toda and Daressy 1920; Vernier 1911, 18, pl. 2; Hayes 1959, 414, 416; Desroches-Noblecourt 1976, 170–171,

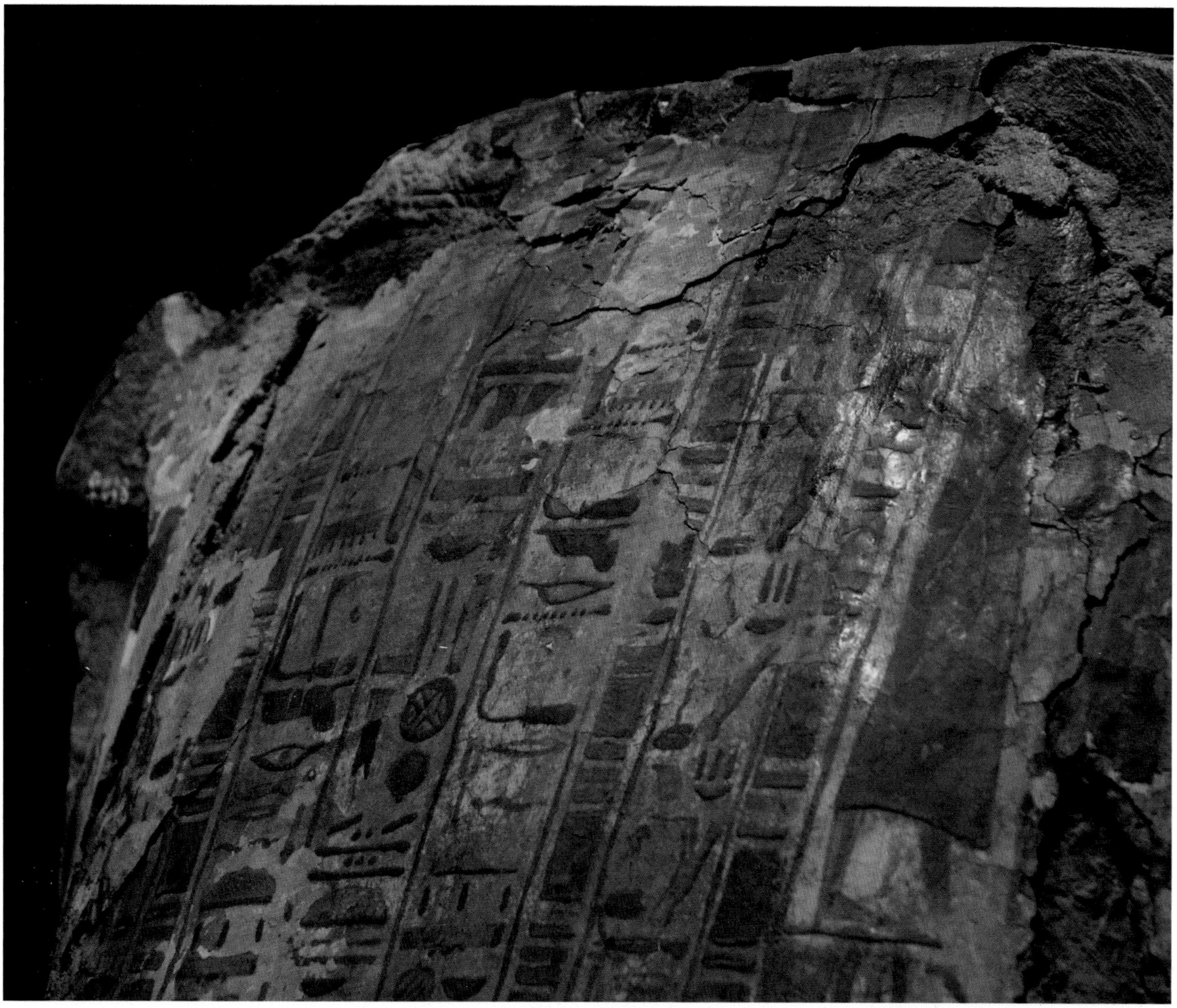

Fig. 66: Outer coffin of an anonymous individual (Museo Archeologico, Florence, Inv. 8525). In the mid 21st Dynasty a key pattern of reuse becomes clear, especially in the Bab el-Gasus cache, but not restricted to it: varnished blank spaces or names. Photo by Neil Crawford

pl. 37; Niwiński 1988a, 118; Tiradritti 1999, 272). Gender modifications were still common in the mid-Twenty-first Dynasty, as evidenced by the anonymous coffin in Paris, Louvre AF 9593 (Niwiński 1988a, 167), modified from a female body container for a Mistress of the House and Chantress of Amen for a man (both female titles were retained along the side seam of the lid, and the new masculine name was never filled in). Here in the mid-Twenty-first Dynasty, we see the skill set the reusing draftsman was now able to apply. The hands and breasts were removed, a new pectoral added; if it were not for the half moon outlines of the breasts, these modifications would be practically invisible to the eye as the reusing draughtsmen relied on the same red and yellow ochre, the same carbon black, Egyptian blue, and manufactured green as the previous decoration layer, blending new painting in with the old around the collar and upper body. This Louvre coffin proves that by the Twenty-first Dynasty, decoration changes could and did include the previous decoration layer, seamlessly updating it with similar styles so that the new paint layers are hardly visible.

Indeed, the anonymous coffin of Turin 2221 (Niwiński 1988a, 171) shows us how much the craft of reuse had improved from the poorly done reuse of the Twentieth and early Twenty-first Dynasties (**Fig. 67**). Turin 2221 is a complicated coffin with evidence of multiple uses and reuses. Both the case and lid show

Fig. 67: Inner coffin of Tamutmutef (Museo Egizio, Turin, Inv. 2228). Craftsmen did not modify the bodily undulations or the arm position of this coffin, both of which are typical of a much older Nineteenth Dynasty style. Such indicators of multiple reuse as well as decorative reuse and a blank space for a name suggest reuse rather than archaisation. Photo by Remy Hiramoto

multiple layers on the surface. The case interior reveals a previously painted plaster layer underneath the current painted plaster. The wood on the case interior was also chiselled down, ostensibly to make more space for a mummy board (although no mummy board was brought to Turin with the set), suggesting another previous use. The case once had stepped ledges, but they were chiselled down and made flat, only to be made stepped again with a plaster addition. The mortises are thus too close to the coffin interior, as the width of the case sides was originally wider. The lid of Turin 2221 has flat seams and shows two decorative uses, including a gender change. It does not seem that lid and case were originally crafted together. Indeed, it is possible that the case was older as it has at least two previous uses before the exterior decoration was added. The lid shows just two decoration levels – the yellow of the lower body, and the later gender change which included wig, collar, hands and embellishments on the lower body. The text at the feet ends with Osiris, but the craftsmen never added the name, instead varnishing over a blank space in the text.[7]

Multiple reuses are also visible on the mid-Twenty-first Dynasty coffin of Nany in the Metropolitan Museum of Art (Niwiński 1988a, 161), but they are harder to spot. A divot at the top of the case shows wood modification, but instead of plastering over the damage, the carpenter left the area unfinished, and the draftsman decided to just paint his decoration directly into the dent. Second, there is a clear name reuse on this piece, in which none of the decoration was changed; the name was changed from a certain Ta(net)Behnet, probably the mother of Nany, and reinscribed for Nany. Obviously, sometimes

[7] I would like to thank conservator Elsbeth Geldhof for confirming these reuse layers on this complicated piece.

it was believed that no decorative updates at all were required, just a change in the name.

As we leave the Twenty-first Dynasty behind, reuse becomes harder and harder to spot, so skilled do the carpenters and draughtsmen get at performing it better. Indeed the stola coffins of the late Twenty-first Dynasty and early Twenty-second Dynasty suggest that the Egyptians were also able to abandon reuse as new wood sources became available. Very few stola coffins have shown evidence of anything beyond name reuse. I have never identified another layer of decoration or wood modification on a stola coffin. I should not expect to find any, perhaps, as Renee van Walsem has proven that stola coffins were, overall, longer and narrower than the typical Twenty-first Dynasty coffin (van Walsem 1997), indicating that if stola coffins were reused, they were made of broken down reused wood, not of entire body containers. To test this theory, I ran a series of Carbon 14 dates on the stola coffin in private collection now on display in the Houston Museum of Natural Science. The case seems to have been made of reused wood; indeed the four case wood samples show calibrated dates between 1393 and 931 BC, while the four samples from the lid range from 998–822 BC. The one tenon sample of 877–811 BC is the youngest date. Clearly, as Egypt moved into the Twenty-second Dynasty, new wood was available for the first time in larger amounts, either through regularised cultivation of native wood species or from trade, or both, allowing coffins made with new, fresh pieces. By the early Twenty-second Dynasty, reuse was not as common, at least not for the elite who could afford the special stola variety.

Reuse patterns through time follow a bell curve pattern, increasing in the Twentieth Dynasty and decreasing in the Twenty-second Dynasty. Reuse patterns within caches show different patterns, because many of these caches cover a broader span of time. The Bab el-Gasus cache dates from the Twenty-first to early Twenty-second Dynasties and displays a variety of reuse actions and patterns; in this cache, overall reuse is quite high, while gender modification is significant. The Royal Cache from Deir el-Bahari 320 also shows a broad span of time, the highest rate of reuse at a remarkable 100% (probably because of my complete access to all sides of a given coffin and to almost every interior), but in this cache, gender modification is practically non-existent (**Fig. 68**). In other words, the family-driven reuse of the Bab el-Gasus cache drove gender modification as coffin sets were, ostensibly, reused within family units, while the

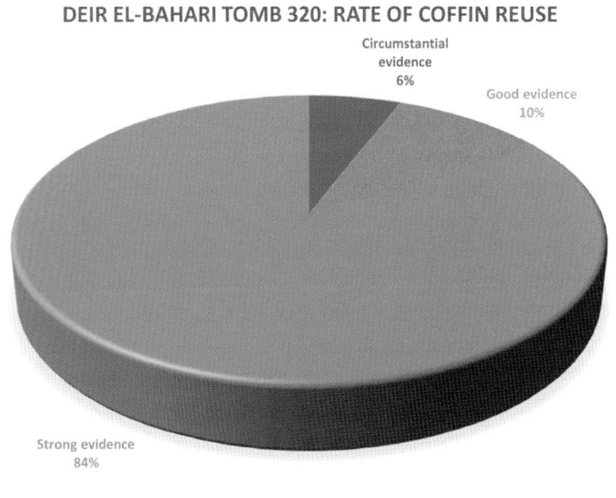

Fig. 68: The Royal Cache from Deir el-Bahari (TT320): rate of coffin reuse

Royal Cache was not reliant on coffins from previous family generations, but from a wider source area than the family unit, including even royal coffins from the Valley of the Kings, as Pinedjem I was buried in the reused coffin of Thutmose I (Daressy 1909, Pl. XVIII). Only the cache of the stola coffins, assuming there was once such a cache opened in Luxor in the early 19th Century, shows a decrease in such coffin reuse. All the other caches or groups – Bab el-Gasus, Royal Cache, or the Metropolitan Museum of Art Group – display high rates of reuse in comparison in keeping with their earlier dates.

Typology conclusions, economic conclusions, caching behaviour

Returning the question raised at the beginning of this discussion, we can ask again: what did it mean to own a coffin? How did the Egyptians conceive of ownership of a body container that was reclaimed and remade from those pieces of the ancestors? Indeed, why were so many of these pieces eventually buried and not pulled out of the tomb to be used again, especially when so many of them still retained blank name spaces, varnished over and ready for another inscription? (**Table 2**)

The behaviour of coffin caching is the final layer of this discussion. Indeed, caching marks the moment when a coffin was no longer easily fashioned into something else, when current coffin styles had shifted so irrevocably into something so new that it became difficult to use the old body containers to make them. Caching also marks the moment when freshly cut wood becomes

Table 2: Rate of reuse for coffin groups analysed thus far

Provenance	Coffins	No reuse	Circumstantial evidence for reuse	Good evidence for reuse	Strong evidence for reuse	To be decided	Reuse %
Bab el-Gasus, Deir el-Bahari, Thebes	69	11	20	6	32	0	84.06%
MMA Tombs 59, 60, 358 & Pit 1016	18	4	2	0	12	4	77.78%
Royal Cache, Deir el-Bahri 320	31	0	3	3	25		100%
Totals	**118**	**15**	**25**	**9**	**69**	**4**	**87.29%**
Totals for reuse with high confidence				**9**	**69**		**66.10%**

Period	Coffins	No reuse	Circumstantial evidence for reuse	Good evidence for reuse	Strong evidence for reuse	To be decided	Reuse %
19th Dynasty	58	57	1	0	0	0	1.72%
20th Dynasty	41	15	7	4	15	0	63.41%
21st Dynasty	188	45	36	18	81	8	71.81%
Late 21st Dynasty–Early 22nd Dynasty	45	23	10	1	11	0	48.89%
Totals	**332**	**140**	**54**	**23**	**107**	**8**	**46.5%**
Totals for reuse with high confidence				**23**	**107**		**39.16%**

available on the market again, cutting down the demand that old wooden containers be broken down for scrap wood. Every single cache, including both the first and second Deir el-Bahari caches, have early Twenty-second Dynasty coffin examples in them as the latest objects in terms of style, indicating the date of final deposit. After this time, not only did the use of these cache deposits stop, but coffin styles changed so much that the coffins within these caches were ostensibly less economically useful to families and to craftsmen, especially with so much new wood flooding the market.

When pressed with scarcity, the Egyptians decided, *en masse*, as a culture, certainly according to reuse percentages of over 60% for the coffins examined thus far from the Twentieth to Twenty-first Dynasties, to use funerary objects short term as transformative devices, rather than as long term objects to be owned in perpetuity by one man or woman. Long term funerary ownership was expensive, both in materials and in labour for security. When old social systems broke down, the Egyptian moral system of funerary production changed with it. But when prosperity returned, elite Egyptians who could afford a coffin closed down the old family tombs and caches, unneeded and forgotten, dispensing with the repeated reuse of all those older body containers. This is why most of the coffins in these caches are later examples and why so few of them date to the earlier Twenty-first Dynasty. Reuse had occurred unabated within these social units until the practice became unnecessary in the Twenty-second Dynasty, as political and economic systems began to heal.

In the early Twenty-second Dynasty, coffin styles changed so drastically for a variety of reasons. First, political pressures foisted a northern style upon a Theban population who likely lost much of their influence in the shift of power over the High Priesthood of Amen. Second, none of the elites wanted to look like they were engaging in coffin reuse any longer. The characteristics of the new northern style imported into Thebes include unpainted bare wood, ostensibly to display prestigious woods with fine grains, a means of broadcasting that eternal ownership was again prized by the Theban elite.[8]

[8] John Taylor has argued convincingly that the Twenty-second Dynasty coffin type was an import into Thebes (Taylor 2009, 378–379).

Cartonnages with painted and moulded decoration from the Twenty-second Dynasty

Fruzsina Bartos

In the most recent seasons, the excavation of the spoil heap on the north-east hill-side of Sheikh Abd el-Qurna in the surroundings of TT 65 has produced some fragments of an interesting and uncommon type of cartonnage. The special interest of these fragments derives from the manner of their decoration. Based on the small number of this type of cartonnage, it might be reasonable to assume that they were made by the same workshop. Their provenance – if we accept that all of them are from Thebes – and the similarities in their designs may also support this assumption.

The excavation of the spoil heap in the surroundings of TT 65 in Sheikh Abd el-Qurna at Thebes has produced some fragments of an interesting and uncommon type of cartonnage. The special interest of these cartonnage fragments derives from the manner of their decoration. A plastically modelled surface has been enhanced by a painted design on the front of the cartonnage, while the back and the head have only the usual painted decoration. The blank spaces between the motifs on the frontal part are sunk approximately 1–2 mm into the white plaster coating, in which the designs are also moulded. The hieroglyphic signs of the central offering formula are also sunk into the surface. After this plastically modelled layer was formed, the whole surface of the cartonnage was covered with painted polychrome decoration. The entire frontal surface may have been varnished, judging by the remains of resin.

The aim of this paper is to specify the date of origin of these fragments comparing them with cartonnages with a parallel design. I know at present five examples of complete cartonnage cases on which painted and modelled decoration is combined:[1]

- the cartonnage of Padimut (Harvard Semitic Museum 1901.9.1; Farell, Snow and Vinogradskaya 2006; Hollis 1987) (**Fig. 69, left**),
- the cartonnage of Nakhtefmut (Fitzwilliam Museum E.64.1896; Quibell 1898, 10–11; Vassilika 1995, 42; Strudwick and Dawson 2016, 198–200) (**Fig. 70**),
- the cartonnage of Tjentdinebu (National Museum of Ireland 1881.2228) (**Fig. 69, right**),
- the cartonnage of Panehsy (Rijksmuseum van Oudheden AMM 17-e) (**Fig. 71**),
- the cartonnage of Ankhhor (Norwich Castle Museum and Art Gallery 196.928; Dawson 1929, 189–190, pl. XXXVII) (**Fig. 72**).

As for the workmanship, although they form an uncommon type, their decorative pattern follows the usual iconographic designs of Twenty-second Dynasty cartonnages (Aston 2009, 279–285; Elias 1993, 395–417; Taylor 2001b, 172–173; Taylor 2003, 104–107). Since the majority of these examples cannot be dated certainly on the basis of external evidence, it was necessary to establish a hypothetical chronological order among them. Detailed analysis and comparison of iconographical details on these cartonnages formed the only point of reference for placing the excavated fragments into this sequence.

Two of the five cartonnages can be firmly dated and

[1] A small fragment of the same type of cartonnage is kept in the Fitzwilliam Museum (E.GA.2891.1943), and some other fragments were discovered by the Hungarian excavation led by Dr Gábor Schreiber in TT -400- at el-Khokha.

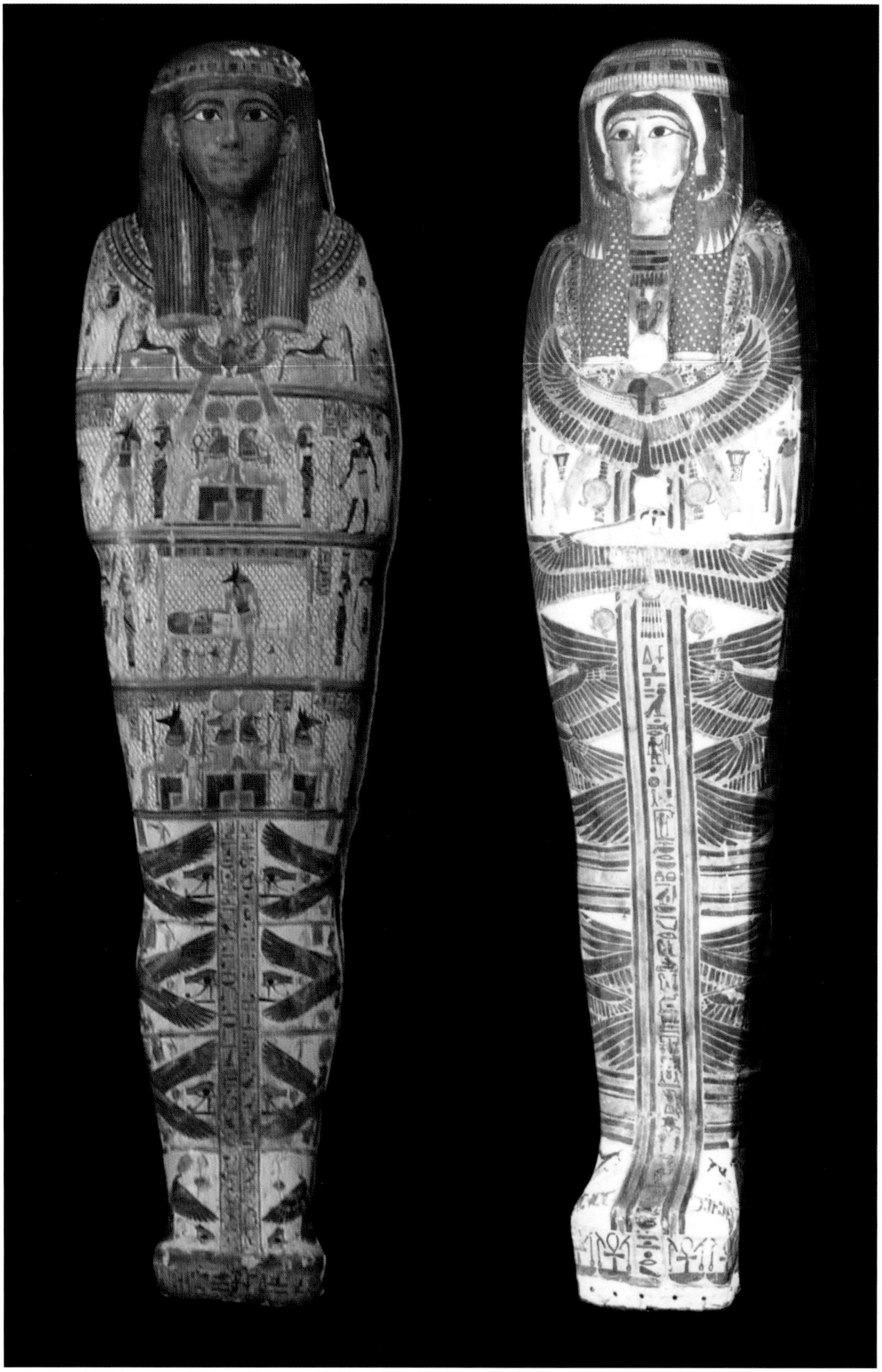

Fig. 69: left: cartonnage of Padimut, Inv. No. 1901.9.1 (© Harvard Semitic Museum); right: cartonnage of Tjentdinebu, Inv. No. 1881.2228 (© National Museum of Ireland)

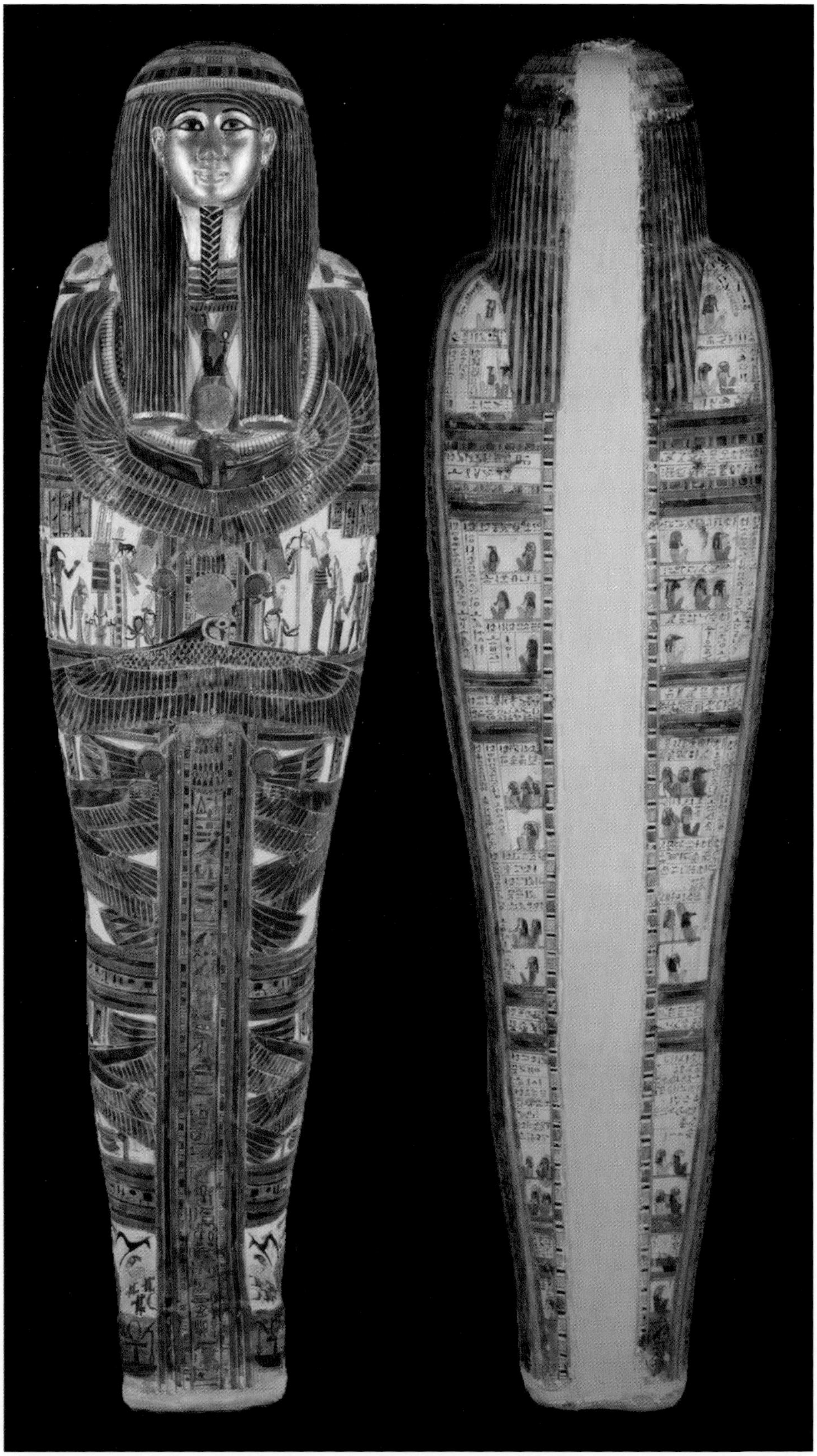

Fig. 70: Cartonnage of Nakhtefmut, Inv. No. E.64.1896 (© The Fitzwilliam Museum)

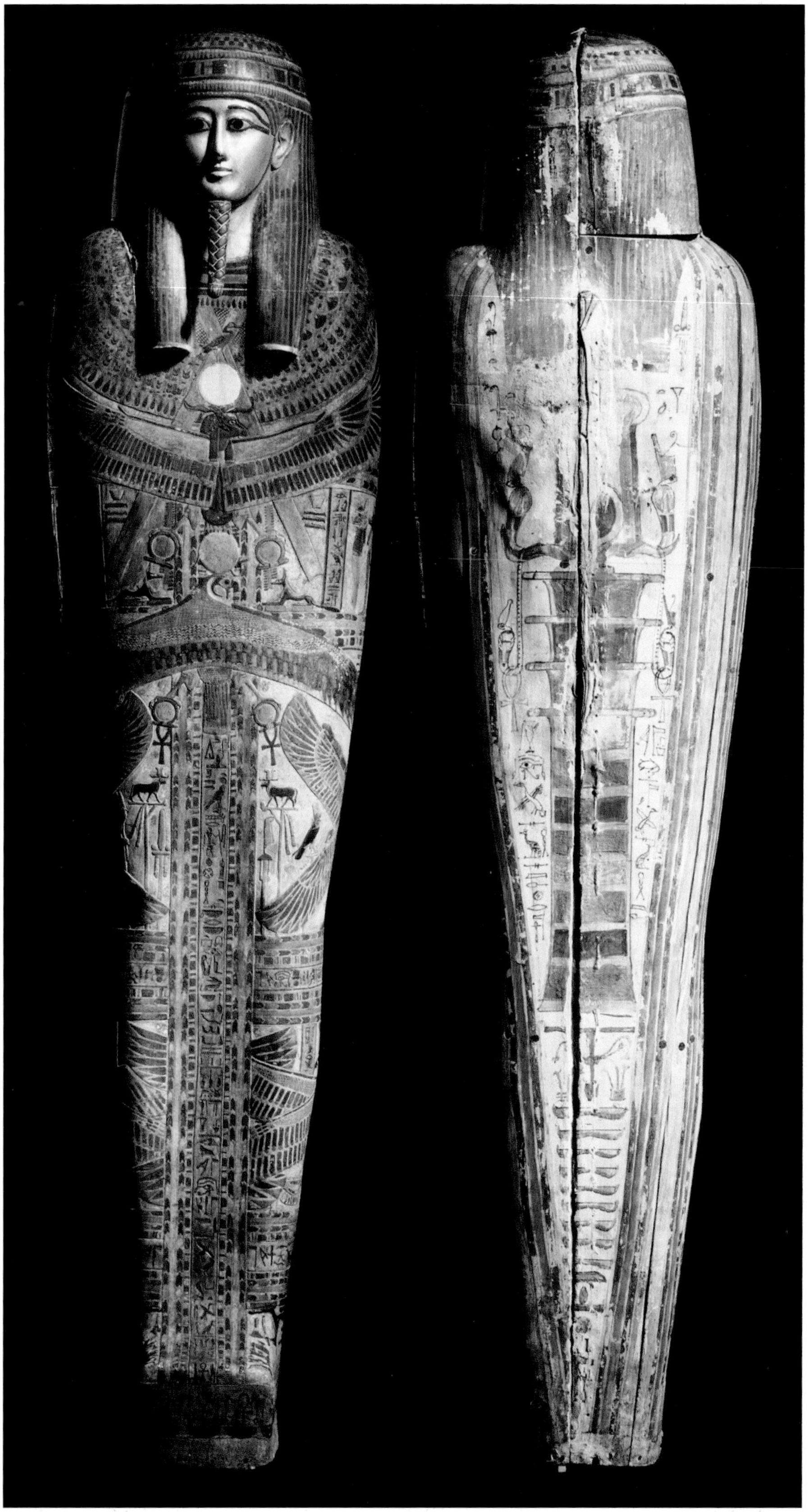

Fig. 71: Cartonnage of Panehsy, Inv. No. AMM 17-e (© Rijksmuseum van Oudheden)

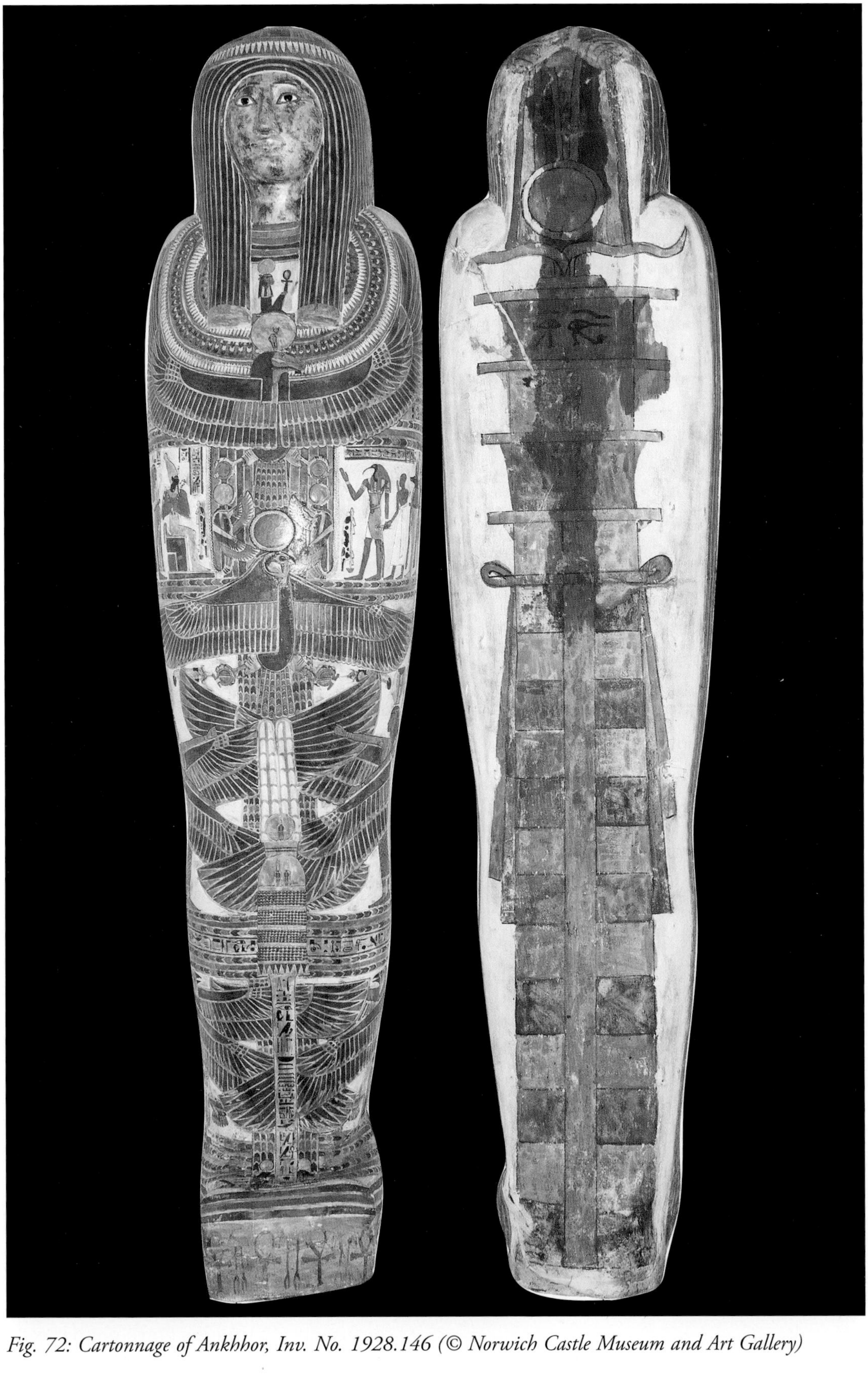

Fig. 72: Cartonnage of Ankhhor, Inv. No. 1928.146 (© Norwich Castle Museum and Art Gallery)

their provenance is known. One of them is the cartonnage of Padimut (Fig. 1 at left), who was a *wab*-priest and metal engraver of Amun-Re. This cartonnage was found by Th. M. Davies and P. E. Newberry in 1901 in a wooden coffin inside a large wooden sarcophagus in Sheikh Abd el-Qurna (Farell, Snow and Vinogradskaya 2006, 2; Hollis 1987, 165–166). The cartonnage was cut in half longitudinally when it was opened in the same year. It contained among other things a pair of leather bands crossing over the chest of the mummy, stamped with the name of Sheshonq I (*c.* 945–925 BC) which gives us the date of the burial.

This is the earliest among the examples, not only because of its certain date but according to its iconographic design as well. In this regard, this is the only one which differs from the others. While the other four cartonnages have a two-falcon motif (Aston 2009, 281; Taylor 2003, 105), on that of Padimut the scenes are arranged in registers horizontally on the upper body and divided axially by a double column of inscription on the legs. This design is typical in the earlier part of the Twenty-second Dynasty (Aston 2009, 281; Taylor 2003, 105).

Padimut wears a collar that consists of four rows of flowers. Over the collar, a red stola and a winged scarab can be seen on his chest. Below the collar there are four registers with white background.

In the first register, on the proper left side, Re is shown seated on a throne, with four cowering figures under it. A mummiform figure stands in front supporting a balance. On the proper right side there is an adoration scene, with the deceased standing in front of the seated deified Amenhotep I.

In the second register, two hawk-headed gods are shown sitting in the centre with figures of Hathor in front of them. On the proper left, Anubis brings forward the justified deceased to present him to the gods. On the proper right the gods observe the weighing of the heart.

The third register shows a scene of the mummy on a bier: Anubis is in his shrine, standing next to the mummy, Isis and Nephthys are on the proper right and proper left side of the shrine respectively. Behind the goddesses there is a nome standard with a recumbent jackal on the top and with the adoring deceased under it.

In the fourth register Thoth and Re are seated in the middle with two anthropomorphic figures of Anubis seated in front of them. On each side the deceased adores these gods.

On the lower part of the case four more registers can be found. They are divided axially by a double column inscription, the two *ḥtp-di-nsw-t* formulae reveal the offices of Padimut, namely wab-priest and metal engraver of Amun-Re, and mention his mother, Ankheseniset and his father, Nespaher(en)tahat(?). The registers on the two sides of the inscriptions are nearly identical. Each of them contains a bird facing centre, with a Sn-ring and a *wḏꜣt*-eye between their spread wings.

On the back of the cartonnage a large figure of Amenhotep I can be seen with two offering formulae, addressed to the deified king himself on the left side and to his mother, Aahmes-Nefertary on the right side. On the footboard is another figure of Amenhotep I, seated on a throne, with an *imiwt*-fetish in front of him. A single line of inscription runs along the front and the sides of the foot-case, starting from the centre towards left and right.

The other cartonnage that can be securely dated is that of Nakhtefmut (Fitzwilliam Museum E.64.1896) (**Fig. 70**), a priest of Amun. It was found by J. E. Quibell in the Ramesseum in 1896, enclosed within three wooden coffins (Quibell 1898, 10–11). The mummy was removed by the excavators. Among other things, a leather *menat* counterweight was found, stamped with the cartouche of Osorkon I (*c.* 925–890 BC). The inscription of year 33 on the mummy bandage serves as terminus post quem for the burial at the very beginning of the 9th century BC.

Nakhtefmut is the second in the chronology. The iconographic details that correspond to this early 9th century BC date are his simple collar, consisting of one row of petals, and the curve of the wings of the ram-headed bird, which follows the edge of the collar up to the shoulders (Aston 2009, 281; Elias 1993, 400). In addition, the metope and the simple red-green-red bands around the inscriptions also support this early date (Aston 2009, 281; Elias 1993, 400). The red stola lies on his chest with the figure of Maat at its crossing-point. On the top of his head a plastically modelled scarab can be seen.

The layout of the decoration on the front of the case shows features typical of the two-falcons design (Aston 2009, 281–283; Taylor 2003, 106). The main motifs are:

- the two solar falcons, one ram-headed and one falcon-headed on the upper body, both of them with gilded sun disks on their heads and holding Sn-rings in their claws;
- the inscription running down on the legs and dividing, axially, the lower part of the field;

- and the pairs of winged goddesses and falcons in the compartments on each side of the inscription.

The space between the ram-headed and the falcon-headed bird is usually occupied by figures of the Sons of Horus or other deities and representations or personifications of certain places (Aston 2009, 281; Elias 1993, 401–402; Taylor 2003, 106). Here on the proper right side, Thoth stands in front of an Abydos fetish with two of the Sons of Horus, Imsety and Qebehsenuef, while on the proper left side Horus pours a libation for Osiris with the other two Sons of Horus, Hapi and Duamutef, behind him.

Under the tail of the falcon-headed bird a column of inscription starts. The *ḥtp-di-nsw-t* formula names Nakhtefmut as the Fourth Prophet of Amun, son of Nesperneb. On each side of the inscription there are three pairs of compartments: two on the legs and one on the feet. On the legs, in the upper compartments are winged figures of Isis and Nephthys, while in the lower ones their manifestation as *ḏrti*-falcons can be seen (Aston 2009, 281; Elias 1993, 402; Taylor 2003, 106). The wings of the goddesses as well as those of the falcons cross each other behind the inscription. The compartments on the feet contain two jackals standing on a standard, identified as Wepwawet. Between the compartments *imȝḫy-ḫr* formulae run horizontally from the centre towards the sides. The pedestal-like foot-case is decorated with a repeated *ꜥnḫ-nb-wȝs* motif, which is intersected in the middle by the inscription running down as far as the bottom of the case.

As for the back of the cartonnage, there is a wide re-plastered section in the middle, which was probably damaged when the mummy was removed. Both sides of this area, where once the central motif was placed, is divided into small compartments decorated with figures of deities and with the text of the Negative Confession (Elias 1993, 324–327, especially for the cartonnage of Nakhtefmut see 327, n. 10, 350, 373–374).

The provenance of the three other cartonnages, those of Tjentdinebu, Panehsy and Ankhhor, is not recorded but they are believed to be from Thebes. Because they cannot be dated by external evidence and their decoration is so similar, study of the iconographic design as a whole does not provide us with sufficient data to establish a relative chronology among them. Therefore, the main aspect of the examination has to be the presence or absence of characteristic and variable attributes of the design. Accordingly, I have focussed on the following attributes:

- the collar, which becomes wider, more complex, and spreads more and more over the shoulders towards the end of the Twenty-second Dynasty (Elias 1993, 400–404);
- the wings of the ram-headed bird, which usually follow the edge of the widened collar or, if not, partly cover it (Aston 2009, 281–283; Elias 1993, 400–404; Taylor 2003, 106);
- the opening out of the wings of the falcon-headed bird in the middle making its body widely visible; this is a feature of the late Twenty-second Dynasty, approximately during the 8th century BC (Aston 2009, 285; Elias 1993, 408);
- the appearance of a ram figure on standard between the wings of Isis and Nephthys, which is the emblem of the *ba* spirit of Osiris: it is closely associated with the Abydos fetish and also serves as a sort of substitute for it. It is frequently present, usually together with a small fetish at the beginning of the central inscription, during the early to middle of the 9th century BC (Aston 2009, 283; Elias 1993, 402);
- the large Abydos fetish involving the central inscription line, which becomes dominant during the 8th century BC (Aston 2009, 283; Elias 1993, 404–405; Taylor 2003, 106);
- the complexity of the decorative stripes around the inscriptions: next to the simple metope bands and red-green-red bordering stripes, the single and two-parted chevron bands appear in the first half of the Twenty-second Dynasty, while the tripartite chevron bands appear only around the late 9th century BC (Aston 2009, 281–285; Elias 1993, 402–403, 405–406);
- the depiction of the Apis bull on the footboard alone or with the deceased on its back: the bull is usually represented alone but when it is depicted with the deceased it may suggest a later date, perhaps rather early in the 8th century.[2]

As I observed, there seem to be some further characteristic attributes which change or disappear during the Twenty-second Dynasty, although I cannot specify a closer date in these cases:

- the stola, which is usually present in the early Twenty-second Dynasty but disappears after a while;

[2] The Apis with the deceased mainly occurs on coffins from the Twenty-fifth to Twenty-sixth Dynasties but examples already appear on some cartonnages as well (Taylor 2003, 106, n. 115). However, according to Elias (personal communication), the appearance of the deceased on the back of the Apis bull does not indicate any dating criteria.

- the different colouration of the sun-disks of the ram-headed bird, which is gilded, and the falcon-headed bird, which is painted red, as well as the depiction of a uraeus inside one or both of them: this feature seems to be connected with the appearance of the large Abydos fetish in the centre;
- the covering, or otherwise, of the tail of the ram-headed bird: the tail is usually covered when the sun-disk of the falcon-headed bird is gilded and revealed when it is painted red, so in some respect it may also be connected with the presence of the large Abydos fetish;
- and finally, the extension of the central inscription to the bottom of the foot-case, intersecting the *ꜥnḫ-nb-wꜣs* motifs. This seems to be a characteristic of the first half of the Twenty-second Dynasty, as well as the only special iconographic feature of this type of cartonnages because I have not seen this on any other cases.

According to these criteria, the cartonnage of Tjentdinebu remains third in the chronology (purchased from a dealer in Dublin in 1881) (**Fig. 69, right**). Tjentdinebu is the only woman among the owners of these cartonnages. Small rosettes have been added to the other floral motifs on her collar. It overspreads the shoulders and is partly covered by the wings of the ram-headed bird. This feature dates Tjentdinebu to slightly later than Nakhtefmut, probably to the middle of the Twenty-second Dynasty, around the middle of the 9th century BC.[3] The compartments between the two birds are occupied by Hapi and Duamutef on the proper left side, with the shrine of Buto behind them, and Imsety and Qebehsenuef on the proper right side, with the shrine of Nekhen behind them. The appearance of the two shrines is a characteristic feature of the early to middle 9th century cartonnages, which also supports the date above (Aston 2009, 281; Elias 1993, 401–402). The wings of the falcon-headed bird are opened out in the middle, although not significantly. The decorative bands around the inscriptions are still simple. The *ḥtp-dỉ-nswt* formula, which extends down to the foot-case, informs us that Tjentdinebu was a sistrum player of Amun-Re. The cartonnage seems to be unfinished, as the horizontal bands for the *ỉmꜣḫy-ḫr* formulae and the small columns above the Sons of Horus are left blank.

As regards the decoration of the top of the head, the back and the bottom, I do not have any information.

The next one is the cartonnage of Panehsy (**Fig. 3**), the prophet of Amun, which shows more minor variations in the design. The collar is wider, covers the shoulders and consists of lotus flowers, buds and other floral motifs. The size and complexity of the collar, as well as the moderate curve of the wings of the ram-headed bird, suggest a date later in the Twenty-second Dynasty, perhaps during the second half of the 9th to first half of the 8th century BC.[4] At the crossing-point of the stola the figure of Maat is replaced with that of a benu-bird. In the compartments under the ram-headed bird, Hapi and Duamutef are depicted on the proper left side and Imsety and Qebehsenuef on the proper right side. The design of the wings of the falcon-headed bird, however, differs from all of the other cases, even from the wings of the ram-headed bird above it. Instead of the dark green outer feathers and the light green innermost feathers, these two colours alternate on the feathers, and plumes are imitated in black and white above them. Even the tail of the bird is different: it consists of vertical stripes in contrast with the chevron-band design of the others. Under the bird, the wings of Isis and Nephthys do not cross each other but flank a ram figure on a standard, the appearance of which indicates a date during the early to middle of the 9th century BC (Aston 2009, 283; Elias 1993, 402). The decorative bands around the inscriptional fields show not only the metope band and red-green stripes but parted chevron ribbons as well (Aston 2009, 285; Elias 1993, 402–403). The column containing the *ḥtp-dỉ-nswt* formula finishes above the foot-case and does not intersect the *ꜥnḫ-nb-wꜣs* motifs. On the bottom of the case an Apis bull is depicted carrying the deceased on his back. This latter somewhat contradicts the dates mentioned above because this depiction did not seem to appear much earlier than the 8th century BC (see above note 2). In this case we should consider that this is an early example of the depiction of the Apis bull with the deceased and a late one of the ram figure on standard. Accordingly, a middle or late 9th century BC date might accord with the cartonnage, in

[3] Taylor suggests an early Twenty-second Dynasty date on the basis of the type of unguent cones represented on the cartonnage (Taylor 2003, 106, n. 104).

[4] According to the shawl-like pectorals on the coffins, Elias dates the cartonnage of Panehsy to the first half of the 9th century BC (Elias 1993, 404, n. 8). Taylor suggests an early Twenty-second Dynasty date, based on the same iconographic attribute as in the case of the cartonnage of Tjentdinebu, see above n. 23. Considering the stylistic features of both the coffins and the cartonnage, a middle or late 9th century date of origin might be suggested.

view of the fact that all the iconographical criteria more or less fit in this time interval. As for the decoration of the back, a *djed* pillar dominates the field with short text lines around it. On the top of the head a scarab can be seen.

The last one in order is the cartonnage of Ankhhor (**Fig.** 72) which also shows new features in the design. There is still a scarab on the top of the head but the stola is missing. Between the two birds on the upper body, Hapi and Duamutef are shown on the proper left side, with Thoth leading the deceased forward to present him to Osiris, who is seated on the proper right side in front of Imsety and Qebehsenuef. Interestingly, but not unusually, the names of Hapi and Qebehsenuef are confused in the labels above the figures. A uraeus appears inside the sun-disk of the ram-headed bird, and the sun-disk of the falcon-headed bird is not gilded but painted red with a yellow borderline. These features together with the presence of the tail of the ram-headed bird and the absence of the stola indicate a later date, sometime during the 8th century BC. The wings of the falcon-headed bird open out significantly, which tendency starts around the beginning of the 8th century BC (Aston 2009, 285; Elias 1993, 407–408). The wings of Isis and Nephthys under the falcon cross each other again, now behind a large Abydos fetish involving the central inscription line, a characteristic feature of the 8th century BC (Aston 2009, 283; Elias 1993, 404–405; Taylor 2003, 106). The *ḥtp-di͗-nsw·t* formula, which ends above the foot-case, tells us that Ankhhor was a god's father of Amun and a wab-priest with free entry into Karnak, and his father was Bes. The signs of the inscriptions are only painted in black, while on the other examples they are carved into the plaster, as well as painted. Tripartite chevron bands, which appear in the late 9th century BC (Aston 2009, 285; Elias 1993, 406), flank the Abydos fetish and the central inscription but not the horizontal *i͗mꜣḫy-ḫr* formulae or the figural scenes on the sides. The decorative motif running round the foot-case consists of only *ꜥnḫ-wꜣs* symbols; the nb signs are missing. The back of the cartonnage is decorated with a large *djed*-pillar which occupies the whole field. The footboard depicts a galloping Apis bull.

In this case, the middle coffin of Ankhhor also helps us to specify the date. Its decoration, the scene of the weighing of the heart on the chest, and the text of the Negative Confession below it on the legs, is a typical design during the late Twenty-second to early Twenty-fifth Dynasty, around the second half of the 8th century BC (Taylor 2003, 108).

And how do the fragments from the excavation fit in this chronological order? I use the drawing of Nakhtefmut, published by Quibell (Quibell 1989, pl. 16), as a template, to allocate the original location of the fragments (**Fig.** 73). Besides the head part, most of the fragments belong to the front surface of the cartonnage. The following attributes can be recognised on them:

- the feathers and the leg of the ram-headed bird;
- the stola;
- one of the sons of Horus, namely Qebehsenuef and a part of the shrine of Nekhen;
- the head of the falcon-headed bird with a red sun-disk, both ends and the middle part of its wings, and one of its claws;
- the wings of Isis crossing the wings of Nephthys;
- parts of a large Abydos fetish and the beginning of the central inscription;
- parts of the *ꜥnḫ-nb-wꜣs* motifs on the foot-case, intersecting at the end of the central inscription;
- and finally, the proper right side part of the foot-case where Wepwawet was originally depicted standing on a standard, but only the pole of the standard can be recognised and parts of its horizontal elements with red dots on a white background.

There is also a large fragment from the back of the cartonnage, on which part of a large *djed* pillar can be identified.

Although there are only a few characteristic attributes on the fragments, the simple red-green-red decorative bands between the scenes and the intersection of the *ꜥnḫ-nb-wꜣs* motifs by the central inscription suggest an earlier Twenty-second Dynasty date, but the presence of the large Abydos fetish in the axis and the red colouration of the sun-disk on the falcon-headed bird widen the date to the 8th century BC. According to these I would put the manufacture of this cartonnage somewhere between those of Tjentdinebu and Ankhhor, close to the date of Panehsy, in the late 9th to early 8th century BC.

Acknowledgements

For the permission to use and publish the images of cartonnages used for comparison, I am grateful to the Fitzwilliam Museum, Cambridge; the Harvard Semitic Museum, Cambridge, Massachusetts; the National Museum of Ireland, Dublin; the Norwich Castle Museum and Art Gallery, Norwich; and the Rijksmuseum van Oudheden, Leiden.

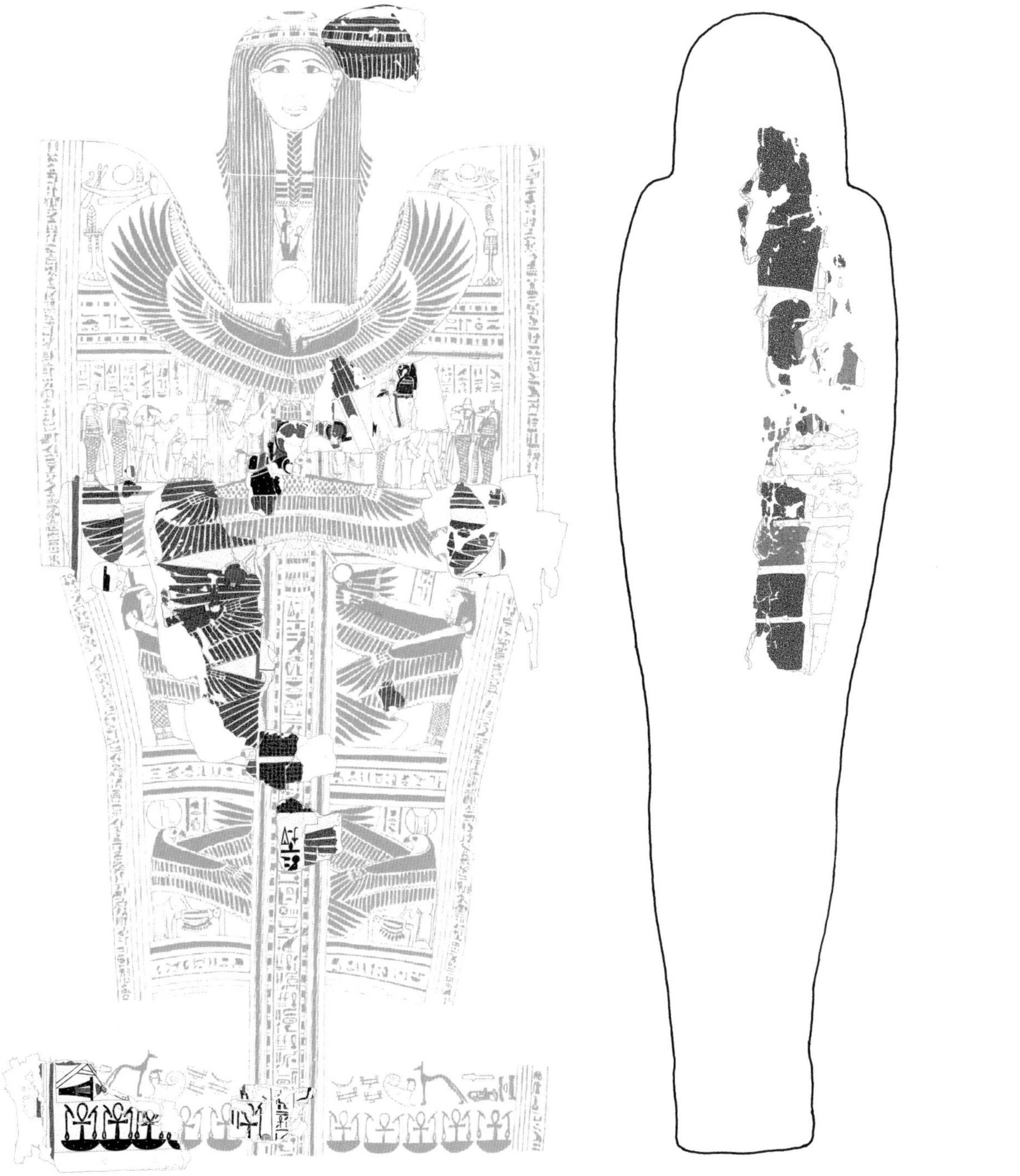

Fig. 73: Original location of the fragments found at the excavation of TT 65 on the front side of a cartonnage based on the drawing of the cartonnage of Nakhtefmut, after Quibell 1898, pl. 16.

A Libyan singer in the Karnak temple choir

The cartonnage of Shauamunimes (Egyptian Museum Cairo TR 21.11.16.5)

Cynthia May Sheikholeslami

A Twenty-second Dynasty cartonnage in the Egyptian Museum, Cairo (TN 21.11.16.5), which can be securely dated to the reign of Osorkon I, belongs to a female 'singer of the interior of the temple of Amun' named Shauamunimes. This paper discusses this cartonnage and its parallels, and the results of recent radiographic investigation and a CT scan conducted on it. The Libyan ancestry of Shauamunimes is also considered. Pieces from the burial ensembles belonging to other 'singers of the interior of the temple of Amun' also named Shauamunimes are examined to address the question of whether such women, sometimes thought to be virgins, took on a 'temple name' when they joined the temple choir in Thebes.

An intact cartonnage case in the Egyptian Museum Cairo (EMC) belonging to Shauamunimes (TR 21.11.16.5) is one of the documents attesting to the group of approximately one hundred women entitled *ḥsyt n ẖnw n imn* "singer of the interior of the temple of Amun",[1] mostly from Thebes and Abydos, in the Twenty-second to Twenty-sixth Dynasties. On the basis of cartonnage cases with parallel decoration, the burial of Shauamunimes, daughter of a *ms* of the Libyan Meshwesh tribe, may be dated to the reign of Osorkon I (Taylor 2017, 453–458). The cartonnage has recently been X-radiographed and CT-scanned to provide information about the mummy of the woman inside (Sheikholeslami and Ikram 2017, especially 25–26; Ikram *et al.* forthcoming).

The unopened cartonnage case containing the mummy of Shauamunimes was entered in the Temporary Register (TR) of the Egyptian Museum Cairo on November 21, 1916 (Koch 2012, 244 (no. 59)). No provenance is recorded, but her title, the style of decoration, and the cartonnage technique indicate a Theban provenance. In the TR 21.11.16.5 entry is a reference to "Guide 1884 no. 4937" (a sticker with the number is visible in **Fig. 78**), referring to Maspero's *Guide du Visiteur au Musée de Boulaq* (Maspero 1894, 307, 311). Actually, the cartonnage of Shauamunimes is first mentioned in the Guide published in the previous year (Maspero 1893, 307, 311), where it is stated that it was purchased in Thebes in 1882, and according to the seller (if he could be believed) came from Sheikh Abd el-Qurna. Maspero dated the cartonnage to the Twenty-third Dynasty. Since burial equipment belonging to two other praise singers who had (or took) the same name has been recovered in excavations by the Egyptian-Polish mission working at the Deir el-Bahari temple of Hatshepsut (Barwik 2003, 122–125), it is quite possible that this cartonnage came from the same area on the west bank at Thebes. The wooden funerary stela of the *ḥsyt n ẖnw n imn* Shauamunimes in the Houston Museum of Natural Science (30.1997.328) (Saleh 2007, 210 (cat. 56); Koch 2012, 244–245 (no. 61)) almost certainly belongs to the same person, although her parentage is not mentioned on the stela.

Description of the cartonnage of Shauamunimes

The cartonnage case (L 1.80 m) enclosing the mummy of the praise-singer of the temple of Amun Shauamunimes

[1] The title is often translated as "singer or chantress of the interior of Amun", but it should be distinguished from the title *šmˁyt n imn*, usually translated as "chantress of Amun", and I therefore prefer a more literal translation related to the root *ḥs*.

Fig. 74: Cartonnage case of Shauamunimes, left side head and shoulder profile (EMC TR 21.11.16.5, photo by C. M. Sheikholeslami, Courtesy Egyptian Museum Cairo)

Fig. 75: Cartonnage case of Shauamunimes, falcon-headed winged scarab on breast and ḥr-nḏ-it.f leading deceased to wn-nfr in first register of frontal body field (EMC TR 21.11.16.5, photo by C. M. Sheikholeslami, Courtesy Egyptian Museum Cairo)

is still intact, so the exact method of its construction cannot be determined. However, the method of closing the case around the body indicates it must have been made in the same way as other cartonnages of the period (Taylor 2003, 104). There is a vertical opening down the centre of the back, the edges of which were laced together and covered over with a linen strip pasted over the lacing. Around the back of the head, at the same level as the band above her forehead on the front and sides of her wig, there is a horizontal slit with holes in each side, which have also been laced together and covered over with a plain linen strip (visible in **Fig. 74, right**). Around the base of the foot are a series of holes used to lace the bottom of the foot to the body of the cartonnage (visible in **Fig. 78, left**). The separate flat piece has roughly the same form as the outline of the bottoms of the feet. Possibly a linen strip originally covered the lacing, and the bottom of the footpiece was also plastered over after the lacing was completed.

The face and neck of the cartonnage case are covered with thin pieces of gold leaf, some cut in rather large squarish pieces, and applied directly over the plaster body of the case, up to the edges of the wig with its lappets and a collar visible between the lappets, sometimes

Fig. 76: Cartonnage case of Shauamunimes, deceased embraced by mꜥt, mistress of the west, left end of first register of frontal body field (EMC TR 21.11.16.5, photo by C. M. Sheikholeslami, Courtesy Egyptian Museum Cairo)

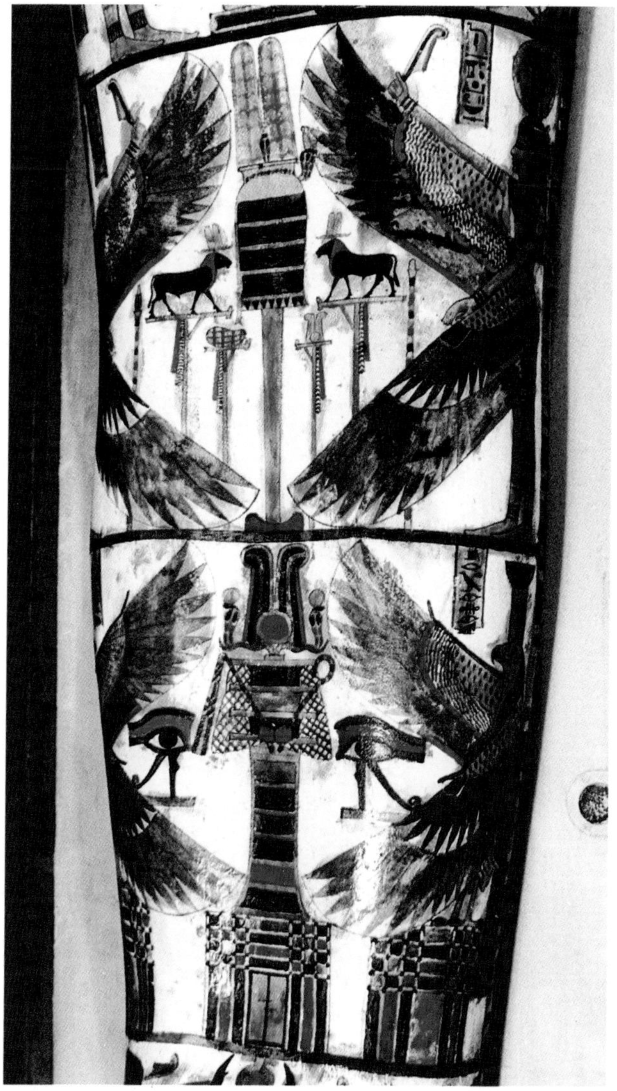

Fig. 77: Cartonnage case of Shauamunimes, emblems of Osiris protected by Nephthys and Isis as goddesses and ḏrtyw in the second and third registers of the frontal body field (EMC TR 21.11.16.5, photo by C. M. Sheikholeslami, Courtesy Egyptian Museum Cairo)

overlapping the painted surfaces (see **Fig.** 74, especially over the cheek and along the jaw). The eyes have a dark pupil set into a white cornea enclosed in a thick blue paste outline below slightly arched paste eyebrows applied over the gold leaf. The wig, which now appears dark blue-black, has gold rectangles evenly spaced in a chequerboard pattern (see **Fig.** 74), flaked off in a few places on the left side and the lappets. The wig extends to the multicoloured rectangle border that runs vertically the length of the cartonnage case on each side. Each wig lappet has a gold leaf-covered band at the bottom. Around the top of her head is a wreath of white flower petals, each with a red dot at the base on a blue-black ground, suspended from a green and white band, mostly covered by a wash of varnish (now yellowed) above a coloured rectangle band. Both elements extend to the side of the wig, but do not continue around the back of the head. The entire top of her head is covered by an oval painted plain black, which has scraped or flaked off in some places. Between the lappets is a collar consisting of blue, red, blue, green and blue bands with golden yellow borders and round red beads alternating with blue teardrop beads suspended from the lowest row. Below this, on a gilded ground, is a mummiform figure of the goddess Maat in a blue shroud with an *ꜥnḫ* sign on her knees and a green symbolic ostrich feather on her head, seated on a flat blue base in the shape of the *mr* sign outlined in gold, with four blue *sꜣ* signs with gold knots separated by green leaves suspended from it (**Fig.** 75).

Over the breast of the cartonnage case, on the white plaster of the case itself, is a falcon-headed winged scarab holding a gilded solar disk between its front legs and a green *šn* sign with a red centre between its rear legs (**Fig.** 75). The falcon's face is gilded, with black markings for the eyes, beak and tripartite wig outlined in yellow, and the body and six legs of the scarab beetle are blue with yellow outline. The falcon's outspread wings are divided into three feathered sections: three rows of black dots on a yellow-beige ground for the marginal coverts of the shoulders, ending with pointed red-tipped green alulae at the top, a row for the blue-green primary and green secondary (with red tips) coverts on a red ground in the middle, and the bottom row of primary and secondary (with red tips) feathers on a red ground. The green feathers are outlined with yellow. The wings curve upward on either side of the scarab, with the tips of the primary feathers meeting the edge of the lappet on each shoulder of the cartonnage case (**Fig.** 74).

Above the curve of the falcon wings is a floral collar extending below the wig lappets, following the curve of the wings (**Fig.** 75). The top row has pendants resembling a drawing of the hieroglyphic sign for the heart (in black, white and blue) with green suspension loops on a red ground with round red separators. The second row has white eight-petalled rosettes with red centres on a triangular green leaf alternating with open triangular shaped blossoms suspended from the green base of the flower opening to red and blue bands. The two rows of the collar are separated by a narrow yellow band.

In the triangular area between the horizontal blue line, demarcating the top register of the body field below, and the curve of the falcon wings above are kneeling figures, each with an ostrich feather on the head and holding a flail, with their backs at the band of multicoloured rectangles running down the two sides of the case. The figure on the proper right is falcon-headed, while the figure on the proper left is lioness-headed (see **Fig.** 74). The garment worn by each figure is dark orangey gold; the face, arms, hands, feet and ostrich feather green (with black markings for the falcon face); the tripartite wig blue for the falcon and red for the lioness; the collar and flail blue and yellow. Parts of these figures have been covered with varnish (now yellowish), with the varnish extending beyond the boundaries of the figures.

Most of the area between the wig lappets and over the floral collar and the falcon-headed scarab with outspread wings appears to have been painted over with varnish (now yellowish), except the areas that are actually covered with gold leaf. The red and blue coloured rectangles with white-black-white separator rectangles, forming the border of the frontal decoration on each side of the cartonnage case, has also been varnished (the varnish is now yellowish), not always neatly within the borders of the bands (see **Fig.** 74).

The decoration of the frontal body field of the cartonnage case of Shauamunimes belongs to Taylor's Design 1 type (Taylor 2003, 104–106; Taylor 2017, 453–458). It is divided into three horizontal registers by blue-black dividing lines and extends over the abdomen and legs of the cartonnage case. The first register (**Fig.** 75) consists of a scene: on the proper left, the falcon-headed anthropomorphic deity *ḥr-nḏ-it.f* leads the deceased *ḥsyt n ḫnw n imn šꜣwy-imn-m-im.s*, embraced from behind by the goddess *mꜣꜥt ḥnwt imntt* (**Fig.** 76), into the presence of *wn-nfr nṯr ꜥꜣ nb pt mꜣꜥ ḫrw*, who stands at the centre.

The god *ḥr-nḏ-it.f* has his right hand raised in adoration and his left hand holds the right hand of the deceased woman (**Fig.** 75). He has blue skin on his arms and legs and wears a green feathered corselet with straps and a straight kilt with a bull tail. His tripartite wig is also blue, with the lappets falling over the broad collar, edged with blue pendants, over his shoulders. The markings around the eyes of his falcon head and his beak are black. He wears armlets, wristlets and anklets. The entire figure has had varnish daubed over it, not evenly covering all parts and often extending beyond the outlines of the divine figure.

The elegant and graceful figure of the *ḥsyt n ḫnw n imn šꜣwy-imn-n-im.s* is outlined in black, like the other figures in the scene (**Fig.** 76). She wears a heavy tripartite wig with wavy edges showing the feathery hair of which it is made, and three separate strands spread over her left shoulder. Her pleated garment is edged with blue and worn so as to provide wide sleeves and a lower edge draped over the tops of her feet. Her broad collar has alternating blue and green bands, and she wears yellow and blue wristlets. The top of her wig is encircled by a red and white ribbon, tied in a bow at the back of her head with the ends hanging down below, and on top is a lotus stem with the bud projecting above her forehead and a cone set in the middle, with red drips running down its sides. Her thighs, visible through the thin pleated linen of her garment, are full and fleshy, in the preferred style of the Twenty-second to Twenty-third Dynasties. Her left arm is bent upwards at the elbow across her chest to grasp the hand of Maat standing behind her, with her left hand at the top of her right shoulder.

The goddess *mꜣꜥt ḥnwt imntt* embraces the deceased from behind, with her right hand on the woman's right shoulder and her left hand placed flat on the woman's left hip (**Fig. 76**). The goddess wears the emblem of the west on her head, and her straight tripartite wig is encircled with a white and red ribbon around the crown, tied in a bow at the back. She wears a red tunic ending below her breasts with white straps and a white belt around her waist with its ends hanging down the length of her close-fitting garment. The goddess wears a blue and green banded broad collar and blue and yellow wristlets.

The mummiform god stands on a horizontal *mꜣꜥt* sign and holds a long-handled *wꜣs* sceptre and a short-handled *ḥqꜣ* sceptre with a *nḫḫ* flail in his two hands emerging from his white shroud (**Fig. 75**). Over his shoulders is a red and green broad collar with blue droplet pendants at the lower edge and a yellow counterpoise on the back with crossed red bands below the collar. He wears a tall white crown with a uraeus and his blue face has a curved beard suspended from his chin. In front of his figure is an *imy-wt* emblem. Varnish (now yellowish) has been daubed over his figure and the staffs and emblem.

Behind the god *wn-nfr*, on the right side of the scene, are *ꜣst wrt mwt nṯr nb(t) pt* (**Fig. 75**) and *nb(t)-ḥwt smn wḏt nṯrw*. Each goddess wears a tight-fitting garment (blue for Isis and red for Nephthys), ending below her breasts, with white straps and tied around the waist with a white belt with the ends falling the length of the skirt, and a blue and green banded broad collar, and blue and yellow armlets, wristlets and anklets. Each has a plain tripartite wig with a uraeus over her forehead and a red and white ribbon tied around the crown with a bow in the back and the ends hanging down. In front of each goddess is a column with the legend *ir sꜣ wsir ḥsyt n ḫnw n imn šꜣwy-imn-n-im.s mꜣꜥt ḫrw*, "protecting the Osiris praise-singer of the interior of temple of Amun Shauamunimes justified". Each goddess wears her emblem on a yellow modius on her head: a blue seat for Isis and a blue *nb* basket on top of a yellow and red *ḥwt* for Nephthys. Isis has her arms at the back of the mummiform *wn-nfr*, the left hand raised behind his neck and the right extended towards his buttocks (**Fig. 75**). Nephthys has her left hand raised behind the right shoulder of Isis, and her right arm hanging along her body holding an *ꜥnḫ* sign.

The label texts for the scenes have been covered in yellow varnish. The figures of the deities and the deceased have also been covered with varnish (now yellowish), not always completely, nor always within the lines of the drawing of the figures. The feet of all the figures in the scene of the first register rest on a blue register line that also forms the upper boundary of the second register below.

In the centre of the second register is the Abydos fetish of Osiris, with two tall plumes with a uraeus between them at the base on a modius on top (**Fig. 4**). Double uraei, wearing the white and red crowns, project below the modius towards the proper right. The Abydos fetish is flanked by standards: on the right, the first standard bears double *šw* feathers (the emblem of the Thinite nome) and the second taller one has a ram with double plumes on his horizontal horns; the third is a blue-yellow-red striped pole with a *ḥtp* loaf on top. To the left, the standards bear an ovoid package (the placenta), another plumed horizontal-horned ram, and another striped pole with what appears to be a beer jar or situla on top. The Abydos emblem and the standards have been daubed with varnish (now turned yellowish). To the left and right, goddesses extend protective winged arms holding an ostrich feather in the hand of their uppermost arm. The underside of the wing is shown attached to the uppermost arm, with distinctive black rippled lines for the covert feathers. Each goddess is dressed in a tight-fitting red garment with a blue-green banded broad collar and a yellow disk containing her emblem resting on top of her head, with a white ribbon tied around the crown of her blue-back tripartite wig, and the wing feathers wrapping around her torso and buttocks. The goddess on the proper left has the emblem of Nephthys in the disk, and a label text reading *ḏd mdw in nb(t)-ḥwt ḫwy nb.s* "recitation by Nephthys protecting her lord". The goddess on the proper right side has the emblem of Isis in the disk on her head, and the same label text, except with her name Isis.

The third register of the frontal decoration of the cartonnage case of Shauamunimes has a *ḏd* pillar standing atop a niched façade shrine with a double-leafed door in the centre (**Fig. 77**). Shoulders and arms covered with a blue bead net project from the top of the *ḏd* pillar, ending in hands that grasp a *nḫḫ* flail on the right and a *ḥqꜣ* sceptre on the left, with red hands below the lowest crosspiece of the pillar. Atop the pillar are horizontal

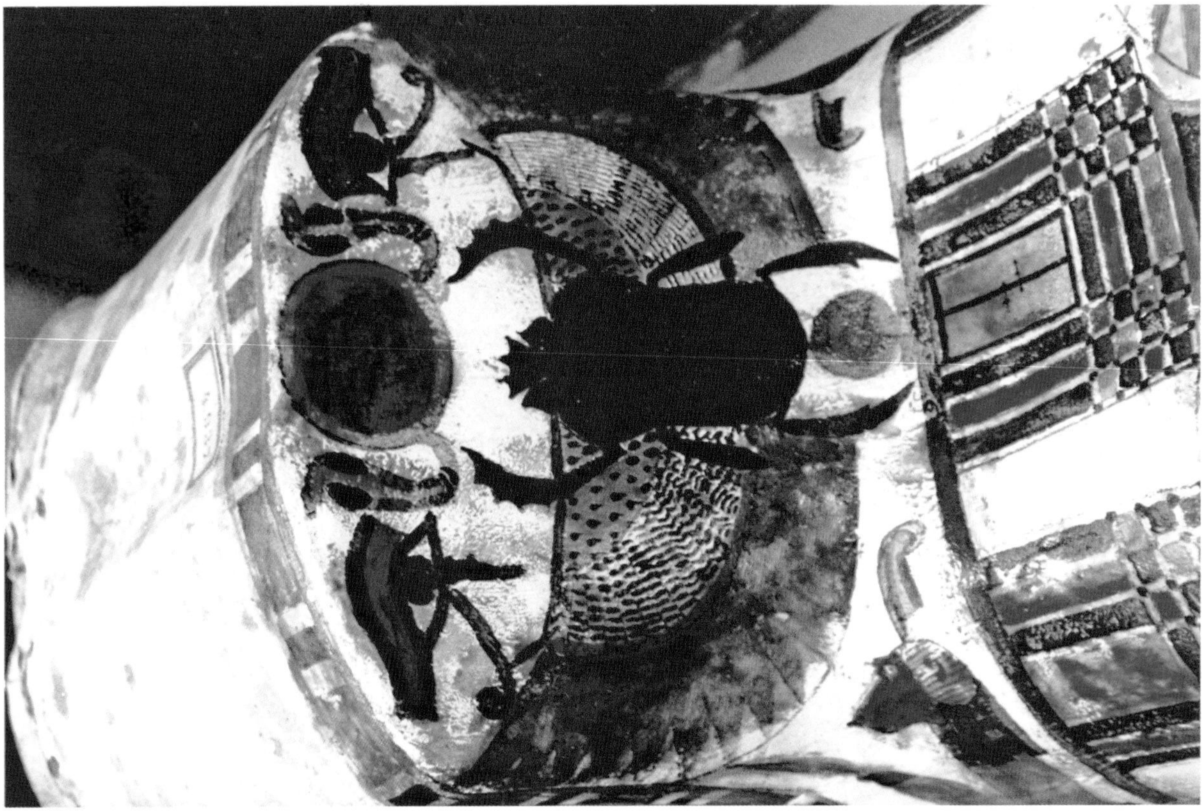

Fig. 78: Cartonnage case of Shauamunimes – winged scarab on foot with solar disk, wḏꜣt eyes and protective divinity with cynocephalus head and knife (EMC TR 21.11.16.5, photo by C. M. Sheikholeslami, Courtesy Egyptian Museum Cairo)

ram horns with a uraeus with a disk on its head at each tip, with ostrich feathers flanking a red disk with a gold border at the centre. Flanking this emblem of Osiris are falcons standing on top of the same type of niched façade shrines as the *ḏd* pillar, with their outstretched wings enclosing *wḏꜣt* eyes on either side of the pillar. The falcon on the proper right has the emblem of Isis on its head, and the one on the proper left has the emblem of Nephthys. The label column above the uppermost wing in front of the beak of each bird has the same text: *ḏrt ỉrt sꜣ wsỉr*, "the *djerty* bird protecting Osiris". The coloured emblems and figures and the label texts have all been somewhat unevenly daubed with varnish (now yellowish).

The blue line below the third register marks the separation between the frontal field decoration of the body of the cartonnage case of Shauamunimes and the decoration of the top of the footpiece, which is oriented towards the tips of the toes, rather than the top down orientation of the body decoration. Over the tops of the feet is a large black winged scarab, here with the wings shown from the underside rather than from above, as is the case of the winged falcon-headed scarab over the breast above (**Fig. 78**). Over the beetle's front legs is a red disk with a yellow circular border and a uraeus suspended from each side flanked by a pair of *wḏꜣt* eyes facing towards the disk in the centre. The rear legs of the beetle frame a blue *šn* sign with a red centre. To the left and right over the ankles are mummiform protective divinities holding green knives. They are seated on green rectangles that rest on the multicoloured rectangular border that runs the length of each side of the cartonnage, and wear orangey-yellow shrouds with green collars and blue tripartite wigs. The divinity over the proper left ankle has the head of a cynocephalus ape, and the one over the proper right ankle has the head of a hippopotamus with its tongue sticking out between its teeth. As above, the coloured figures have been daubed with varnish (now yellowish). The border of multicoloured rectangles continues at the top edge of the vertical section of the footpiece, and the white surface of the plaster below has a substance (perhaps a varnish, now brownish-yellow) unevenly painted over it above the lacing holes, formerly covered with a now missing linen strip.

The rear of the cartonnage case of Shauamunimes

is also decorated. A large *ḏd* pillar occupies the centre and most of the length. The top supports double ostrich plumes painted green with a white outline on top of each, and the outer edge of each painted red. At the centre of the base of the plumes is a *šn* sign with a white ring and red centre. They rest on horizontal twisted ram's horns with a uraeus with a white disk on its head at each end.

The top two segments of the *ḏd* are flanked by hooded cobras with lioness heads with green faces, white ruffs and red tripartite wigs. The one on the proper right side has the outline of the emblem of Nephthys on its head, and the one on the proper left has the emblem of Isis painted green on top of its head (partly visible in **Fig. 74, right**). Shoulders and arms painted red with white armlets and wristlets extend from the third segment from the top of the *ḏd*; the arms are bent upwards at the elbow with the hands laid flat, palm down, embracing the sides of the cartonnage at the level of the winged falcon-headed scarab decoration on the breast of the frontal field (see **Fig.** 74).

Below each elbow is the profile figure of a goddess wearing a tight-fitting garment ending below the breast with a strap leading up towards the shoulder, and a black wig hanging down the back having a red ribbon around the crown tied in a bow at the back with ends hanging down. The goddess on the proper right side has the *ỉmntt* emblem outlined on her head and her garment is painted red with a white belt. The goddess on the proper left has the *ỉꜣbtt* emblem drawn in outline on her head and her garment is white with the ribbons of her belt painted red. Each goddess is drawn with a single arm raised in protective adoration of the *ḏd* pillar.

Both goddesses stand on a blue ground line that intersects the *ḏd* pillar at the base of the third segment from the bottom. This line, the border of multicoloured rectangles running down the sides of the cartonnage case, and the flaring base of the *ḏd* pillar form a roughly triangular space that has a rectangle painted red set into the apex, partly hidden behind the bottom segment of the *ḏd* pillar on each side; this resembles a diagonally truncated *ḥwt* sign. The eight lower segments of the *ḏd* pillar are painted alternately red and blue, and the ninth segment from the base, the first with projections to the sides, is pale yellowish-beige. The top three segments are blue-red-blue. The separations of the segments and the four projections to the sides at the top are painted pale yellowish-beige. The outline of the pillar is painted yellow. On the right side, the outline has been corrected to be further to the right before the pillar was painted.

Slightly to the left of the centre of the third to sixth segments from the top of the *ḏd* pillar, a vertical band is painted yellowish-beige. It seems it may have demarcated a central section of the *ḏd* pillar, which was left undecorated to accommodate the lacing and linen strip closing the opening into which the mummy was inserted, elsewhere covered over by the plain linen strip over the lacing; the horizontal segments of the pillar do not perfectly line up on either side of the vertical opening.

Dark brownish stains are visible on the bottom of the plume and top segments above the shoulder of the arm on the proper left side of the *ḏd* pillar, and also in an area in front of the goddess with the *ỉꜣbtt* emblem on her head. These are probably due to fluids that seeped out of the mummified body inside the cartonnage case.

Below the base of the *ḏd* pillar at a level approximately corresponding to the lower legs of the cartonnage case of Shauamunimes is a *sḫm* sceptre painted yellowish-beige with a yellow disk on top. This occupies the centre and the laced opening covered with linen runs vertically through it. Flanking the sceptre and facing away from it are two mummiform protective deities, each with a blue tripartite wig, a red-blue-yellow collar around the shoulders with blue teardrop pendants at the bottom, and a red belt knotted over the abdomen with a streamer hanging down the front. The shrouds have been partly painted with varnish (now turned yellowish). The divinity on the left has the face of a cynocephalus ape painted red, and the one on the right that of a falcon only drawn in outline. The sceptre and the feet of the mummiform deities rest on a band that extends the multicoloured rectangle border at the top of the base of the feet on the front of the cartonnage case, but it is only drawn in outline.

Some yellowish and beige varnish has been applied around the lower end of the vertical laced slit that extends down the back to the footboard. Traces of the same treatment are visible around the horizontal laced slit that crosses the top of the vertical laced slit around the back of the crown of the head.

The mummy of Shauamunimes

The mummy of Shauamunimes (Sheikholeslami and Ikram 2017, especially 25–26; Ikram *et al.* forthcoming) is of a woman who was about 1.63 m tall in life. The head was some distance away from the top of the cartonnage case enveloping the mummy. She died while a teenager (about 17 or slightly younger), as may be determined by the fact that her long bones were still fusing and by her dentition.

The body was well wrapped, with differing layers of bandages over various parts, and extra pads or folded pieces of linen used to provide bulk, particularly around the legs. In the wrapping over the legs and the torso there are several layers of textile with a resinous layer in between. Her arms, wrapped separately, are extended with her hands resting on her thighs. Linen bundles fill the area between her separately wrapped legs. Long lamellated bands that appear to be from some sort of plant (papyrus stems or palm leaves, though it is just possible that these are made of finely pleated linen) were placed over the skin of her thighs, helping to thicken them so they are more like the fleshy thighs seen in the representation of Shauamunimes on the exterior of her cartonnage (see **Fig. 76**); these are not documented elsewhere.

The skull of Shauamunimes was excerebrated via the ethmoid, with some linen introduced into the cranial cavity. Her mouth and neck were stuffed with a grainy substance (mud or sawdust) mixed with oils, probably to give her face a more life-like appearance, a practice commonly noted in Twenty-first and Twenty-second Dynasty mummies. She was eviscerated from the left side, with the four visceral packages carefully replaced in the thorax and abdomen, each with a pierced tab-like metal amulet, presumably bearing the protective likeness of the relevant son of Horus. The incision was covered by a square plate with a hole in each of the four corners, possibly having a representation of the *wḏꜣt* eye on it. Her heart remained in the body, but it seems to have been wrapped.

The mummy of Shauamunimes was richly supplied with amulets: a string of at least twelve (*tyt, ḏd, wꜣḏ*, possibly *ib*, a foot, possibly images of standing deities, rectangular and stela-shaped objects with suspension loops) is around her neck; a scarab was placed within the wrappings at the base of her throat; and a few other amulets (including a rectangular plaque, perhaps decorated with a winged scarab, apparently over her heart) were scattered in the area of the thorax, and a small rectangular plaque near one of the visceral packages. Shauamunimes also had two amulets (rings?) at her wrist and hand.

Shauamunimes has a butterfly vertebra, a rare congenital malformation that causes no harm to its owner. It was not possible to determine whether or not she ever gave birth. The cause of death is unclear.

The dating of the cartonnage case of Shauamunimes

The cartonnage case of the praise-singer of the interior of the temple of Amun Shauamunimes, daughter of the Meshwesh *ms* Takelot, may be dated to the reign of Osorkon I on the basis of its stylistic similarity to the cartonnage case Berlin Ägyptisches Museum 7325, as the mummy enclosed in the latter was provided with leather bretelles stamped with the cartouches of this Twenty-second Dynasty ruler.[2] The group of related cartonnage cases is particularly distinguished by the presence of the winged falcon-headed scarab, probably representing Khepri, on the breast. Some, such as Berlin Ägyptisches Museum 7325, Chicago Art Institute 1910.238 and St Louis Art Museum 109.1989, also display a distinctive manner of painting the coverts on the underside of the falcon's wings in the third register with rippled lines that may indicate the hand of a single painter.

The title *ḥsyt n ẖnw n imn*

The role of these "praise singers of the interior of the temple of Amun" is not well understood.[3] Their singing (or perhaps chanting) most likely accompanied ritual performances in the inner parts of the Karnak temple of Amun in Thebes. The title is the only one held by these women. As title-holders, they were high status individuals, as is indicated by gilding that may appear on their burial containers.[4] Some, like Shauamunimes, were daughters of members of the Libyan or Kushite elite or royal families or of high-ranking persons or individuals in the entourage of the God's Wife of Amun. However, for the most part their parents seem to have been of relatively humble origins. The women may have been placed in temple service by their parents. Land could be donated to a temple for their support; nevertheless, they could inherit, buy and sell land and own slaves. The fact that a number of names are common in the group – at least four named Shauamunimes are known[5] – suggests they might have been given "temple names" when they received the title. It is not known how many *ḥsyt n*

[2] See the comprehensive discussion of the related group of cartonnage cases in Taylor 2017, 453–458.

[3] See Koch 2012, 185–186, 188–196 (discussion of the title), 230–254 (most recent publication of the corpus), 282–283.

[4] For example, in addition to the cartonnage of Shau-amun-im-es (Koch no. 59), the outer anthropoid coffin of Di(mutshepen) ankh, CCG 41061 (Koch no. 90).

[5] Koch 2012, 243–245, nos. 57–61; nos. 59 and 61 probably belonged to the same woman.

Table 1: Individuals entitled *ms, ms wr* or *ms wr ꜥꜣ n (nꜣ) mšwš/mꜥ*

[* with  after *ms*]

(in chronological order of dated/datable monuments)

Document	Title	Name	Date	References
letter from "el-Hibeh" archive, pAberdeen 167bd+168k+168o	*ms n nꜣ mšwš*	*ꜥnḫ-f-(n)-ímn*	Twenty-first Dynasty; also a *ḥm-nṯr* priest of Haroeris (of Qus)?	Müller 2009, 255 with n. 47, 263 with n. 123.
lintel reused in Heracleopolis tomb; JE 94748	*ms wr ꜥꜣ n mꜥ* *	*wsrkn*	2nd half/end Twenty-first beginning Twenty-second Dynasty (original date of lintel, by style)	Jansen-Winkeln 2007a,165 [11.1].
Dakhleh stela Ashmolean 1894.107a	*ms wr nꜣ mꜥ*	*wyḥꜣst*	Sheshonq I, yr 3; date of stela referring to his unnamed son coming to oasis	Jansen-Winkeln 2007b, 23–36 [12.28].
cartonnage case Egyptian Museum, Cairo TN 21.11.16.5	*ms wr mꜥšwš*	*ṯkrt*	Osorkon I (date of daughter's cartonnage)	Jansen-Winkeln 2007b, 392 [44.21].
stela Elephantine	*ms wr nꜣw mꜥ/////*	[-----]	Osorkon II	Jansen-Winkeln 2007b, 120–121 [18.33]
donation stela Moscow 5647 = I.1.a 5647 (4128)	*ms n wr ꜥꜣ rbw* *	*pꜣ-wrdw*	Shoshenq III, yr 31	Jansen-Winkeln 2007b, 202–203 [22.34].
Serapeum stela Louvre IM 3078	*ms wr ꜥꜣ n rbw*	*ꜥnḫ-ḥr*	Shoshenq V, yr 37; cf. stela JE 407168 of his daughter where titled *wr ꜥꜣ n rbw ꜥnḫ-ḥr* Shepenwepet I ca. 736–714? BC	Jansen-Winkeln 2007b, 286–287 [28.32].
secondary text around base of group statue Berlin 9320, Memphis?	*ms wr n mꜥ*	*p-n-sḫmt*	late Twenty-second/Twenty-third Dynasty; father of following	Jansen-Winkeln 2009, 302 [51.65].
secondary text around base of group statue Berlin 9320, Memphis? (see above and Jansen-Winkeln 2007b, 202–203 [22.34]	*ms wr n mꜥ*	*ns-ptḥ*	late Twenty-second/Twenty-third Dynasty; son of previous	Jansen-Winkeln 2007b, 389 [44.13].
scarab from Heracleopolis	*ms wr ꜥꜣ mꜥ*	*ššnq*	Twenty-second to Twenty-fourth Dynasty; Libyan period; son of following	Jansen-Winkeln 2007b, 416 [45/39].
scarab from Heracleopolis (see above and Jansen-Winkeln 2007b, 286–287 [28.32]	*ms wr*	*pꜣ-di-nꜥrt*	Twenty-second to Twenty-fourth Dynasty; Libyan period; father of previous	Jansen-Winkeln 2007b, 416–417 [45.40].
coffin set Berlin 7478	*ms [n] wr mꜥ*	*ḥr-wḏꜣ*	Twenty-second to Twenty-fourth Dynasty (date of daughter's coffin)	Jansen-Winkeln 2007b, 415 [45.35].
bronze statuette Louvre E.7693	*ms wr n [r]b[w]?*	*pꜣ-šꜣsw?*	Twenty-second to Twenty-fourth Dynasty	Jansen-Winkeln 2007b, 417 [45.42].
axe Cairo JE 36513	*ms wr ꜥꜣ nꜣ mꜥ*	*wsirḥrt*	Twenty-second to Twenty-fourth Dynasty	Jansen-Winkeln 2007b, 337–350 [35.1].
stela of Piankhy Cairo JE 48862, ll. 18–19	*sꜣ-f smsw ms?/wr? wr n mꜥ*	*nsnꜣꜥy*	Twenty-fifth Dynasty, yr 21 Piankhy	

ḫnw n ỉmn could hold the title simultaneously, but it seems likely more than one (however, possibly their term of office was only short), even though they remained a small elite group. The mummy of Shauamunimes indicates quite young women could have held this temple position.

In contrast to many priestly and other offices during the Third Intermediate Period, the title seems never to have been inherited within a biological family. It has been much debated whether or not such women were celibate or not, but there is no definitive evidence to answer this question.[6] Women with this title are not clearly known to have biological children (no *ḥsyt n ḫnw* is named alongside a man as parents of a child), and they are hardly ever entitled *nbt pr* "house mistress", indicating a married woman. The supposed (grand) mother-(grand)daughter relationship between some of them is more likely one in which the "(grand)mother" adopts her younger colleague or successor as her biologically unrelated "(grand)daughter", a practice well known for the God's Wives of Amun of the period, who were adopted into office by their predecessors with no biological relationship between "mother" and "daughter".

The father of Shauamunimes

In the label text above the figure of Shauamunimes in the first register, her father is named as Takelot (see **Fig. 76**). Whether his title is to be read as *ms* or *ms wr (n mšwš)*, however, is problematic.[7] As **Table 1** shows, there are two documents where the word *ms* has the determinative of a sitting child (𓀔), so that the word *ms* has recently been interpreted as the Egyptian word "child", whereas earlier it had been connected to the Berber word mas meaning "leader". On the cartonnage case of Shauamunimes, the word *ms* is followed immediately by a variation of the determinative which may be used also as an ideogram for *wr* "chief" (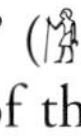, with a feather projecting forward from the top of the man's head), and sometimes a genitival *n* appears between the two, so the current interpretation of Takelot's title is *ms (n) wr n mšwš*, "child of the Meshwesh chief". However, if  is taken as the determinative of *ms*, the title could be *ms* of the Meshwesh. It is possible that *ms* was taken as a homophone of the Egyptian word for "child", and if it is not to be connected with the Berber word *mas*, then it could be either an unknown Libyan word or an Egyptian designation for a person in the Meshwesh or Libu tribal hierarchy different from a *wr (ꜥꜣ)*. It does not seem to indicate a genealogical relationship between a *wr (ꜥꜣ)* and a *ms*, since both a father and son could be entitled a *ms*. In any case, it is clear that the father of Shauamunimes had a position in the Meshwesh tribal organisation.

Concluding remarks

The decoration of the Twenty-second Dynasty cartonnage case of the praise-singer of the interior of the temple of Amun is of very high quality. The gilding on the face and breast and the fineness of the drawing and careful painting, as well as the numerous amulets adorning the mummy, indicate the high status of Shauamunimes, or at least the economic resources available for her burial. This could be due to her position as a *ḥyst n ḫnw n ỉmn* and/or to her father's status as a *ms* in the Meshwesh tribal hierarchy, which was apparently still influential in the reign of Osorkon I. Although it has been claimed that the varnish (now turned yellowish) that covers most of the figures and texts on this cartonnage case highlights their sacred nature, in this case it seems intended to fix the colours; it is not applied to any of the gilded areas. It is clearly worth singing the praises of the cartonnage case of Shauamunimes as a masterful example of early Twenty-second Dynasty Theban funerary art.

[6] For a discussion of the question, see Sheikholeslami 2002, 1112–1114; Koch 2012, 190–195 (the evidence presented is inconclusive since there are alternative interpretations for some of the prosopography), 282–283.

[7] See the discussion in Meffre 2015, 269–270 with earlier references, and the review of the role of Libyan chiefs and their associates in Egypt during the Twenty-first to Twenty-third Dynasties in Jansen-Winkeln 2017, 218–226.

The rediscovery and conservation treatment of Tanetmit's outer coffin

(Louvre N 2588) – Twenty-second Dynasty

Patricia Rigault

The Louvre Museum holds in its collection the set of coffins of the 'mistress of the House' and 'Songstress of Amen-Re' Tanetmit. She was the wife of the priest Horudja, son of Iufaa, and probably lived in the middle of the Libyan period. This set of coffins arrived at the Louvre during the nineteenth century, but its provenance is unknown. Until quite recently, only the inner coffin (Louvre N 2587–N 2633) and the cartonnage case (Louvre N 675), both bearing her name, were identified. The outer coffin was considered lost. The history of the rediscovery of the outer coffin and its restoration are detailed in this communication.

The Musée du Louvre has for many years held in its collection an inner coffin and cartonnage case belonging to the Lady Tanetmit, "Noble lady, mistress of the House" and "Songstress of Amen Re".[1] Both works came into the Louvre's collection at the beginning of the nineteenth century and were then listed in the Napoleon inventory, which was created around 1850 under Napoléon III.

The inventory entries read as follows:

- N 2587, "partie postérieure du cercueil de la dame Tent-cha", which is the box of the coffin;
- N 2633, "Couvercle du cercueil de la momie d'une dame nommée Tent-cha", which is the lid of the coffin;
- N 675, "Dessus de cercueil de momie portant le nom de la dame Tent-cha", which is the cartonnage case. This number had been lost soon after, so a temporary one was provided: AF 83[2].

The Napoleon inventory includes all the Egyptian antiquities held by the Louvre at this time. They were classified by typology, without taking into consideration their provenance or even their entry date into the collection. As the given descriptions are often very simple, it is difficult to identify them accurately, for instance, when the number is lost or no more associated with the object. It was, therefore, difficult to find out more about these two pieces belonging to a woman called by the writer "Tent-cha".

The inner coffin and the cartonnage case (Fig. 79)

The Lady Tanetmit's inner coffin is of mummiform type. It shows an image of the deceased wrapped in her shroud and wearing a large, plain wig ornamented with a headband. The rather simple decoration on the lid is painted directly on the reddish wood and has been preserved in very good condition. The large collar is composed of several rows and shows different patterns, such as little coloured squares and flower petals. Below the collar is a winged disc flanked by uraei. The inscriptions in the middle column, an offering formula dedicated to

[1] The inner coffin and cartonnage case are unpublished. They are mentioned in: Taylor 2003, 98; Payraudeau 2003, 135 and Payraudeau 2005, 202–203 (coffin mentioned under the database reference no. AE029174 and cartonnage case with its AF number as original ones had not yet been retrieved).

[2] The AF inventory was created around 1900 by Georges Bénédite and included the first objects that entered the collections and had lost their inventory numbers. AF numbers are normally "temporary" numbers for objects waiting to be identified in the inventories.

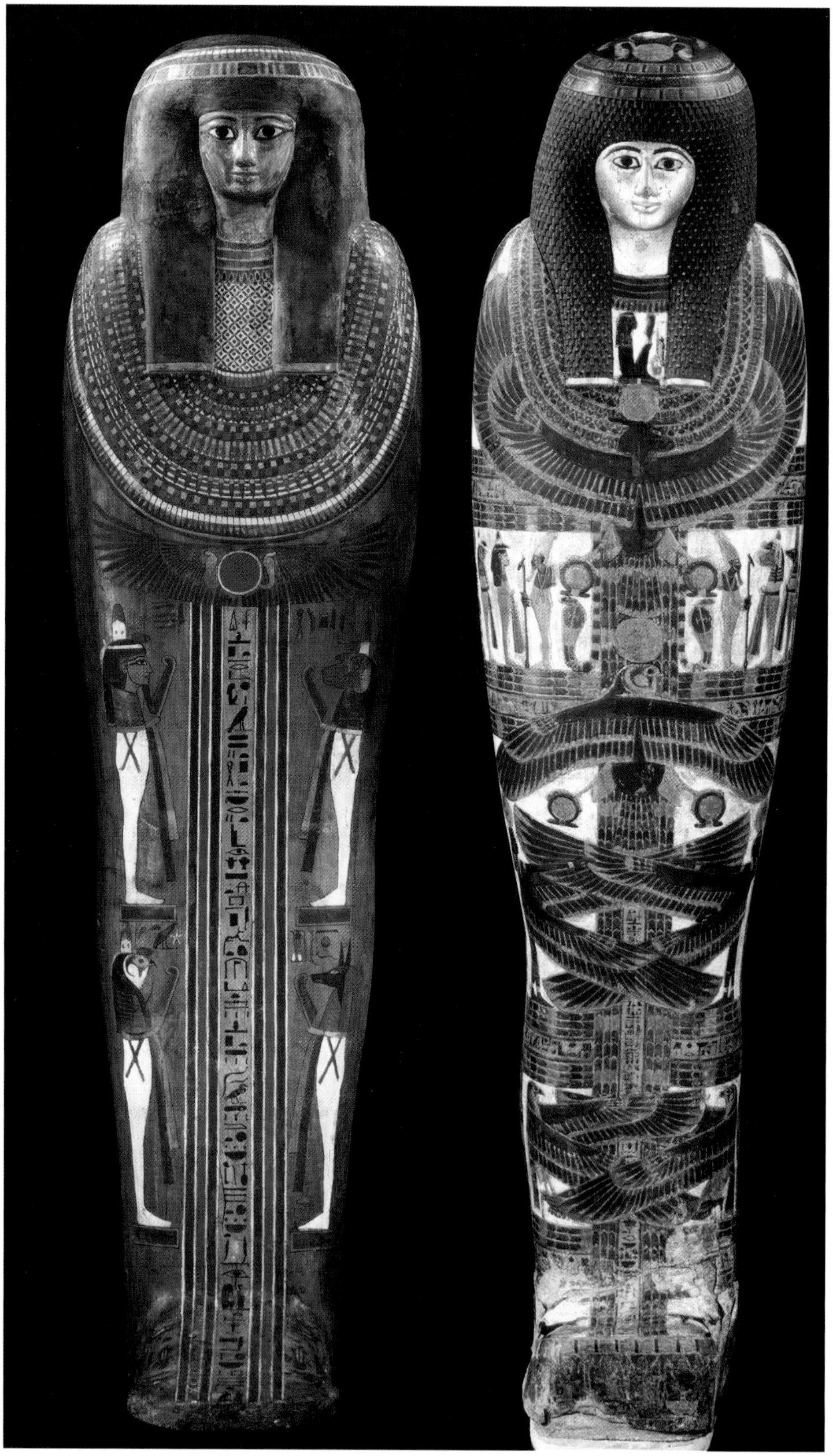

Fig. 79: Inner coffin and cartonnage case of Tanetmit.© 2004 Musée du Louvre / Georges Poncet

Ra-Horakhty, Ptah-Sokar-Osiris and Anubis, give the name and titles of Tanetmit. On each side stand the four sons of Horus, Imsety and Qebehsenuef on the right, Hapi and Duamutef on the left.

As usual, the cartonnage case features an elaborate decoration with beautiful polychrome images and inscriptions. It is of a kind of cartonnage well attested during the 22nd Dynasty[3]. Again, the dead Tanetmit is wrapped in her shroud but she wears a different wig adorned with little square curls. She also wears a headband and her face is completely covered with gold. The goddess Maat is painted between the lappets of the wig. The collar is less important than the collar of the coffin and the beads have less colour. Beneath there is a ram headed bird wearing a golden solar disc and a horizontal band, showing Imsety and Qebehsenuef on the right, Hapi and Duamutef on the left. Then, on each side of the central column of inscriptions, an offering formula dedicated to Osiris, two goddesses and two falcons with open their wings to protect the body of the dead. The inscriptions and the scenes are delimited by a triple band of motifs in the form of short feathers.

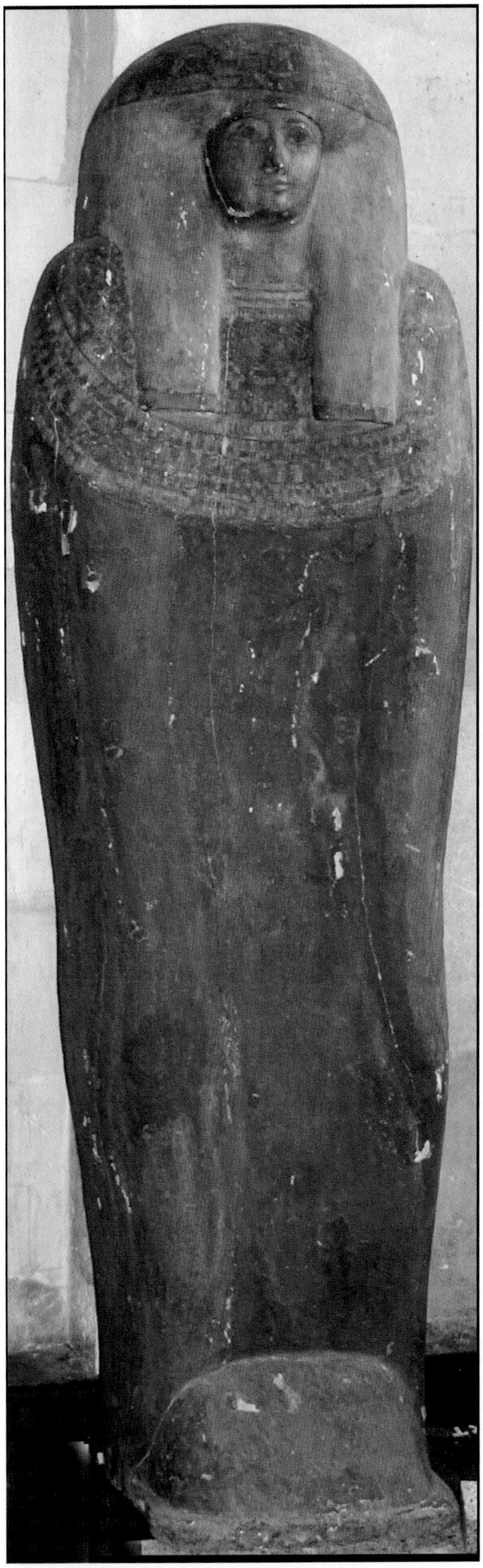

Fig. 80: Anonymous unnumbered outer coffin © Musée du Louvre/Patricia Rigault

Who was Tanetmit?

The name of Tanetmit, *tꜣ-nt-mỉt*, is clearly a reference to the goddess Bastet (Ranke, PN I, 360, 8). She was the wife of a priest of Amen called Horudja, himself the son of Iufaa, priest of Montu and Amen and governor of Thebes. Iufaa is quite well known. One of his statues, dedicated by his son Horudja, shows cartouches of Harsiese engraved on the shoulders (Cairo Museum JE 37374. See Payraudeau 2005, 197–207). Thus, according to what we know about her family, Tanetmit lived in the middle of the Libyan period, approximatively around the reign of Osorkon II or just after (See Payraudeau 2014, 9–25). Tanetmit and Horudja had a son called Djedkhonsuiufankh, who was himself priest of Amen, Mut and Nekhbet and whose set of coffins is also kept in the Louvre's collection (Outer coffin: N 2582, inner coffin: N 2578 and cartonnage case: N 2617). These also have been owned by the Louvre since the beginning of the 19th century, but their origin remains unknown. However, we can guess that the two sets come from a familial tomb.

Until recently, only the inner coffin and the cartonnage case, both with the name of Tanetmit, had been

[3] On the development of cartonnage cases during the Twenty Second dynasty, see Taylor 2003, 104–107 ; Elias 1993, 395–431.

identified in the Louvre's collection. The conservation treatment they underwent a few years ago gave us the opportunity to examine them closely.[4] Some stylistic details led us to compare them with an anonymous, unnumbered, outer coffin, usually dated, in quite an imprecise way, to the Ramesside period or to the beginning of the Third Intermediate period.

This large anonymous coffin (**Fig. 80**) was very dark and dull. It was also entirely covered with a thick coat of grey paint. There was a black coating on the interior. It was simply decorated with a floral headband on the wig and a large collar with a lot of overpainting and some traces of varnish. No text or number enabled us to identify it or establish its precise origin.

Some stylistic details could be compared with those on the Tanetmit coffin and cartonnage case. There was some facial resemblance between the coffins; the eyes had something very similar in their shape, in the look and in the shape of the eyebrows. Also, the floral headbands display many similar features such as the same alternation of rectangles and lines, the same colours on the cartonnage case, the same petals on the inner coffin. Finally, the floral collars presented the same diamond shaped drawing on the neck, a similar alternation of small coloured squares and bi-coloured flower petals and the same red dots between these petals. These similarities led us to consider a possible link between this outer coffin and Tanetmit's inner coffin and cartonnage case.

Technical examination

A technical investigation of these coffins was undertaken to confirm or dispel this hypothesis. The conservators who had worked on the inner coffin and cartonnage case examined the outer coffin and found many technical similarities between the two coffins, in the original decor and in the way they had been conserved previously.

The two boxes have sparse decoration and had not been restored. By contrast, the two lids are more elaborately decorated, show more extensive restoration and also the same types of restorations. For instance, the same white mastic had been used to fill the cracks; the same overpainting imitating the original decor was present using the same colours.

It was thus evident that the two coffins had been conserved together, in a way that was not the rule for the coffins of the Louvre. So, at some time in their modern history, these coffins had been linked together. They could, for instance, have entered the collection at the same time and been conserved together, probably by the same persons.

Then it was found that the smaller coffin was perfectly adapted to the anonymous outer coffin. The boxes and the lids fitted exactly and this could not be by accident. The two coffins had probably been made as a set; otherwise, they could not have been so well adjusted.

Looking more thoroughly inside the box of the anonymous coffin, it could be observed that the black coating was worn, especially near the left shoulder and the head, more lightly near the feet. These traces correspond exactly to the shape of Tanetmit's inner coffin. On the other hand, traces of black painting on Tanetmit's box surface match with these missing patches inside the anonymous box.

Technical analysis

A number of technical analyses were then undertaken on the anonymous coffin, mostly on the lid. This allowed us to understand the relationship between the restored surfaces and the original polychromy. The technical analysis was carried out in the Centre de Recherche et de Restauration des Musées de France (C2RMF).[5]

X-radiography revealed that the lid had been built from several long planks of wood fixed together with long dowels. A single sculpted block of wood had been used for the face and this had been fixed to the planks with dowels. The feet were made of several planks too. Some modern metal screws were also visible.

The lid has been comprehensively examined and recorded photographically with different light sources:

Ultraviolet photography helped us characterise the organic coating on the surface and see the restored areas. The presence of varnish was detected on part of the face. Overpainting was evident on the surface of the collar, the neck, the rest of the face and on some places on the wig, which showed no trace of varnish.

With infrared light the carbon based pigments below the existing surface appeared clearly as dark images on the lower part of the body, the drawing of the collar, the

[4] Conservation treatment carried out by Sophie Joigneau and Marie Louis, Conservators.

[5] We want to thank particularly for the technical analysis in the C2RMF: Thierry Borel, radiography; Daniel Vigears, Sandrine Pagès-Camagna: UV, IR examination; Sandrine Pagès-Camagna, Eric Laval: pigment identification; Anne Chauvet: photography; Juliette Langlois, organic analyses.

headband, the pupils, and absolutely not on the restored zones of the collar, especially on the left of the lid.

Pigments were identified by X-ray fluorescence spectrometry (XRF), without removing any sample, on the specific areas seen on the ultraviolet photographs (Pagès-Camagna and Vigears 2006). This identification has shown:

Fig. 81: Anonymous unnumbered outer coffin during conservation treatment © Sophie Joigneau/Marie Louis

- Egyptian blue on the wig and on the collar, covered in modern times with a coating containing chrome and lead;
- iron, calcium, lead, copper and chrome on the restored areas (on the left elbow especially)
- copper based green, but no Egyptian green;
- iron oxide or red earth;
- orpiment and yellow earth mixed on the face and on the yellow stripes at the end of the lappets;
- calcium (white) and carbon-based pigment (black). Conservation treatment (Louis and Joigneau 2007)

It has been possible to remove the modern grey paint on the wig and with it the dust it has recovered when it has been applied.

The original colours have reappeared (**Fig. 81**): Egyptian blue for the wig, white for the back of the head, and the original glossy black coating on the body. This thin black coating was also present inside the box and the lid. Applied on an ochred layer of rendering which filled the missing patches and sealed the joints between the planks, it looked very much like bitumen. The analysis of very small samples with pyrolysis and gas chromatography-mass spectrometry (GC-MS) showed the presence of bitumen and fat, but no trace of Pistacia spp. resin was found.[6]

Removal of the modern coating also allowed the original decor drawn in yellow to reappear (**Fig. 83**). Below the collar is a beautiful kneeling winged Nut and in the middle of the lid a column of yellow hieroglyphs runs down to the feet, giving the name and titles of Tanetmit. This is again an offering formula dedicated to Osiris (**Fig. 82**).

Getting back to the inventory

Thanks to the conservation work, an ancient number was found on the reverse of the lid, N 2588, which corresponds in the Napoleon inventory to a "Cercueil extérieur d'une momie dont le nom est illisible".

[6] The composition is not described by Serpico and White. See Pagès-Camagna and Langlois 2007.

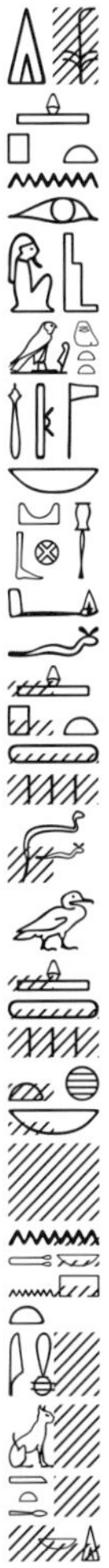

Fig. 82: Inscriptions on the outer coffin

Thus, at the time this inventory was written, the name of Tanetmit, easily readable on the inner coffin and the cartonnage case was no longer visible on the outer coffin. We may suppose therefore that the first conservation took place before the mid-nineteenth century.

And finally, now that the set is complete, we are able to confirm its origin. It probably came to the Louvre with the Salt collection in 1826. Before arriving in the Louvre, this collection had been inventoried by Champollion in Livorno. The first entry (no. I a, b, c, d, e) in the Champollion inventory mentions the complete set of a woman, including two boxes with two lids painted inside and outside and a mummy in a painted cartonnage with a gilded face. Among the sets of coffins in the Louvre collection, especially those that arrived in the nineteenth century, the set of Tanetmit is the most complete and the only one that could correspond to such a description.

Fig. 83: The previously anonymous outer coffin of Tanetmit after conservation treatment © 2007 Musée du Louvre / Georges Poncet

Non-invasive diagnostic techniques in the authentication and study of Egyptian coffins

The case of the anthropoid coffin of Pakharu, son of Panehesy and the cartonnage of Asetirdis in the Stibbert Museum, Florence

Marco Nicola, Simone Musso and Simone Petacchi

Since its beginnings, the study of Egyptian antiquities has generated interest and fascination and the widespread production of fakes and pastiches since the nineteenth century has been a complicating factor in its development. Due to such a common phenomenon, collections have acquired fakes together with original pieces throughout the centuries, often retouched in modern times but so similar to the genuine ones as to make it hard to distinguish them. In the last few decades, chemistry and physics have helped in this research by providing important support in the identification of genuine artefacts, and in the study of their state of conservation, as well as the techniques used to assemble the pieces. Recently, several analytical techniques have been introduced for the diagnostic study of artworks as well as for archaeological finds. Among them, the most important are those that are non-invasive. These latter techniques are highly successful in providing useful data without altering the original state of the object. In this paper, we present our current research on two cases in which Visible-Light Induced Luminescence (VIL) was applied: the anthropoid wooden coffin of Pakharu, dating to the first half of the Twenty-fifth Dynasty and the "painted wooden board", (Twenty-second to Twenty-fifth Dynasties), which was made by re-assembling two different fragments of the same cartonnage onto a wooden support mounted within a golden frame.

Introduction

Visible-Light Induced Luminescence (VIL) is a very useful analytical tool for detecting and identifying Egyptian blue pigments on the painted surface of Egyptian artefacts. In particular, this technique is important not only for the blue areas but also for the green and black ones, where Egyptian blue could be present in mixtures or in altered form. Portable diagnostic techniques such as VIL allow a quick and direct intervention on the artefact without moving it from the museum or archaeological site.

VIL is an imaging technique applied to the examination of a surface: it is used to recognise and map the spatial distribution of pigments. Some pigments, including cadmium yellow, cadmium red, and especially Egyptian blue, Han blue and Han purple (both of these are barium copper silicate synthetic pigments developed in China), are characterised by a strong luminescence in the infrared following the absorption of visible light. VIL photography captures the luminescence of pigments that are sensitive to the technique. In this way, a non-invasive imaging technique provides the opportunity to analyse an artefact and to detect Egyptian blue and the other pigments, even when they exist in only a very tiny quantity, pure or mixed.

Egyptian Blue

Egyptian blue was called *ẖsbd-ỉryt* ("artificial lapis-lazuli") in ancient Egyptian, or "uknu" in the Assyrian language. It is considered to be the oldest synthetic pigment ever

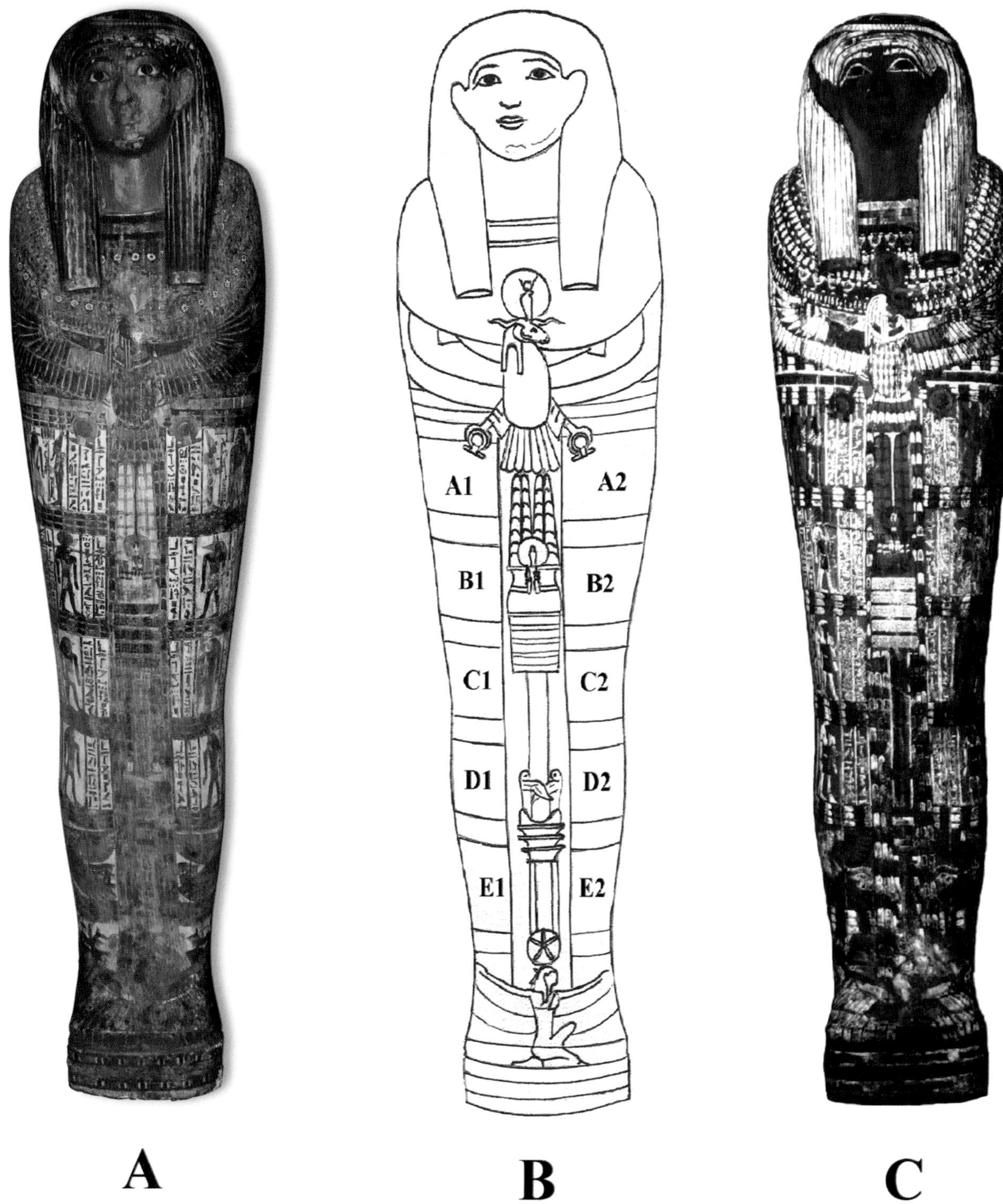

Fig. 84: The lid of the coffin of Pakharu (Museo Stibbert, CV 11169). © Musso-Nicola-Petacchi, 1b: drawing by Simone Musso, 1c: photo by ADAMANTIO lab.

Fig. 85: The coffin of Padiashaikhet at the Nicholson Museum in Sydney (Nicholson Museum, NMR. 28). © *Musso-Nicola-Petacchi*

produced by man (Riederer 1997). Egyptian blue is the common name for the pigment made up of a mixture of silica, lime, copper and alkali (Warner 2011). The blue colour is due to the calcium-copper tetrasilicate ($CaCuSi4O10-CaO-CuO-4SiO2$) (Garcia-Fernández *et al.* 2016), commonly existing in nature as the mineral cuprorivaite (Mazzi and Pabst 1962). This mineral is found in such tiny concentrations that it is not possible to use it as a source for pigments (Warner 2011). In Egypt and in the Near East, Egyptian blue was synthesised from as early as the late Predynastic Period (reign of King Scorpion) (Newman 2015; Corcoran 2016). It was widely used from the Fourth Dynasty until the end of the Roman occupation (Riederer 1997). After the collapse of the Roman Empire, it gradually disappears during the Middle Ages (Gaetani *et al.* 2004; Nicola *et al.* 2018). The compound was prepared by firing a mix of limestone powder, copper (copper metal or copper alloy such as scrap bronze or a copper mineral such as malachite), silica and soda at a temperature between 850°C and 1000°C. The best pigment produced was powdered and fired again to be purified. Several studies have been made in recent years, however, the process of production of Egyptian blue is still not entirely clear (Jaksch *et al.* 1983; Riederer 1997; Etcheverry *et al.* 2001; Warner 2011; Johnson-McDaniel and Salguero 2014).

When excited by visible light, Egyptian blue shows a very strong luminescent response in the near infrared, emitting infrared radiation (Pozza *et al.* 2000). This phenomenon is called photo-induced luminescence. The peak of excitation in this material is centred in the red range of the electromagnetic spectrum (at about 630 nm), while the emission spectrum is centred in the near-infrared region (at about 910 nm) (Accorsi *et al.* 2009).

The infrared radiation emitted by the pigment can be recorded with a camera that is sensitive to it (Verri 2009). The radiation appears on the image in the form of a glow, as a very bright white area. The infrared emission of cuprorivaite is exceptionally strong and the length of excitation, i.e. the length of luminescence, is consistent. These factors make it an excellent luminescent marker, useful even for identifying lost decorative patterns that cannot be seen with the naked eye. Another important aspect of synthetic cuprorivaite is that it is a stable material. For this reason, we can be sure that even examples that are a few thousand years old could show luminescence, which neither the environment where they have been stored (humid or dry) nor their eventual exposure to the visible light would have modified over the years (Accorsi *et al.* 2009; Warner 2011).

The images are taken using a digital camera that has been modified. In the present research we used as a light source an LED lamp (YONGNUO YN300) that has a very low emissions in the infrared (IR) range. The luminescence was recorded with a digital camera EOS 400D from which the IR filter had been removed. The sensitivity of the camera is up to 1000 nm. VIL images were produced using a B+W IR (093) BW72487 filter which allows the passage of not more than 1% of the radiation at 800 nm up to 88% at 900 nm.

It is important to note that the small amount of IR

light emitted by the lamp plays an important role in this specific VIL technique used. Indeed the result gives enriched information: in black are visible IR absorbing materials (e.g. many black pigments), in grey are shown reflecting materials while the emitting materials (i.e. Egyptian Blue) glow in white. In this way the pure VIL result is put into context and can be more useful and easy to understand than the mere data sometimes reported.

Two artefacts from the Stibbert Collection: the lid of Pakharu's coffin and the "painted wooden board"

The Stibbert collection (Di Marco 2000) contains a group of Egyptian artefacts bought by the owner on the antiquarian market between 1864 and 1869. Among them, two relevant objects are the lid of the anthropoid coffin of Pakharu and a painted wooden panel. Since 2013 we have been charged by the management of the Museum with the study and publication of the Egyptian collection. From the beginning, we were convinced of the authenticity of these items despite the opinion of previous scholars who thought they were fake (a hypothesis that was never scientifically proved however). The application of the VIL technique revealed that the figurative decoration in blue, present on both of the artefacts, was created with real Egyptian blue. In addition, stylistic and epigraphic elements corroborated the date of the objects and their authenticity.

The lid of Pakharu's coffin (Museo Stibbert, CV 11169) 170 x 42 cm (**Fig. 84**), has such a close parallel in the style and iconography of Padiashaikhet's coffin on display at the Nicholson Museum in Sydney (Nicholson Museum, NMR. 28) (**Fig. 85**; Taylor 2006, 263–291), that these two items, dating from the first half of the Twenty-fifth Dynasty, could come from the same workshop. Of the original anthropoid coffin of the deceased only the lid survived, cut from just one wooden block, plastered and painted. The face, coloured red, is framed by a striped wig in yellow and blue. The eyes are sculpted and painted, and the mouth has only a hint of a smile. The chin was adorned with a false beard, now lost, of which the remains of the wooden tenon are still present. Around the forehead there is a painted floral diadem. On the top of the head on a white background, a sacred scarab is painted in black, a symbol of the god Khepri, the daily hypostasis of Re who confers rebirth to the deceased with his rays. The lid is divided into zones across the body featuring panels of various gods. Under the large and polychrome *wesekh* collar, Amun-Re is shown standing in the form of a falcon with a ram's head topped by a solar disc with a uraeus; he stretches out his wings in a protective manner. *Shen* rings, symbolic of the solar circuit and eternity, are grasped in his claws. A significant iconographical element is the presence, at the same time, of both curved and corkscrew horns. This is not uncommon among the coffins of the Third Intermediate Period.[1] Under the solar falcon, in a central register, is the Abydos fetish.

From the sides of the diadem which frames the reliquary, two lion-headed falcons display their wings to protect the base of the central shaft. In the centre is a column of hieroglyphs painted on a yellow background, registers G1 and G2, reads as follows (**Fig. 84**b):

ỉnḏ ḥr=k ḫnty-ỉmntt wnn-nfr mꜣꜥ ḫrw nb ꜣbḏw dỉ=f prt ḫrw (n kꜣ n) wsỉr p(ꜣ)-ḫꜣrw mꜣꜥ ḫrw
"Hail to you, Foremost of the West, Wennefer, true of voice, Lord of Abydos, may he give to you invocation offerings (for the ka) of the Osiris Pakharu, true of voice".[2]

Below the *ḏw* symbol, at the level of the ankles of the coffin, the djed pillar is depicted. In the centre of this Osirian symbol, on a yellow background, a column of hieroglyphs reads as follows:

wsỉr nb ḏd·w ỉrỉ(=k) sꜣw wsỉr p(ꜣ)-ḫꜣrw mꜣꜥ ḫrw
"Osiris, Lord of Busiris, may you protect the Osiris Pakharu, true of voice".

Under the aforementioned emblem, at the level of the foot, there is a kneeling goddess with open wings for protection. She wears a tripartite wig topped by a blue disc containing a yellow star, emblem of the Duat, the Hereafter. She represents the personification of the Duat who hosts and protects the divinised deceased.

Each lateral side of the lid is painted with images of the dead and the gods, within five registers, on a white background and framed by *rishi*-like borders.

Two horizontal inscriptions on a yellow background framed by two lines of *rishi*-like borders contain the following texts:

Right inscription, in section I1 (Fig. 1b):
ỉmꜣḫ(w) ḫr nṯr ꜥꜣ nb qrst p(ꜣ)-ḫꜣrw mꜣꜥ ḫrw

---

[1] For parallels, see Taylor 2006, pl. 51; Musso and Petacchi 2014, 441–452.

[2] This funerary invocation is less common than the *ḥtp-dỉ nsw* one, but it is recorded on coffins and inscribed materials dating to the Twenty-third to Twenty-fifth Dynasties. See Taylor 2006, 277–281, pl. 51.

"The one honoured by the great god, lord of the tomb, Pakharu, true of voice".

Left inscription, I2:
imȝḫ(w) ḫr nṯr ꜥȝ nb qrst p(ȝ)-ḫȝr[w mȝꜥ ḫrw]
"The one honoured by the great god, lord of the tomb, Pakhar[u, true of voice]".

In register A1 of Fig, 1b, the deceased is followed by two of the four Sons of Horus in front of Osiris. In the right scene Pakharu is standing and wears a short kilt and a transparent overdress. The chest is bare, apart from the white strip of cloth across his chest which attests to his religious function. On the head, a short wig topped by an unguent cone is decorated with a closed lotus flower. Behind, Osiris is dressed in linen wrappings and he wears the white crown. Behind him, three columns of hieroglyphs give Pakharu's titles and his pedigree.

Inscription A1:
1) wsir mry nṯr ḥnk nw·w iwnw šmꜥ p(ȝ) 2)-ḫȝrw mȝꜥ ḫrw sȝ mi nn 3) p(ȝ)-nḥsy mȝꜥ ḫrw (nb) imȝḫ
1) "The Osiris, the one beloved of the god, the one who offers *nw* bowls in the Heliopolis of the South, 2) Pakharu, true of voice, son of the one who bore the same titles 3) Panehesy, true of voice, lord of favours".

The left scene is approximately the same and Pakharu is depicted in the same way. Behind him are the figures of Qebehsenuef and Duamutef, with the symbol of the East behind them. Three columns of hieroglyphs give Pakharu's titles and the name of his father:

Inscription A2:
1) wsir mry nṯr ḥnk nw·w iwnw šmꜥ ꜥbw m 2) ipt-swt p(ȝ)-ḫȝrw 3) mȝꜥ ḫrw sȝ mi nw p(ȝ)-nḥsy
1) "The Osiris, the one beloved of the god, the one who offers *nw* bowls in the Heliopolis of the South, the wab priest in service at 2) Karnak temple, Pakharu 3) true of voice, son of the one who bore the same titles, Panehesy".

The lower scenes, on the right and left side, quote a part of Chapter XLII of the Book of the Dead, the formula "to repel any evil and injury done in the necropolis". The limbs of the deceased are divinised and associated with specific gods. Even though this chapter is relatively common on funerary papyri and on the walls of tombs, it is not found on coffins before the Twenty-fifth Dynasty.[3]

Register B1 shows an image of a falcon-headed Re topped by the solar disc with Hathor looking towards the left side.

Five columns of hieroglyphs accompany the figures:
1) wsir mry nṯr ḥnk nw·w iwnw šmꜥ ꜥbw m ipt-swt 2) p(ȝ)-ḫȝrw (iw) ḥr=f m rꜥ 3) wsir mry nṯr ḥnk nw·w iwnw šmꜥ p(ȝ)-ḫȝ 4) rw mȝꜥ ḫrw iw irty=f(y) m 5) ḥwt-ḥr nb·t iwn·t
1) "The Osiris, the one beloved of the god, the one who offers *nw* bowls in the Heliopolis of the South, the wab priest in service at Karnak temple 2) Pakharu, his face [is] that of Re; 3) the Osiris, the one beloved of the god, the one who offers the *nw* bowls in the Heliopolis of the South, Pakha- 4) ru true of voice; his eyes are those of Hathor, Lady of Dendera".

In the left scene, register B2 shows Anubis and Isis moving towards the right. Five columns of hieroglyphs accompany the figures:
wsir mry nṯr ḥnk nw·w iwnw šmꜥ p(ȝ)-ḫȝ 2) rw iw spty=fy m inp(w) 3) iw ḥn=f 4) m ȝst mwt nṯr ḥwt-ḥr nb·t iwn·t
"The Osiris, the one beloved of the god, the one who offers *nw* bowls in the Heliopolis of the South, Pakha- 2) ru; his two lips are those of Anubis; 3) his neck is 4) [the neck] of Isis, mother of the god, and Hathor, lady of Dendera".

The right register below, C1, shows the figure of a standing god who is described, using a plural form, as Lords of Kher-Aha, together with a figure of a female divinity, identified as Nut. Both are looking towards the left side.

Four columns of hieroglyphs accompany the figures:
1) wsir mry nṯr ḥnk nw·w iwnw šmꜥ p(ȝ)-ḫȝ 2) rw mȝꜥ ḫrw iw=f m nb·w 3) ḫr-ꜥḥȝ iw šn· 4) w=f m nwt
"The Osiris, the one beloved of the god, the one who offers *nw* bowls in the Heliopolis of the South, Pakha- 2) ru, true of voice; his limbs are those of the lords of Kher-Aha; 3) his hairs are those of Nut".

The left register, C2, shows the goddess Serqet, together with Wepwawet who is shown with a human appearance, as opposed to the more common image of him with a jackal head. Both are standing and looking towards the left. Three columns of hieroglyphs accompany the figures:

[3] The same text decorated the inner coffin of Tashepenkhonsu that is now lost. It was previously on display in the former Giza museum as we can infer from some old postcards which show clearly that the coffin of Tashepenkhonsu has a stylistic affinity with that of Pakharu from the Stibbert Museum. See Munro 2009, 19–20, pl. 14.

1) wsỉr mry nṯr ḥnk nw·w ỉwnw šmʿ p(ꜣ)-ḫꜣ 2) rw mꜣʿ ḫrw ỉw ỉbḥw=f (m) srqt 3) ỉw ʿnḫwy=f(y) m wp-wꜣwt
"The Osiris, the one beloved of the god, the one who offers *nw* bowls in the Heliopolis of the South, Pakha- 2) ru, true of voice; his teeth are those of Serqet; 3) his ears are those of Wepwawet".

The lower right register, D1, includes the god Ptah wearing the dress of the living, looking towards the left followed by a goddess who is not identified. Two columns of hieroglyphs read as follows:

1) wsỉr mry nṯr ḥnk nw·w ỉwnw šmʿ p(ꜣ-)ḫꜣrw 2) mꜣʿ ḫrw ỉw rdwy=f(y) m ptḥ
"The Osiris, the one beloved by the god, the one who offers the *nw* bowls in the Heliopolis of the South, Pakha- 2) ru, true of voice; his feet are the ones of Ptah".

On the other side, register D2 shows a god wearing the dress of the living, looking towards the right. The inscription describes him as Osiris. Behind him is a female figure, but she is not identified. The text, divided in two parts, reads as the follows:

1) wsỉr mry nṯr ḥnk nw·w ỉwnw šmʿ p(ꜣ)-ḫꜣrw 2) mꜣʿ ḫrw ỉw ḥnn=f(y) m wsỉr
1) "The Osiris, the one beloved of the god, the one who offers *nw* bowls in the Heliopolis of the South, Pakha- 2) ru, true of voice; his phallus is that of Osiris".

Sections E1 and E2 are a mirror image of each other, showing a falcon with wings stretched out towards the djed pillar in the centre, in a gesture of protection. Between the wings there is a *wedjat* eye.

Sections F1 and F2 are also a mirror image of each other, with a black jackal depicted crouching on a plinth with a cavetto cornice, from which an uraeus comes out. The inscription identifies the jackal on each side as Anubis. Under the plinth, within a yellow band, which is framed by a block border in alternating colours, there are two hieroglyphic inscriptions with an apotropaic central ankh sign.

Inscription H1:
ḏd mdw gb r-pʿ nṯrw ỉrỉ(=k) sꜣw wsỉr p(ꜣ)-ḫꜣrw
"Words spoken: Geb, Lord of the gods, may (you) make the protection for the Osiris Pakharu".

Inscription H2:
ḏd mdw ỉnp(w) nb tꜣ-ḏsr ḫnty sḥ-nṯr ỉrỉ(=k) sꜣw wsỉr p[(ꜣ)-ḫꜣrw]
"Words spoken: Anubis, Lord of the sacred land, the one who presides over the divine pavilion, may (you) make the protection for the Osiris P[akharu]".

There was originally almost certainly decoration under the feet, but this is now lost. The inner part of the coffin is plastered and painted uniformly with a gold-yellow background.[4] It is interesting to note that the inner part, at the level of the face and the wig, was carved out, in order to better preserve the face of the mummy by avoiding damage when the coffin was closed. The Egyptian blue pigment used to decorate the surface of the coffin appears in the VIL image as a series of bright white areas (**Fig. 84**c).

Genealogy of Pakharu's family

The inscriptions on the lid give information about the personal details and priestly titles borne by Pakharu and his father Panehesy. He worked both at Thebes and at Armant, as did his father before him. Priests with the same names and titles are named on two block statues: the first one, which is complete, is Cairo Museum, JE 36998;[5] the second one is more fragmentary (Cairo Museum, JE 36971).[6] Both belonged to the priest of Montu named Nespasefy also named as Senu-shery, who was the son of Pakharu. They were found by Georges Legrain in the Karnak cachette at the beginning of the twentieth century.

We can suppose that Pakharu should be identified with Pakharu II, quoted on both the two aforementioned statues, and Nespasefy Senu-shery can be equated with Nespasefy I, one of the forefathers of the well-known Besenmut family. He was the nephew of Pakharu I, who was the son of the God's servant of Montu, Hor (**Fig. 86**). Furthermore, we can also suggest that the coffin of Pakharu has the same provenance as two other coffins that are on display in the Stibbert Museum, the coffin of Nespasefy III and that of his wife, Iretiru, who must have been important members of that family on the basis of the quality and artistic accomplishment of these objects.[7] These two coffins may come from Deir el-Bahari (Wiedemann 1889), where several tombs of the family of Besenmut have been discovered containing coffins and other unspecified items of funerary equipment

4 A similar case is Padiashaikhet's coffin. For this coffin, there is no doubt of its authenticity. See again Taylor 2006, 292, pl. 46.
5 http://www.ifao.egnet.net/bases/cachette/?id=203 (accessed 27 July 2018).
6 http://www.ifao.egnet.net/bases/cachette/?id=165 (accessed 27 July 2018).
7 The two artefacts are under study by the present writers and they will be the main topic of a forthcoming monograph.

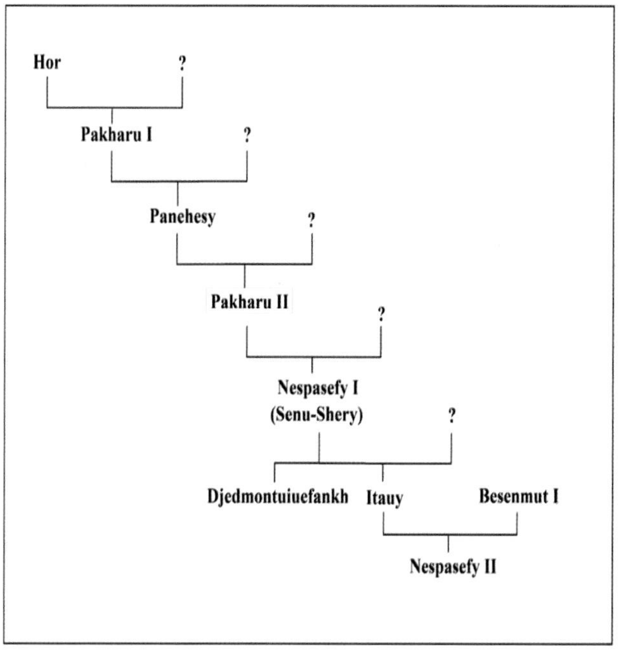

Fig. 86: Genealogy of Pakharu. Reconstruction made by Musso & Petacchi

that are now scattered in private and public collections worldwide, some of which are now lost.

The "painted wooden board"

The so-called "painted wooden board" (Museo Stibbert, Dipinti n° 198) (**Fig. 84**) is 64 cm long, 32 cm high, and 0.7 cm in width. It is not a nineteenth century "divertissement" as suggested by previous scholars.[8] It was created by assembling two different fragments of the same cartonnage on a wooden support within a gilded frame. It dates to a period between the Twenty-third and the Twenty-fifth Dynasties; some restoration of the painting has been added in modern times in order to maintain harmony in the scenes.[9] According to the inscriptions, the cartonnage belonged to the lady of the house named Asetirdis. We can make out the *rishi* friezes, and we can easily read the lightly raised relief hieroglyphs in Egyptian blue on a red background. Using VIL imagery, as in the case of Pakharu's coffin, it was possible to detect the use of Egyptian blue on the *rishi* friezes, on the hieroglyphs of the central and vertical inscription and on the skin of some gods. The VIL images showed as bright white areas the parts where this material has been used (**Fig. 87**, lower image).

Two painted scenes coloured yellow were divided by a central vertical inscription of blue hieroglyphs over a red background framed by two *rishi* friezes. This contains a type of funerary invocation rarely attested elsewhere on coffins from that period (**Fig. 88**).

ind̲ ḥr=k wsir ḫnty-imnt wnn-nfr nb ꜣbḏw di=k wḏꜣ=i m ḥtp r imnt(t) šsp (ḫt) nb(.t)[...]
"Hail to you, Osiris, Foremost of the West, Wennefer, Lord of Abydos, may you cause that I go forward in peace towards the West, <may I> receive every <thing>..."

The left scene shows an anthropoid figure of the god Thoth with an ibis head moving towards the left.[10] He wears a red wig and a strip of white fabric crosses his chest. Before him a text introduces him as:

ḏḥwty nb mꜣꜥt wḏꜣ mdw "Thoth, Lord of Maat, the one who judges the words".

It is noteworthy that Thoth's skin is green but the white fluorescence in the VIL image shows the presence of Egyptian blue. This could be due to various reasons. For example:

[8] See the (now very questionable) note of one of the curators of the exhibition "Frederick Stibbert. Gentiluomo, collezionista e sognatore" in the catalogue of the exhibition of the same name, held at the Stibbert Museum in 2001, 2000, p. 94: "Sorgono però dei dubbi sull'autenticità questo reperto, originati da diversi fattori. Il coperchio infatti si presenta ricavato in un sol pezzo di legno (sic! 'several anthropoid coffins were made from only a single piece of wood'), e mostra l'interno molto levigato e privo di qualsiasi traccia di decorazione o iscrizione. La decorazione esterna inoltre fa sorgere il dubbio che si tratti di una copiatura da sarcofagi autentici non perfettamente capita (sic!), con una mescolanza di motivi che lasciano molte perplessità come la testa di ariete sul petto (sic!) e il disco solare con la stella (sic!). Anche le iscrizioni piuttosto limitate, che porterebbero a far risalire la datazione rispetto agli altri due sarcofagi del Museo Stibbert, contraddicono con la tipologia del coperchio (sic!); inoltre l'iscrizione della fascia centrale, che si suppone trattarsi della formula dell'offerta, appare copiata da un testo non capito (sic!). Sono da ritenere pertanto fondati i dubbi sull'autenticità del reperto (sic!)".

[9] To confer a certain stylistic coherence, the modern artist modified the right scene by painting over, in yellow, the lower part of the horizontal *rishi* frieze which is above the god Khnum and the falcon: he is depicted with only two stylised, yellow feathers rather than the more normal three rows of feathers. The artist has also extended the double feathers of the god Khnum's diadem with the solar disc.

[10] According to the VIL photographs taken, this is the section with the most retouched parts, with different layers of painting made in modern times, especially on the image of Asetirdis and on the two priests. The decorative friezes which frame the central scenes are new except for the *rishi* frieze in front of Thoth.

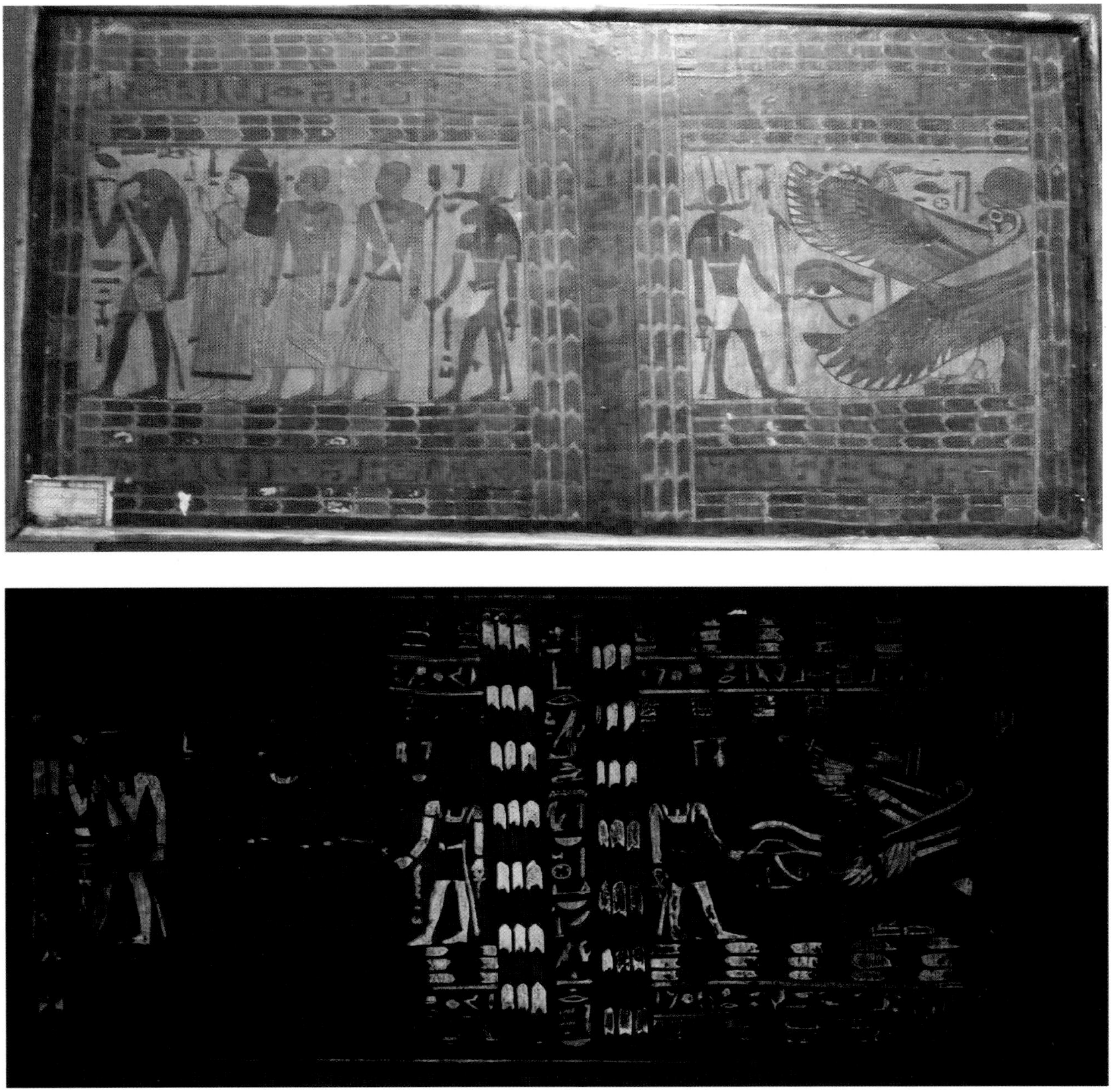

Fig. 87: The "painted wooden board" (Museo Stibbert, Dipinti n° 198). © Musso-Nicola-Petacchi, 4c: photo by ADAMANTIO lab

- a) the pigment is the related synthetic pigment Egyptian green. Egyptian green does not respond to the VIL technique (Verri 2009), however there may be some cuprorivaite present in the final product, or the pigment could be an accidental or intentional mix of Egyptian blue and Egyptian green, so a luminescence could still be seen.
- b) the green is a mixture of Egyptian blue and a yellow pigment. Examples of this are certainly known from the period of the coffin studied in this paper (Scott 2016).
- c) the aspect of the surface is now greenish, but it was originally blue and the yellowing of a binding medium or a resin has changed the appearance (Daniels *et al.* 2004).

It seems however, that there is no luminescence from the face or beak of Thoth. There could be various explanations for this, such as the presence of soot

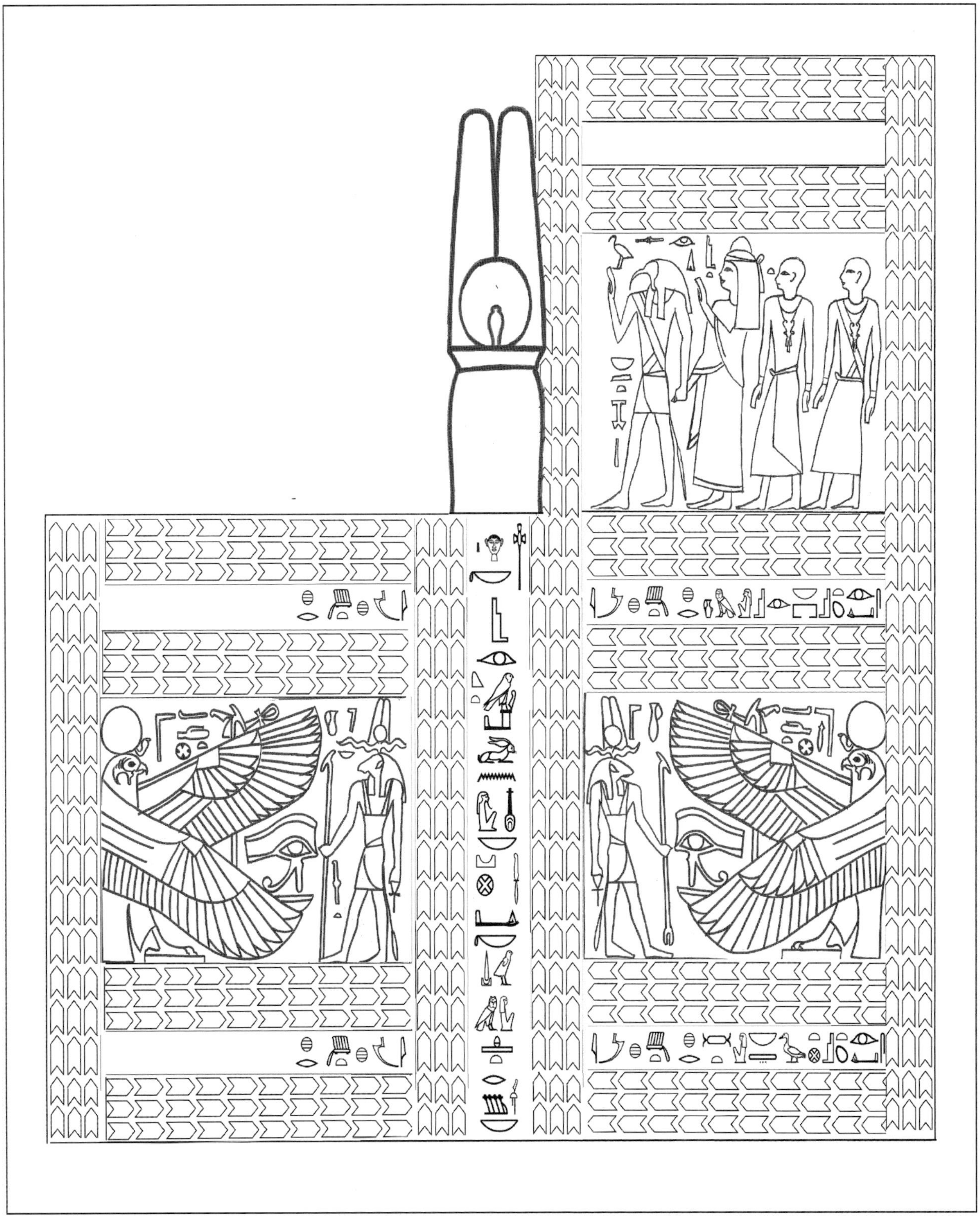

Fig. 88: Reconstruction of the "painted wooden board". Drawing by Simone Musso

deposits or previous Nineteenth Century restorations and repainting.

Thoth raises his right hand in a gesture of greeting and he takes the deceased, Asetirdis, by the arm. Framed by a black wig, she has an unguent cone on top of her head and she wears a long, white and pleated robe. She is shown in the same pose as Thoth. Behind her are two unidentified male figures, each shaven-headed and with a naked torso, who wear short, pleated kilts. Each one has a wesekh collar and a bat pendant on his neck. It is likely that they are two priests of the god Montu, as suggested by that emblem, and they were probably members of the same family as the deceased. Behind them is a figure of Khnum with a ram's head, identified by the hieroglyphic text as:

ẖnmw nb ỉmnt(t) "Khnum, Lord of the West".

The left scene shows the god depicted with skin that appears green, and the head framed by a bipartite wig from which corkscrew horns rise, surmounted by a diadem with two tall feathers and a solar disc. He brings the *ankh* sign and the *was* sceptre. The right scene contains a standing figure of the god Khnum similar to the one on the left.[11] The god is introduced by hieroglyphs which mention his name. In front of Khnum is a falcon with outspread wings on a low plinth. grasping a *maat* sign. Between the wings is a *wedjat* eye on a *nb* basket. The hieroglyphic text above the falcon reads:

bḥdt nṯr ꜥꜣ "Behedet, the great god".

The scene with the god Khnum in the left register, the vertical inscription and the scene currently positioned to the right originally belonged to the same section of decoration, probably positioned in the area between the knees and the ankles of the cartonnage. In front of the scene of Khnum, according to Egyptian symmetry and the sacredness of figurative images, there should have been a mirror image of Khnum and the falcon with opened wings on the other side.

This is also confirmed by the direction of the horizontal hieroglyphs which frame the top and bottom of the figured scene. The inscriptions of the left scene were traced at the time the two fragments were reassembled: the artist, probably Frederick Stibbert himself, who was a well-known painter but not an expert in the ancient Egyptian language, completed the missing part by repeating the surviving text, in the upper band and in the lower part, without understanding the meaning. The only original parts of the inscription are the ones including the last hieroglyphs at the right which form the words *ỉmꜣḫ(w·)t ḫr* "the one honoured by…", which is the beginning of the original inscription written right-to-left, now lost, together with the rest of the figural scene. The original hieroglyphs can be distinguished from the ones added in modern times by the fact that they were painted with a dense pigment which pooled along the edges as it dried..

The scene in which Thoth is shown accompanying Asetirdis followed by two priests is rather rare for this type of funerary artefact, and probably belongs to another register of figures, which was on the front right side of the cartonnage in the area between the chest and the hips. We read:

ỉmꜣḫ(w)·t ḫr ẖnmw wsỉr nb(·t) pr ꜣst-ỉrỉ-dỉ=s
"The one honoured by Khnum, the Osiris, lady of the house, Asetirdis".

On the bottom:

ỉmꜣḫ(w)·t ḫr nt nb(·t) sꜣ(w)·t wsỉr nb(·t) pr ꜣst-ỉrỉ-dỉ=s
"The one honoured by Neith, Lady of Sais, the Osiris, lady of the house, Asetirdis".

On the left side: *ỉmꜣḫ(w)·t* "The honoured one…".

It is interesting that the inscriptions mention two gods whose local cult centres are geographically far away from one another: for Khnum, this was the area of the cataracts at the southern frontier with Nubia, while Neith was the tutelary goddess of the Delta, in the northern part of the country. Our attempt to reconstruct the original decorative plan of the cartonnage is supported by comparing the panel with other cartonnages of the same style and similar decoration.

We hope that in the future, the aforementioned non-invasive technique could be used more often in supporting philology and stylistic studies in order to clarify better the authenticity of artefacts, and to provide data about the social status and provenance of the individuals to whom they belonged.

[11] There is no luminescence from the central part of the bodies of the Khnum figures, nor from their faces or horns. As already noted in relation to Thoth, this maybe because of nineteenth century restorations and repainting in these areas.

A coffin lid of an unidentified person from the Late Period

Observations on the wood and construction

Antje Zygalski

The Heinrich Schliemann Institute for Ancient Sciences (H.Sch.-Institut für Altertumswissenschaften) of the University of Rostock owns an archaeological collection, including ancient Egyptian objects from Abusir el Meleq. The investigation and conservation of the coffin lid, the subject of this paper, has been divided between two universities: the Egyptology department of the University of Cologne and the Cologne Institute of Conservation Sciences of the Technical University of Cologne. The coffin lid under discussion was made for an unidentified person (Inv.Nr. 148, I, 3). It reached the University of Rostock as a gift in 1903 from the Deutsche Orient-Gesellschaft Berlin. Since that time, the coffin lid has not undergone any treatment. It consists of single boards that are plastered with Nile mud and painted. In this paper, science and art technological results from examinations of the wood are presented. The species of wood used, the production of the single parts and, at least, the construction of the lid are described in detail.

This paper makes use of an extensive glossary of woodworking terms, which will be found at the end of the paper.

1. Introduction

In the Cologne Institute of Conservation Sciences (CICS), it is a requirement that documentation is completed for every conserved object. The general structure of the content is as follows:

1 Short description with art historical facts
2 History of condition
2.1 Original condition
2.2 Treatments to which the object has been subject (e.g. reuse, conservation interventions)
2.3 Current condition
3 Conservation concept
4 Conservation treatments

In every subsection of "2 History of condition", all layers of the object have to be described (for example, supports and decorative surfaces). For a wooden support this would include the following aspects in this order: materials used, the production of the individual elements, the construction of the object itself. The order helps the reader as it represents the production process. In contrast to the description order, the order of the previous examinations must be set out the other way around: construction, production of individual elements, materials. Therefore, the sections in this paper are organised in the examination order. Additionally, each section shows the steps of investigation in which CICS students have been trained: the results of research first, then the examination of the object.

The examination of the wooden support was carried out in 2014 within the Bachelor of Arts studies of the author.

2. Short description of the object

The coffin lid (Inv.-No. 143, I, 3; **Fig. 89**) is part of the collection of the University of Rostock, Heinrich Schliemann-Institut für Altertumswissenschaften. It is from the coffin of an unidentified person and has been dated to the Late Period by Katharina Stövesand (K. Stövesand, personal communication, 5 April 2016). It

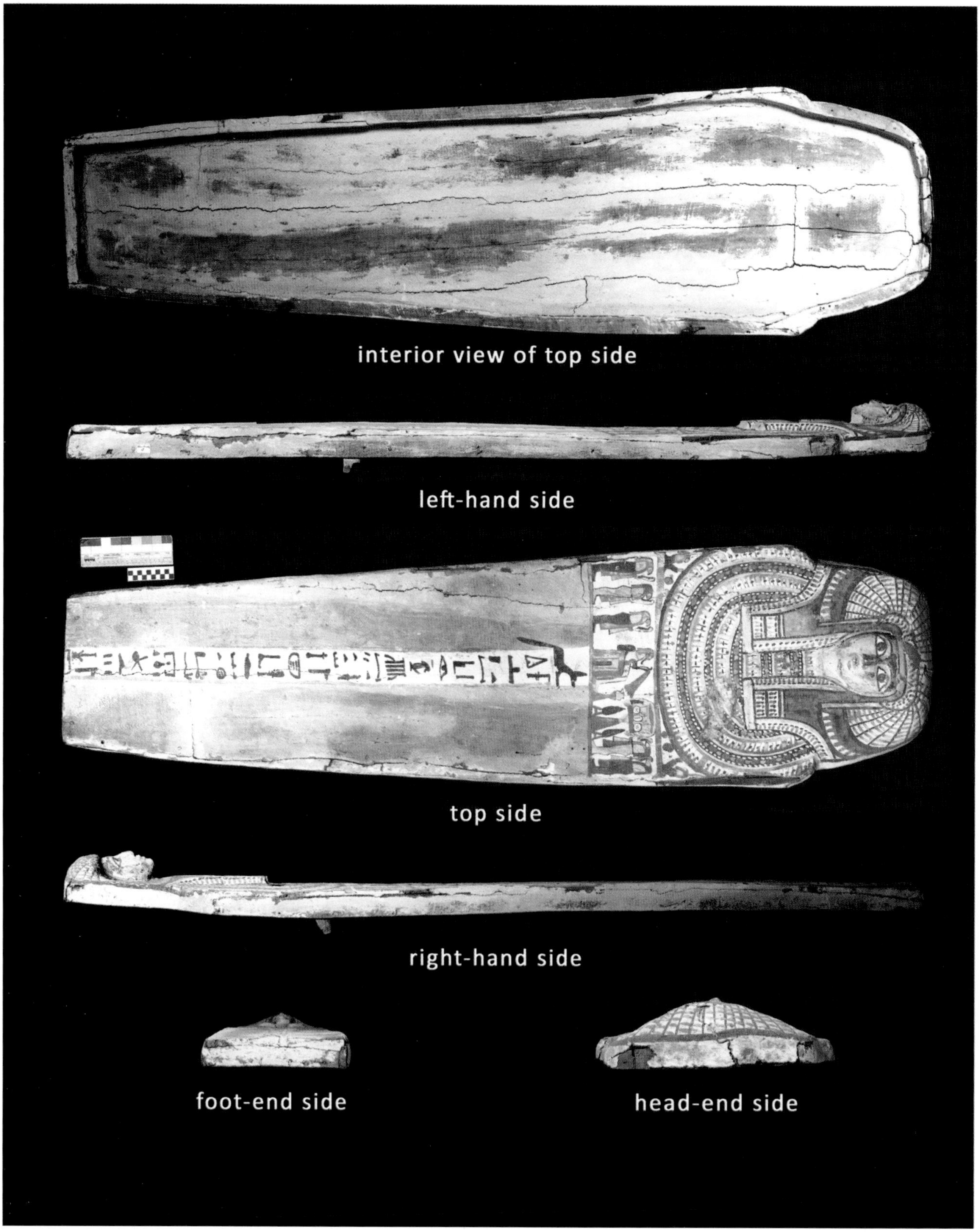

Fig. 89: Coffin lid dated to the Late Period and found in Abusir; photographs of condition before conservation

was found in Abusir el-Meleq as noted on a label on the left-hand side of the coffin lid and in the inventory book of the Heinrich Schliemann-Institut für Altertumswissenschaften (Stövesand 2012, description for fig. 39). Its measurements are 182 cm (width) / 12 cm (height at nose) / 54 cm (depth at shoulders).

The layer stratigraphy of the exterior differs between the part with the decorative scheme and the rest. A first layer of mud-straw paste was applied on the whole coffin to cover timber features and build up the shape of the coffin. Over this the decorative scheme is composed of a white gypsum layer and several polychrome paint layers. The rest of the outside shows a chalk-based layer located only over the mud-straw areas – obviously to cover the dark appearance. Finally, a now brownish appearing glaze was applied on the white area and the area where the wooden support is visible. The intention was maybe an imitation of wood after covering the wood features. The inside of the coffin lid has just the mud-straw paste and the chalk-based layer.[1].

3. Construction

In order to identify the construction of the coffin lid, research into typical construction techniques was undertaken. This was followed by visual examination and X-radiography to clarify, on the one hand, the outlines of the individual timber elements with their fibre direction and the type of joints used and, on the other hand, the fasteners.

3.1 Research on typical coffin constructions

To supplement the limited information available on typical construction techniques for coffins, literature on furniture construction was consulted. Ancient Egyptian Woodworking and Furniture (Killen 1994) was a starting point for possible joint types and mechanisms.

3.2 Examination of individual timber elements, types of joint and fibre direction

A visual examination was undertaken to investigate the individual timber elements used, as well as their grain direction. The examination concentrated on parts that were not painted originally, parts with lost polychromy and cracks in the polychrome areas. Small cracks mostly occur over timber features in individual elements. Larger cracks can be seen on construction joints between two elements due to the shrinking and swelling movements of the timber in response to changing environmental conditions. Many outlines can be mapped just through observation. X-radiography completed this examination and showed the last missing outlines of individual pieces.

Basically, the coffin lid is constructed of a top surface with a connected frame construction underneath to create an internal space (see **Fig. 90, Fig. 91**).

The top surface is made from three rows of elements. The middle and the left-hand row consist of a main board with an additional piece to achieve the required width. In the middle row the additional board is placed at the head end and in the left-hand row it is placed at the foot end. This configuration stabilises the construction, thus avoiding the weak point that would be created if the additional boards were each placed on the same end. Additionally, a very small lath was added to the left row to create the shoulder. The row on the right-hand side is built up from two laths, both of which are too short and too thin to reach the required measurements. Thus, a large hole was created and the intended outer shape could not be achieved. The connection between all of these elements is made from simple butt joints secured with pegs. The fibre direction of all pieces is horizontal.

The right-hand side of the frame construction is a single lath. The left-hand side and the head-end are each constructed from three separate pieces. Presumably, no adequate material with the full length for this purpose was found.

The short laths on the left-hand side are connected to each other by scarf joints (a), whilst the laths on the head-end side (b) have simple butt joints.

For the corner constructions of the foot-end sides to the long sides (c) again the simplest construction technique is used: simple butt joints. The term "corner construction" could also be used to describe the simple butt joint between the head-end laths and the long sides (d) although the orientation is not rectangular but diagonal.

The type of joint used for the connection of the head area to the body area i.e. at the shoulder (e) is specific: the laths from the head area can be described as engaged in the laths of the body area. This connection can be called "bird´s mouth".

The fibre directions of the frame elements are different too. The laths of the long sides and the foot- end are oriented horizontally like the front timber pieces. The laths on the head-end are oriented vertically. Since timber shrinks mostly along the growth rings (circa 10 %), the connection between two fibre directions is always a

[1] The material analyses were carried out by Dr Elisabeth Jägers, CICS.

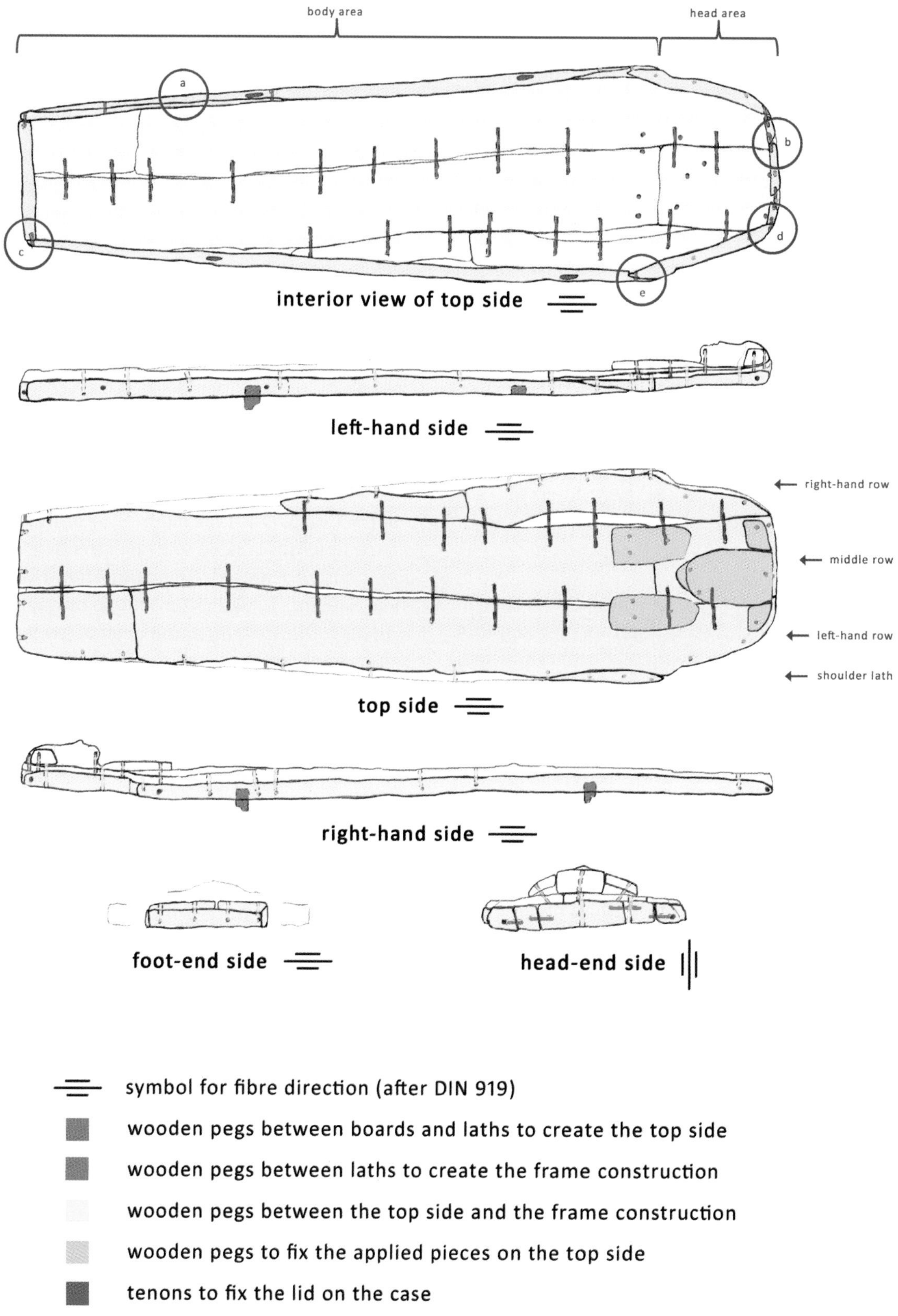

Fig. 90: Coffin lid: sketches of construction features (1)

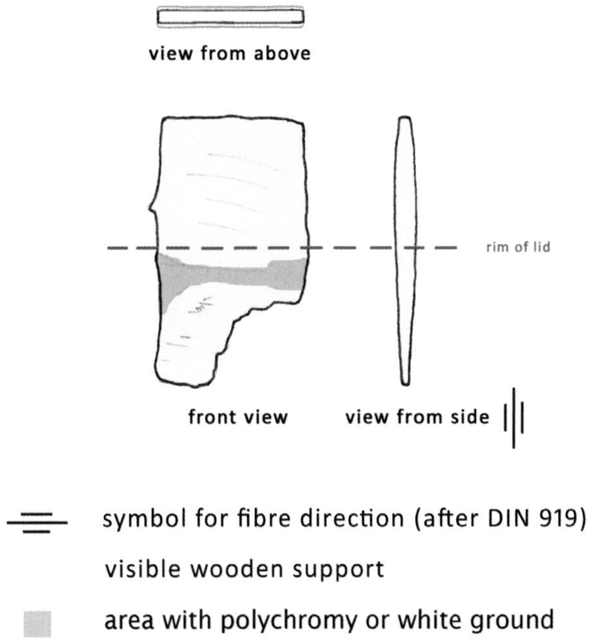

Fig. 91: Coffin lid: sketches of construction features (2)

problematic point. In this case it would mean that the long sides stay dimensionally stable in their horizontal dimension but the laths of the head-end side will shrink horizontally. This may be what has happened and is why today the laths are movable and no longer fit together.

The connection of the top side to the frame is harder to describe because the construction seems random. At certain points, simple butt joints were used but, on major areas of the long sides, the waney edges of timber pieces were used to create a mitre.

The face and wig are created from five single pieces of timber applied to the top surface – one piece for the face, two similar pieces either side of the forehead area and another two for the lappets of the wig. The edges of the small laths to the sides of the forehead are prepared with butt joints. The fibre direction of all pieces is horizontal.

3.3 Examination of fasteners

Visual examination was sufficient to identify most of the joint connectors at corners (because of different shrinkage directions between individual timber elements and pegs) and within the applied pieces of wood (because of the very thin polychromy). The fasteners between the timber elements of the top surface were identified by X-radiography. Three of the four rim tenons – two on each long side – could be taken out of their mortises and investigated by visual examination. (The fourth tenon was broken and the remains of it were wedged in the mortise).

The examination showed that only wooden pegs were used as fasteners. Between the rows within the top surface, on the corners of the frame and to fix the applied pieces they were used in straight orientation and between the top side and the frame construction in diagonal orientation (see **Fig. 90**).

For the safe attachment of the lid to the case, four loose tenons were used. These sit in mortises on the underside of the lid rim. Basically they can be seen as cut laths with their fibre direction oriented vertically. The shape of the three tenons examined is interesting (**Fig. 91**). Regarding the edges of the laths, they each form the shape of an upside down droplet. This shape allows the tenons both to stay in the lid mortises without the use of glue[2] and to be placed in the rim mortises of the case very easily as the lid is put in place to close the coffin. Additionally, the face side of all tenons is not rectangular as is usual. All three tenons show a cut area at the bottom corner that is oriented to the head-end, with the cut area presenting nearly a quadrant. It is possible that these cut-outs were made because the tenons did not fit into the rim mortises of the coffin case, but this theory cannot be checked as the case is lost.

[2] The absence of glue was confirmed by examination with ultraviolet radiation.

4. Production of single timber elements

In order to understand the construction of the lid, firstly research was carried out into typical woodworking tools and the marks they leave. This was followed by visual investigation. There is space in this short paper only to give an overview of the results of the examination.

4.1 Typical woodworking tools

Examples of tools used by carpenters can be seen in museums (e.g. British Museum, London EA 6037, EA 6040, EA 6042–44, EA 6046, EA 6055, EA 6061), and representations of tools in the carpenters' workshop model from the tomb of Meketre (Egyptian Museum, Cairo JE 46722) and depicted on wall paintings, for example in the tomb of Rekhmire at Thebes. The model and the wall paintings show that logs were bound to a pole and sawn into boards. To shape and smooth the surfaces, adzes and small blocks of sandstone were used. To produce holes for fasteners for example, chisels with mallets (for mortises) and bow drills (for peg holes) were employed.

4.2 Examination of toolmarks and production techniques

Traces of tools used were investigated by visual examination. Therefore, tool marks could only be recognised where there is no polychromy. Characteristics of tool marks that help to identify the tools are the imprint of marks, their length, depth and outline, the combination of single marks and their orientation on the timber element (which can be described by reference to the angle of the fibre direction).

On half of the boards from the top side and some laths of the frame construction, similar marks could be seen (**Fig. 92**, the marks are just shown schematically). They are straight and always extend over the whole width of the face side. Additionally, they are very deep and have rough outlines. In combination they appear almost parallel but not to the extent that machine-made tool marks would. It is clear that they are tooth marks made by a saw. An interesting feature is that the angle changes within the length of the top side main boards. At one end the angle could be described as 45 degrees but after approximately 20 cm the angle changes to 90 degrees. The reason for this practice may be found in the relation between the height of the carpenter and the height of the standing round timber. The saw kerf (incision) was placed on an arris, resulting in a starting angle of around 45 degrees. Whilst continuing sawing it was necessary to change to a right angle in order to achieve an even, precise cut. Comparing these marks on the two main boards, it seems possible that both were cut from one trunk. Other features of these boards were checked for similarities. These included both the presence and the area of pith, the locations, sizes and kind of knots, measurements of the boards, outlines of the boards. This investigation confirmed the hypothesis: the main boards were cut out of one trunk. The board in the middle row is oriented as it was cut and the board in the left row was turned over its cross-section side. Since both boards contain parts of the pith, it is clear that they are heart boards.

The loose tenons show different features to those seen on the boards and laths. The marks on the face side are slightly rounded and are mostly oriented from the upper and lower edge to the middle of the face side. This is a first hint for the production technique because if the same tool was used then, within the production process, the tenons must have been turned around. Furthermore, the marks are only a few centimetres long – so not crossing the whole surface. Also, they are deep with very sharp outlines. The individual marks are not parallel to each other and there is no combination of them, which shows that the tool was taken away from the surfaces within the process. The tool that was used is an adze with a slightly rounded blade.

5. Wood

For the examination of wood species used, the research focused on functions for which different wood species might be expected to have been used (e.g. surface elements, applied pieces, fasteners).

From an understanding of the types of wood most likely to be found in coffin construction (see for example: Davies 1995, 146–148; D'Auria et al 1992, 76, 105, 110f, 131, 174; Gale et al 2009 [reprint of the 2000 edition], 335–352; Liptay 2011, 7, 23, 32, 43, 58, 71; Meiggs 1982, 404; Polz 2007, 107; Weisser 2012, 22–29, 34–37, 40–44) and from an examination of samples under an Olympus BH2-UMA microscope at magnifications of ×50 (to distinguish hardwoods from softwoods) and at ×200 (to look for diagnostic features for species), conclusions were drawn and are proposed below. Samples were taken of the transverse, radial and tangential sections and prepared on microscope slides covered with cover glasses.

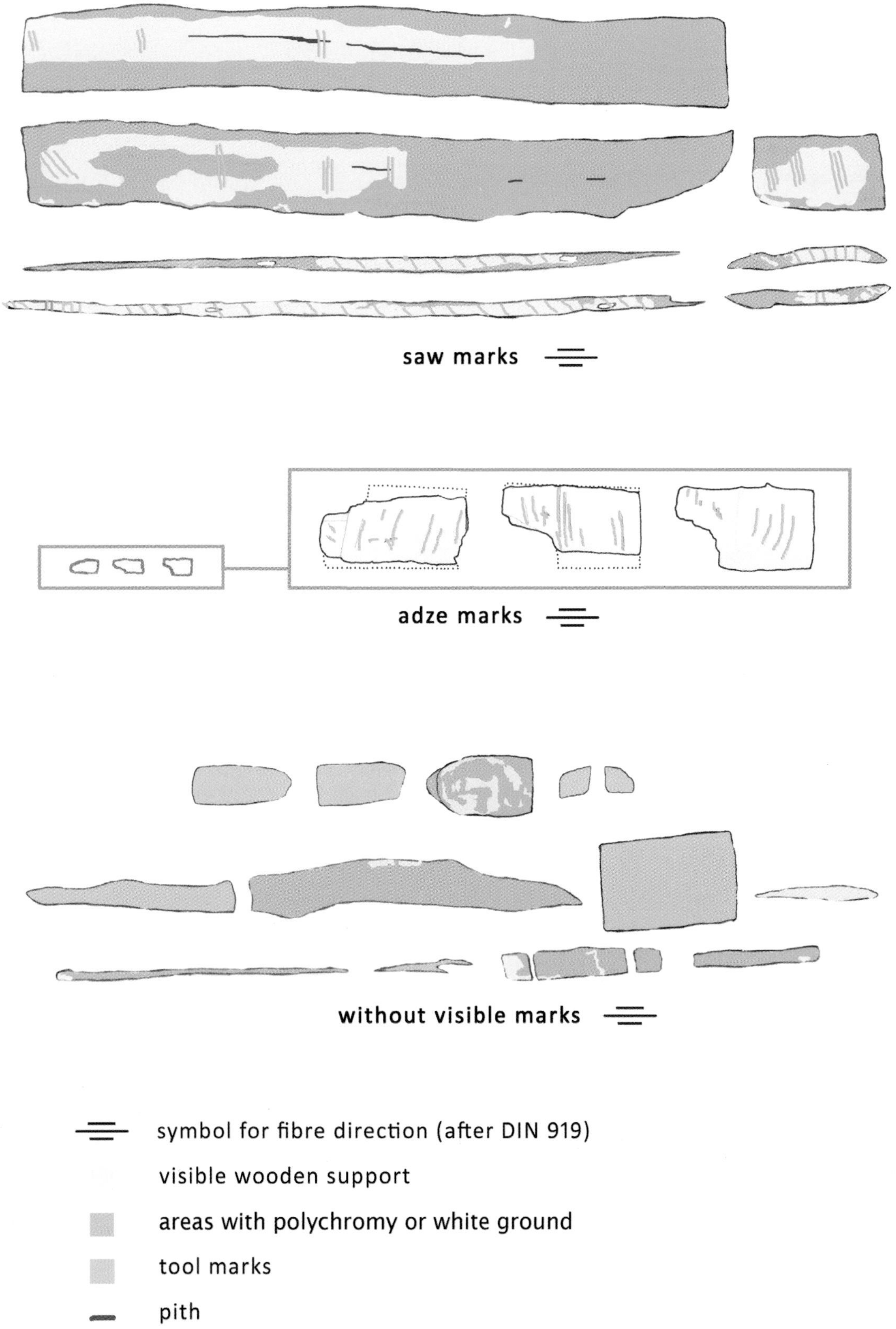

Fig. 92: Coffin lid: sketches of single elements with tool marks

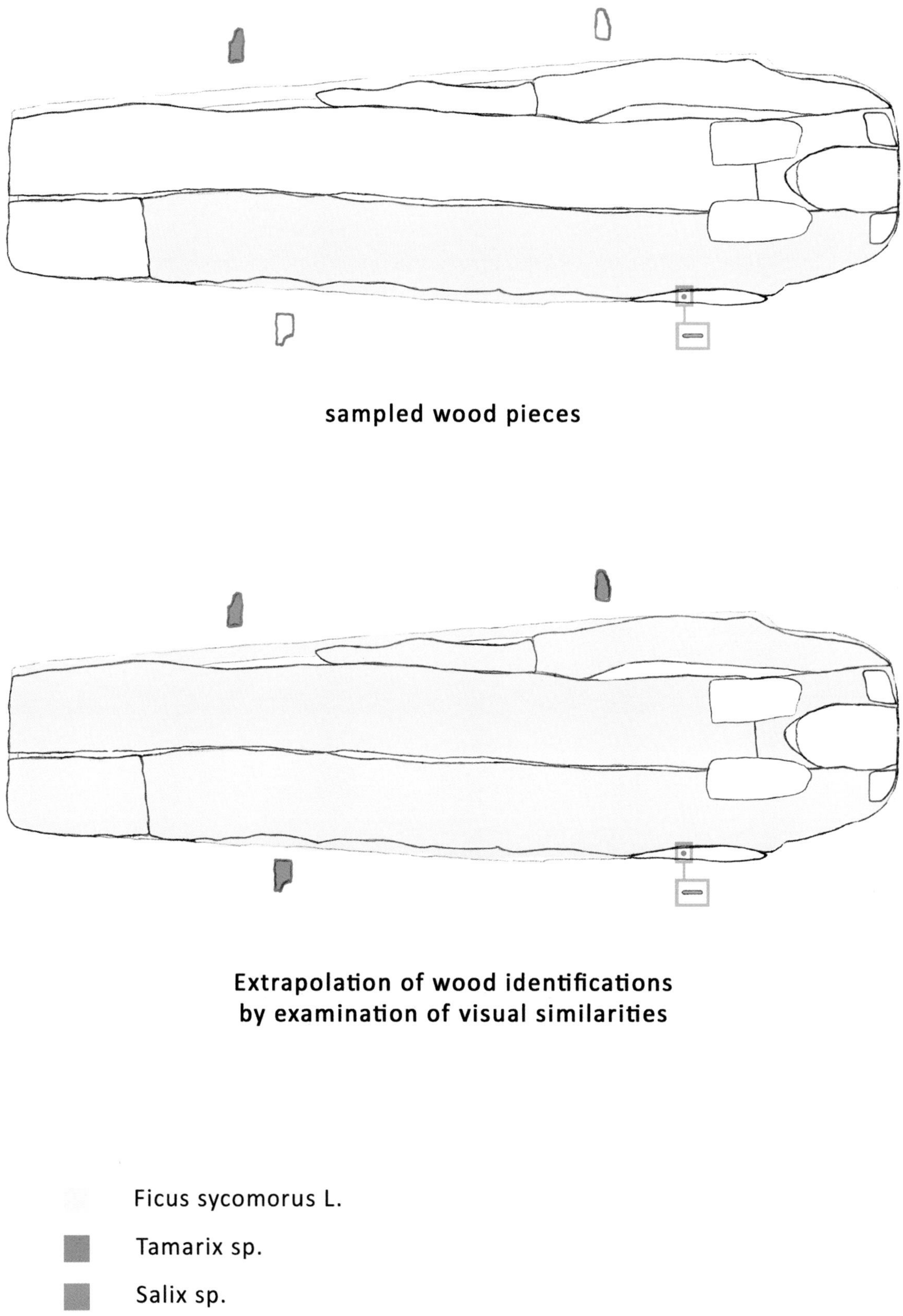

Fig. 93: Coffin lid: wood identifications and suggested extrapolation

5.1 Typical woods used in ancient Egyptian coffins

As with the construction of furniture today, it would be expected that a wooden coffin, would not be made from just one type of wood, but that different species with different properties would be selected to fulfil different purposes in the construction. A modern chest, for example, could consist of a cheap softwood species as a support, covered with an expensive veneer, such as walnut, and jointed with dowels made of beech, for example. In the case of Egyptian coffins, different species might therefore be expected for the following different functions:

1. surface elements (such as boards and laths):
   top and bottom – main elements,
   sides / frame constructions – main elements,
   top and bottom, sides / frame construction – step joints / scarf joints
2. fasteners:
   wooden pegs
   loose tenons
   crossing wooden pegs
3. applied pieces:
   face
   head part of the wig
   wig lappets

From authors who have recently summarised understanding of patterns of wood use across Egyptian coffins of all types, for example Cartwright (2016) and Asensi Amorós (2017, 46), it is clear that this is the case.[3] Sycomore fig, from which relatively large pieces of wood can be taken, is by far the predominant native wood used for surface elements, although there are results of tamarisk for small structural pieces as well. The most common foreign wood for the same purpose is cedar. Dense native woods such as tamarisk and acacia were frequently chosen as fasteners such as wooden pegs and tenons, in order to give strength and stability to the structure. For carved applied pieces again sycomore fig was often used.

5.2 Examinations of wood species

Before the microscope examination of wood samples from the lid was carried out, literature on the microscopic characteristics of likely wood species was collected as reference material (Fahn *et al.* 1986, Grosser 1977, Jagiella and Kürschner 1987, Scheingruber 1990, Schoske 1992, Weisser 2012); reference slides were not used.

Areas for sampling were chosen in relation to the different functions of parts of the construction: a board from the top side, a lath from the frame construction, a wooden peg and a tenon. It was not possible to sample from the applied wooden elements because of the intact polychromy.

From the x50 magnification examination, the four samples were all classified as hardwood, thus ruling out cedar of Lebanon or any other softwood found in Egyptian artefacts. The examination of the samples at x200 magnification indicated three species of wood (see **Fig. 93**).

Part of coffin lid	Wood species
1. Sample of top	*Ficus sycomorus L.*
2. Sample of frame	*Ficus sycomorus L.*
3. Sample of wooden peg	*Tamarix sp.* *(T. nilotica (Ehrenb.) Bunge ?)*
4. Sample of tenon	*Salix spp.*

The sampled top board and lath of the frame are made of sycomore fig and the wooden peg of tamarisk, results that are consistent with previously observed uses. For the wooden peg it was possible to check the ray width which shows that larger rays are commonly 4- to 10-seriate. This might indicate that within the genus of tamarix, the species *Tamarix nilotica* (Ehrenb.) Bunge was used. However, the indigenous species of tamarix in Egypt are difficult to distinguish (Neumann *et al.* 2001).

The identification of the tenon as willow was surprising for the reason that within the research in 2014 willow was found just once: as a side element of the lid from an Eighteenth Dynasty coffin in the Staatliche Museum Ägyptischer Kunst Munich (ÄS 1627; Weisser 2012, 40–44).[4] From the point of view of a carpenter, using willow as a joint means, especially for tenons, makes sense (Duhme and Senge 2015, 106). Firstly, willow is generally very elastic, which aids the process of putting a heavy coffin lid (with tenons already in it) onto a coffin case and then securing the tenons with crossing pegs. This property ensures that the wood will

[3] Asensi Amorós summarises from her database of identifications of 500 Egyptian coffins dating from Prehistory to the Byzantine period and comments briefly on her findings to date from the Vatican Coffin Project.

[4] Subsequent to this research, and after I gave this paper in Cambridge in 2016, identifications of willow in the construction of Third Intermediate Period coffins has been reported by Asensi Amorós (Asensi Amorós 2017, 46)

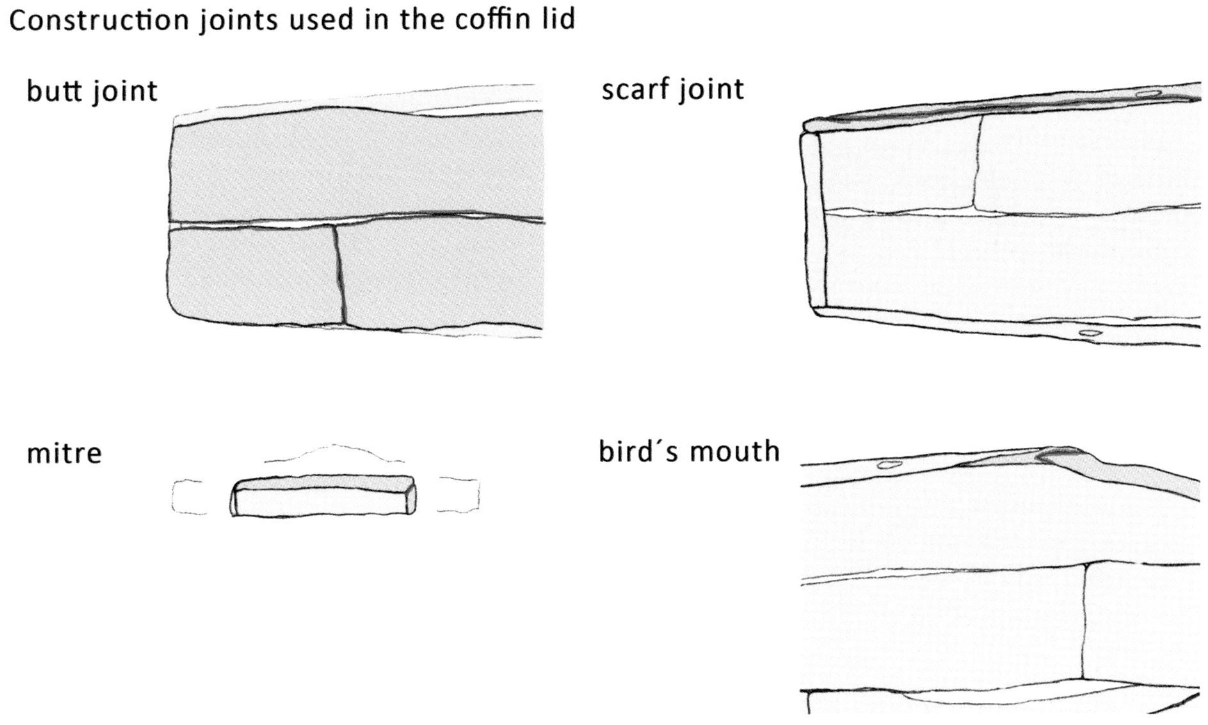

Fig. 94: Construction joints used in the coffin lid

not crack easily. Secondly, the timber can be carved very easily with cutting tools.

In the light of the results from the four samples, specific visual features on the remaining elements were checked again, for example, the colour, the condition of the surface, the texture of the cross section (where it was possible to see this), the occurrence and kind of knots and the elements with insect attack. Nearly all boards and laths representing the top side and the frame construction show the same features, so a tentative extrapolation was made that all are sycomore fig. Only the small lath that creates the left shoulder is of different appearance and assumed to be a different wood. Since the pegs in one coffin are often made of different species, the identification of one as tamarisk cannot provide any clues to the identity of the others. By comparison, the other three rim tenons are all similar in colour, texture and cross section characteristics to the sampled one and may therefore also be of willow.

6. Conclusion

The examination techniques described above have provided evidence towards an understanding of the production process of the coffin lid.

Sycomore fig may have been used for the main elements of the lid, i.e. boards and laths. Indeed, the main boards of the top side appear to have been cut out of one trunk as they are also both heart boards. These elements were generated by sawing the trunk with a hand saw while the trunk was standing in a vertical position, as the tool marks indicate. The presence of waney edges implies that the whole cross section of the timber was used for each plank. The wood of the applied face and wig could not be examined through the taking of a sample. To create fine carving with a smooth surface, a chisel followed by a sanding tool must have to be used for the preparation of these elements.

The individual pieces of the coffin lid were joined mostly using butt constructions with wooden pegs. However, because of the waney edges, the corner joints between the top side and the frame construction employ a mitre joint in places. The pegs (the sampled one identified as tamarisk) were probably cut with an adze or a hand knife. This could not be determined more precisely as it was not possible to remove a peg. Lastly, tenons (one of which appears to be willow) were fashioned with an adze and were put into the mortises to connect the lid with the case.

Glossary of woodworking terms in this paper

Standards

DIN:	Deutsches Institut für Normung (English: German Institute for Standardisation)
EN:	Europäische Norm (English: European Standard)
ISO:	Internationale Organisation für Normung (English: International Organisation for Standardisation)

For timber elements

round timber	"Felled tree crosscut at the top, with all branches removed, that may or may have not been further crosscut [...]" (according to DIN EN 844-2:1997)
individual timber elements:	general term for timberware (such as boards and laths) used to create surfaces and 3D-constructions.
lath:	a piece of timber that is less than 80 mm in width and less than an area of 32 cm2 in section thickness (according to DIN 68252-1:1978, ISO 1032:1974).
board:	a piece of timber which measures more than 80 mm in width and between 8 and 40 mm in section (according to DIN 68252-1:1978, ISO 1032:1974).
heart plank:	"Piece of sawn timber that contains the pith" (according to DIN EN 844-12:2000).
sides of individual elements:	longitudinal sides (face sides and edges) and cross-sections.
face side:	"Either of the wider longitudinal opposite surfaces of sawn timber or any longitudinal surface if the timber is of square cross section"(according to DIN EN 844-3:1995).
edge:	"Either of the narrower longitudinal opposite surfaces of square edged timber." (according to DIN EN 844-3:1995)
cross-section:	"Section at right angles to the longitudinal axis of a piece of timber." (according to DIN EN 844-3:1995)
arris:	"Line of intersection of two faces or a face and an edge:" (according to DIN EN 844-3:1995)
wane:	"Original rounded surface of a log, with or without bark, on any surface or edge of sawn timber" (according to DIN EN 844-3:1995).
fastener:	item used to provide attachment of two or more separate parts, components or assemblies. For example: fasteners have the junction of locking the parts together and providing the structural load path between the parts or, if used as a securing part, to ensure proper locating of the parts to be secured (according to DIN EN 16603-33-01:2018, English version), e.g. nails, pegs, pins or screws.
wooden dowel:	fastener in the form of a rod of solid wood that is routed or pressed by machine with standardised measurements, e.g. 10 x 30 / 35 / 40 / 45 / 50 / 60 mm and is made of beech, oak, ash, robinia or utile (according to DIN 68150-1-1:2016). Therefore, this term should not be used in relation to the construction of ancient Egyptian coffins.
wooden nail:	1:1 translation from German "Holznagel", which describes a fastener from solid wood that is handmade, without standardised measurements or specific wood species, but this term is not commonly used in English (G. Killen, personal communication, 5 April 2016).
wooden peg:	better term for "Holznagel" / "wooden nail" (Chaballe and Vandenberghe 1982, Killen 2016).
crossing wooden peg:	a wooden peg that crosses another fastener (in this case a tenon) with its fibre direction oriented in a 90 degree angle to the piece that it crosses.
timber features:	"Physical, morphological or growth characteristic of timber which could affect its use." (according to DIN EN 844-1: 1995) Examples are the presence of pith, loose or unsound knots or areas with problematic ingredients such as resins.
tooth marks:	"Scoring caused by a saw tooth"(according to European standard EN 844-3:1995).

For timber constructions

terms for sides:	top side (side with face), left-hand side, right-hand side, foot-end side and head-end side. (The coffin is described from the lying position because it is considered as furniture, which would be described from this aspect.)
long side(s):	general term for the two longer sides of a constructed object, in this case the left-hand side and right-hand side.
narrow side(s):	general term for the two narrower sides of a constructed object, in this case foot-end side and head-end side.

dimensioning:	width / height / depth (according to DIN 406-10:1992 for three dimensional objects). The coffin lid is described from the lying position with the describing person standing opposite to the left-hand side.
butt joint:	"Two pieces of wood joined together along the edges with a plain square joint" (according to Corkhill 1979). See **Fig. 94**.
scarf joint:	"A lengthening joint, in structural timbers, that does not increase the cross-section area" (according to Corkhill 1979). See **Fig. 94**.
mitre:	"The intersection of two pieces or mouldings forming an angle" (according to Corkhill 1979). See **Fig. 94**.
notch:	"A V-shaped cut or slot" (according to Corkhill 1979)
end notch: bird´s mouth	"A re-entrant angle at the end of a piece of timber to allow the end to sit astride the corner of a supporting timber" (according to Corkhill 1979). This term is used in schemes for erection of dwelling-houses and flats where the "supporting timber" is oriented horizontal and the "timber with the re-entrant angle" is oriented vertical. However, as there is no term that describes the ancient technique where a lath is notched diagonally into another lath (both oriented in the same way), this term is adopted because of the shape of the notch.

The coffin of the Anthropology Museum in Padua and others

A peculiar type of Late to Ptolemaic Period wooden anthropoid coffins

Susanna Moser

In the Anthropology Museum of the University of Padua there is a wooden anthropoid coffin of a rather unusual type. The apparent inconsistency of the decoration, together with the necessity of a chronological attribution, has led to a search for other examples of this type of coffin. The resulting group of coffins is spread all over the globe: eight coffins are exhibited in The Egyptian Museum, Cairo, and single examples are found in the Royal Ontario Museum, Toronto; the British Museum in London; the Staatliche Sammlung Ägyptischer Kunst, Munich; and in Bombay and other cities.

The Museo di Antropologia of the University of Padua possesses, among its archaeological collections, a wooden anthropoid coffin from Egypt, with no inventory number.[1] It has appeared in several publications so far,[2] but it has not received a thorough study yet.

The coffin (**Fig. 95, Fig. 96**), together with an unwrapped male mummy, arrived in Padua in 1835 as a present to the University by Giuseppe Acerbi, who had been General Consul of the Austrian Empire in Egypt (Carrara, Menegazzi and Moser 2010, 20; Menegazzi, Carrara and Moser 2013, 228). It is said to have been bought in Thebes (Catullo 1836) and it has been stated that it is made of sycomore fig wood.[3] The lid and the box have each been carved from a single piece of wood, probably both from the same tree trunk. On the left side (from the observer's viewpoint) of the head, on the lid, there is a long, deep fissure that seems to be a defect in the growth of wood. The external surfaces appear to be carefully polished, while the internal ones have been left rough and uneven, so that the marks of the artisan's chisel are still clearly visible. The colour of the surfaces varies greatly, from a glossy black on the exterior to the natural golden colour of the wood internally. This difference is not due to the application of a varnish, for there are no traces of it anywhere on the coffin, but most probably to polishing, perhaps with beeswax. Traces of a black substance occur in different spots on the lid. At the level of the chest, where the coffin is wider, some abrasions are present. Woodworm holes are visible almost everywhere.

[1] The present work started in 2009 in the form of the final essay for the Second Level Professional Master's Programme ("Master Universitario di II livello") in Egyptology, organised by Università degli Studi di Torino and Centro di Restauro "La Venaria Reale" in Turin (Moser 2009/2010). The Conference in Cambridge seemed the perfect opportunity for sharing some new data that had been acquired in the meantime.

[2] The coffin is mentioned for the first time in Catullo 1836, 44–64, 3. It then appeared in a number of exhibition catalogues and articles: Drusini *et al.* 1982, *passim*; Rippa Bonati and Drusini 2000, 103–117 *passim*; Carrara, Menegazzi and Moser 2010, 20; Menegazzi, Carrara and Moser 2013, 228–229; Zanovello and Ciampini 2013, 70–72, 84–89; Le mythe Cléopâtre 2014, 108; Cleopatra y la fascinación de Egipto 2015, 163. The only element which has been studied in some detail is the hieroglyphic inscription engraved on the coffin's chest (Crevatin and Bertani 2008, 75–80).

[3] Rippa Bonati 1987, 93: the author quotes an old description of the coffin, dating back to 1835 and part of the modern archive of the University of Padua: "cassa in Sicomoro con geroglifici…". It has not been possible to identify who was the first to state the wood is sycomore fig or how the identification has been carried out. Further investigations should be carried out in order to obtain a definitive wood identification.

Fig. 95: Front of the coffin of the priest Baankh, Museo di Antropologia of Università degli Studi di Padova (courtesy of Museo di Antropologia).

Fig. 96: Back of the coffin of the priest Baankh, Museo di Antropologia of Università degli Studi di Padova (courtesy of Museo di Antropologia).

	Height	Width – head	Width – shoulders	Width – waist	Width – feet	Depth (max)
Box	199	45	60	55	36	36
Lid	200	45	60	55	37	15

The dimensions of the coffin (in centimetres) are shown at the top of the page.[4]

From an iconographical point of view, the proportions of the head and face are strongly emphasised. The wig is smooth, with two straight lappets on both sides of the face, whose features are very delicate. The mouth is shaped as almost smiling. A short braided divine beard is present. The hands are absent, and only the line marking the separation between neck and shroud is carved. Underneath the feet a rectangular base is present, while on the back of the box there is a flat back pillar.

The inscriptions (Fig. 97)

Until recent years, only two lines of carved hieroglyphs running from right to left had been recorded on the chest. A painted inscription, again on the lid, was discovered in 2009 (Moser 2009/2010, 21–25): it consists of five vertical columns of black hieroglyphs, very badly damaged and only partially visible, to be read from right to left and running from below the carved lines to the feet. Lastly, when the mummy was finally removed from the box on the occasion of the Paris exhibition in 2014 (Le mythe Cléopâtre 2014, 108), it was possible to see that the back pillar is also inscribed with two columns of black painted hieroglyphs, from right to left. These too, unfortunately, are damaged and not completely readable. The inscriptions run as follows:[5]

Lid, carved Line 1

ḏd mdw i͗[n] i͗mꜣḫ(y) n wsi͗r ḫtmw-nṯr i͗my-rꜣ wꜥbt n… n ḥwt-ḥkꜣ n i͗r-[n]-wḏꜣt m

Lid, carved Line 2

i͗wnw wꜥb n i͗b-n-rꜥ rḫ-i͗ḫt ḥry-sštꜣ i͗wꜥ Nb-r-ḏr bꜣ-ꜥnḫ sꜣ wnn-nfr i͗r n nb(t) pr di͗=s-ꜥst mꜣꜥ-ḫrw

(1) Words to be said by the *imakhy* of Osiris, seal-bearer of the god[a], overseer of the *Wabet*[b] of (?) …[c] of the *ḥwt-ḥkꜣ*[d] of That-who-was-born-from-the-*Wedjat*-eye[e] in (2) Heliopolis, *wab* priest of the Heart-of-Re[f], learned man[g], in charge of secrets, heir of the Lord-of-Everything[h], Baankh[i], son of Wenen-nefer[j], born by the lady of the house Di-es-aset[k], true of voice.

As it will become clear from the following comments, the orthography of the text is often careless, perhaps due to the difficulty of rendering in hieroglyphs a master copy which was written in hieratic or demotic.

[a]  is to be read *wsi͗r ḫtmw-nṯr*, with haplography of the *netjer* sign. Since this title is often attested (Hannig 2006, 67, n. 24635–24639 and Sauneron 1952), the group of signs  on the back pillar has to be interpreted as an even more defective writing of the same title. As convincingly demonstrated by Serge Sauneron (Sauneron 1952, 151), it implied a role during embalming and, during the Late and Ptolemaic Periods, had a special connection with the Memphite area.

[b] In , the round sign must be interpreted as the determinative for 'city', as the comparison with the text on the back pillar proves. Nevertheless, the usual determinative for the *Wabet* is that for 'house' (Wb I, 284, 4–5; Wilson 1997, 214 and Hannig 2006, 198, 7034–7046). Notwithstanding this problem, the reading of the title as *i͗my-rꜣ wꜥbt* seems sure,[6] especially if considered that it is often associated with *ḫtmw-nṯr* (Sauneron 1952, 155), thus setting the owner of the coffin in the milieu of embalming priests.

[c] The group of signs , that appears on the back pillar as , is highly problematic. In addition, the reading of the determinative is contested by Crevatin (Crevatin and Bertani 2008, 75), who says that the similarity of the carved sign with  is only due to a scratch in the wood. Given the structure of the text, it seems likely that this is the beginning of a new title,[7] connected with the subsequent words.

[d] The most plausible reading of the group  seems to be

[4] Measurements have been taken by the author considering the coffin as standing. Taking into account the Egyptian units of measurement (as described in *LÄ* III, 1199–1200; Hannig 2006, 1319) and how they could have varied in time, it seems likely that the intended height of the coffin was roughly 4 cubits, a hypothesis reinforced by the fact that many of the other coffins used as comparative material (see below) have the same height of 210 cm, that is exactly 4 "royal cubits" of 52.5 cm.

[5] The following conventions are used in the transliteration: ( ) for endings that are not usually written at this stage of the Egyptian language but are necessary for the understanding of the grammar; [ ] for signs that should be present in the inscriptions but are not, either because of a scribal forgetfulness or of a lacuna; < > for signs that are present but should not be there.

[6] The same is proposed also in Crevatin and Bertani 2008, 75.

[7] In Wilson 1997, 563, the word *ndm* as "lord" is attested. This might account for half of the signs, but the rest would still remain obscure.

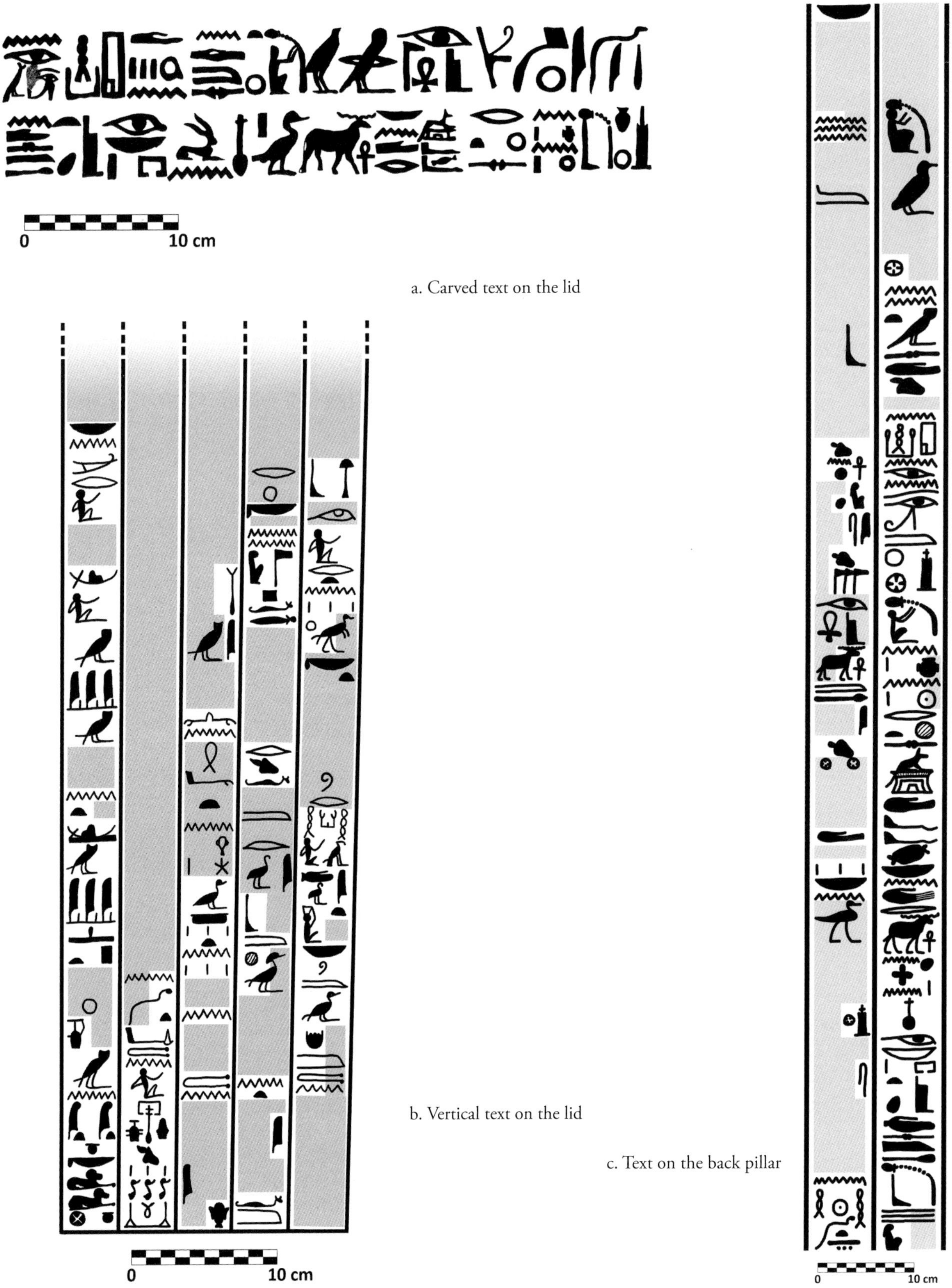

Fig. 97: Facsimile of the inscriptions on the coffin (drawing by S. Moser).

ḥwt-ḥkꜣ, a temple of the local form of the goddess Hathor in the city of Heliopolis.[8]

[e] (written on the back pillar) must be, then, the epithet through which the goddess is named. A good reading is that proposed by Crevatin,[9] who interprets the *wedjat* eye as a cryptographic writing of Re and the whole passage as "the temple of the Eye of Re (i.e. Hathor) in Heliopolis".[10] I would like to add that the spelling of the epithet on the back pillar allows for another interpretation: *ỉr-n-wḏꜣt* can also be translated "The one born by the *Wedjat* eye (i.e. the god Re)".[11] The author of this inscription was probably well aware of this ambiguity, intended perhaps as a display of erudition.

[f] *ỉb-n-rꜥ* is a well attested and frequent divine epithet, connected in particular to the god Thoth (LGG I, 208–209; see also Crevatin and Bertani 2008, 75).

[g] I agree with Crevatin (Crevatin and Bertani 2008, 75) in considering as a form of *rḫ-ỉḫt* (Wb II, 443, 27 and Hannig 2006, 506, 18227), with haplography of the round sign and a misinterpretation of the determinative, which should be .

[h] appears as in the temples of Edfu and Dendera, respectively as an epithet of the god Khonsu-em-Behedet and of the *ỉḥy-wr*, both in the context of ritual scenes of the Graeco-Roman Period.[12] The phonetic writing *dr* for *ḏr* does not pose any problem.[13]

[i] Thanks to the inscription on the back pillar, where appears, it is certain that the name of the owner of this coffin is . Largely attested as divine epithet (LGG II, 668–670) and read as *bꜣ-ꜥnḫ*, "the living ram", it does not seem to be attested as a personal name previously.[14]

[j] The father's name is written and, on the back pillar, . This name, in contrast, is widely attested, corresponding to the Greek Onnophris (Ranke, PN I, 79, 19), even if written quite oddly with the inversion of *wnn* and *nfr* in the first occurrence and with (Gardiner sign M42) in the second.

[k] The name of the mother is less straightforward. Written (and on the back pillar), it best corresponds to Ranke, PN I, 397, 19, *dỉ=s-ꜥst*, taking the hand sign as the verb *rdỉ*, 'to give' (Daumas 1988, 190 n. 871 and Kurth 2010, 47 n. 71).

Lid, Column 1

[…]

…wbꜣ=ỉ r-tn ꜣḫ=k(wỉ) …· r ḥkꜣw=ỉ ỉdwt nbw m <sꜣ> [ꜣḫ] … ḥm=ṯn…

Lid, Column 2:

[…]

… rḫ=k(wỉ) [r]n n nṯr pf ꜥꜣ … r fnḏ=f [tk]m r[n=f] ỉw [w]b[ꜣ] m ꜣḫ[t] … nt [pt] ỉ[w] … f m

Lid, Column 3:

[…]

…sbỉ[w] ỉm … nn šnꜥ=ṯn ḥr sbꜣw=ṯn …n … =ṯn …ỉ ḥr …

Lid, Column 4:

[…]

…n ḏt dỉ=ṯn n=ỉ prt-ḫrw tꜣ ḥnqt kꜣw ꜣpdw šs mnḫt

Lid, Column 5:

[…]

… nb n mr=ỉ [ḥdỉ]=ỉ m … m? sḫt-[ỉꜣrw] ḫnt=[ỉ] m sḫt-ḥtp … ḫnm=n[=ỉ] mꜣꜥty ỉnk rwty

Back pillar, Column 1:

…wꜥb… n ḥwt -ḥkꜣ n ỉr-n-wḏꜣt m ỉwnw wꜥb n ỉb-n-rꜥ rḫ-ỉḫt ḥry-sštꜣ <d> ỉwꜥ [n] nb-r-ḏr bꜣ-ꜥnḫ sꜣ wnn-nfr ỉr [n] nb(t) pr dỉ=s-ꜥst mꜣꜥ-ḫrw wꜥb …

Back pillar, Column 2:

nb ꜥnḫ … nṯrw wsỉr ḫtmw[-nṯr] bꜣ-ꜥnḫ mꜣꜥ-ḫrw …nb n …nḥḥ ḏt

As far as the fragments of painted inscription on the lid are concerned, they are luckily sufficient for identifying the text as BD Spell 72.[15] On the basis of several features of the remaining text[16] it appears that

[8] Gauthier 1927, 115. It is noticeable too, that this is an archaising spelling of the temple's name: the temple of Dendera has (Chassinat 1932, 126, 12).

[9] Crevatin and Bertani 2008, 75.

[10] This would be a newly attested epithet, since LGG VIII, 354, lists among the epithets of Hathor only that of *ỉrt-rꜥ-m-ỉwnt*, "Eye of Re in Dendera".

[11] An epithet with the same structure is attested in Graeco-Roman times (LGG I, 453): the god Hor-sema-taui-pa-khered is referred to as in the temple of Dendera.

[12] LGG I, 178. On the title *ḥry-sštꜣ* see Rydström 1994 and Balanda 2009.

[13] Crevatin and Bertani 2008, 75, could of course not be sure about the presence of the , which is confirmed by comparison with the text on the back pillar, unknown to him at the time. (The same is true also for the rest of the line, whose reading is only confirmed by the text on the back pillar.)

[14] It is not present in Ranke, PN, nor in Michelle Thirion's additions to it (see articles in *Revue d'Égyptologie* 21 to 50 (1979–1999), 65–87) or in the *Demotisches Namenbuch* (Lüddeckens *et al.*, 1980–2000).

[15] Moser 2009/2010, 21–25. The identification was independently made also by Emanuele Ciampini (Zanovello and Ciampini 2013, 71–72). This spell in particular has been studied by Günter Vittmann (Vittmann 1994), allowing some conclusions to be drawn even from the scant remains of text on the coffin in question.

[16] (end of Vittmann's section d of the spell) appears not to be attested in this form in Late Period sources with

the present version of BD 72 is more similar to Günter Vittmann's Versions I and II, the ones dating back to the Eighteenth Dynasty. This of course does not have any chronological implications for the date of the coffin, since this occurs also on a stone rectangular sarcophagus of the Twenty-sixth Dynasty from Saqqara (Egyptian Museum, Cairo, CG 29312).[17] The only possible conclusion is that the copyists had, both for the Cairo sarcophagus and for the coffin under examination, access to an old and uncorrupted source, which, in the writer's opinion, is likely to have come from a long-established and important temple archive.

The two columns of text on the back pillar are also very fragmentary. The first one repeats in an almost identical way the carved text on the lid, and it has already been taken into account in the previous comment. The preserved words of the second column are unfortunately too few and too common to identify the text.

However, if the interpretation of Baankh's titles is correct, the choice of naming the gods he served not directly but through epithets, together with the archaising version of BD 72, hint not only at a priest involved in the embalming process, but also to a very learned man who was proud of the knowledge he acquired thanks to the possibility of accessing the temple archive in Heliopolis.

Type and iconography (Fig. 98, Fig. 99)

To the writer's knowledge, the closest parallels to the coffin of Baankh are:[18]

1) Inner coffin of Petosiris (Cairo Egyptian Museum, JE 46592)

Lefebvre 1920, 112–113 and Lefebvre 1923, 100–101, pl. LVII.
Titles: the Greatest of Five, master of the seats, great *wab* priest, prophet of the Ogdoad, chief of the *wab* priests of Sekhmet, chief of the third- and fourth-class priests, royal accountant scribe of all the things in Hermopolis temple, second prophet of Khnum-Re and of Hathor, phylarch of the second-class priests of the temples of Her-weret and Neferusyt, prophet of Amun-Re and of the gods and their temples.
Family: son of the Greatest of Five, master of the seats, second prophet of Khnum-Re lord of Her-weret and of Hathor lady of Neferusyt, Nes-shu[19] and of the mistress of the house Nefer-renepet.
From Tuna el-Gebel, 1919
End of 4th to beginning of 3rd Century BC
Height 1.93 m; max. width 0.57 m; depth 0.45 m
Wood (Pinus halepensis), polychrome glass paste, bronze (inlaid brows). The blackish colour is said to be due to "une macération" (Lefebvre 1923, 100).
Text: BD 42

2) Inner coffin of Nes-nehemet-awi (Staatliches Museum Ägyptischer Kunst, Munich, ÄS 31)

Staatliche Sammlung ägyptischer Kunst 1966, no. 79 and Staatliche Sammlung ägyptischer Kunst 1976, 166–168.
No titles
Family: daughter of the Greatest of Five, second

the exception of Nesy-Thoth's sarcophagus (Egyptian Museum Cairo, CG 29312), while it appears on Eighteenth Dynasty versions (Vittmann 1994, 236); personal pronoun =*ṯn* in (section w) is used mostly in older variants of the spell (Vittman 1994, 245); (end of section hh) appears in this form only in Eighteenth Dynasty sources (Vittmann 1994, 251); (section ii+jj), though incomplete, seems to be closer to the variants found on papyri dating back to the Eighteenth Dynasty (Vittmann 1994, 251); (section kk) is found in Eighteenth Dynasty papyri, even if it is also attested in Vittmann's version III from the Late Period (Vittmann 1994, 252). It must also be said that, naturally enough, some minor differences with respect to the sources quoted by Vittmann are present, but given the condition of the text it is impossible to determine if they are simple writing mistakes or not.

[17] Vittmann 1994, 231, 236. This sarcophagus was found by Quibell at the bottom of a 20 m deep shaft of a Saite mastaba in Saqqara (next to Apa Jeremias' monastery), and it is of an unusual type (Quibell 1912, 32, 142, pl. LX n. 5). The exterior of the box has been left rough, while the flat lid is decorated in high relief with the figure of a mummiform coffin among two seated jackals and two falcons at the corners, with no inscriptions. Hieroglyphic texts and figures of deities are present only on the interior of the box, where, on the western side, BD 72 appears. It is worth noting that not only the version of the spell is archaising, but also the layout of the decoration, which recalls quite closely late New Kingdom red granite sarcophagi like the one belonging to Suty-nakht in Trieste (Civico Museo di Storia ed Arte, Trieste, inv. no. 12088; Crevatin and Vidulli Torlo 2013, 66–73). In the relevant volume of the *Catalogue Général* two other interesting facts are pointed out (Maspero and Gauthier 1939, 60, 66): the sarcophagus is said to be unusual for Memphis, but of a type much more common in the Theban necropolis during the Saite Period, and to have been left unfinished.

[18] I am indebted to all the Museums' curators and staff who greatly helped me in my search. I heartily thank them all for their efficient and kind assistance.

[19] The only titles of Nes-shu that appear on Petosiris' coffin are Greatest of Five and Director of the seats (Lefebvre 1923, 100). Petosiris' family is of course well known: for the other relatives, see Lefebvre 1924, 3–9.

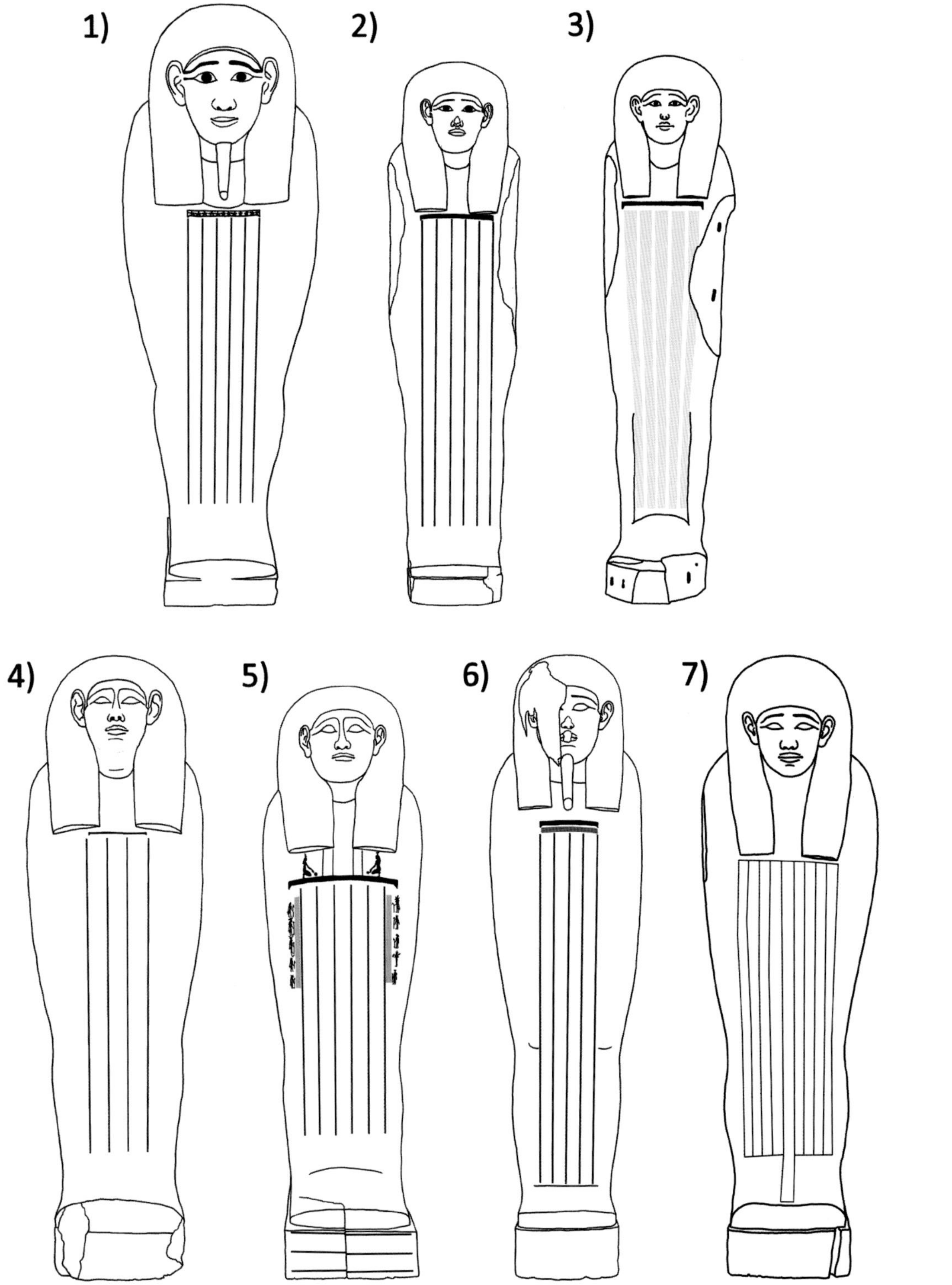

Fig. 98: Parallels to Baankh's coffin (1):
1) Egyptian Museum, Cairo, JE 46592;
2) Staatliches Museum Ägyptischer Kunst, Munich, ÄS 31;
3) Royal Ontario Museum, Toronto, ROM 930.103.1,2;
4) Egyptian Museum, Cairo, JE 87822;
5) Egyptian Museum, Cairo, TR 24.2.21.5;
6) Musée du Louvre, Paris, E 18842;
7) Fine Arts Museum, San Francisco, 2002.2a-b
8) Egyptian Museum, Cairo, JE 67859;
(drawings by S. Moser)

prophet of Khnum-Re Lord of Her-weret and of Hathor Lady of Neferusyt, Nes-shu and of the mistress of the house Nefer-renepet (possibly a sister of Petosiris)
Presumably from Hermopolis
About 300 BC
Height 1.74 m
Cedar wood, carved
Text: carved, five columns, with BD 72

3) Coffin of Ta-sherit-ihet (Royal Ontario Museum, Toronto, ROM 930.103.1,2)

Royal Ontario Museum 1964, 11 and Trumpour 2006, 6–7.
No titles
Family: daughter of the Greatest of Five, master of the Two Seats, chief priest, priest of the twice-great Djehuty, Lord of Khemennu, the priest Djed-Djehuty-iuef-ankh, and the mistress of the house Setja-iret-binet; niece of Nes-nehemet-awi
380–300 BC
Height 1.76 m
Wood (Cupressus sempervivens), carved, eyes outlined in black
Text: carved, five columns, with BD 72

4) Coffin of Pa-sheri-en-ta-ihet (Cairo Egyptian Museum, JE 87822)

Hassan 1941, 223–226.
No titles
Family: son of Kheper-petef and of the mistress of the house Tjeteb
From Giza (Mastaba I, to the north of Queen Khentkaues' pyramid), excavations of Selim Hassan for the University Fouad I, 1932
"Late"
Height 2.00 m; width 0.70 m
Wood, carved. Hieroglyphs bear traces of a white filling. "The upper part of the forehead is coloured blue while the eyes, eyelashes and eyebrows are all black" (Hassan 1941, 226). The skeleton within had a plaster gilded mask.
Text: carved, three columns under a *pet* sign, with BD 72

5) Coffin of Psamtek (Cairo Egyptian Museum, TR 24.2.21.5)

Unpublished.[20]

[20] This coffin is on display, together with the others from the Cairo Museum, in Room 49 on the ground floor. The data here presented were gathered during an autoptic examination of the coffins by the author; the same holds true for the other unpublished coffins.

No titles
Family: son of (father's name not written) and of the mistress of the house Setja-iret-binet
Height: about 1.90 m
Wood, carved. Small figures of Isis and Nephthys kneeling on a large *pet* sign. At both sides of the inscription there are five figurines of standing deities. Hieroglyphs bear consistent traces of a white filling.
Text: very crudely carved; five columns, two lines on the front of the plinth

6) Coffin of Iahmes (Musée du Louvre, Paris, E 18842)

Galliano 2011, 102.
Titles: father of the god, beloved by the god, *sem* priest, servant of Ptah, *wab* priest in the temples of Memphis
Family: son of Ib-hemes (mother)
Presumably from Memphis; transferred from Musée Guimet to the Louvre in 1948
6th to 4th century BC
Height 1.99 m; width 0.51 m; depth 0.37 m
Cedar wood, carved, no traces of painting
Text: carved, one small line under a pet-sign and four columns, with BD 72

7) Coffin of Iret-hor-irou (San Francisco Fine Arts Museum, 2002.2a-b)

Dreyfus 2007, 21; Karlstrom and Kam 2013, 78.
No titles
Family: son of  (?) and of the mistress of the house Ta-di-Usir
Museum purchase, gift of Diane B. Wilsey in memory of Alfred S. Wilsey
Thirtieth Dynasty or very early Ptolemaic Period
Height 1.98 m
Cedar wood, carved, with traces of paint
Text: carved, with multicoloured inlays, nine columns (BD 72)

8) Coffin of the priest Hep-men, called Iah-mes (Cairo Egyptian Museum, JE 67859)

Kamal 1938, 2–14.[21]
Titles: father of the god, beloved by the god, prophet of

[21] The coffin is also present in the Bonn University Totenbuch-Projekt website (http://totenbuch.awk.nrw.de/), though listed under the number JE 67858. This number was taken from an article by A. el-Toukhy (el-Toukhy 1993, A, pl. I–II), which is the only bibliographical reference cited and that unfortunately the writer was unable to access. However, Kamal (Kamal 1938, 2) not only clearly labels the coffin as JE 67859, but assigns (op. cit., 2, 15) the number JE 67858 to an offering table. In the

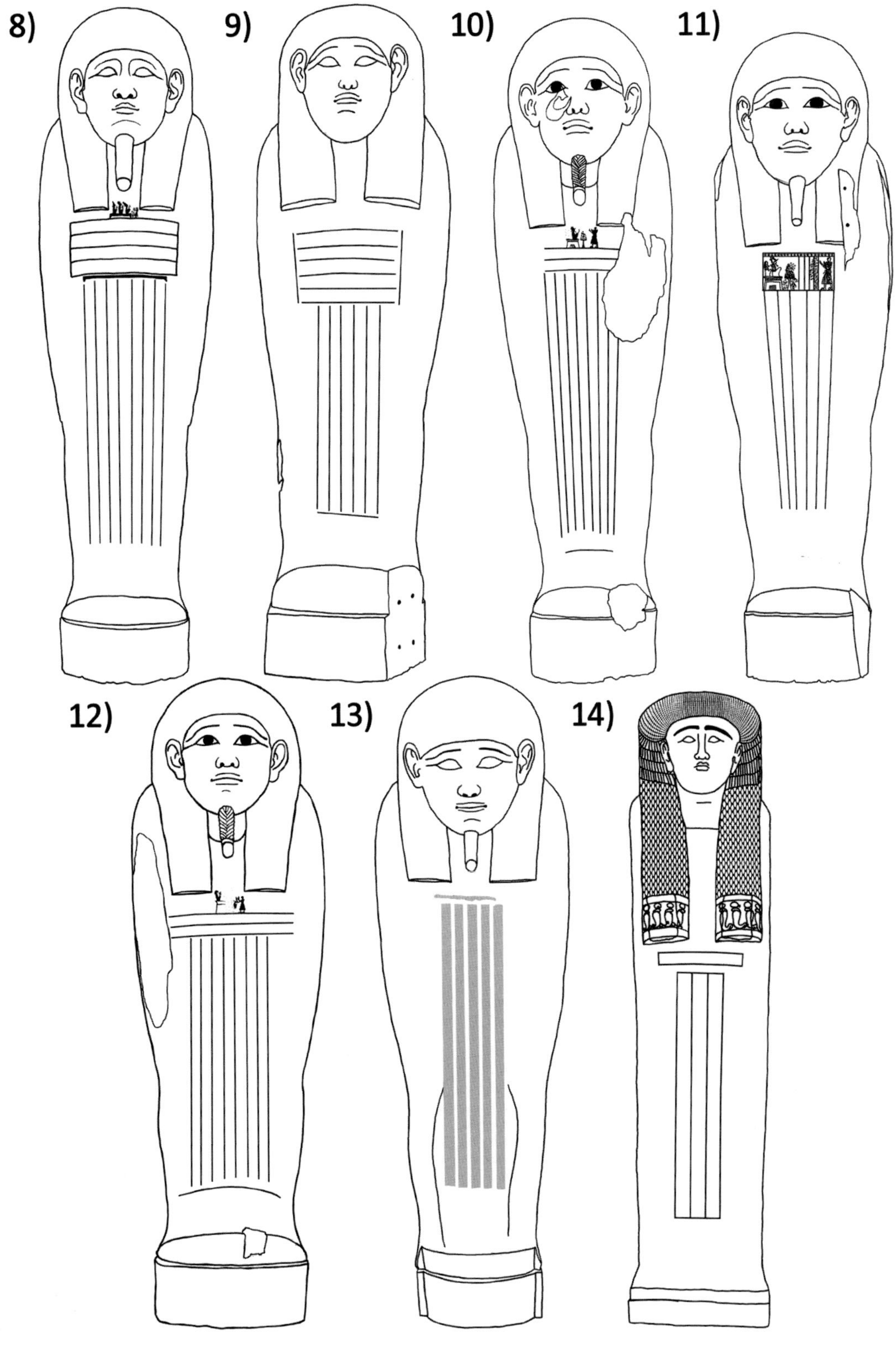

Fig. 99: Parallels to Baankh's coffin (2):
9) Egyptian Museum, Cairo, TR 27.2.21.8;
10) Egyptian Museum, Cairo, TR 26.2.21.5;
11) Egyptian Museum, Cairo, TR 27.2.21.6;
12) Egyptian Museum, Cairo, TR 26.2.21.1;
13) Musée d'Archéologie, Marseille, 264;
14) Fondation Gandur pour l'Art, Geneva, FGA-ARCH-EG-0315
(drawings by S. Moser)

Ptah, *wab* priest of the temples of Memphis, prophet of Ptah in Avaris, prophet of Osiris in Avaris, scribe of the Gold-House of the temple of Ptah, prophet of Sopdu in Iaati, prophet of the gods of the House of Sopdu in Iaati, prophet.
Family: son of the mistress of the house Ta-di-Imhotep
Bought in England by King Farouk I, 1937
Thirtieth Dynasty ?
Height 2.19 m; max. width 0.64 m; depth 0.50 m
Wood, carved. Hieroglyphs are sometimes partially filled with a white substance (blackish one in other instances).
Text: carved, five lines and seven columns, with BD 72.

9) Lid of the coffin of  (Cairo Egyptian Museum, TR 27.2.21.8)

Unpublished (see n. 20, above).
No titles
Family: son of Djed-hor and of the mistress of the house Ta-di-Usir
Height 2.20 m
Wood, carved.
Text: carved, five lines and five columns, with BD 72 and other unidentified spells

10) Lid of the coffin of Pa-di-Ptah, called (P)samtek-em-wedja (Cairo Egyptian Museum, TR 26.2.21.5)

Unpublished (see n. 20, above).
Titles: father of the god, beloved by the god, king's acquaintance, servant of Ptah, [...]
Family: name of the mother only, but illegible
Height 2.15 m
Wood, carved. Small offering scene (vignette of BD 72) painted on top of the inscription.
Text: painted, two short lines and seven columns, with BD 72

11) Lid of the coffin of *Nb-š-mḥty* (?) (Cairo Egyptian Museum, TR 27.2.21.6)[22]

Titles: father of the god (?), king's acquaintance, servant of Ptah, scribe of Pharaoh of the Gold House, accountant of everything in the temple of Ptah, prophet [...]
Family: not mentioned
Height 2.10 m
Wood, carved. Offering scene (vignette of BD 72) painted on top of the inscription.
Text: painted, four short columns in the vignette and five columns, with BD 72

12) Lid of the coffin of An-em-hor, called Hor-nedj-itef (Cairo Egyptian Museum, TR 26.2.21.1)[23]

Titles: father of the god, beloved by the god, king's acquaintance, servant of Ptah, [...] scribe [...]
Family: son of Her-ib (mother)
Height 2.10 m
Wood, carved. Hieroglyphs are painted in black.
Small offering scene (vignette of BD 72) on top of the inscription, between the wig lappets.
Text: painted, two lines and seven columns, begins with BD 72 (the rest is almost illegible)

13) Coffin of Pa-di-hor-nedj-itef (Musée d'Archéologie, Marseille, 264)

Maspero 1889, 47 no. 64 and Niwiński 1996a, 46–49.
No titles
Family: son of the lady Ta-nebet-nehi-(resi)
From Saqqara
Probably 2nd century BC
Height 2.10 m; width 0.60 m; depth 0.45 m
Wood, carved and painted; "the careful polishing of the surface testifies to the intention of the artist to imitate stone coffins" (Niwiński 1996a, 46); the foot part seems to have been reworked.
Text: carved and filled with blue colour (in antiquity?), a line in demotic and five columns of hieroglyphs, with BD 72 (hardly identifiable signs).

14) Coffin of Hor-em-akhet (Fondation Gandur pour l'Art, Geneva, FGA-ARCH-EG-0315)

Sotheby, Wilkinson and Hodge 1921, lot 349 and Bianchi 2011, 248–251.
No titles
Family: son of the lady Aset-em-akh(bit)
Formerly in the collection of Lord Amherst
3rd to 1st century BC[24]
Height 2.05 m

writer's opinion it is advisable, therefore, to retain JE 67859 as the correct inventory number for this coffin.

[22] This coffin is mentioned in the article by el-Toukhy (1993, D, Pl. VII–VIII) (see n. 41 above). It is otherwise unpublished.

[23] This coffin is mentioned in the article by el-Toukhy (1993, B, Pl. III–IV) (see n. 22 above). It is otherwise unpublished.

[24] Twenty-first to Twenty-fifth Dynasty according to Bianchi 2011, 248. The dating proposed by the writer is due to the comparison of the coffin's face with the head from a colossal Parian marble statue of a woman wearing a sakkos, from the temple of Athena Polias, Priene (Turkey), dated to about 350–325 BC (British Museum, London, BM 1870,0320.138) and of the peculiar wig on a cartonnage case from Akhmim (BM 29585) dated to the 1st century BC to the 1st century AD. Furthermore, the palaeography of the inscriptions is very similar to that of the other coffins in the present list.

Wood, carved. Eyes inlaid with white and blue glass. Eyebrows made of plaster; perhaps some very small traces of gilding on the right cheek.
Text: painted in black, one short line and three columns, hardly readable.

The only certain chronological data of this series relates to the coffin of Petosiris in Cairo (no. 1), which dates to around 300 BC. It is nevertheless worth noting that, even in this small sample of artefacts, there is an evolution in the proportion of the face and in the distribution of the inscribed text: numbers 1 to 7 have smaller faces and only columns of inscription (all of which, except for no. 7, surmounted by a pet-sign),[25] while numbers 8 to 13 have larger faces and T-shaped inscriptions. It is tempting to assume that the second group is slightly later in date, according to the principle that during the Ptolemaic Period greater and greater emphasis was given to the head (Taylor 2001a, 241) of coffins and sarcophagi. This would result in a date for the first group spanning the end of the Pharaonic Period (perhaps as early as the Twenty-sixth Dynasty) to the beginning of the Ptolemaic Period, with the second group dating well into Ptolemaic times: all the unpublished coffins from Cairo (nos 9–12) and that in Padua would then date back to the 3rd to 2nd centuries BC.[26]

As far as provenances are concerned, we have the following data: Petosiris' coffin comes from Tuna el-Gebel, that of Pa-sheri-en-ta-ihet (no. 4) from Giza and that of Pa-di-hor-nedj-itef (no. 13) from Saqqara. In addition, the texts mention the cities of Heliopolis (Baankh's coffin), Avaris and Iaati (coffin no. 8) and the temple of Ptah (nos 6, 10, 11 and 12), almost certainly the one in Memphis. It seems plausible, then, that this type of coffins belong to a Lower Egyptian (if not specifically Memphite) tradition, though coffins of similar type seem to have been found also in Thebes (Budka 2008, 70 and Budka 2010, 57).

Lastly, some technical features are worth mentioning: all coffins were hewn out of a single tree trunk; the wood of most of these coffins (except for numbers 6 and 7) is more or less polished; there are sometimes deep gashes or lacunae (nos 2 and 3, in particular) due respectively to growth defects and to an insufficient size of the trunk, and these were filled or completed with pieces of the same wood attached with dowels; some coffins (nos 4, 5, 7, 8 and 13) bear traces of a white substance on the surface. The latter point hints at a massive loss of – possibly polychrome – decoration, especially if compared to the coffin of Pef-tjau-awi-aset (Civico Museo Archeologico, Milan, E 0.9.40147), dated to the Twenty-sixth Dynasty and showing the same polishing of the wood together with a polychrome collar painted on a white preparation layer.

If this is true, are we sure to be dealing with a group of coffins that belong to the same type? As far as the coffins that have no remnants of painted decoration are concerned, it is generally assumed that they imitated contemporary stone sarcophagi (Buhl 1959, 212 and Niwiński 1996a, 46 (see above)) and that that is why they were not polychrome. But, as a look at the examples exhibited in Room 49 on the ground floor of the Egyptian Museum in Cairo shows, stone sarcophagi were in many cases brightly coloured and/or gilded. Furthermore, it seems unlikely that the patches and other flaws in the wood were left in plain sight. A possible explanation could lie in the 'conservation' practices of the past: it might be that the painted decoration detached very easily from its support, and when the coffins were discovered small remnants of colour were scraped off in order to have a more attractive object for exhibition or sale. As there is no certain provenance for the coffins that have no trace of colour, there is yet another possibility: these ones might come from a workshop and be still unfinished.

Conclusions

Baankh's coffin of the Museo di Antropologia in Padua belonged to a high ranking funerary priest who probably lived in the city of Memphis between the 3rd and 2nd centuries BC. This monument has either undergone treatments, since its discovery, that deprived it of its original polychrome decoration or was left unfinished. A more detailed knowledge of the practices of past conservators and antique dealers could help determine which of the two possibilities is correct, and similarly scientific analyses to identify microscopic traces of paint might also assist with this. In any case, in the study of coffins and sarcophagi, a closer cooperation between Egyptologists and conservators will certainly lead to better results.

[25] Only Petosiris' coffin (n. 1) has a somewhat larger face, but the text distribution is identical with the others.

[26] These conclusions, as well as those on the provenance, match the ones by Marie-Louise Buhl about stone sarcophagi (Buhl 1959, 196 and following).

Late Period Coffins from Qubbet el-Hawa Tomb 33

Yolanda de la Torre Robles

During the works carried out in tomb 33 in the necropolis of Qubbet el-Hawa in archaeological seasons from 2008 to 2015, many coffins were unearthed. They can be dated to different periods (Middle Kingdom, New Kingdom and Late Period) which correspond with the three phases of occupation in the tomb. In the present paper, different types of coffins, which date to the Late Period, from the Twenty-sixth to Twenty-seventh Dynasties are discussed. They were made of stone and different types of wood, and it is possible to observe that the pattern and the stylistic motifs follow, in general, those of the Theban region, but with some local peculiarities.

Introduction

The Spanish Project from the University of Jaén is currently working on the Qubbet el-Hawa necropolis located in the south of Upper Egypt, in front of the modern city of Aswan, and to the north of Elephantine Island. It is important to mention that the island is closely related to the necropolis because that is the place in where the governors of the town, as well as their family and officials, were buried during the Old and Middle Kingdom.

Qubbet el-Hawa comprises, at least, one hundred rock tombs dug into the hill, which are located in several levels. The top level was reserved for important persons, while the lower ones were for people of lesser importance (Jiménez Serrano 2013, 29–37).

Since the Nineteenth Century several excavations have been carried out in Qubbet el-Hawa. The first work was begun in 1885/1886 by General Grenfell, who was the highest military official in charge at that time in Aswan, but the actual fieldwork was carried out by Major Plunkett, one of his officials (Budge 1887, 31). During the work, several tombs were discovered,[1] and it is thought that Tomb QH33 was discovered at this time on the basis of several different pieces of evidence (Jiménez Serrano 2015b, 154). The tomb was never excavated, probably due to the absence of decoration; moreover the tomb was burnt as well. Thus, there was nothing of interest for Grenfell and Plunkett. Another early reference to Tomb QH33 is a plan of the tomb, which was published by de Morgan in 1894 (de Morgan 1894, 142), but only the pillared room was drawn.

There is no further information about Tomb QH33 until 1938 when Müller recorded inscriptions and architectural details from the Middle Kingdom tombs on the hill (Müller 1940, Taf. XXIa), and there is evidence that this tomb was completely covered by sand at this time. After that, we have to wait until 1959/1960 when two members of Elmar Edel's team, J. Karig and F. Komp, from Bonn University recorded the basic dimensions of Tomb QH33 (Edel 2008, 430). It is only a brief reference (half a page) in which the pillared room, the niche and north shaft are mentioned. The surface material is described as Late Period.

No proper study of Qubbet el-Hawa tomb 33 had been carried out until 2008, when a team from the

[1] Tombs QH25, 26, 27, 28, 29, 30, 31, 32, 33, 34, 35 and 36.

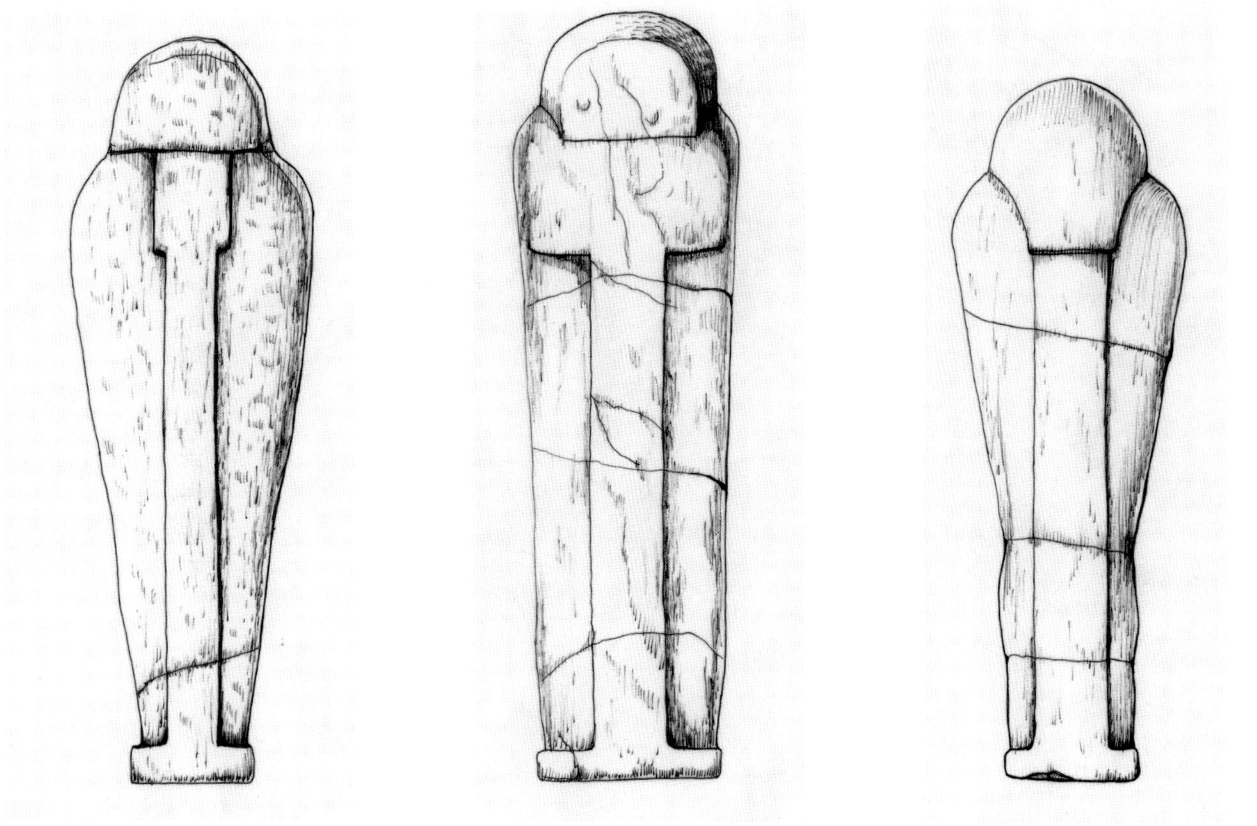

Fig. 100: Stone sarcophagi from the pillared hall of Tomb QH33. Drawing: Martinez Hermoso after a reconstruction by the author

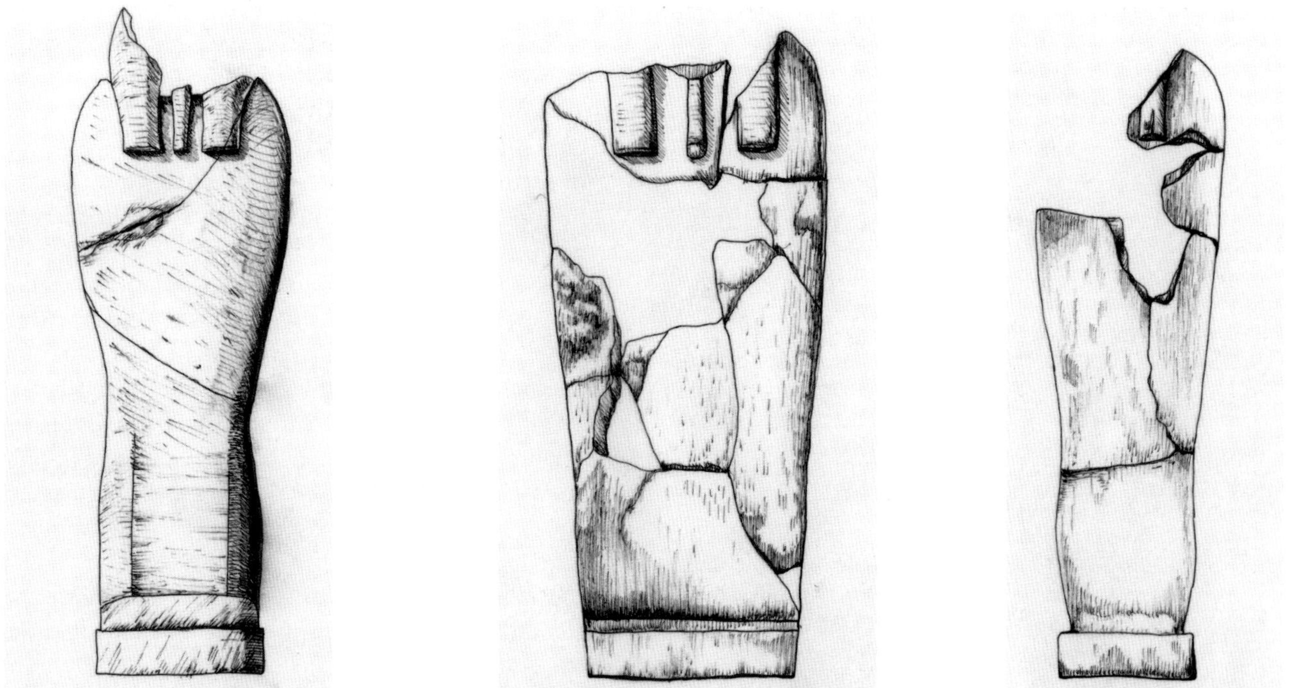

Fig. 101: Stone sarcophagi dating to the Persian Period. Drawing: Martinez Hermoso after a reconstruction by the author

University of Jaén began its project there.[2] Since the start of the excavations there, funerary complex 33 of Qubbet el-Hawa has revealed itself as a rich source of material and information[3].

According to our current findings,[4] construction of tomb QH33 started in the Middle Kingdom, during the reign of Senwosret III and Amenemhat III (1837–1773). Its owners were two governors of Elephantine Island, Heqaib (III) and Ameny-Seneb (Jiménez Serrano and Sánchez León 2015a, 117–130).[5] The state of the tomb nd the remains from it reveal that the tomb was reused after the Middle Kingdom, hundreds of years after the original owners' burials, during at least in two different periods: in the New Kingdom, from the transition between the Seventeenth and Eighteenth Dynasties to the reign of Thutmosis III,[6] and in the Late Period, during the Twenty-sixth and Twenty-seventh Dynasties.[7]

Description of some of the coffins from QH33

The following coffins and sarcophagi come from two chambers and the pillared room in tomb QH33.[8]

Firstly, there are several uninscribed sarcophagi, made of sandstone, probably from local quarries.[9] These sarcophagi were located in an overlying layer of debris, resulting from the looting and disturbance of the tomb. Due to the current data available and the disposition of them it is not clear whether all the sarcophagi found in the same level originate from a Late Saite/Persian Period context associated with tomb QH33 or whether they are from a context outside the tomb.

The state of conservation is rather poor because they were burnt during a fire which took place at some time after the Late Period. In addition, the sarcophagi were broken into several pieces during the period of looting suffered by the tomb (**Fig. 100, Fig. 101**).

The date of the objects is based on the associated pottery which was found in the same upper layer of debris. This included pottery that has been identified as dating to the Late Saite/Persian Period: a deep bowl with incurved walls and red-slipped surface (for example, see Wodzinska 2010, 270 and also Aston 1999, 224–225, plate 69, fig. 1987); a small jar with wide neck, spout and flat base, smoothed (Wodzinska 2010, 255 and also Aston 1999, 210–211, plate 65, fig. 1898); also a jar with wide cylindrical neck and rounded base with red-slipped surface (Wodzinska 2010, 251 and Aston 1999, 224–225, plate 69, fig. 1996), and a jar with cylindrical neck, rounded base, with a faience stopper (Defernez 2001, 245–246, Pl. LII, 141). As regards parallels for these sarcophagi, there are some examples in Copenhagen, for instance, and in The Egyptian Museum in Cairo that are similar in style, but they are later in date, coming from the Thirtieth Dynasty (Buhl 1959, 73, figs 34, 35 and 77, and fig. 39).

In sector C18 we found a rectangular coffin with a vaulted per wer-shaped lid, made of wood. Inside was an anthropoid coffin. Both have yellow decoration on a black background. The decoration of the external coffin shows representations of several deities inside chapels on the long panels, and there is a representation of Isis on the foot end and Nephthys on the head end. The coffin has a cavetto cornice on which there is a representation of the sun god, Re, flanked by two cobras. Around the entire surface of the lid and upper part of the box there is a decorative motif which is meant to represent a *khekher* frieze and also possibly a snake, which is encircles the entire lid. The function of the snake in this case would be protective. There are three

[2] http://www.ujaen.es/investiga/qubbetelhawa.

[3] More data about Qubbet el-Hawa excavations made by the University of Jaén can be consulted in Jiménez-Serrano *et al* 2008, 35–60; 2009, 41–75; 2010, 65–97; 2012, 102–123; Jiménez Serrano 2011, 182–197; 2015,169–176; Jiménez Serrano et al 2013, 7–85; 2014, 7–48; de la Torre Robles and Martinez de Dios 2015, 27–34; de la Torre Robles and Martinez de Dios 2016, 12–15; de la Torre Robles 2017, in press; Martinez de Dios and de la Torre Robles 2018, forthcoming.

[4] The excavations of the main shaft were finished in 2018. The chambers located there did not show evidence of the owner, only traces of Middle Kingdom remains belonging to coffins. Due to this the theory about the owner cannot be confirmed. Martínez de Dios and de la Torre Robles 2018.

[5] In this paper the authors propose Ameny as the owner of Tomb QH33.

[6] The dating is based on the discovery of a scarab carved with the name of Thutmose III, as well as from the pottery and coffins remains which are still under study. See Jiménez Serrano *et al.* 2010, 67 and López-Grande and Valenti Costales 2008, 129–130.

[7] The objects mentioned in this paper come from this period and they were found on the upper level of the debris of the tomb, some of them partially buried. Other grave goods, mainly pottery vessels confirm these dates. The pottery from the New Kingdom is currently under study by Dr Maria José López-Grande. For pottery from the Third Intermediate Period and Late Period see López-Grande 2016, 113–144

[8] The tomb was divided into archaeological sectors at the beginning of the excavations.

[9] The sandstone of the sarcophagi is still under study but it is suggested that it came from the quarry at Gebel el-Silsila (personal communication Mellado-García geologist of the team, 2017).

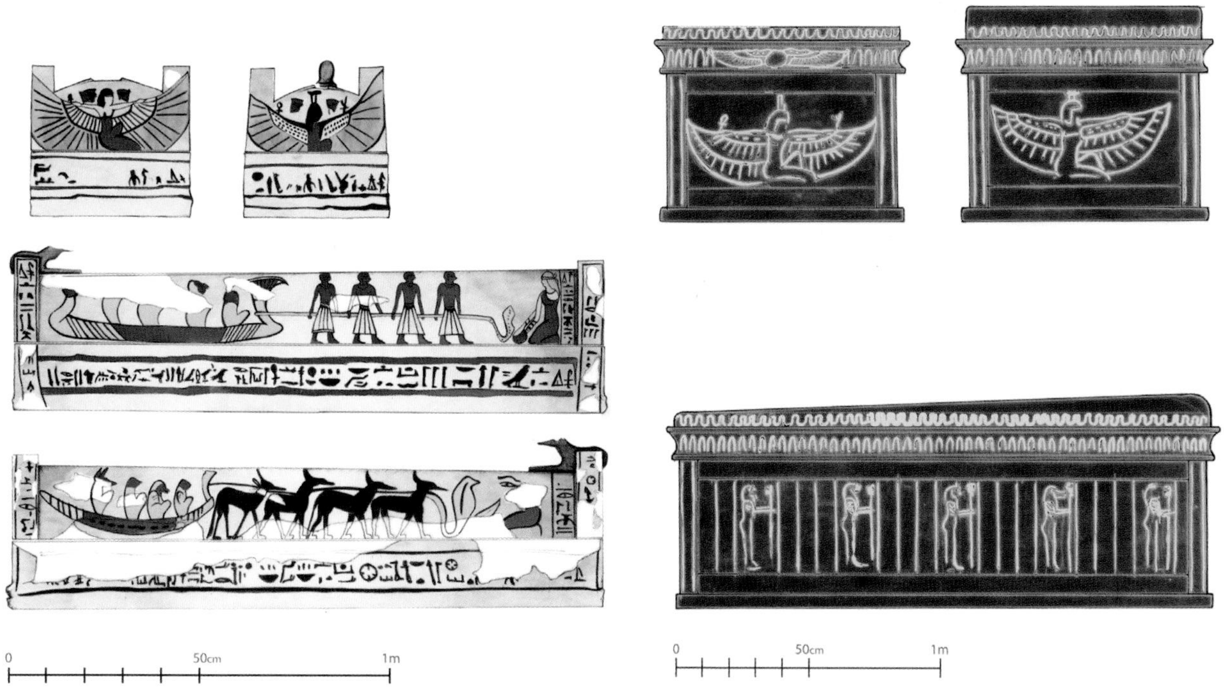

Fig. 102: Left: Coffin of Hor-Wedja. Right: Coffin of Psamtik from sector C18 of Tomb QH33. Drawing: Jiménez Iglesias after a reconstruction by the author

lines of text on the lid, which contain the classic *ḥtp dỉ nsw* formula. The decoration of this coffin is very reminiscent of those of the New Kingdom, such as the outer coffin of Khaemwese in the Brooklyn Museum (accession number 37.15E). Although there are clear differences in decoration, the typology is the same in essence: black background with iconographical features in yellow, showing a number of deities in each panel; and the presence of a *per wer* shaped lid (Ikram and Dodson 1998, 254–259. Wilkinson 2004, 154). This coffin was in a very bad state of conservation when it was found, due to the activities of termites and it proved to be impossible to conserve it. However, it was possible to make a reconstruction of the whole coffin.

The inner coffin was anthropomorphic in shape, and decorated with the same colours as the outer rectangular coffin. Its state of preservation was also very precarious and we were only able to save part of the face belonging to the mask. Inside the coffin was a mummy with a bead net and amulets in the form of the four Son of Horus with a winged scarab.

From an inscription written on the Ptah-Sokar-Osiris figure, which was placed on top of the outer coffin we know that this set of coffins was made for a man named Psamtek (*psmṯk* (Ranke, PN I, 136, 8)), which is a very common name in Late Period Twenty-sixth Dynasty. The inscription contains the classic offering formula, and also the filiation of the deceased is mentioned.

A coffin of another type is that of a child called Horwedja (*ḥr-wḏꜣ* (Ranke, PN I, 246, 23)). This coffin is a typical example from the Late Period, with yellow background and hieroglyphs mainly in black and red. It is rectangular, with four pillars in the corners and a vaulted lid, qersu type. In addition, there were figures of a recumbent jackal, Anubis, and a falcon representing the god Sokar on the lid (at the foot and head). The coffin decoration may show scenes from the Book of the Amduat (Hornung 1999), but this is still under study. On the front, four jackals are shown pulling a rope to drag the solar boat, in which the four Sons of Horus are depicted. On the back is a similar scene showing four priests dragging a similar barque. On both the front and the back, this group is preceded by a giant cobra goddess with a kneeling female figure facing the procession. It is interesting to note that the female figure has covered her eyes. Isis and Nephthys are depicted on the head and the foot ends.[10] The classic *ḥtp dỉ nsw* formula is inscribed around the sides of the coffin together with the genealogy of the deceased. There is no figurative or epigraphical decoration inside the coffin, but it is painted

[10] This coffin is currently under study.

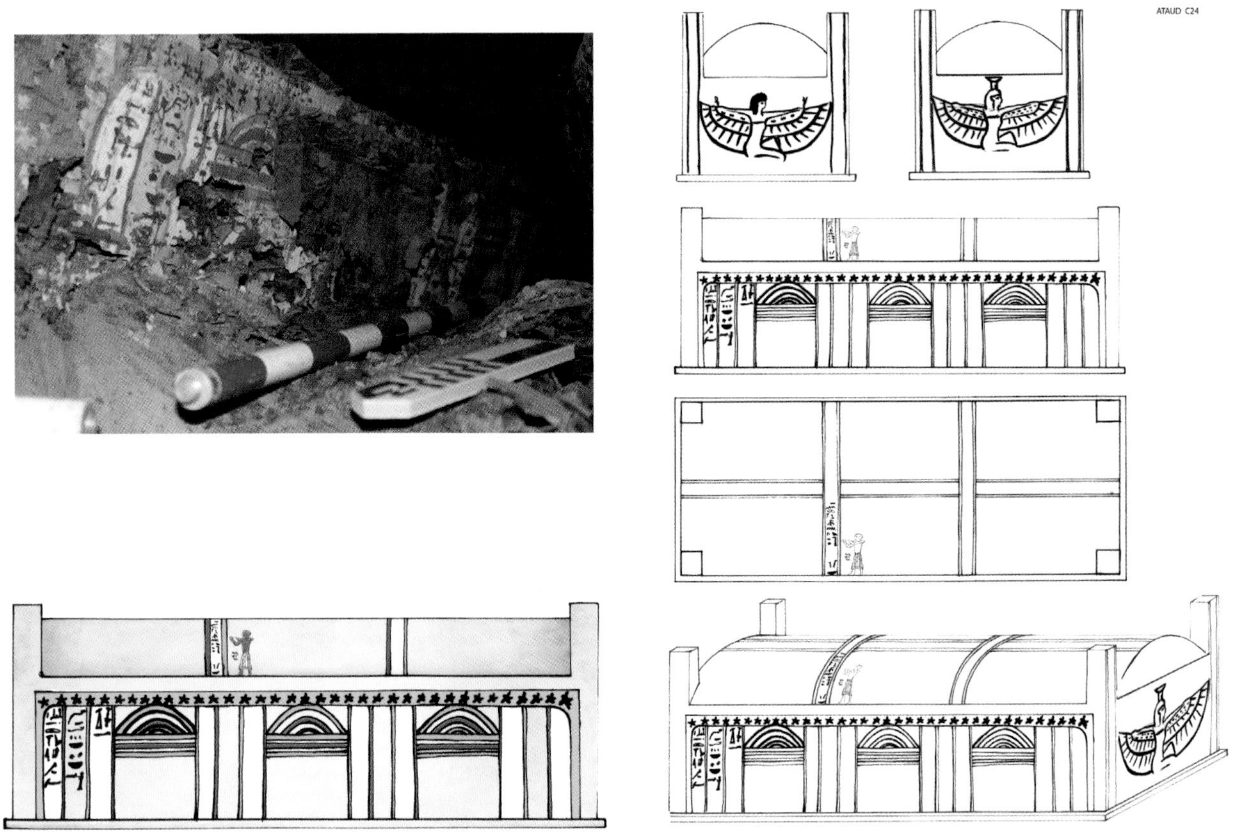

Fig. 103: Coffin of Psamtik from sector C24 of Tomb QH33. Drawing: Jiménez Iglesias after a reconstruction by the author

with yellow ochre, similar to the background colour of the exterior (Ayora Cañada *et al.* 2015). In spite of its poor condition when found, it was ultimately possible to conserve the majority of it (**Fig. 102**).

As regards chronology, this coffin clearly dates to the Late Saite/Persian Period not only on the basis of the Ptah-Sokar-Osiris figure associated with it but from the pottery which confirms a Twenty-sixth/Twenty-seventh Dynasty date. This included some of the same types mentioned before: a deep bowl with incurved walls and red-slipped surface, for instance (see p. 170). There was only a piece of this pottery, which was found broken inside a box. We also found a New Year flask with the name of King Amasis, which confirms the chronology suggested.[11]

Another set of coffins was found in sector C24, located in the main northern shaft, consisting of a rectangular coffin with two associated anthropoid coffins. These belong to another Psamtek (psmtk). The exterior rectangular coffin has four pillars and a vaulted lid, decorated with a yellow background and iconographical elements painted in different colours (blue and red). These include a representation of the sky, in the form of a line of stars on a light blue background. Below this is a series of funeral chapels with divinities, alternating with columns of hieroglyphs in white and yellow columns. They are probably a representation of the Third Hour of the Underworld in the form of the *per nu* chapel (Wilkinson 2004, 155). At the head end is a depiction of Nephthys as a winged deity, and there was probably an image of Isis at the foot end, but no evidence for this survives. At the top, there is a depiction of the procession of the night hours and several deities but its fragmentary condition makes difficult to understand the whole decorative programme.[12]

The first inner anthropoid coffin is yellow and white, and has a green face. The nemes is decorated with red and green stripes on a yellow background. On top of the head, is a depiction of the solar disk is flanked by

[11] In an unpublished report of the work done in 2015.

[12] This coffin is similar in shape to that of Horwedja (*ḥr-wḏꜣ*) from C18 discussed above.

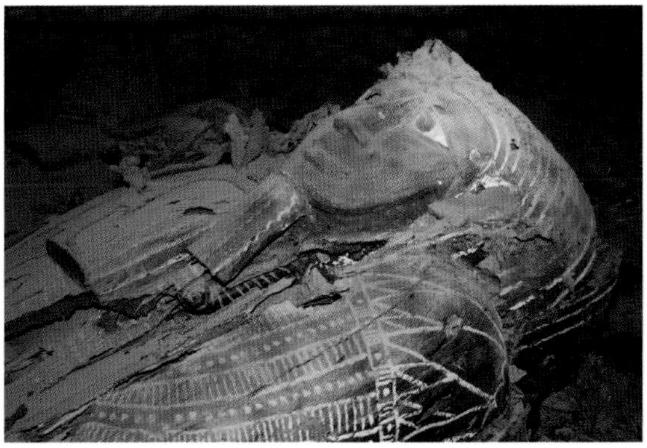

Fig. 104: Coffin of Horwedja from sector C24 of Tomb QH33. Drawing: Jiménez Iglesias after a reconstruction by the author

two cobras. Below the wesekh collar is a single line of hieroglyphic text containing the offering formula and the name of the deceased.

The second inner coffin is also anthropoid, with decoration in orpiment (Ayora Cañada *et al.* 2015) on a black background. The face is green. Below the necklace there would normally have been several columns of hieroglyphic text, but they have not been preserved. Insufficient has survived to be able to be sure about the decorative programme, but it is likely to have been similar to other anthropoid coffins documented in QH33 (see below) (**Fig. 103**).

This assemblage also consists of two very similar anthropoid coffins. The only different between them is in the colour of the face: the first is red while the second one is green.

The outer coffin is decorated with a black background, and the text and iconography are painted in orpiment. The head has an Osirian beard and a nemes head cloth. Feathers are depicted on the shoulders, perhaps as harkening back to the decoration of coffins of the rishi type. Below the feathers there are two kneeling divinities. On the front, below the wesekh necklace there is a kneeling deity with outstretched wings holding two ankhs. Below this decoration, the mummy is depicted lying on a lion-shaped bier, below which are arranged the four canopic jars with lids in the form of representations of the Four Sons of Horus. The ba flies over the mummy. Below this section of decoration there are lines of hieroglyphic text, arranged both horizontally and vertically, and each one associated with a particular divinity. Although the texts are barely preserved, sufficient remains to be able to identify the figures as protective deities such as Qebehsenuef or Duamutef. The name and filiation of the deceased can also be seen.[13] This information is supported with the texts from the Path-Sokar-Osiris figure associated to this burial (**Fig. 104**).

The inner coffin shows the same features as the outer coffin with one exception: the face of the inner coffin is green. This is due to the fact that it was made to be closer to the body of the deceased and therefore shows his assimilation to the God Osiris. In the case of the outer coffin, the red face may be intended to show that the deceased is still human. The chronology of these pieces is supported again by finds of pottery, a bead net and some Ptah-Sokar-Osiris figures associated with them.

[13] More recent study has revealed the name of the owner to be Horwedja (*ḥr-wḏꜣ*).

The preliminary study of the pottery shows it dates to the Twenty-sixth to Twenty-seventh Dynasties.[14]

This set of coffins has a good parallel in the coffins belonging to the Prophet of Montu, Djeddejhutyiufankh in the Ashmolean Museum (Ikram and Dodson 1998, pl. XXXI. Raven 1981, plate 7). The exterior decoration is similar to our rectangular type, but the two anthropoid coffins are different in colour. As regards the coffins with black background and yellow decoration presented here, there are two examples that can be considered as parallels although they have some slightly differences.

The first one is located in a place as far away as the Saqqara necropolis, from tomb q1C. It belongs to a certain Iahmes.[15] This coffin shows the same black background and yellow decoration, but it differs in one aspect: the presence of polychrome blue and red in some of the vignettes and also the presence of an wesekh n bik collar instead of the usual wesekh and feather pattern. The date for this coffin is established as the Twenty-sixth/Twenty-seventh Dynasty, the same as the examples from Qubbet el-Hawa.[16]

The other example is the coffin of Irethorrou from Akhmim, now in the Fine Arts Museum of San Francisco (42895). This coffin shares some of the same aspects of its decoration: it has a black background with yellow decoration. It differs in its iconographical pattern. This coffin is dated to around 500 BC (Twenty-seventh Dynasty).[17]

Conclusions

To summarise, it is possible to say, on the basis of current findings, that there are some coffins found in the Qubbet el-Hawa necropolis that appear to be slightly different. Some of them have a clear resemblance to the New Kingdom coffin type with a black background and yellow decoration, typical of the Tuthmoside period in the Eighteenth Dynasty (Taylor 2001a, 225), and this, for unknown reasons, seems to have reappeared in the Late Period in Qubbet el-Hawa. Until now, this type of coffin has usually been thought to be typical for the Theban area in New Kingdom and one that does not occur at later periods as it now appears to have been the case in the south of Egypt. The same type of coffin with, a black background and yellow/orpiment decoration, and also the same decorative programme, can be observed from other tombs of Qubbet el-Hawa, such as Tomb QH208 (Edel 2008, 2014, Fig.3).

The dating of these coffins is further supported by the pottery, examples of which are described above, and also by the Ptah-Sokar-Osiris figures found in each of the burials. These examples have gilded faces and blue lines framing the hieroglyphic inscription on the base. The size of the figures is also larger. The latter figures belong to Raven's type Iva (Raven 1976, 266–271). However, they establish a dating of the Twenty-sixth Dynasty, within the Late Period, although it might be possible to date them to the Twenty-fifth Dynasty.

The coffin with four corner posts and a vaulted lid, documented in QH33, has also parallels in this necropolis, for example in tomb QH207. Edel recorded an example of this type of coffin, but with slight differences in the texts and some details of the decoration (Edel 2008, 1897, Fig. 48 and 49; 1904, Fig. 105; 1905, Fig. 106).

As regards the anthropoid stone sarcophagi, as noted at the beginning of this paper, is difficult to be certain whether they are from tomb QH33 or whether they originate from elsewhere, maybe from others tomb of the necropolis. The pottery indicates a dating in the Persian Period, probably Twenty-seventh Dynasty, but the sarcophagi themselves are similar to examples belonging to the Thirtieth Dynasty or later on the basis of the parallels noted above. Additionally, recent discoveries by a Mission from the Ministry of State for Antiquities (MSA) of some tombs situated south of Qubbet el-Hawa necropolis, in the so-called Aga Khan Tombs, have included at least one stone sarcophagus similar to the one from tomb QH33. However, there is a difference in the materials: sandstone in the example from tomb QH33 and limestone in the new example(s) from the Aga Khan Tombs. It is also reported that these new sarcophagi date to the Ptolemaic Period.[18]

The works and study will continue on the funerary complex of tomb QH33 in the coming seasons and we hope that we will be able to shed more light on this fascinating tomb and the rest of the necropolis of Qubbet el-Hawa.

[14] The study of the pottery points to the Twenty-sixth Dynasty (López-Grande 2016).

[15] Ziegler 2013, 292–295 (volume I).

[16] Ziegler 2013, 124–129 (volume II).

[17] Dreyfus and Elias n.d..

[18] Thanks to Osama Amer, inspector of the Supreme Council of Antiquities, for this information.

Regional identification of Late Period coffins from Northern Upper Egypt

Jonathan P. Elias and Carter Lupton

Typology is no longer an academic exercise. The accelerated looting of Egyptian cemeteries in the 21st century has elevated the accurate identification of coffin styles in Egypt to the level of the "absolutely essential". If sites are to be adequately protected, it no longer suffices to suggest an object's point of origin just generally. It needs to be specified much more exactly so that areas under attack can be properly secured. There are several coffin styles dating to the Late Period that still defy geographical localisation. Heracleopolis' stylistic dominance in Northern Upper Egypt is examined relative to neighbouring sites, such as el-Hibeh, and the likelihood assessed that Abusir el-Melek is the find location of coffins belonging to this alternate style (resembling that of Gamhud, but not "of Gamhud").

Introduction[1]

There can be little doubt that the past thirty years have witnessed steady improvement in coffin typology. Understandably, much of this work has related to Thebes. Therefore, Theban coffins of different time periods have inspired separate analyses, for example coffins of the Twenty-first Dynasty (Niwiński 1988) and those of the Twenty-Second to Twenty-Sixth Dynasties (Taylor 2003). Typological interest has been extended to other regions where large numbers of coffins have also been found: Akhmim (Brech 2008), and different sites in northern Upper Egypt, including the trans-regionally attractive necropolis of Abusir el-Meleq (the so-called "Abydos of the North") (Rubensohn and Knatz 1904; Limme, 2009; Meffre 2012a), and the locally-used cemetery of Gamhoud (Kóthay 2012b; Schreiber 2012). This is all exciting work, but much more remains to be done to clarify stylistic development, and to explore how "types" developed within regions and how regional products may have been distributed in commerce. Our focus is Northern Upper Egypt (**Fig. 105**).

It is the problem of distribution which needs to be addressed most carefully. A coffin may be made in one place and buried at another. The situation becomes complex in regions that may have had multiple independent workshops churning out container "types" within relatively limited areas. This is our opinion respecting Northern Upper Egypt. One look at Botti's catalogue of coffins found at el-Hibeh (Botti 1958) shows that a given cemetery will contain the products of many workshops; some of these products reflect the design sensibilities that developed at or near el-Hibeh; others are from workshops located elsewhere (and therefore represent an independent tradition) which produced objects buried at el-Hibeh. Such is the case with Twenty-second Dynasty coffins excavated at el-Hibeh that are indistinguishable from those found at Sidmant or Illahun, and presumably represent an imported "tradition".

Typological evaluation is a process of untangling

[1] The authors wish to thank Dr. Robert Cohon, Curator of Ancient Art at the Nelson-Atkins Museum for his assistance during our visit to Kansas City. Special thanks also are extended to Dawn Gorman Frank, Senior Registrar, and Catherine Sawinski, Assistant Curator of Earlier European Art, at the Milwaukee Art Museum. Our study of Milwaukee M1967.20 originally produced two letter-reports (1997 and 2003) on file with the museum.

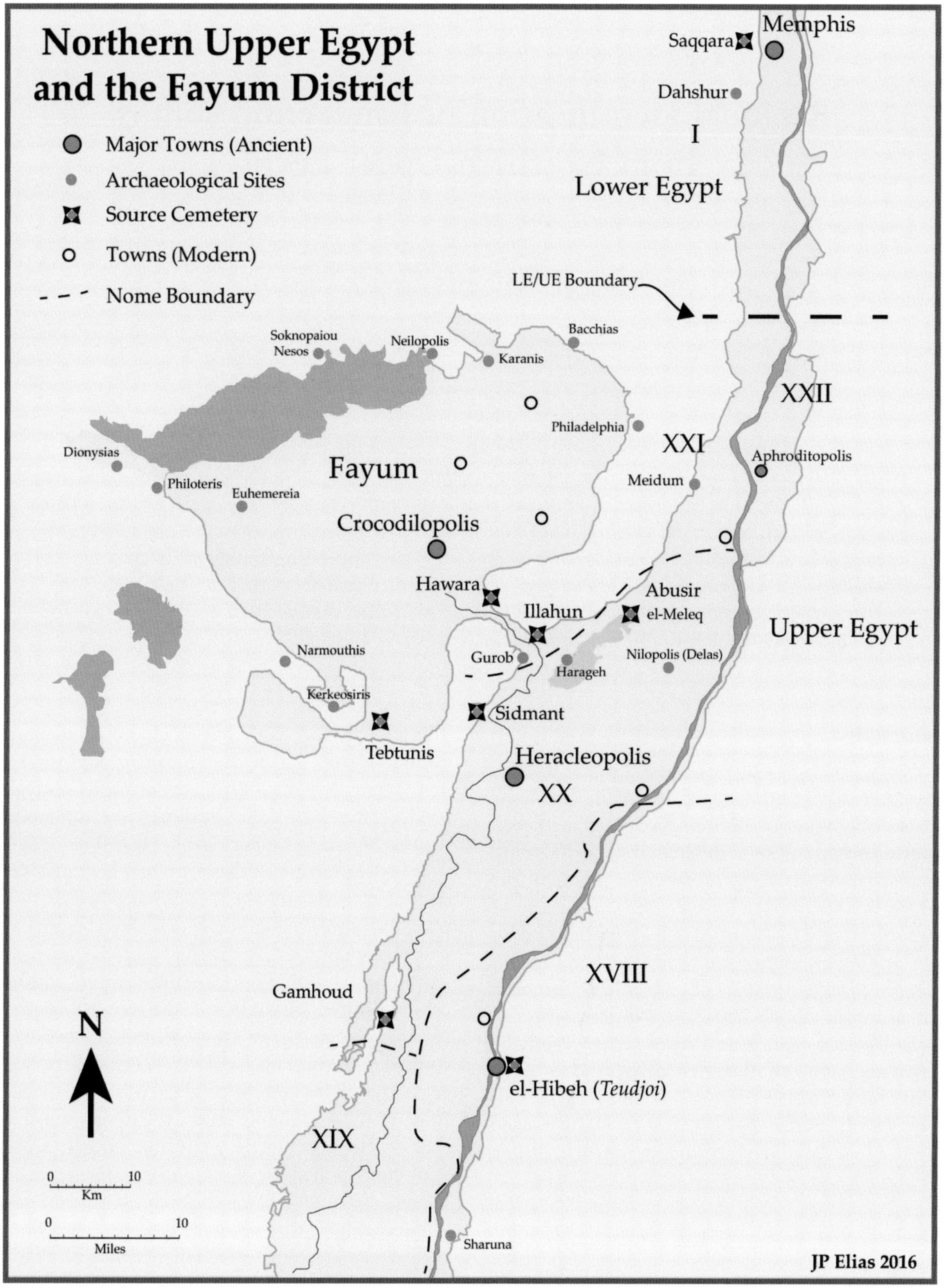

Fig. 105: Map of Northern Upper Egypt and the Fayum District

the patterns making up a "type" so that workshops can be identified and the "types" connection to particular cemeteries be determined. We aim at finding affinities between objects in time and space. These affinities are stylistic ones, but more than that: they are the result of conditions of manufacture, arising through the sharing of methods, ideas or templates by groups of artisans.

Two coffins of problematic origin

The typology of two Egyptian coffins belonging to different museums in the American Midwest is considered here. The first of these is the anthropoid coffin of the man "Pediusiri" (Padiousir) in Milwaukee, Wisconsin (Milwaukee Art Museum, M1967.20); the second is the anthropoid coffin of the woman Meretites in Kansas City, Missouri (Nelson-Atkins Museum, 2007.12.2 A,B). The latter is part of a luxurious ensemble that includes a *qersu* coffin, the wooden figures of the goddesses Isis and Nephthys which adorned the *qersu* coffin's vaulted lid, more than 300 faience shabtis, and the mask and trappings of cartonnage which once adorned Meretites' mummy. These coffins are distinguished by "reddish yellow" bodies (about Munsell 5YR 7/8) and text columns of light blue and yellow on which hieroglyphic inscriptions with black silhouette glyphs are written; both have large collars in which powerful decorative content appears. Padiousir's coffin is dominated by an image of Nut inserted over a mummification vignette in which Anubis holds a vessel beneath a "heaven band filled with stars". Meretites' coffin has a winged Khepri beetle above the Nut figure (Khepri supra Nut), an arrangement of the zone separating the collar from the text apron that is known in Late Period coffins deriving from northern Upper Egypt (Galerie Antiker Kunst N. u. Dr. S. Simonian 1978).

Both coffins are massive. Padiousir's coffin is 213.36 x 78.11 x 34.93 cm. It was said to have come from Aswan, but we feel that this "provenance" was attached to it by a dealer eager to associate the coffin with the Aswan High Dam very much in the news in 1966/67. The cover (C) and box (B) of Meretites' coffin measure as follows:

	Cover	Box
Length	191.77	220.98
Width	85.09	82.55
Depth	38.1	21.59

They can be classed as: "Seven-footers" or, perhaps better, as "213s" best thought of as dimensioned as an "outer anthropoid coffin" (*c.* 15 percent larger than an inner anthropoid coffin would be). More to the point, the amount of wood and coating materials embodied in them is truly grand and approach in scale the anthropoid sarcophagi made for high status persons in northern Egypt from the 26th Dynasty up to the end of the 4th century BC (Taylor 2001a, 241). Both coffins date to the end of the fourth century BC, and represent what was available to the Egyptian elite at the end of the Second Persian Period (343–332 BC) or when Egypt came under early Macedonian administration.

As with so many Egyptian artefacts, no specific details exist to tell us where these magnificent works were excavated. An origin in Hermopolis has been suggested rather informally for each (though never argued in print). Our typological evaluation suggests other possibilities. So here we ask the simple question: is it possible, when lacking all provenance information for a coffin, to determine the district in which it was manufactured?

Typology has been used to address many archaeological issues, but our primary purpose right now is to use it to solve chronological and locational questions. We are trying to develop a method which can deal with what we suspect is a great deal of stylistic diversity within a comparatively limited area. Furthermore, we believe that typology improves by identifying features of interest and naming them distinctively so they become memorable. In this way, the eyes of future typologists will focus on what truly distinguishes an object as a product of a particular region.

Regional affinity needs to be established for many styles of Egyptian coffin. The similarity of these particular containers, both of which have a "swollen" morphology implying manufacture in the late fourth century BC or early Ptolemaic Period, is immediately recognizable, but their typological relationship has not been studied formally. Despite the beauty and importance of these products, their place of origin has remained a mystery. Anyone quickly looking at the Milwaukee and Kansas City specimens would admit that they both resemble Ptolemaic coffins discovered at Gamhoud (Kamal 1908). Nevertheless, Gamhoudian patterns are distinct and the workshops producing them should not be supposed to have manufactured either of these coffins. We now need to reflect on what these coffins "say to us" stylistically and piece together, if we can, clues which will give us a better idea of the point of manufacture.

Circumstantial Clues to Origin

One of the reasons why the regional affinity of the coffins has been so puzzling is that there is, as yet, no closely comparable material known from secure excavations. For the region in question, despoliation is not only historical, but it has continued unabated into our own times (e.g., Vittmann 1981). Typological associations are, more often than not, severed.

The Coffin of Meretites: Nelson-Atkins Museum 2007.12.2 A,B came into the collection of Sayed Bey Khashaba in the early twentieth century. Descending from an aristocratic family of the Asyut region, Khashaba backed "concession excavations" in the period of the First World War. For example, he supported the work of Ahmed Bey Kamal at Asyut (1913–1914) and nearby, at Meir (1914–15). Through *partage*, Khashaba's collection grew, and using his various connections, he put together what he termed "The Khashaba Museum". This was eventually broken up and its contents exported. In this way, Meretites' ensemble eventually came into the possession of a dealer in Germany from whom the Nelson-Atkins Museum purchased it in 2007.

Although there is no perfectly straightforward path to recover provenance for either coffin, regionally suggestive factors are present. The name Meretites harks back to those of several important Old Kingdom women. Most prominent among these is the Fourth Dynasty queen Meretites I, (also known as Mertitytes, wife of Khufu) who was the mother of Djedefre, Khafre, Kawab and Hetepheres II. She was buried at Giza. Others so-named, it turns out, were Hathor priestesses. One of these is the wife of Kahai, buried in a tomb at Saqqara datable to the reign of Fifth Dynasty king Niuserre, (Moussa and Altenmüller 1971). The other is a Hathor priestess discovered in a Sixth Dynasty tomb at Thebes (TT 405, Porter and Moss 1960, 445). "Meretites" is, in fact, counted in the Graeco-Roman Period as a distinct name of Hathor (Leitz 2002, III, 346), "one beloved of her father". One might conjecture that families naming their womenfolk in this way were expressing respect for the cult of Hathor. Cult allegiance could itself have regional implications.

There is, admittedly, remarkable use of Thoth imagery on Meretites' coffin, particularly on the rear facet of the wig (taking the form of seated ibises flanking a Hathor cow) and a vignette just above the text apron showing the deceased standing in the presence of Thoth, Lord of Hesret. Nevertheless, Thoth's strong connection with the Fayum and elsewhere in the north must not be overlooked in order to favour Hermopolis. A Fayumic (or peri-Fayumic) origin may possibly be the reason for Thoth elements being so prominently represented on her anthropoid coffin. Significantly, whatever elements of Hermopolitan collar style (Fourth century BC or later) are known about, and they are admittedly few, they do not seem strongly represented in Meretites' coffin. An example in contrast is the coffin of Shen-Ptah from Tuna el-Gebel (Aubert 1997, 31).

Strong *Stundenwachen* (hour-vigil) content on the *qersu* coffin and on the flanks of the box of Meretites' anthropoid coffin is also noteworthy. Such content is widely distributed in Late Period coffins and sarcophagi, all of it dedicated to making the burial container capable of protecting "the majesty of the one weary-of-heart"; the function of the deities arrayed on coffins is to guarantee the safety of Osiris at his low ebb, exhausted upon his bier (Leitz 2011, 3). We will discuss aspects of *Stundenwachen* patterning below in terms of regionality, particularly in connection with the anthropoid coffin of the Heracleopolitan priest Ankhemmaat, likely to have been excavated at Abusir el-Meleq.

The Coffin of Padiousir: Because it was obtained by purchase, the origins of Milwaukee Art Museum M1967.20 are equally mysterious. However, the genealogical texts on it are suggestive of origins within Northern Upper Egypt. Its owner was "Padiousir, son of Shesepenbast (var. Shesepbast)". These names occur within the context of spell formulae derived from Pyramid Text spell 368, arrayed within a text "apron" below the mummification bier vignette, and in the texts found in the three long text columns written on the back "column" of the box in black silhouette glyphs on alternating yellow and light blue grounds. The zone carries a system of vertical dark blue, light blue and yellow stripes resembling a serekh niche (**Fig. 106**). The text (much of which is destroyed) is a common "Nut" spell which was widely used during the Late Period. We were equally fortunate to find the name Shesepen-bast on a section of the lid from a fourth century BC *qersu* coffin in Amsterdam (Allard Pierson Museum, 8898, Scheurleer and Van Haarlem, 2006). This vaulted lid is decorated with standing figures of the goddesses who represent the first to sixth hours of the day. They wear alternately green and red; disks on their heads are alternately red and yellow. Below them is a frieze consisting of tripled kheker decoration alternating with jackals reclining on pylon-shaped shrines (van Harlem 1995, 50–52). The same system of decoration appears

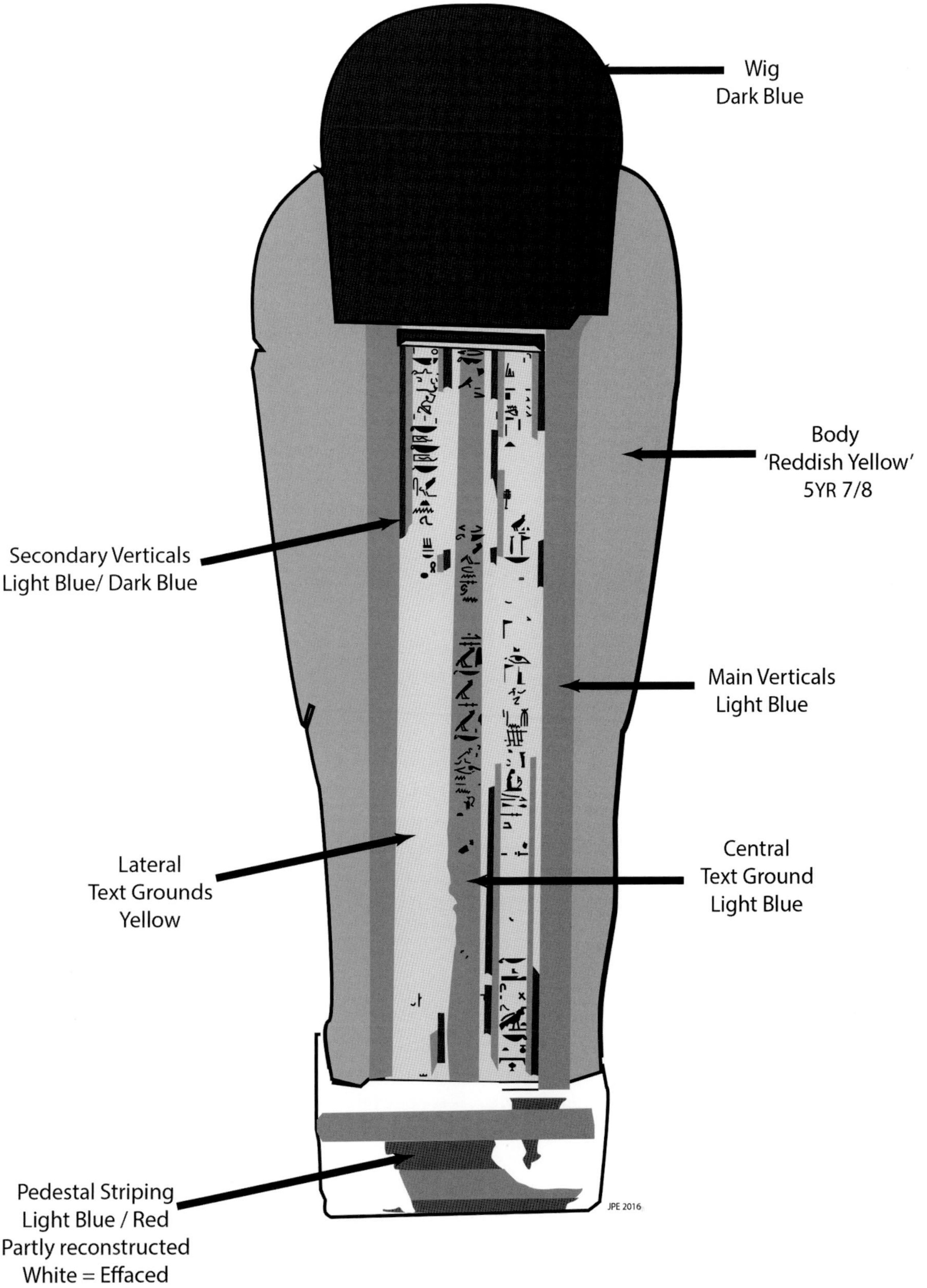

Fig. 106: Rear face of the coffin of Padiousir (Milwaukee Art Museum M1967.20) Diagram: J. Elias

on the *qersu* coffin of Meretites. It has a long history in the decoration of outer coffins and stone sarcophagi extending back to the New Kingdom, but the handling is distinctive enough in its colour and layout to support the argument that the ensemble of Shesepenbast and that of Meretites were produced using a similar template and probably in the same location.

Methodology for the analysis of style

We recommend that the collar designs on anthropoid coffins become a focus of typological research. Ancient artists lavished a good deal of energy on these colourful designs, and many coffin collars are tours-de-force of graphic design. Typological evaluation is pursued advantageously by discovering distinctive features that indicate shared allegiance to templates or approaches to producing graphic forms. It is important to be as specific as possible in describing these features. It is not enough to say that a band of decoration consists of "eight-petal rosettes"; it is necessary to determine how these rosettes have been formed. On the coffin of Padiousir, for example, the petals of these "eight-petal rosettes" are frequently angular rather than gracefully rounded at the tip. Small black dots "mark" each white petal. The approach we take to naming patterns is quasi-heraldic in detail specifications.

The sub-lappet section of the Padiousir coffin's collar expands outward from basket-work checker patterning inside the lunate zone. The following patterns occur:

- "Tied & Folded Leaf", variant 1–red crossing blue on a light green field, revealed as isosceles triangles;
- "Eight-petalled rosettes brown-centred, marked", on a dark blue field;
- "Lotuses with drooping calyx leaves", variant 1–a single yellow eight-stigma row and light blue volute petals /alternating with yellow buds on a red field, inverted;
- "Palmate blossoms-divided", variant 1– two six-petal rows in white, separated by a wide triangular brown spikelet, entwined;
- "Tied rectangular tabs marked with white dots" (alternating light green and red) on a dark blue field;
- "Lotuses with rigid calyx leaves", variant 1–two yellow six/seven-stigma rows separated by a spikelet and light blue petals, alternating with light blue buds on a red field, entwined; and,
- along the perimeter, (g) "Wide Bangles" (**Fig. 107** and **Fig. 108**).

Three observations are of importance: (1) the "tied & folded leaf" pattern is the main separator band of this collar design system; (2) the pattern of tied rectangular tabs commonly found in collar designs originating in the Fayum is the central band in the composition; (3) the general colour palette (light green, dark blue, deep red mixed with yellow elements) seems to have an association with the area of Heracleopolis going back to the seventh century BC, noted in Papyrus Cologne 10207 (illustrated in Verhoeven 1998, 486, fig. 114).

The sub-lappet section of the Meretites coffin is similar. It expands from a lunate zone filled with basket-work checker design. The collar bands consist of the following patterns: "Tied & folded leaf" variant 1; Palmate foliage divided, variant 2– two seven-petal rows in light blue separated by a wide triangular yellow spikelet, on a dark blue field, all connected; and "Lotuses with rigid, flaring calyx leaves", variant 2– two five-stigma rows separated by a spikelet (yellow) and light blue petals alternating with light blue buds on a red field, all connected and "Palmate blossoms undivided", variant 1– six/seven petals in single row alternating with light blue buds with yellow bodies, on a dark blue field, all connected. There is general comparability to the collar on Padiousir's coffin, for example in the use of the "tied & folded leaf" pattern as main separator. The palette is "Herakleopolitan".

We have found that the direct-copy method (tracing) is useful in discovering typologically distinctive features because in this way the typologist is compelled to understand what is required to complete the design. Adobe Illustrator™ is excellent for doing these tracings digitally. The pen tool creates the requisite lines and curves, and the analysts' eye learns how the ancient artist "composited" the designs.

The artist responsible for the coffin of Padiousir includes "virtuoso" bands within its collar which are filled with alternating motifs of ostensibly "standard" floral forms. In each of these, the way the artist has "constructed" the blossoms is the same. The major work is done by creating rows of tube-shaped petals or stigmas using a fine-tipped implement to create narrow black lines which are then in-painted. The creation of these "petal-tubes" allows the artist to fill quickly entire bands of collar decoration neatly and expressively. The same narrow line tube technique is used in the virtuoso bands of floral decoration seen on the coffin of Meretites.

The 4-layered wings of the goddess Nut are handled similarly (**Fig. 109**). Below the semi-circular or shield-shaped plumage adjoining the goddess's arms, rows of

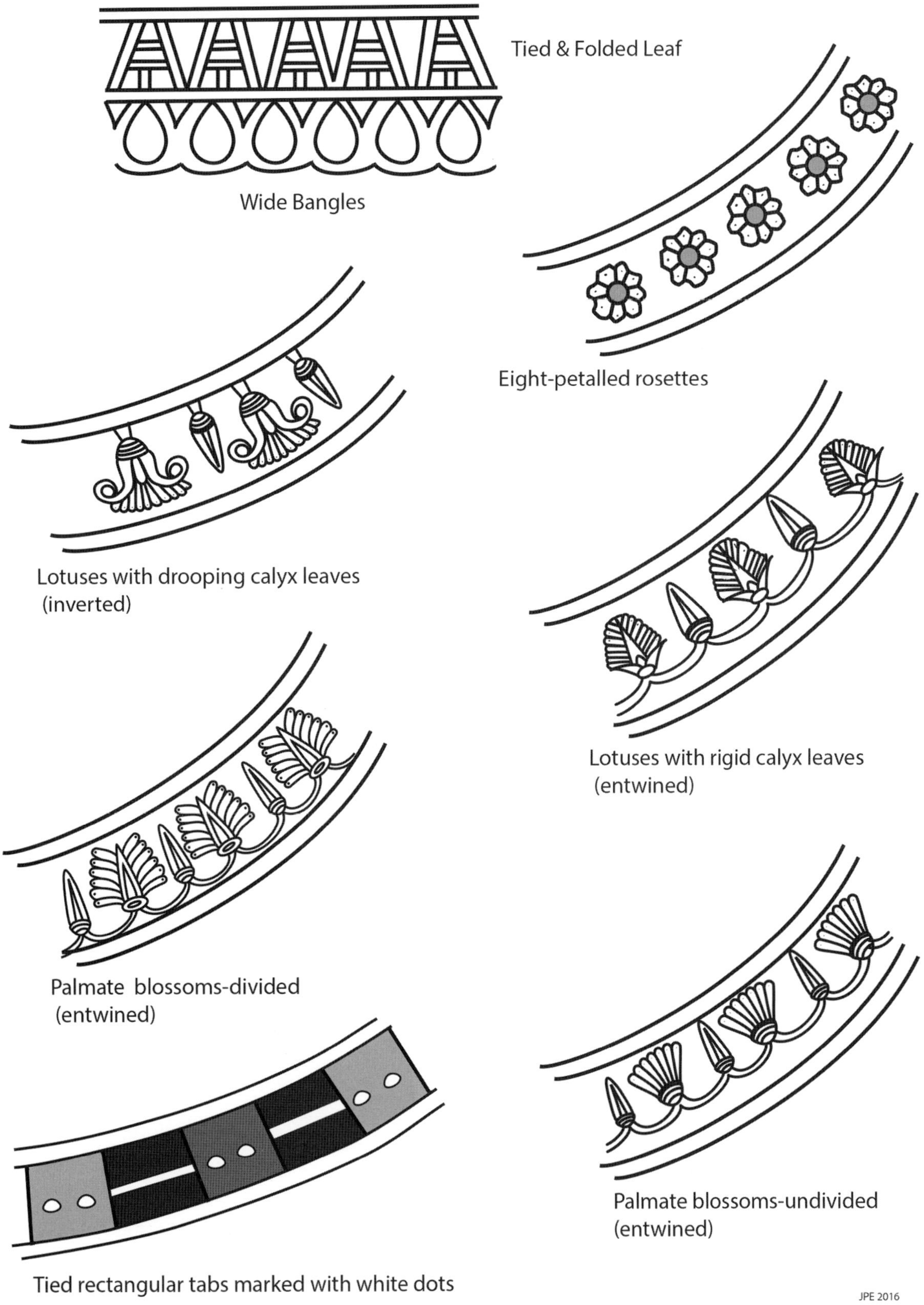

Fig. 107: Collar Patterns. Diagram: J. Elias

tube-shaped feathers with red tips fill in the remaining three echelons of plumage. The technique even extends to the coffin instep to represent the grooves in the cavetto cornices on which the Wepwawet jackals recline. In our view, the work is being done by Egyptian artists, but the floral fantasies created are stylistic amalgams. They bring to mind the architectural motifs of earlier and non-Egyptian structures, such as the frieze of the Treasury of Massalia at Delphi (*c.* 530 BC), or decorative borders found in glazed brickwork at Susa.

This graphic technique appears earliest in the Nut renderings of coffins produced in the Memphite region, perhaps toward the end of the Twenty-sixth Dynasty (late sixth century BC) and adopted by artists whose products are believed to be associated with the region surrounding the Fayum, including, significantly, Heracleopolis (e.g., Mariemont, Ac. 95/1, the coffin of Irethorerou, son of Nesheneb, Limme 2009, 355) and similar coffins with large-format polychrome hieroglyphs inscribing Book of the Dead spell 72, including the famous coffin of Peftauneith (Leiden, AMM 5, Schneider and Raven 1981, 127–128), and the coffin of Psamtik, son of Sebarekhy(t) (Musée des Beaux-Arts de Grenoble, no. 125, Kueny and Yoyotte 1979, 106–109)).

Other regional diagnostics emerged. One of these relates to the rendering of the jackal deities Anubis and Duamutef. Their heads have long, sinuous mouths which terminate with several short ticks, which fill them with tense energy. This feature connects our two coffins with other objects, including an unnamed canopic box in Baltimore (Walters Art Museum, 62.6) which could be that of Meretites herself.

Revealing similarities to the coffins of Padiousir and Meretites are found on the coffin of the woman Ta-akhet-weret, daughter of a house mistress, called by the usually masculine name Djed-hor. Again, unfortunately, we are confronted by unprovenanced material. It entered the Kikugawa Egyptian collection in Japan and was there described by Jiro Kondo (Kondo *et al.* 2004, 100–101). Like the other two coffins, Ta-akhet-weret's is distinguished by text columns of light blue and yellow on which hieroglyphic inscriptions with silhouetted bird glyphs abound. The lower part of this coffin's neck has a vignette (in gold upon a red ground) showing the deceased praising Osiris and the Fetish of Abydos. This distinguishes the area between the wig lappets above the semi-lunate of the collar. This same feature is seen in the coffin of Meretites. The rear of the wig shows a three-part motif consisting of the Hathor cow (striding), flanked by two seated ibis deities (forms of Thoth), each of which wears an *atef* crown with emerging (lunar) disks. Again, a close connection with Meretites' coffin is apparent, for the latter has the same motif in the very same position. The presence of the Hathor cow in this position is reminiscent of the arrangement seen in contemporary hypocephali (Mekis 2015). In view of the prime space dedicated to Hathor, it can even be suggested that the tradition of Atfih (Aphroditopolis) on the east bank of the Nile opposite Meidum is reflected here. This possibility is supported independently by the repetitive use on Ta-akhet-weret's coffin of a peculiar decorative pattern of red and blue triangles separated by white ones with a black tick or dot (looking like circus decoration) in rectangular slots, on which the figures of hour goddesses stand. It is a pattern noted on Ptolemaic cartonnage trappings called "Fayumic" but in several cases associated with Atfih (in particular NMS A.1911.201.3, see Manley and Dodson 2010, 116–118).

The central pillar of Ta-akhet-weret's coffin box is decorated with two compartments arranged vertically above five columns of text. They contain imagery long associated with the troughs of coffins. The upper of the two contains a motif of an anthropomorphised but acephalous *djed* column, flanked on its right by Isis and on its left by Nephthys. It is equipped with an *atef* crown, with blue–red–blue separations between the upper four vertebrae; its white-shirted body springs from a five-sectioned belt at the top of the lower shaft, and its arms are bent at the elbow. Hands emerge, meeting fist-to-fist, holding a crook (*heqa* sceptre in the proper left hand) and flail (*nekhakha* sceptre in the proper right hand). A collar hangs from the shoulders. The lower shaft is decorated with bands of alternating colour.

This iconography of the *djed* column helps to align Ta-akhet-weret's coffin regionally and chronologically. An extremely similar *djed* column is found on the posterior face of the canopic box of Ankhemmaat (private collection) (Bruwier 1998, 68, 74; Meffre 2012c, 164–165). The assemblage of Ankhemmaat, a *sameref* priest and prophet of the god "Herishef-who-hears-prayers" must have originated from Abusir el-Meleq. This has been ably established by Bruwier, but if any doubt remains, it is further dissipated by finds made by Petrie at Abusir el-Meleq of inscribed materials originating from the burial of Ankhemmaat's maternal grandfather, the *sameref* priest and prophet of Hor-bes in the midst of "Abydos of the North" Ousirnakht (Petrie, 1891, pl. XXVIII).

Fig. 108: The coffin of Padiousir (Milwaukee Art Museum, M1967.20), Collar Patterns. Photo by C. Lupton

Fig. 109: The coffin of Padiousir (Milwaukee Art Museum, M1967.20), figure of the goddess Nut. Photo by C. Lupton

Ankhemmaat's burial occurred in the late Thirtieth Dynasty or Second Persian Period (*c.* 350–330 BC), and the stylistic qualities of his equipment represent what the Heracleopolitan elite was interested in using at that stage.

Ankhemmaat's inner anthropoid coffin, like many coffins of the mid-fourth century BC, lacks broad collar designs altogether; its designers concentrate on hieroglyphic texts instead, and these are engraved into the wooden surface and then coloured with pigmented infills (Meffre 2012a, 161). Again, like other coffins of its era, the interior of the lid is decorated in the Stundenwachen tradition, with an elongated image of Nut (with upward-streaming hair), her feet springing off a *shen* hieroglyph (compare the image on sarcophagus of Tanehetep's sarcophagus, Louvre D 39, Buhl 1959, 65–67), giving birth to the sun, and this is flanked by the names of the hour-goddesses of night and day derived from the *Livre du jour et de la nuit* (for example, Anđelković and Elias 2015).

The lower of the two compartments on Ta-akhet-weret's coffin box contains a figure of Nut, standing with relaxed wings pointing down diagonally. Meretites' coffin is similarly organised. The treatment of the *djed* column is similarly white-shirted like that on Ta-akhet-weret's coffin, also flanked by Isis and Nephthys, but has adoring baboons added in above them. The *atef* crown is replaced by *shuty* plumes, but it emanates *atef* accoutrements like flanking cobras, ram's-horns and a solar disk on its axis. Even greater comparability is seen in the rendering of the *djed* column found on Meretites' *qersu* coffin.

Further Regionalisms

Coffin pedestals are rarely subjected to much regional analysis, but this misses their potential. The pedestal of Meretites' coffin consists of six decorative compartments (three on the lid and three on the trough). The imagery is dominated by papyrus barques and skiffs. The three sections on the trough show a barque carrying seated figures of Thoth, a beardless male god, and Ra (rear face), a sun disk alone in a small barque (proper right) and the craft decorated with a serpent head fore and aft, loaded with a stairway, floating at the end of a channel (proper left). The latter is known from the lowest register of the vignette of Book of the Dead spell 110.

The compartments of the pedestal belonging to the lid are all from BD 110 and they are arranged in the order they are presented in the original spell vignette: a priest bows reverently after positioning a falcon atop a box in front of a mummy (proper right); an image in which the deceased paddles along by himself (front face); and finally, a group of three seated deities: rabbit-headed, cobra-headed, and bull-headed (proper left).

Book of the Dead spell 110 concerns primarily the "Field of Hotep", a mythological realm suggesting peace and plenty. As is well-known, the Field is depicted, above all, as an agricultural zone filled with canals and islands. These form the geographical features through which the barques and skiffs navigate. Coffin pedestals do not generally sport such imagery. Other patterns, such as the serekh, are much more commonly painted upon them. So why is it present in this example, and in the far more fragmentary examples that appear from time to time in the market? (For example, an unpublished pedestal fragment from Bonham's auction 1 May 2013 [no. 20668 Lot 350] shows a barque with five seated deities upon it.)

We suggest that the images connected with the Field of Hotep were selected for the Meretites pedestal by artists interested in creating a visual analogy to their own region. While the Field might be said to resemble the agricultural configuration of anywhere in Egypt, we are interested in the possibility that its imagery was selected by artists from the Fayum as a proud representation of their own region. Meretites' coffin is the most complete example known. An unpublished pedestal front panel, showing the deceased paddling in a skiff, appeared in a 2017 online auction (Goldberg Auctioneers 2017, Sale 99, lot 444).

If this conjecture proves to be correct, it suggests the further possibility that sites such as Abusir el-Meleq contain coffins produced by Fayumic artisans (and representing a Fayumic/peri-Fayumic stylistic tradition), and indeed others produced by competing workshops located outside the Fayum, probably at el-Hibeh. The cemetery of Abusir el-Meleq emerges as a zone of stylistic heterogeneity in which styles contributed from many areas (and representing different traditions) are part of a mosaic of funerary artistry best described as "cosmopolitan".

Further investigation of a Ptolemaic wooden coffin lid from Abusir el-Meleq in the Egyptian Museum, Cairo

Nour Mohamed Badr, Mona Fouad Ali, Nesrin M.N. El Hadidi and Mohamed Abd El Rahman

Investigations in the basement of the Egyptian Museum in Cairo led to the rediscovery of a coffin lid of unknown provenance belonging to smꜣ-tꜣwy son of iʿḥ-ms (JE.36806). The lid was covered with two textile layers made from linen that do not belong to the coffin lid. According to the excavation Journal of Otto Rubensohn, the coffin was found in a family tomb at Abusir el-Meleq, Northern Middle Egypt. Non-destructive methods (Portable X-ray radiography, Reflectance Transformation Imaging (RTI), Environmental scanning electron microscopy (ESEM) and Fourier Transform Infrared Spectroscopy coupled with Attenuated Total Reflection (FTIR-ATR) were used to identify tool marks and carpentry technology used during the Ptolemaic era in ancient Egypt. The lid was composed of six pieces of Tamarix *sp. wood that were joined together with scarf joints and wooden dowels. Only the outer surface of the lid was covered with ground preparation layers that had been applied directly on the wooden support by brush, hiding any tool marks that were clearly obvious in the inner side of the lid. The detailed study of the coffin that was made in the necropolis workshop is a good example of woodworking techniques applied during that period.*

Introduction

Investigations in the basement of the Egyptian Museum in Cairo led to the rediscovery of a coffin lid covered with two linen layers (**Fig. 110**). It was of unknown provenance and with an incorrect register number (JE 35806) (Badr *et al.* 2018). Thorough studies proved that the lid belonged to *smꜣ-tꜣwy* son of *iʿḥ-ms* and the correct number is (JE 36806). The excavation diary of Otto Rubensohn (unpublished in the archive of the Neues Museum, Berlin), is an important reference which mentions that the coffin was found intact in a family tomb at Abusir El-Meleq in the northern part of Middle Egypt in 1903–1904. It was decorated with many colours, but due to bad preservation conditions during centuries of burial, severe contraction in the wooden support had occurred and parts of the paint ground or paint layers were detached (Rubensohn 1904; Kischkewitz *et al.* 2009).

The coffin box of *smꜣ-tꜣwy* son of *iʿḥ-ms*, with its mummy and cartonnage are exhibited in the Museum under a totally different number (TR.25/8/19/3). It is not clear why the lid was separated from the box, which has been on exhibition for many years. The presence of textile layers on the lid of this coffin is another interesting issue. After investigation and study with infrared reflectography it turned out to be an Osiris shroud, which most probably was not part of the coffin of *smꜣ-tꜣwy* but comes from another burial excavated during Rubensohn's third campaign (1904/05). There is a possibility that the Osiris shroud was laid over the coffin/mummy of *smꜣ-tꜣwy* during its transportation to Cairo. (Rubensohn 1904; Kischkewitz *et al.* 2009).

Removal of the textile revealed the painted decoration on the lid. Below the pink face with blue beard and wig, there is a multicoloured broad collar made of rows of floral and geometric shapes. Below this, the

Fig. 110: Coffin lid covered by two textile layers (Cairo Museum JE 36806).

sun-god is depicted as a winged scarab beetle. The central full-face figure is Nut with open wings and the sun disc on her head. Chapter 89 of the Book of the Dead is written beneath her body and to either side of this there are deities: the four Sons of Horus and the goddesses Isis and Nephthys (fig.6). In a previous study, pigment analysis confirmed the use of Egyptian blue, haematite (red), a mixture of haematite, calcite and gypsum to obtain the pink tone, and a mixture of Egyptian blue, goethite, calcite and gypsum to obtain the green tone. A proteinaceous material was used as binding medium in the painted and lower ground layers of the lid. Carbon black pigment mixed with a gum (probably gum Arabic) as a binding medium was used to make the drawings on the linen textile layer (Badr *et al.* 2018).

The current paper focuses on further investigations to identify materials, tool marks and carpentry techniques used on this coffin lid.

Methods used in the study

Portable digital X-radiography

Portable digital X-radiography using a Cuattro Slate, 25 x 30 cm wireless Cesium-I Detector system with a tablet monitor was used to study the construction technology (Davis 2005; Kariya *et al.* 2010; Parkes and Watkinson 2010).

Reflectance Transformation Imaging (RTI)

RTI is a computational photographic technique that captures an object's surface shape and colour and enables the interactive re-lighting of the object from any direction. Multiple images are taken of the surface from a fixed camera position but with the direction of the light varied for each shot. The lighting information is then mathematically synthesised creating a model of the surface morphology of the object (Cultural Heritage Imaging 2013).

Fourier Transform Infrared Spectroscopy coupled with Attenuated Total Reflection (FTIR-ATR)

To identify the organic binding media and some inorganic functional groups, sample fragments were analysed with a FTIR spectrometer Vertex 70 (Bruker) using an ATR crystal attachment (Platinum diamond ATR) and standard MIR source at 2mm/s in the spectral region ranging from 4000 to 500 cm^{-1} with 4 cm^{-1} resolution.

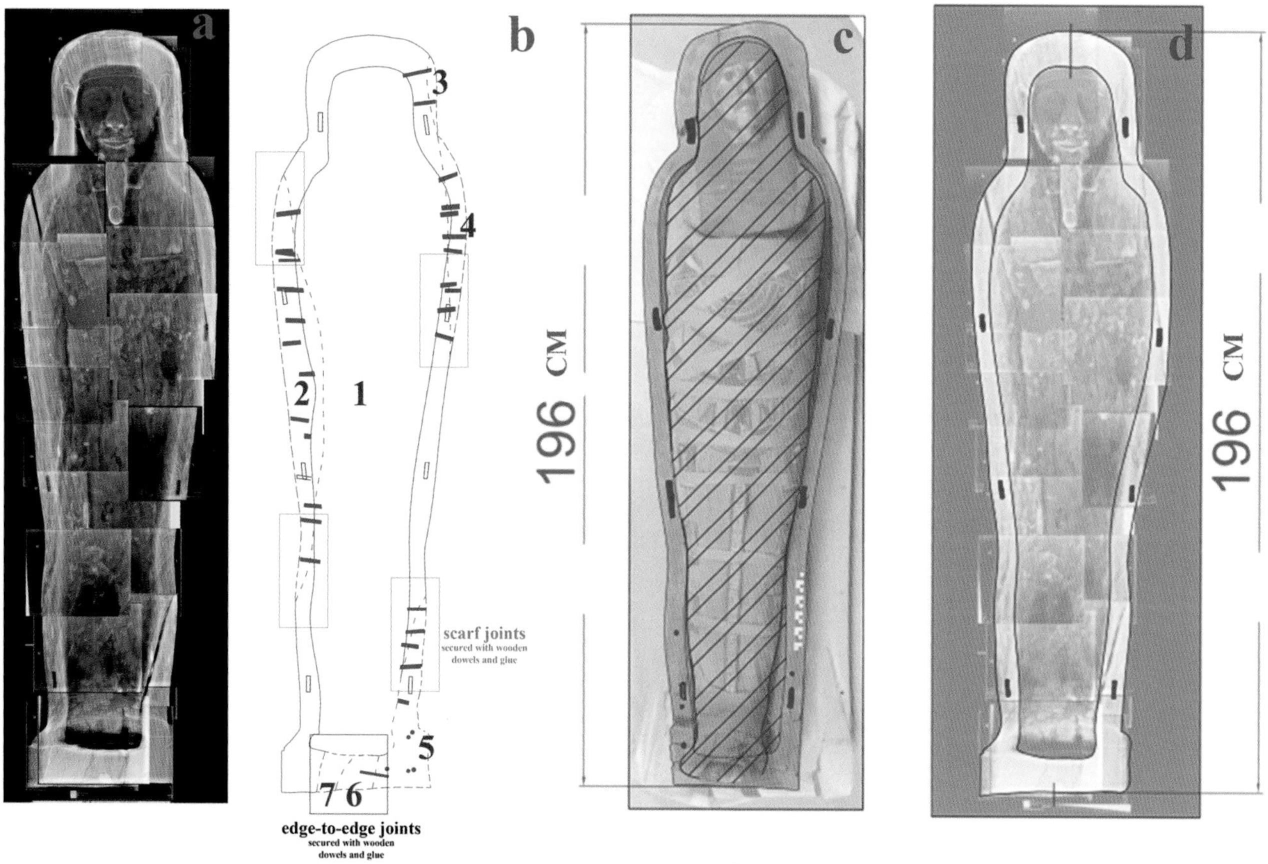

Fig. 111: Coffin construction and relationship between the lid and the box: (a) Composite X-radiograph image of the coffin lid constructed from one large hollowed out tree trunk, with scarf joints and edge-to-edge joints secured with wooden dowels attaching the six additional pieces to the main piece. (b) Technical 2D drawing showing scarf joints and edge-to-edge joints secured with wooden dowels. (c, d) Comparison of the coffin box (c) and coffin lid (d) show the similarity of dimensions of both and the dimensional and position similarity in the rectangular rim mortises and rebate joints..

Environmental scanning electron microscopy (ESEM)

The wooden support, textile and cross sections of the painted gesso layers were examined with a Quanta 3D 200i environmental scanning electron microscope made by FEI. The accelerating voltage was between 10–15kV in a range of magnifications.

IR reflectography

The textile was studied with infrared reflectography in order to penetrate the thick layer of dust that covered it. Illumination was provided by an IR LED lamp and a Sony A6000 digital camera modified to full spectrum with a 90C IR filter was used to capture the images.

Results and Discussion

Wooden support

The *smꜣ-tꜣwy* son of *ỉꜥḥ-ms* coffin provides data about woodworking technology in the Ptolemaic era in Egypt such as tool marks, techniques and materials.

Portable digital X-radiography was used to understand the construction technology of the coffin lid, which had been hollowed out of a tree trunk. The face and body were carved out from the main piece, to which six pieces were joined with scarf joints and edge-to-edge joints secured with wooden dowels and glue (**Fig. 111** a, b) (Gale *et al.* 2000).

As already stated, the lid of the coffin of *smꜣ-tꜣwy* son of *ỉꜥḥ-m* had been given a different registration number and was left behind in the basement when the coffin box, with its mummy and cartonnage were put on display in the Museum. Accurate measurements of the coffin lid and coffin box taken as part of this study showed a similarity in the position of the four rectangular mortises with glued wooden loose tenons on each side and of the rebate joints on the rims (**Fig. 111** c, d).

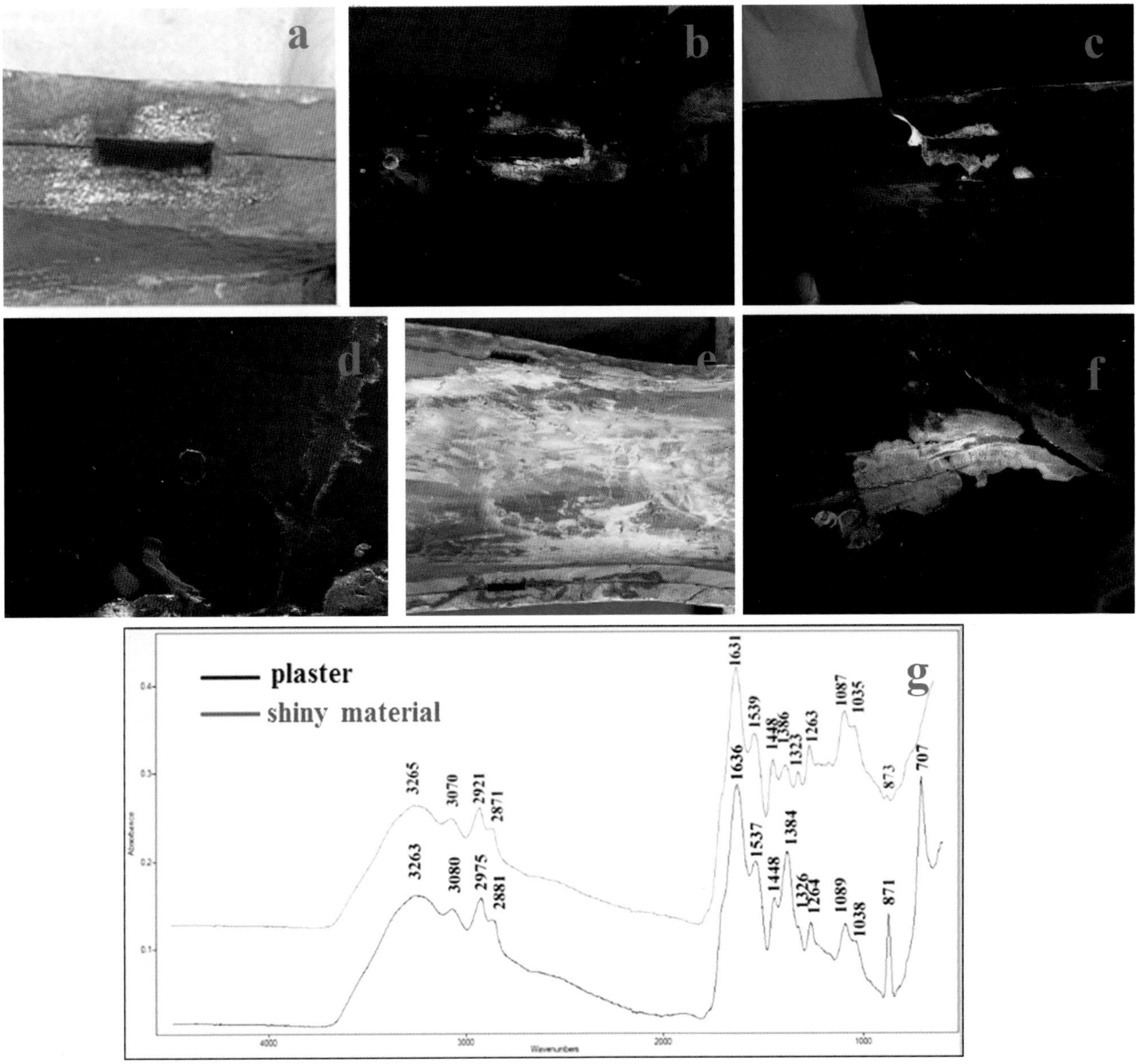

Fig. 112: Shiny material and yellow plaster. (a) Shiny material surrounding the mortise. (b–c) The fluorescence of the shiny material under UV light is attributed to organic material that surrounds the mortise opening and dowels. (e) Yellow plaster which was used to cover the separation between wooden pieces in the coffin lid interior. (f) Fluorescence of the yellow plaster under UV light is attributed to (probable) animal glue mixed with plaster. (g) FTIR-ATR spectrum of shiny material (red) and yellow plaster (black).

Samples from the main piece of wood were identified by optical microscopy as *Tamarix* sp. (Badr 2018). These results were confirmed by examination of the sections with ESEM and were reviewed with botany specialist Ohyama Motonari, Botanical Gardens, Tohoku University, Japan (motonari@m.tohoku.ac.jp).

Some of the wooden pieces had been glued together using a shiny material that also surrounded the mortise openings and dowels. The fluorescence under UV light in those parts of the lid may be attributed to an organic material (**Fig. 112** a–d) (García-Moreno *et al.* 2013, 110). Additionally, a yellow plaster was used to cover the separation between wooden pieces in the coffin lid interior (**Fig. 112** e–f). The FTIR-ATR spectrum for the shiny material indicated that it is a proteinaceous substance, probably animal glue, with the following spectral features: a C=O stretching (amide I) band at ≈1631 cm^{-1}; a C–N stretching and N–H deformation (amide II) band at ≈1539 cm^{-1}

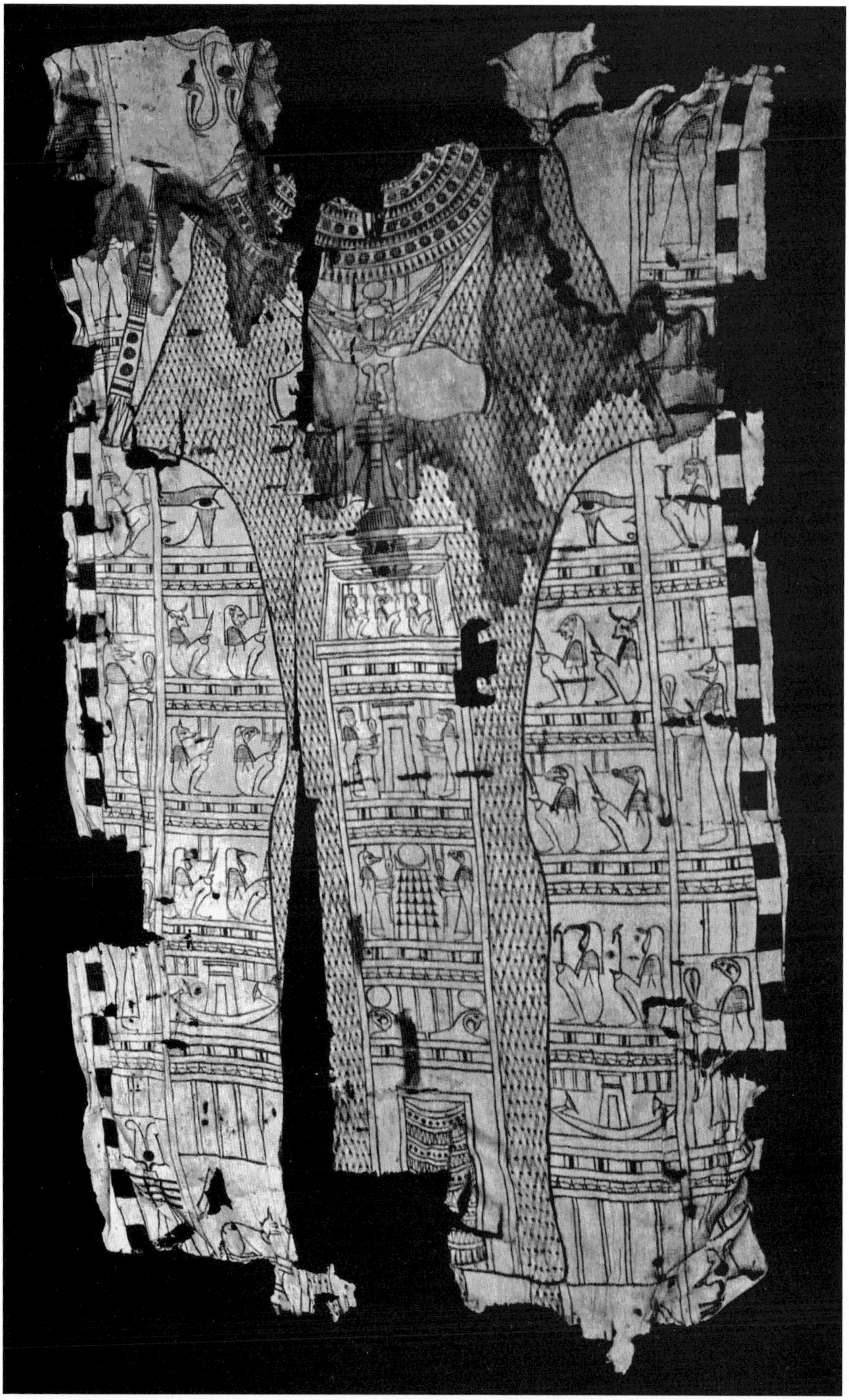

Fig. 113: IR reflectography images of the textile layer showing the Osiris shroud.

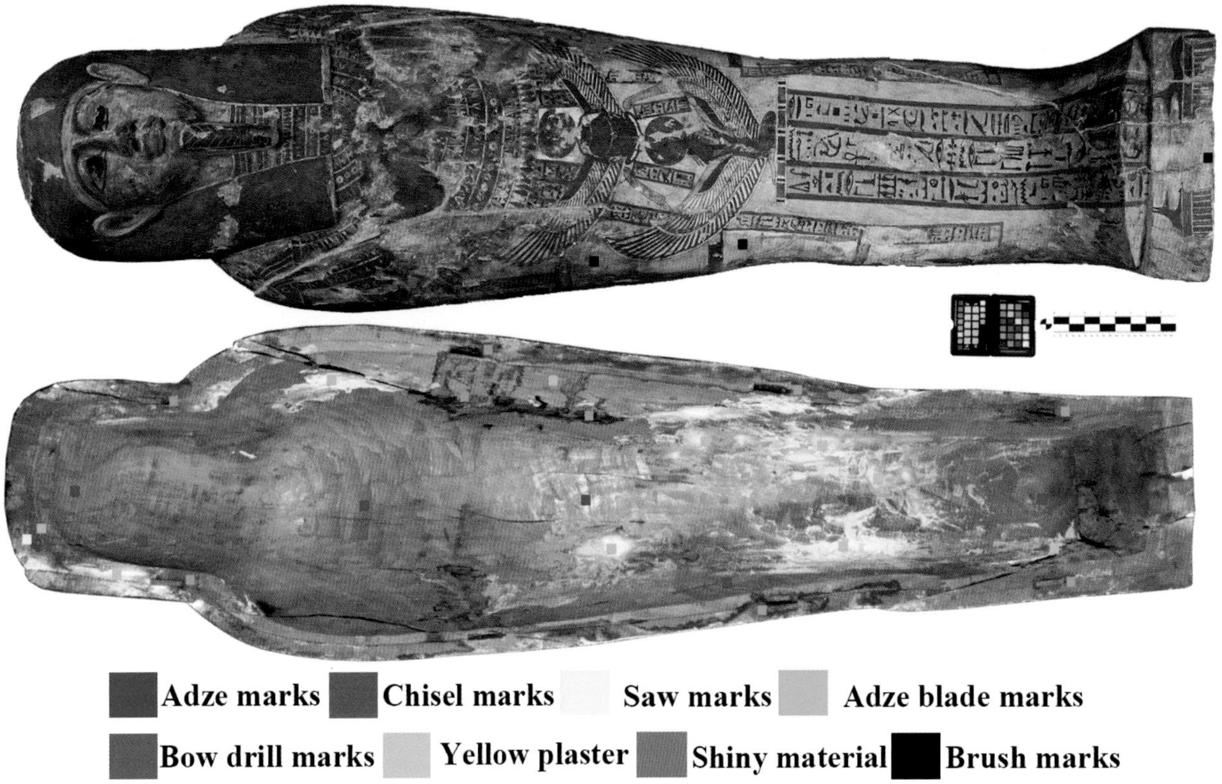

Fig. 114: Colour mapping of tool marks and materials, which were observed on the smꜣ-tꜣwy son of iꜥḥ-ms coffin lid exterior and interior.

and a C–N stretching and N-H bending (amide III) band at ≈1263 cm^{-1}. In addition to these characteristic bands, there are other typical protein O-H and N-H stretching bands at ≈3265 and ≈3070 cm^{-1} as well as C-H stretching bands at ≈2921 and ≈ 2871 cm^{-1}. C-H bending bands were found at ≈1448 and ≈1323 cm^{-1}. The FTIR-ATR spectrum for the yellow plaster exhibits further bands: an asymmetric CO_3 stretching band at 1384 cm–1, an O-C-O bending band at 707 cm–1 and a symmetric CO_3 deformation at 871 cm^{-1} that are attributed to calcite mixed with (probable) animal glue (**Fig. 112** g) (Derrick *et al.* 1991; Kong and Yu 2007; Dallongeville *et al.* 2016).

Textile covering

There are a few references in the literature to coffins covered with textile ('shrouded coffins') (Bruyère 1929; Museum of Fine Arts 1982; El-Enany 2010) but, at the beginning of this study, it was not clear whether the textile that lay over the lid belonged with this coffin. The textile was covered in dust, which made it difficult to take good images in the early stages of the documentation. IR reflectography was used to study the designs on the two textile layers. Twenty images were taken, merged together and improved with Photoshop™. They show drawings which indicate that the textile is an Osiris shroud (**Fig. 113**) (Badr 2018). Osiris is depicted standing and facing frontwards (the face missing unfortunately), holding the flail and the shepherd's crook in his hands, which are clenched over his chest on which there is a winged scarab sun-disk (Riggs, 2006). The decoration surrounding the figure of Osiris is framed on either side by a vertical column of depictions of deities, including at elbow level, on the proper right, a seated figure of Isis and, on the proper left, a similar figure of Nephthys. At the bottom of the proper right column is a djed pillar with an Atef crown. In front of Isis and Nephthys, close to the figure of Osiris on each side, is a wedjat eye, below which on each side are three registers of seated divinities with knives, a barque and (on the proper right) a jackal on a shrine. On the centre of the figure of Osiris is a vertical panel of decoration in registers, including three gods within a shrine (an unclear god, Horus and Isis), below which are two registers of divinities (probably the Sons of Horus), two Sokar hawks, back-to-back, and an uncertain area of decoration resembling part of a broad collar.

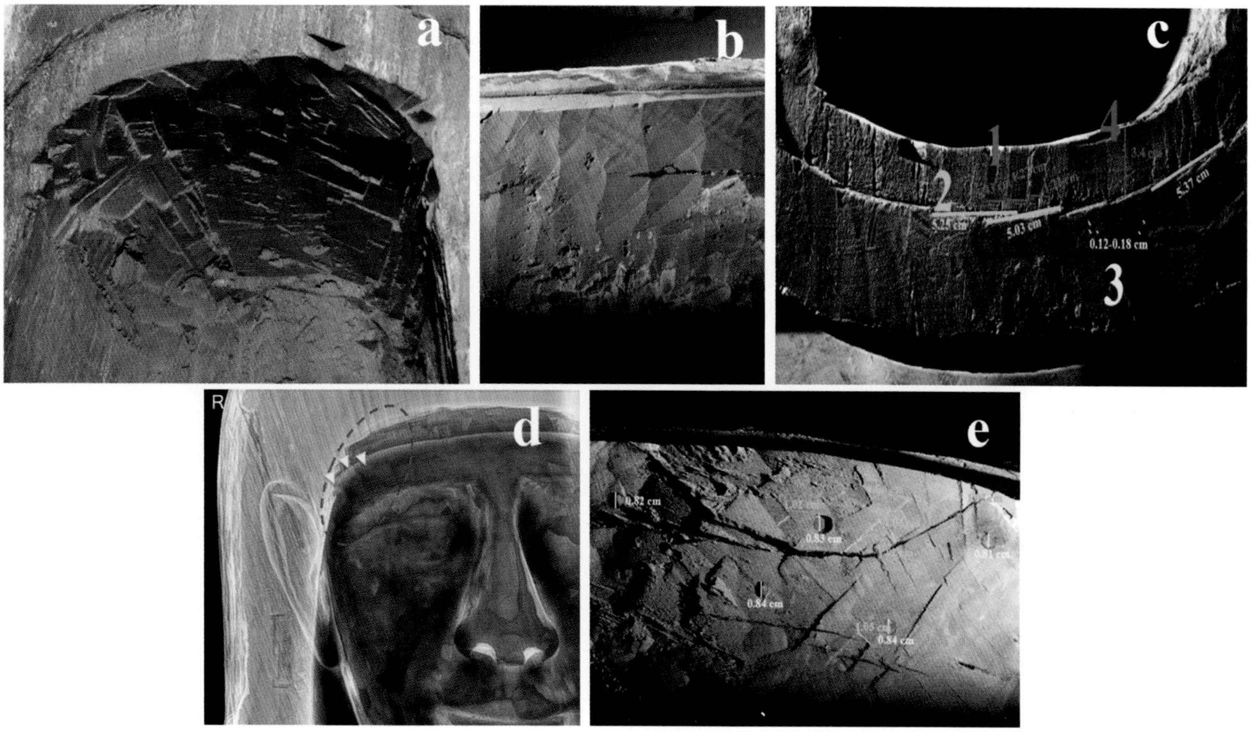

*Fig. 115: Carpenter's tool marks: (a, b) The adze marks on the coffin lid inner surface under raking light. (a) Marks left after using an adze for carving and hollowing out the tree trunk. (b) Marks left after using an adze for smoothing the surface. (c) RTI image of tool marks left after making the rebate joint in the coffin lid rim. Key: **1**. Chisel blade marks, with the size of the chisel blade ranged between 1.2 and 1.5 cm. **2**. The marks left after use of the adze or axe blade to make a sharp cut before using a chisel to complete the rebate joint. **3**. The marks left from using a saw to divide the tree trunk. (d) X-radiograph of marks left after using a chisel for carving out the coffin face. (e) RTI image of marks left after using a chisel for carving and smoothing the surface, the size of chisel blade ranging between 1.0 and 1.06 cm. The diameter of wooden dowels which were used in scarf joints are measurable from the image (0.81–0.84 cm).*

There is a sharp cut in the centre of the textile, which may be due to the use of tools such a knife or scissors. The IR images also indicated the types of deterioration in the textile, which included loose parts, tears in the textile fabric, stains and crumbling especially at the edges due to the fragile and dry state of the fabric.

Tool Marks

Numerous scenes in tomb paintings, the highly detailed model of a carpenter's workshop discovered in the Eleventh Dynasty tomb of Meketre and many examples of securely provenanced and dated full-size and model tools give us clues about the way in which carpenters worked (Dawson *et al.* 2016; Killen 1994; Killen 2017). How tools and techniques were adapted over time to meet the demands of a changing culture and the development of new products made of wood deserves more examination. Detailed study of the technology of individual coffins, such as the Ptolemaic lid discussed here, is vital in building a body of evidence for such investigations.

Many tool marks (from both carpenters and painters) have been observed in the *smꜣ-tꜣwy* son of *ỉꜥḥ-ms* coffin lid (**Fig. 114**). The tool marks of an adze, which has a copper or copper alloy blade attached to a carved wooden haft by means of a leather binding (Killen 2017; Killen 1994), were observed in the main piece of the lid (tree trunk) where it had been used to hollow out the lid and smooth the surface (**Fig. 115** a–b). Another function for the adze blade was to make a sharp cut before the chisel was used (**Fig. 115** c). Ancient Egyptian carpenters used a metal pullsaw for cutting and dividing the wooden trunk (Dawson *et al.* 2016). Tool marks observed on the rim of the coffin lid are attributed to the saw (**Fig. 115** c). The carpenters had several types of chisel for different purposes: the mortise chisel has a thick blade, so that it is strong enough to lever chips of wood out of a deep mortise, and a long wooden handle to withstand repeated blows from a mallet. The firmer chisel, used for

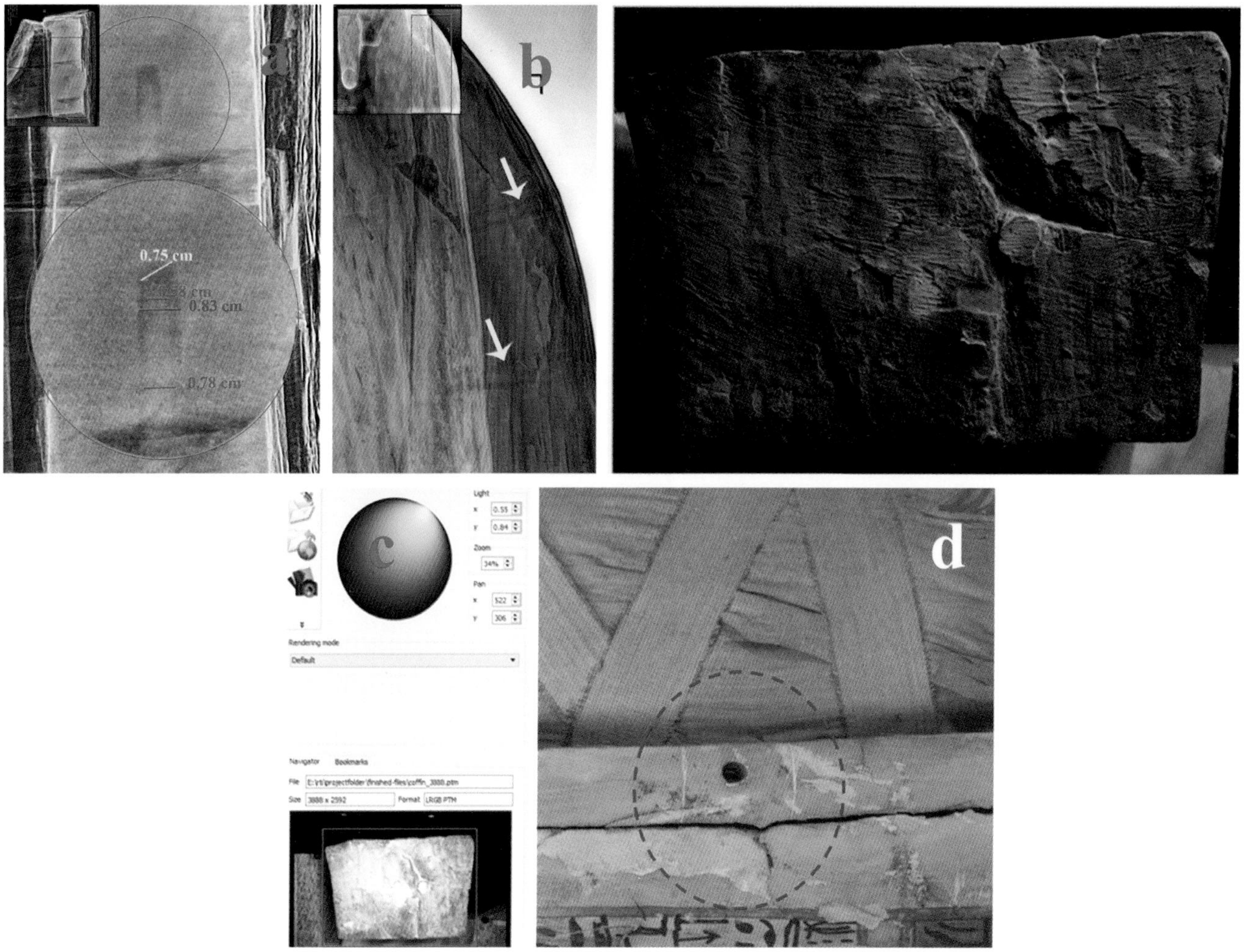

Fig. 116: Tool marks. (a, b) X-radiograph of coffin lid showing parts joined by dowels and the tube and cone shape of the dowel holes. (c) RTI images of the coffin lid foot exterior surface with brush marks in the preparation layer. (d) Lines from a small engraving tool, bradawl or scribing instrument on the painted surface to show the position for a pegged tenon. The rim of the coffin box is shown here.

shaping and smoothing work, generally has a thinner and wider blade than the mortise chisel (Killen 1994; Killen 2017).

Chisels were used to carve the coffin face (**Fig. 115** d), smooth the surface (**Fig. 115** e) and make the rebate joint. X-radiography images of the coffin lid show the wooden parts joined by wooden dowels and the dowel holes as a tube and cone shape (**Fig. 116** a–b), indicating that they were made with a bow drill (Dawson *et al.* 2016). After the lid had been carved, the surface was covered with a preparation layer applied by brush, which may have been made of plant fibre (**Fig. 116** c). Marks left after using a small engraving tool, bradawl or scribing instrument on the painted surface to engrave a line for the position of a pegged rim tenon were also clearly seen (**Fig. 116** d).

Conclusion

A detailed study of a coffin lid of unknown provenance, covered with two textile layers, led to confirmation that it is part of the Ptolemaic period coffin of *smꜣ-tꜣwy* son of *ỉꜥḥ-ms* found by Otto Rubensohn at Abusir el-Meleq in 1903–1904 and displayed separately for decades at the Cairo Museum. The textile that covered the coffin has been identified as an Osiris shroud, but its provenance needs further investigation, which is beyond the scope of this paper. A previous analytical study (Badr *et al.* 2018) and this current study on the coffin lid of *smꜣ-tꜣwy* son of *iʿḥ-ms* provide a new example of how, during the Ptolemaic period, woodworkers manufactured and decorated coffins made of native wood.

Acknowledgements

The authors would like to thank Ms. Sabah Abd El-Razeq, General Director of the Egyptian Museum for her continuous help and encouragement. Many thanks to Mr. Moemen Othman, General Director of the Conservation Department at Egyptian Museum, for his support, Mariana Jung, Staatliche Museen zu Berlin, for providing the Otto Rubensohn report, Karim Attia, a specialist in X-ray radiography, and Dr. Hanaa El-Gaoudi for her help.

Poster Contributions

The quality and quantity of proposed papers to the conference was extremely high. This meant that we were forced to ask a large number of participants to present their work in the form of a poster rather than as a spoken presentation. Happily, all the colleagues affected generously consented to this proposal.

In order to integrate the posters more fully into the programme, they were displayed prominently in the conference venue, with a dedicated poster session on the second day. In addition, all the abstracts (including those relating to the posters) were printed together, so that the poster contributions did not disappear into a metaphorical ghetto.

In this volume, the abstracts of all the posters are printed in the following section. The full posters themselves can be viewed on the Fitzwilliam Museum website at

http://www.fitzmuseum.cam.ac.uk/coffinconferenceposters/

together with posters presented at The Coffin Workshop, the three-day practical event which preceded the conference.

Biography of Coffins in The McManus
Dundee's Art Gallery and Museum

Averil Anderson

Dundee was a prosperous Royal Burgh and a busy port from medieval times until the twentieth century. In the nineteenth century, it became a centre for the jute industry. Wealthy factory owners travelled the world for business and pleasure, and used some of their wealth to improve the cultural life of Dundee and its citizens. The 'Albert Institute for Literature, Science and Art', which opened 1867 and in 2010 became "The McManus: Dundee's Art Gallery and Museum", was one such enterprise. It remains Dundee City's main museum, housing the museum's collections: approximately 150,000 items including Local History, Decorative Arts, Fine Art, Natural History and World Cultures.

The Egyptology collection largely amassed in the 19th and 20th Centuries, came into the museum by various routes: donations from individuals and subscriptions to the Egypt Exploration Fund and other organisations. Though key objects have long been part of the Museum's displays, the majority have long been in storage, and were under-researched. Some have now been the subject of volunteer research projects using contextual information from the early days of the Albert Institute including museum reports, magic lantern slides and correspondence as well as collaborations with universities using new technology. These include:

Third Intermediate Period set of coffin, cartonnage and mummy

The cartonnage had little provenance, however it is clearly of the 'northern' type, as is the associated wooden coffin. It is now possible to identify the set from research into the Annual Reports of the Albert Institute and newspaper articles, and an excavation photograph from Édouard Naville's work at Sedment for the Egypt Exploration Fund in 1891.

Roman coffin

This had not been examined since the 1960s. When reassembled, its form could be paralleled by 3rd century AD Roman Period coffins such as the 'twins' in Edinburgh and Hathor-ta-sherit-net-Osiris in Berlin. The decoration proved to be atypical taking inspiration from 25th–26th Dynasty bivalve coffins.

Roman cartonnage mask

This formed a research project for Jean Lambe, University of Lincoln.

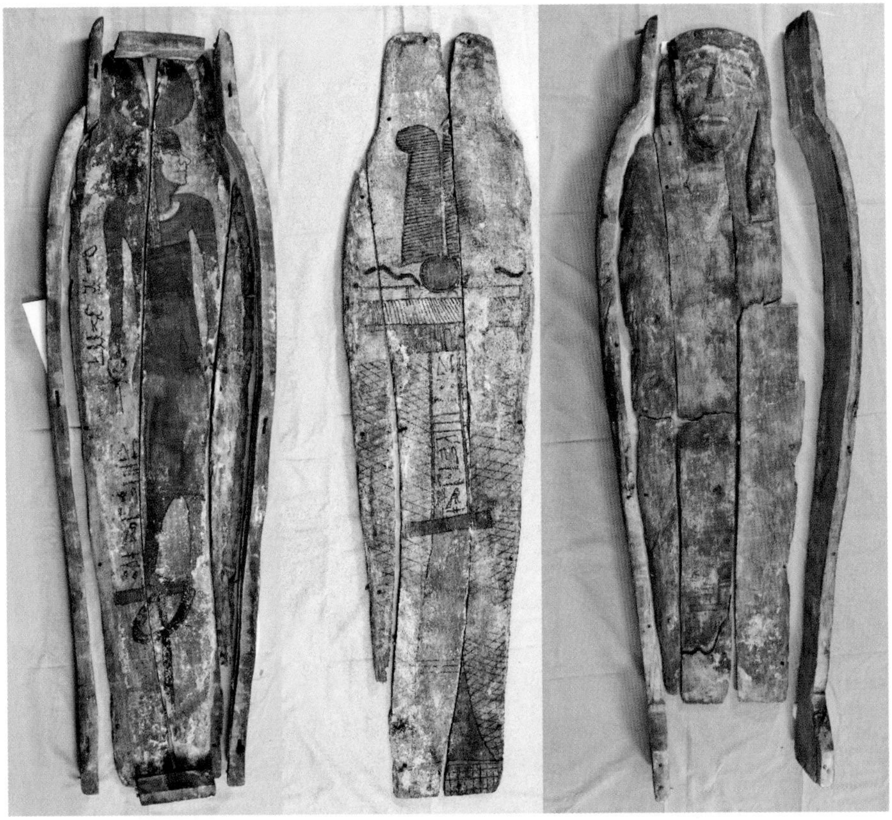

Fig. 117: Roman coffin Inv. 1976–1168, c. 3rd to 2nd Century BC, possibly from Thebes.

Texts for the protection of the body recorded on inner sarcophagi of the Saite-Persian period from Abusir

Dana Bělohoubková, Ladislav Bareš and Jiří Janák

Shaft tombs of the Late Period constitute a key source for our knowledge of religious thought and concepts of an era that was in many ways ground-breaking and unique. The Saite–Persian tombs of Abusir all date to a very narrow period around 525 BC. The inscriptions on the walls of tombs and sarcophagi contain a large variety of religious texts, some originating from the Pyramid Texts of the Old Kingdom, some from coffins of the Middle Kingdom and others from the walls of tombs of the New Kingdom. The deceased was in his tomb and coffins, surrounded by a complex system of religio-magical texts and images, which at that point had already gone through centuries of development and various stages of transmission and editions.

The surface of the inner coffins, situated very close to the body of the deceased, included specific sets of texts. In the case of the tombs of the priest Iufaa and the general Menekhibnekau, the text compositions deal with the idea of connecting parts of the human body with various aspects of the sun god Re as a means of protecting the body of the deceased. Although this particular concept is well-known from a number of other sources, there are as yet no parallels for the specific version found in the Abusir shaft tombs.

Fig. 118: Sarcophagus inside the shaft tomb of general Menekhibnekau.

Private Sarcophagi of the New Kingdom

Isa Böhme

Despite their importance among ancient Egyptian funerary goods and their often prominent display in modern museums and collections, ancient Egyptian sarcophagi are rarely the subjects of comprehensive studies. In the past decades, only five major investigations of stone coffins have been undertaken, of which only three were subsequently published: by A.M. Donadoni Roveri in 1969, on Old Kingdom sarcophagi; by M.-L. Buhl in 1959, on Late Egyptian anthropoid stone sarcophagi; and by W.C. Hayes in 1935, Royal Sarcophagi of the XVIII Dynasty. The extensive works on Middle Kingdom sarcophagi by A. Schwab (1989) and New Kingdom royal sarcophagi of the post-Amarna period by E. Brock were never printed and are only available at certain University libraries.

These fundamental studies laid the groundwork for research on objects of the same kind. But with new finds emerging every year they not only deserve a renewed approach, applying modern research methods, but substantial gaps in the material of various time periods should also be filled. One such gap remains for the New Kingdom. Although Hayes dealt thoroughly with the royal specimens up to the reign of Amenhotep III, later ones were left out of his study, as well as the many examples made for private officials during the five centuries of that period.

This latter group of private sarcophagi consists of approximately 140 examples. These stone coffins are the subjects of a PhD thesis currently being written at the Institute of Egyptology in Leipzig. The thesis comprises a catalogue describing each object, their find spot and history of discovery, the social status and family relations of the owner as well as a detailed translation of the accompanying texts. But more importantly it also includes a comprehensive examination of numerous aspects concerning the genesis and development of private sarcophagi throughout the Eighteenth, Nineteenth and Twentieth Dynasties and their estimated decline at the end of the New Kingdom: the origin, utilisation, and arrangement of the inscribed texts and representations, the usage and preferences of certain stones as raw material and the possible implications of them in comparison to earlier times and in regard to funerary beliefs or potential restrictions to royal convention, the manufacturing process and colouring, the distribution of the objects among the various cemeteries as well as an investigation of the status of the owners in relation to each other and to private officials with the same social standing but differing burial equipment.

Fig. 119: Proper right side of the outer sarcophagus of Pa-Ramesses (reign of Horemheb; Cairo, Egyptian Museum, JE 30707 + 46764). The lid shows the deceased in the dress of a vizier.

Reconstructing the perishable

Perspectives on coffins at the Temple of Amenhotep II in Western Thebes

Anna Consonni and Tommaso Quirino

Recent research undertaken by the Centro di Egittologia F. Ballerini, under the direction of A. Sesana, has brought into focus the intensive funerary use and reuse of the area occupied by the Temple of Amenhotep II in Western Thebes. Twenty-four shaft tombs with one or two irregular chambers at the bottom dating to the Third Intermediate to Late Period were discovered. The work conducted by our team also revealed the presence of funerary structures that predate the construction of the Temple, dating from the early Middle Kingdom to the early Eighteenth Dynasty. Despite the extensive looting of many of these tombs, we were still able, at times, to recover well-preserved or undisturbed burials.

Coffins, along with other perishable materials, have often been badly damaged by humidity and by the actions of white ants and so were preserved only as whitish imprints on the sand. However, careful excavation allowed us to sketch their original shape, to hypothesise the presence of one or more containers and to reconstruct spatial relationships within the assemblage. Sometimes, more remained: areas of different coloured powders, revealing details of the original decoration, figures and texts, hieroglyphs showing the name or title of the dead person, and, rarely, a quantity of gold leaf or a pair of inlaid eyes.

Due to the importance of coffins in establishing the 'use-life' of these tombs and in revealing the identity and social status of the dead, and in view of the difficulties of stabilising and conserving these items, we devoted particular attention to documenting the remains in-situ, going beyond the traditional techniques of drawing and photography.

In particular, during the most recent field seasons the recording of coffins and the related human remains (still anatomically connected) was undertaken using photorectification and photomosaics. The images obtained have been georeferenced in a GIS (Geographic Information System) and vectorised for the creation of final plans. From the 17th field season on, we began using 'Structure from Motion' methods to build 3D models of coffin remains, in order to document the volume of the find and its state of preservation at the time of discovery.

The study of the decoration, on the other hand, is now supported by colour transformation methods. With the aid of imaging programmes and a special plug-in created for enhancing rock paintings (ImageJ and DStretch), we try to bring out figures not clearly recognisable to the naked eye. We will present examples of coffins and cartonnage finds from two recently excavated tombs, along with an assessment of the methodological and archaeological perspectives that they contribute to the reconstruction of the history of this necropolis.

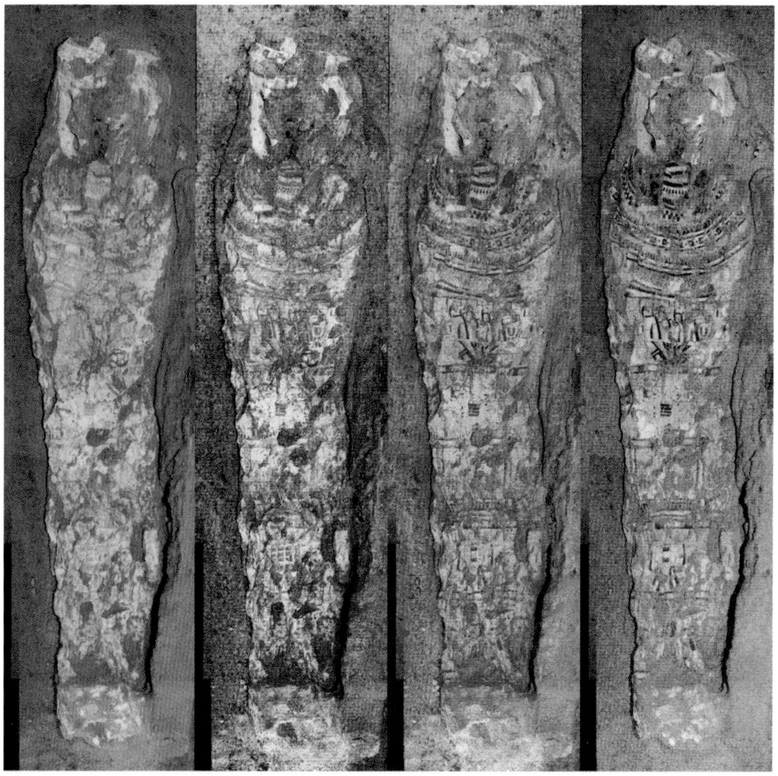

Fig. 120: Cartonnage from chamber E, Tomb D21. Original photograph and (from left to right) decorrelation stretch in colourspace LDS, YBK and YBG.

Creating Egyptian Blue pigment in the laboratory

Practical considerations and insights into the cuprorivaite-forming reaction

Trevor Emmett

Egyptian blue (EB) pigment was first identified as a silicate of copper and calcium in the 19th century. In 1938 Minguzzi discovered the naturally occurring mineral cuprorivaite CaCuSi4O10, in the vicinity of Mount Vesuvius, and approximately 20 years later it was shown that this was the phase responsible for the blue colour of EB. Subsequently, the terms cuprorivaite and Egyptian blue have commonly been used interchangeably but, strictly, this is incorrect. As observed on objects, EB invariably contains significant amounts of quartz so it is suggested here that the term Egyptian blue be reserved for this material. The blue component of this pigment is the artificially-produced analogue of cuprorivaite (but note that, strictly, mineral names should not be used for artificially manufactured phases).

EB pigment available commercially is almost pure cuprorivaite and was not considered for use in reconstructions of coffin paintings carried out in the Fitzwilliam Museum. The author initiated a series of experiments to produce a usable quantity of more realistic-looking EB. In total, 14 experiments were conducted of which 9 produced significant amounts of EB, a total of 107 g in total. Experimental design was informed by a study of the available literature and by the results of experiments conducted by the author some years ago. Some insight was also gained into the nature of the cuprorivaite-forming reaction (CFR).

X-ray diffraction was used to determine the phase composition of all starting materials, intermediate and final products. Quantities of starting materials were determined by calculation from stoichiometry, allowing for a *c.* 25% excess of quartz. Successful runs (those in which the final product was essentially cuprorivaite and quartz) had a molecular CaO:CuO ratio close to 1.0. The amount of flux (Na2CO3) was kept low, generally 5–10% of the total reaction mass. The most consistent results were obtained using a natural limestone (for CaO) and either a powdered bronze (IR350) or powdered copper metal (SP240, for Cu). Finely sieved quartz sand was used in all runs as the source of SiO2.

Fig. 121: Fragment of kiln lining with balls of EB adhering to its inner surface (Fitzwilliam Museum, Cambridge, E.51.1910; © The Fitzwilliam Museum). XRD analysis of a small portion of one ball indicates that the EB consists of cuprorivaite and quartz, with possibly some wollastonite and lime.

The main conclusions of this work are:

- The CFR requires oxidising conditions. At the very least, CO2 evolved during the process must be allowed to disperse.
- The grainsize of the reactants, both initially and during the progress of an experiment, must be kept as fine as possible. At least three stages of manual grinding are recommended.
- The CFR proceeds over a narrow range of temperatures, the lower limit being set effectively by the devolatilisation of calcite (*c.* 800–850° C). The upper temperature was not investigated but is reported in the literature as *c.* 1000° C.
- If quantities of flux are kept to a minimum (as here) the heating needs to be prolonged. The most successful experiments reported here were conducted at *c.* 860° C for in excess of 100 hours.
- The most consistent results were produced using powdered bronze or powdered metallic copper as the source of copper.

Traces of transition

Funerary envelopes from K93.12 in Dra' Abu el'Naga as artistic indicators of political and cultural changes

Stéphane Fetler

A significant number of funerary envelopes have been discovered in the main shaft and inner courtyard of K93.12 in Dra' Abu-el-Naga, being excavated by the German Archaeological Institute Cairo. This tomb forms the northern part of the extensive double-tomb complex K93.11/K93.12 originally cut in the early Eighteenth Dynasty, most probably for king Amenhotep I and his mother Ahmes Nefertari. In the Twentieth Dynasty the site was re-modelled into a monumental tomb-temple by the High Priest of Amun, Ramessesnakht, and his son and successor Amenhotep. The remains of coffins and cartonnages dating from the Eighteenth Dynasty to the Twenty-fifth Dynasty, as does the entire archaeological record, illustrates the multiple reuse of this place and testifies to its long-lasting symbolic importance.

The poster presentation will include the most significant pieces displaying technological, iconographical and/or typological interest. A major, albeit very fragmentary, piece is the coffin of the High Priest of Amun, Amenhotep, dating to the end of the Twentieth Dynasty (Ramesses IX–XI), found in the main shaft of K93.12. Although this person is well attested in ancient Egyptian sources, his burial was not known until its discovery in 2009. His coffin is exceptional in terms of both the period of production and its originality: only very few coffins of the Twentieth Dynasty are known to-date. Moreover, technical and iconographical details show that it was intended to imitate a stone sarcophagus, a rather uncommon feature that illustrates clearly the economic crisis of this period.

In addition, a group of five Twenty-second Dynasty cartonnages (four adults and one child) was discovered in the main shaft, very finely decorated, allowing four of them to be dated to the beginning of this dynasty. They display traces of fire: they are partially burned or covered by soot that darkens or completely masks the decoration. Also, two of them are partially covered with 'bitumen'. Using infrared photography, along with local cleaning, it was possible to expose the decoration beneath the black crust. As a result, the inscriptions were clearly readable and in one case yielded the name, genealogy and the titles of the deceased.

Furthermore, more than 20 lids of 'yellow coffins' dating to the late Twenty-first/early Twenty-second Dynasties were discovered in the inner courtyard of K93.12. They had been removed from their original location by tomb robbers and tossed into the court, partly on top of each other. Although the objects are very fragile, their decoration could be recorded by drawing, revealing interesting typological features. This group of coffins, along with the contemporaneous cartonnages from the main shaft, also provides evidence of a political and cultural change at the transition from the Twenty-first to Twenty-second Dynasties. Being still in their archaeological context, they form a solid starting point for a study of artistic production networks that could improve our understanding of new symbolic values being integrated into Egyptian funerary culture at that time.

Fig. 122: K93.12: Coffin no. 14 from the inner courtyard (photo © Deutsches Archäologisches Institut Kairo).

Examination of a previously untreated polychrome coffin and mummy

Geneva Griswold

This poster discusses the technical investigation and stabilisation treatment of a late New Kingdom (*c.* 1000 BC) Egyptian polychrome coffin and its anonymous mummy, held in the collection of the Fine Arts Museums of San Francisco (20295/2082). The coffin and mummy are considered to originate from Asyut, Egypt. Though the conditions of their departure from Egypt are unknown, they were gifted to the Museums in 1895 by John P. Young. Provenance research continues, meanwhile, the assemblage is being prepared for exhibition.

The anthropoid coffin is composed of a lid (the top) and chest (the bottom), each formed from multiple wood elements of various shape that are dowelled together. Adobe is thickly applied to form the contours of the body on the lid, and further applied as a skim, coating the wood surfaces of the chest. A thin, white ground layer is present over the adobe throughout. The results of pigment identification (X-ray fluorescence spectroscopy, visible-light induced infrared luminescence imaging) and analyses of the yellow, red, black, blue and green paints will be discussed. The extant paint layers are largely stable; however, these are undermined by the fragile adobe support, which is powdering and detached from the wood structure. Consolidation and stabilisation of the adobe will be presented here.

Meanwhile, computed tomography (CT) scans and the forthcoming 3-D reconstruction (to be presented in the exhibition gallery via a publicly accessible Anatomage Table) tentatively identify the mummy as female and illustrate the extreme dislocation of her skeletal structure. It is possible that the coffin structure was not constructed specifically for this individual. The mummy is comparatively small; it was placed 45 cm short of the coffin's shoulders, a conclusion based on the location of exudate staining in the coffin's chest. Ultimately, methods for striking a meaningful juxtaposition between digital reconstruction and preservation of original material (achieved via conservation intervention) require discussion.

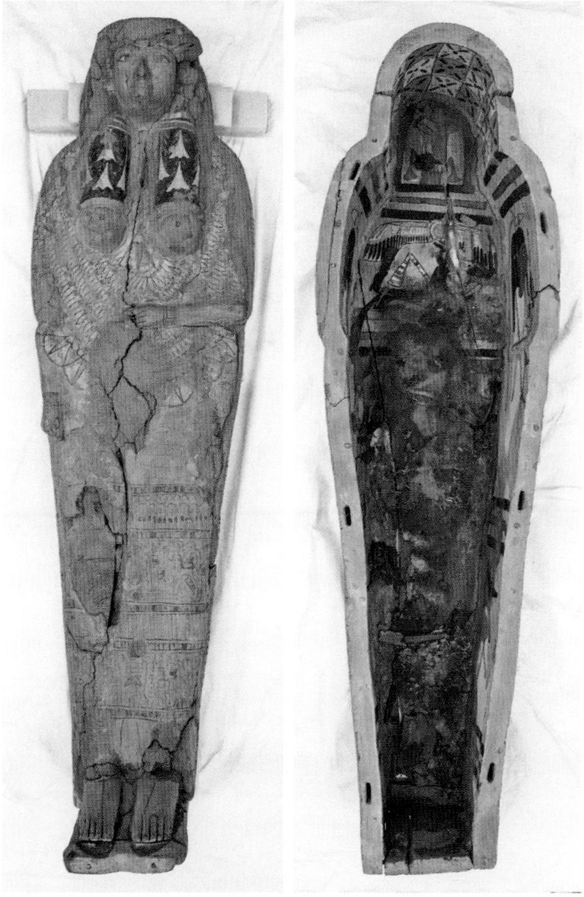

Fig. 123: Coffin 20295.1. Left: lid 190.5 x *56* x *34.3 cm; right: box 190.5* x *54* x *28 cm.*

Sail in peace to the beautiful west

Iconography of the solar barges depicted on *qrsw* coffins from the 'Priests of Montu' group

Dagmara Haładaj

During the middle of the 19th century, a number of anthropoid and *qrsw* coffins with associated burial equipment were discovered beneath the floor of the Hatshepsut Temple, Deir el-Bahari. The "Priests of Montu" group consists of people belonging to the elite of Twenty-fifth/Twenty-sixth Dynasty Thebes, but it is important to note that they are not only connected with the Montu clergy. The coffins of Besenmut and related families can be dated to the Twenty-fifth and Twenty-sixth Dynasties. The development of Theban coffins from the Third Intermediate Period is well described. Coffins of the "Priests of Montu" group can be assigned to Moret's Theban Coffins set type IIIb, which includes a *qrsw* coffin, an outer anthropoid coffin and an inner anthropoid coffin per individual.

In this poster I discuss the central element of so-called "Lid variant B", containing depictions of solar barges being towed by various gods, which first appeared on *qrsw* coffins during the late Twenty-fifth Dynasty. The earliest examples were made *c.* 675–650 B.C and the type is attested as late as *c.* 625–600 B.C. Ten coffins from the "Priests of Montu" group are decorated in this way. Some differences can be seen in the iconography. Deities who tow the boat are not depicted in the same combinations even on the same lid. Numbers vary from three to twelve, mainly consisting of anthropomorphic deities, supplemented by animal-headed gods. Skin colour is invariably blue or red, but details of the garments differ. Other differences between barges take the form of numerous adornments: multi-coloured mats, hawk-headed flagstaffs etc. In interpreting such elements shown in 2-dimensions, analogies from models of solar barges are useful. Apparently there were not any prescribed combinations of gods forming a crew. The only constant feature is the sun god in a naos, but his attributes and immediate surroundings differ. He may be accompanied by the goddess Maat or Merit, snakes or anthropomorphic deities, performing ritual gestures. Another interesting feature of such scenes is the nautical equipment of the solar boat, indicated by the inclusion of paddles, rudders, ropes.

The variety of combinations in such a small number of coffins is thought-provoking. Central features such as the deities towing the barge, the crew or the solar god in a naos were obligatory. However, the variety of details suggest that there was no single mandatory scheme.

The main aim of this poster is to draw attention to the differences between particular scenes and understand the purpose of such diverse compositions.

Solar barge of standard form

Figure 1: Solar barge from the coffin CGC41018

Barge with papyrus terminals

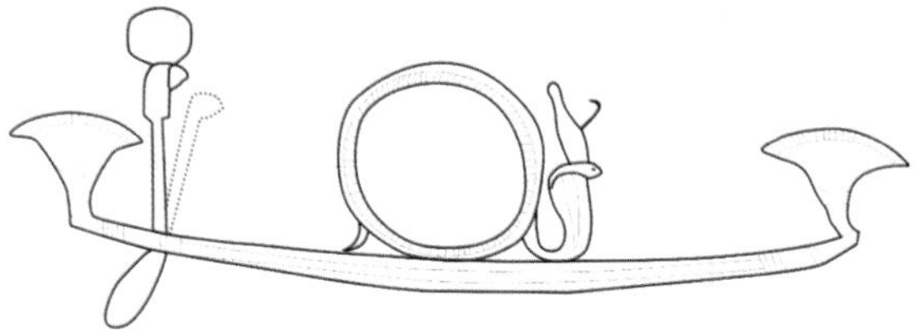

Figure 2: Solar barge from the coffin CGC41031

Barge with animal headed terminals

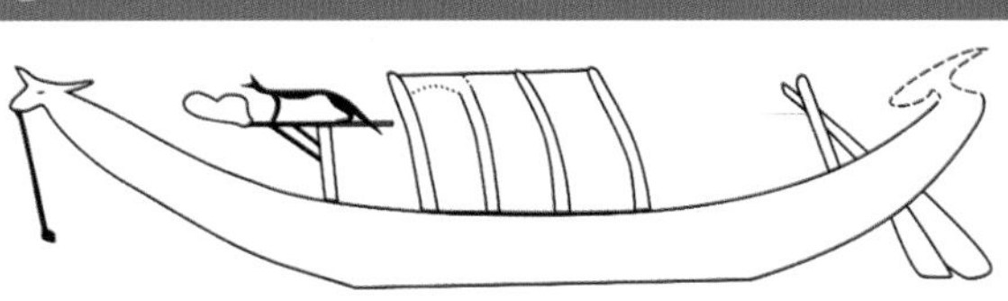

Figure 3: Barge from the coffin CGC41038

Fig. 124: Variation in depictions of solar barges in "Priests of Montu" coffins.

Rest in pieces

Fragments of a Twenty-fifth/Twenty-sixth Dynasty burial ensemble

Charlotte Hunkeler

TT 95 is one of the New Kingdom tombs of the elite at Sheikh Abd'el-Qurna in the Theban necropolis that were reused in the succeeding periods. About two hundred years after the construction of the burial complex and its original sepulchres, the tomb began to be reused. Consecutive reuse took place until the beginning of the Late Period, with an increase towards the end. Unfortunately, like many other tombs in this necropolis, TT 95 was looted on numerous occasions, which resulted in a vast number of fragmentary objects.

The study of approximately six hundred of the more than one thousand coffin fragments revealed elite burials of high quality artistry and craftsmanship that could be allocated to fourteen coffins. This poster will present three of these coffins, which probably belong to a single ensemble dated to the Twenty-fifth or Twenty-sixth Dynasty. The ensemble consists of an anthropoid inner coffin with pedestal and extensive inscriptions, a plain middle coffin and a high quality *qrsw* coffin. Additionally, fragments of a crouching jackal and two complete falcons will be presented since at least some of them must have also belonged to the ensemble.

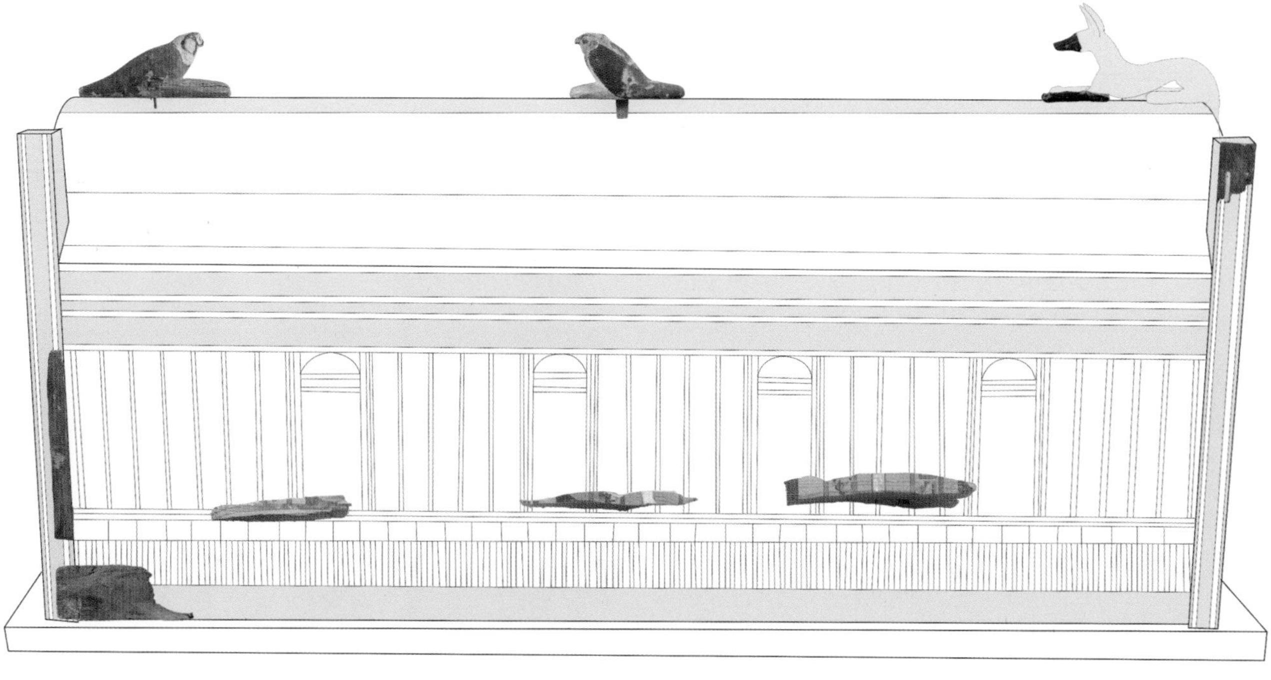

Fig. 125: Reconstruction of a qrsw *coffin found in TT95, Sheikh Abdel Qurna, based on the coffin of Hor (British Museum, EA 15655).*

Conservation treatment considerations for an Egyptian polychrome wood coffin of Pa-mi

Mohamed Ibrahim, Ahmed Ismail, Akram Abd el-Aziz, Ibrahim Salah and Eid Mertah

This poster describes the conservation of an ancient Egyptian polychrome wooden coffin owned by the Egyptian Museum in Cairo. It dates back to the Third Intermediate Period and belonged to a priest called, "Pa-mi", whose tomb was excavated by Alexander Moret in 1913. The wooden coffin is covered with gesso and painted in polychromy; it measures 202 cm in length, 70 to 82 cm width and 55 cm height.

It was constructed from several pieces of wood joined together with wooden dowels, but had been broken into four main pieces. Many gaps were found in the original joints between the wooden planks of the coffin, caused by the pieces shifting out of plane. Movement of the wood had caused cracking and flaking of gesso and paint, as well as numerous areas of surface decoration loss. A heavy superficial dust layer had accumulated on the painted layer. Two unknown black stains of a diameter ranging from 13 to 27 cm were also found on the paint layer. The general condition of the coffin was poor. In addition to loss in the wood surface and gesso, serious flaking/cupping of some pigments and extensive damage in both the wooden support and gesso layer, biodeterioration had caused cracking on the surface and in the structure. The coffin was in need of conservation, especially in areas of missing gesso at the head, and the cracks on the sides.

This poster outlines the investigations and qualitative analysis of a selection of materials from the coffin. Primary investigations were carried out by stereo microscopy. Several analytical methods were employed in the identification process such as the light optical microscopy (LOM), X-ray fluorescence (XRF) and Fourier transform infrared spectroscopy (FTIR). The data obtained were used to evaluate the deterioration status of the coffin, to study the coffin components and to establish suitable treatment methods.

Finally, conservation treatment processes were carried out, including consolidation of detached areas of the paint film, the repair of cracks in the wooden support, and stabilisation of the coffin structure.

Fig. 126: Coffin of Pa-mi in the Egyptian Museum Cairo, prior to conservation.

An unpublished Late Period coffin from Giza, stored in the Museum of Civilisation Magazine

Salwa Kamel

This sycomore fig coffin of a woman, from excavations at Giza by Mohamed Sakr, is now stored in the Museum of Civilisation Magazine under the registration number 485. It dates to the Late Period, Twenty-sixth Dynasty.

This coffin was excavated at el-Mansoreia. The name of the coffin owner is unknown. The coffin is painted in a number of colours including red, white, black and blue. There is a winged scarab on the chest, and below there are two falcons on opposite sides, each surmounted by a sun disc. On the thighs, there is a depiction of the goddess Isis with the disc of the sun on her head and the Maat hieroglyph in both hands. Below, at the sides, there are the four Sons of Horus, the god Anubis and a mummiform Osiris.

Inside the coffin, there is a mummy, with a gilded mask covering its face and neck, a gilded collar on the chest and a gilded inscribed strip.

The coffin's dimensions are given in the magazine register as follows:

Length: 199 cm.

Max. Width: 58 cm.

The actual dimensions as taken by the author are 201 cm (length), 68 cm (maximum width) and 68.5 cm (height).

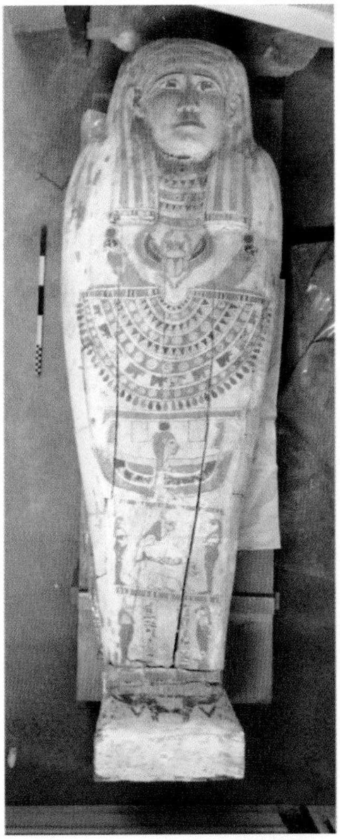

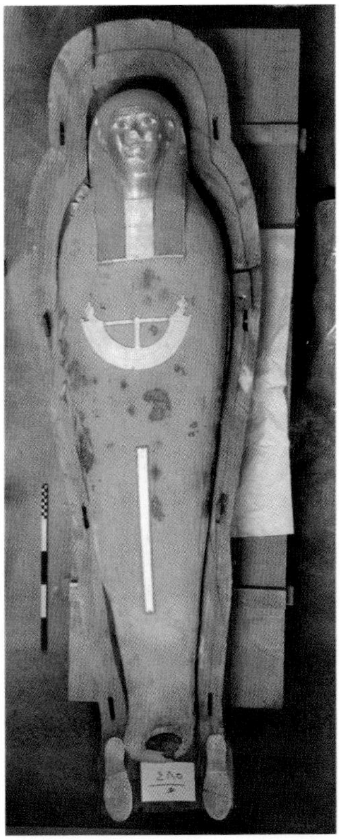

But-har-chonsu's coffin lid (Dynasties 21/22)

A study of ancient Egyptian woodworking and painting techniques and the consequences of a failed 20th century restoration approach

Sylvia Karner

This contribution focuses on the woodworking and painting technique of an ancient Egyptian anthropoid wooden coffin lid belonging to the coffin of But-har-chonsu, a chantress in the cult of Amun, who lived during the Third Intermediate Period (Twenty-first/ Twenty-second Dynasty). The coffin was excavated in Western Thebes in 1891 with several other coffin assemblages from the "Bab el-Gasus" tomb at Deir el-Bahari. Two years later, the outer lid was presented to the Kunsthistorisches Museum, Vienna. The coffin lid was transported to the Museum in several boxes, because the foot end was disassembled into its separate elements. This serious damage in the past, followed by inconsistent and incomplete restoration measures in the 20th century, rendered the lid unsuitable even for safe storage. However, the fragile state of the lid allowed a thorough investigation of its original construction and the decoration techniques used.

The lid is composed of 23 irregular planks, butt-jointed with wooden dowels and loose tenons. In antiquity, the spaces between these planks were filled and covered with preparation material. The disassembled foot end still shows the ancient use of various woodworking techniques, with different wooden joints including square-shaped dowels and holes. Evidence suggests that individual timbers were previously used for another coffin, as was typical for the Third Intermediate Period.

The exterior surface of the lid was primed before it was lavishly decorated with colourful figures on a yellow ground and varnished with a natural resin. Some of the figures, hieroglyphs and sun discs are moulded in gesso. The painted colours of the collar and headband were directly applied after the preliminary drawing on white gesso. The painting technique used by the ancient craftsmen was that of applying mostly separate colour fields for each area.

The goal of the entire project was to reassemble the lid correctly in its entirety and to consolidate the decoration, which had separated from the wood. Implementation of a detailed, step-by-step strategy ensured that the wooden planks could be appropriately and carefully separated in preparation for realignment and final reassembly of all loose pieces of decoration (Karner *et al.* 2015).

Fig. 127: Decorative elements in relief from the exterior surface of But-Har-Chonsu's coffin lid.

The ancient Egyptian perception of *nb ꜥnḫ*

Images of coffins on items from the Pushkin State Museum of Fine Arts, Moscow

Nika Lavrentyeva

The Egyptian coffin was an essential part of burial equipment throughout Egyptian history. The image of the *nb ꜥnḫ* can be found in many different contexts: sculptural models, ushabti boxes, tomb reliefs, mummy shrouds, etc. The Egyptian word *qrsw* depicts an old-style type of coffin, but can also be written with an anthropoid determinative.

The form of coffin images and models can vary from the style of form and décor of full-size coffins used in particular periods and places. We can see the simultaneous use of anthropoid full-sized coffins and box-forms in models and hieroglyphic descriptions. Middle Kingdom "chests " were used in the tombs of nobles together with "old-fashioned " *qrsw*-shaped models as part of the tomb equipment. These differences are considered here.

The collection of the Pushkin State Museum of Fine Arts contains a number of objects with depictions of coffins from different periods that illustrate the variation in perception of this central item of tomb equipment and one of the main themes of Egyptian religious art.

Fig. 128: Burial procession from an unknown tomb. From Saqqara, late Eighteenth Dynasty (Pushkin State Museum of Fine Arts, I.1a.5638 (ИГ 4117)).

Experimenting with adhesives and consolidants for use in the conservation of Egyptian polychrome wooden objects

Giovanna Prestipino

This study presents experiments carried out to identify natural and synthetic adhesives and solvents that can be used in the restoration of Egyptian polychrome wooden objects.

This research forms part of the Vatican Coffin Project, a project of study and research on the constituent materials and techniques used in the manufacture of Egyptian polychrome wooden coffins dating from the Third Intermediate Period. The project was set up in 2008 and is directed by Alessia Amenta, Curator of the Department of Egyptian Antiquities of the Vatican Museums, with scientific contributions from the Diagnostic Laboratory for Conservation and Restoration of the Vatican Museums, directed by Ulderico Santamaria.

The results of the experiments presented here have since also been shared with the Museo Egizio of Turin for the conservation of the polychrome wooden coffins in its collection in preparation for display following the re-organisation of the collection. This work was carried out by the Centro Conservazione e Restauro "La Venaria Reale", with technical and scientific advice from the Vatican Coffin Project team.

The work aims to verify the effectiveness, alteration and deterioration of certain adhesives and consolidants used in the conservation of cultural heritage, in relation to the constituent materials of Egyptian wooden polychrome objects. The research focussed on the identification of natural and synthetic adhesives and consolidants, taking account of the characteristics of their respective chemical formulae. The adhesives tested were Klucel G, Aquazol 200, Acrylic E411, animal gelatine (fish and bovine glue) and Funori. The consolidants tested were Klucel GF, Acrysol WS24, Aquazol 50, Acrilmat, Regalrez 1094 and Funori.

In order to evaluate the behaviour of the products seven samples were prepared using the same materials from which Egyptian polychrome wooden objects were made. To measure the stability of the materials tested, the samples were subjected to an artificial ageing process (UV radiation, variations in temperature and humidity), using colorimetric measurements to characterise numerically the changes induced by the artificial aging process, and at the same time establishing the dimensional stability and effectiveness of the treatments carried out.

Fig. 129: The coffin of Butehamun (Museo Egizio of Turin, Inv. 2236/1-2) during conservation.

From Beds and Coffins to Beds as Coffins?

Beds in the funerary context of Ancient Egypt: an overview

Manon Y. Schutz

Bovine-legged beds dating from the Predynastic Period onward have been found in the funerary context all over Egypt, at Saqqara, Tarkhan, Hierakonpolis and elsewhere. In most cases where beds have been found in situ, the deceased was buried in a contracted or semi-contracted position on top of this piece of furniture. If the dead person, however, was buried inside a coffin, the bed was placed upon this container, contradicting, in a way, its raison d'être. Beds and coffins thus function as two different entities. In the Old Kingdom, lion-legged beds occur next to their bovine shaped counterparts without, however, replacing them – the best-known example of such an early lion bed is probably the restored specimen of queen Hetepheres I, nowadays housed in Cairo. Even though the furniture of Hetepheres I cannot be assigned to the funerary context, the presence of headrests inside coffins of that same period – maybe as a *pars pro toto* for beds –might still hint at a close connection between beds and coffins. It is thus maybe not surprising that in the Middle Kingdom coffins appear that seem to combine the rectangular coffins of that time with the lion bier. What is the significance of this combination? Is it merely a logical development to add feline heads to the already lion-legged beds or does the coffin gain another dimension of meaning through this addition? One might also ask whether, in the Eighteenth Dynasty at Deir el-Medineh, the placing of Sennefer's coffin on top of his completely undecorated bed inside the burial chamber might have had the same significance as the Middle Kingdom specimina or whether this positioning was merely due to a shortage of space. The same combination of coffin and lion bier can be found, for instance, in the wall decoration of the New Kingdom tombs of Paheri and Renni at el-Kab, and Rekhmire at Thebes as well. It is thus highly unlikely that the union of these two objects is a mere coincidence. When in the Graeco-Roman Period the so-called mummy beds appear, they are – as a construct – no novelty anymore, although their decoration and details are very different from the former examples, and place them, without any doubt, in this late Egyptian time horizon. They are no longer simple coffins or beds, but combine features of both.

The aim of this poster is to investigate the occurrence of beds in the funerary context, especially in connection with coffins, to demonstrate how the two objects complement each other throughout the history of Egypt.

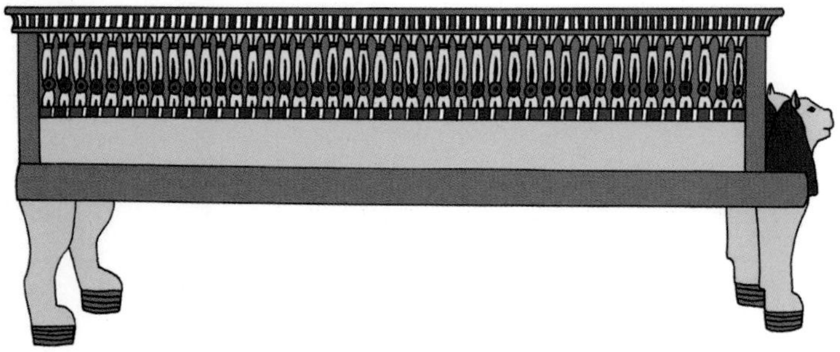

Fig. 130: Mummy bed from the Middle Kingdom.

Pakapu and the choachytes

Cynthia May Sheikholeslami

The Fitzwilliam Museum in Cambridge possesses a Twenty-fifth Dynasty coffin set belonging to a choachyte named Pakapu (E.2.1869). He was buried at Thebes *c.* 675 BC.

His father held the same position. Several other similar coffins from the period belonging to choachytes or other necropolis officials are known. This poster presents the acquisition history of Pakapu's set, brought to England by Edward, Prince of Wales, after his 1869 visit to Egypt. The coffin iconography and parallel examples are illustrated. Some other objects of Twenty-second to Twenty-fifth Dynasty choachytes are also shown, including the statuette Fitzwilliam E.11.1937.

Fig. 131: The mummiform falcon-headed Sokar-Osiris – with whom the mummy is identified – is shown, protected by the goddesses Isis and Nephthys and an encircling cobra, on the inside of the outer coffin of Pakapu. An unusual detail, taken from Theban tomb paintings, is the tree goddess Nut giving water to the ba birds, placed under the mummy's head. © The Fitzwilliam Museum.

A Romano-Egyptian mummy footcase from Hawara in the Fitzwilliam Museum, Cambridge (E.103b.1911)

Analysis of Materials

Ruth Siddall

A Romano-Egyptian period mummy footcase (E.103b.1911) is associated with a fine, gilded, cartonnage mask in the Roman style (E.103a.1911, previously analysed), both housed in the Fitzwilliam Museum, Cambridge. Visual examination suggests that the two artefacts do not "match " and they appear to have been made by different hands and using different materials. There is evidence that the iconography of footcases was relatively standardised, showing, as the Fitzwilliam example does, bound warriors on the base (under the feet of the deceased), one painted in pink and another in red, sides decorated with alternate panels depicting flowers and/or the eye of Horus, and an upper surface with gilded (or painted) feet on a polychrome, chequerboard surround.

The materials used in the construction of the Fitzwilliam footcase, pigments, cartonnage and gold leaf, have been analysed and are presented here. They have also been compared with the analysis of the materials used in the accompanying mask. The pigments indigo, orpiment, red lead, madder, gypsum, ochre and organo-copper compounds have been identified on the footcase. The cartonnage is constructed from a paste of ground calcite, gypsum and quartz bound with an organic glue. The gold leaf used was of a very high purity.

These materials distinguish this artefact from the palette, gold and cartonnage pastes used in the accompanying mask.

Fig. 132: Romano-Egyptian footcase (Fitzwilliam Museum E.103b.1911)
© The Fitzwilliam Museum.

Piecing together coffins of the non-elite at Amarna

Lucy-Anne Skinner, Anna Stevens, Anders Bettum, Corina Rogge, Alexandra Winkels and Rainer Gerisch

Excavations of the South Tombs Cemetery at Amarna, have revealed almost four hundred human individuals. The cemetery is situated in a narrow wadi, about 2 km from the main city site, connecting the Amarna plain and the desert. Almost all the bodies excavated were simply wrapped in vegetable fibre matting and had few burial goods. These modest burials confirm the idea that the cemetery is one of three main burial grounds for the non-elite population of Amarna. Hence, it was a surprise to the archaeologists in 2006 when the first fragmentary remains were uncovered of what came to be (over seven seasons), twenty decorated wooden coffins in various states of completeness, plus pottery and mud coffins.

These coffins are unique in being the only surviving examples of burial containers of the non-elite from Amarna. Conservation and investigative work undertaken over several years, has preserved elements of the vegetable fibre mating, conserved the deteriorated remains and clarified details of the decorative schemes of the wooden coffins.

This poster will describe the different types of coffin and burial container excavated from the South Tombs Cemetery – focusing on materials, technology and iconographic style. It will show how, using the range of analytical techniques available to us in the field, we have been able to determine the pigment palette, the composition of plasters, joinery techniques, plus the species of woods used to construct the coffins.

The analysis is being used to provide fascinating insights into social construction, trade and family life during the Amarna period. There is still much conservation work to do on the coffins but even at this stage, as will be illustrated in this poster, the differences and also similarities in manufacture and style of the Amarna coffins to others of the New Kingdom are clear.

Fig. 133: Digital reconstruction of partially complete proper right side panel of coffin 13262. Image by Gwil Owen.

Connecting coffins and papyri

Social identity and Twenty-first Dynasty funerary iconography

Marissa Stevens

The Twenty-first Dynasty is unique to pharaonic history in several ways. It marks the beginning of the Third Intermediate Period, an era of political and economic destabilisation. With the whole of the Mediterranean region undergoing Bronze Age collapse, the Twenty-first Dynasty, in particular, experienced weakened and truncated kingship, closed trade routes, disruptive migrations of Sea Peoples, and the political rise of the Theban priesthood. All areas of life were affected, including the social identity of elite classes and the funerary materiality of these elites. The correlation between social status and funerary materiality is constant throughout pharaonic history, but the dynamics of the Twenty-first Dynasty ushered in several changes unique to this time period. First, with a lack of connection to traditional kingship ideals, the elite emphasised personal connections to state temples. Second, defensive burial practices required a more concealed and abbreviated funerary assemblage, prompting the widespread use of funerary papyri among the elite. Third, these discrete and singular burials permitted women to utilise their own personal funerary assemblages on a par with men for the first time in Egyptian history. Indeed, half of the Twenty-first Dynasty funerary assemblages represent women, and this, coupled with a new freedom of choice in the content of the papyri led to new and innovative ways of illustrating social identity through funerary materiality for men and women alike.

These funerary assemblages consisted mainly of coffin sets and funerary papyri, as burial space was limited and the threat of theft and reuse was high. Much of the funerary iconography used by Twenty-first Dynasty elites were confined to these two object types. Unfortunately, it is all too often the case that coffins and papyri are disassociated from each other, and consequentially disassociated from their original owners. Reconnecting these pieces into cohesive assemblages and then studying iconography and function as a whole can lead to new insight into the way funerary texts and image were used and provide a social understanding of how the selection of these texts and images reflected the social identity of their owners. It is only by reconnecting these coffins and papyri that one can begin to understand how they functioned in tandem. By looking at a select group of Twenth-first Dynasty funerary assemblages, a greater understanding of social position, self-identification, and personal agency for this unique period in Egyptian history can be understood.

Fig. 134: The Metropolitan Museum of Art, Funerary Papyri of Gautseshen, 25.3.31 and 25.3.32. Rogers Fund, www.metmuseum.org.

Late Period coffins from the Fayum region

A common tradition?

Katharina Stövesand

Late Period coffins originating from the Fayum region are difficult to analyse due to their lack of adequate documentation and study thus far. Insufficiently documented early excavations, their distribution to collections worldwide and their oft perceived minor aesthetic quality have caused scholars to shy away from studying them. However, they may provide a valuable source of information concerning not only the prevalent coffin decoration patterns in this region, but also the organisation of coffin production at that time.

The aim of the poster presentation is to show the distinctive features of the coffins from the different Fayum necropolises through a careful analysis of the coffins' iconographic repertoire. In order to trace the development of coffins in this region, the Fayum area is defined in a much broader geographical sense, extending from Karanis, in the north, to Sedment, in the south, and including the Nile valley cemeteries like Abusir el-Meleq or Kafr Ammar. The overall shape of the coffins, their decoration layout, colour schemes and choice of motifs and texts, as well as details in decorative parts, such as the wig and collar of anthropoid coffins, will be taken into account.

One example are the so-called white coffins,[1] which appeared in the Twenty-fifth Dynasty as wooden bi-valve coffins.[2] Mostly rather plain, with only the facial features, the wig and the painted collar in bright colours, they may also include figurative scenes on their external surface. This type is well attested for many find-spots in the broader Fayum region, but may rarely be found elsewhere in Egypt at that time. As a result, patterns of a common tradition in the Fayum emerge, suggesting a close cooperation between the coffin producers at that time or even a common workshop tradition. Some motifs or coffin types are even unique, which may hint at the Fayum region's innovative craftsmanship.

The implications of this approach for the present study of coffins will be highlighted. Several find-spots in the Fayum have been subject to looting since antiquity, with a surge in modern times. For instance, Abusir el-Meleq has been plundered extensively in the past few years, resulting in severe disturbance to the site. Coffins from illicit excavations often appear on the art market, stripped of their archaeological context and in many cases cut into 'transportable' pieces. However, through identification of these specific patterns, it may be possible to attribute some of these coffins to the broader Fayum region.

[1] For example, the anthropoid coffin from Abusir el-Meleq, University of Rostock, Heinrich Schliemann-Institut für Altertumswissenschaften, inventory number 148.I.2 (see also Meffre, this volume).

[2] These coffins clearly refer back to the first anthropoid coffins of the Middle Kingdom. These were an innovation of the Middle Egyptian region. See for instance the coffin of Userhet in the the Fitzwilliam Museum, Cambridge, E.88.1903.

Mummy-cover fragment Ar–227 in the Lviv Museum of History of Religion

Mykola Tarasenko

The fragment comes from the private Egyptian collection of the family of Polish Princes Lubomirski. It was acquired together with other artifacts during the trip of Andrzej Lubomirski to Egypt in 1887. This collection was kept in Ossoliński estate in Lviv. In 1940 it was nationalised and Egyptian antiquities were transferred to the Lviv Historical Museum. Later, the most significant items, including this fragment, were passed to the Museum of History of Religion, formed in 1973.

The mummy-cover fragment Ar–227 measures 26 cm in length and 51 cm in height. It is inscribed and decorated but does not contain the name of the owner (female). The identification of the name would only be possible if other parts of the coffin could be found. The decorative style of this fragment belongs to Niwiński's type II-c and the object possibly dates back to the middle of the Twenty-first Dynasty. It shows two groups of images, separated by a vertical inscription. To the left of the inscription there are two identical solar compositions with the image of a Khepri-scarab in the centre, which are separated by ornamental registers. To the right of it, there are three tiers of identical composition showing Osiris and Isis, separated by a frieze of cobras and two horizontal inscriptions. The closest parallels to these scenes are found on the mummy-cover Florence 2174.

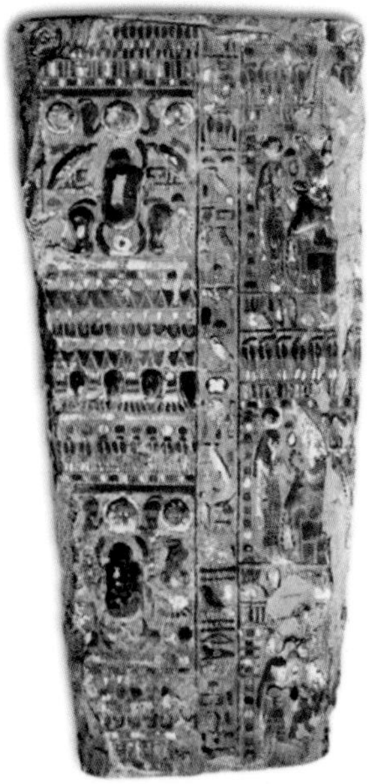

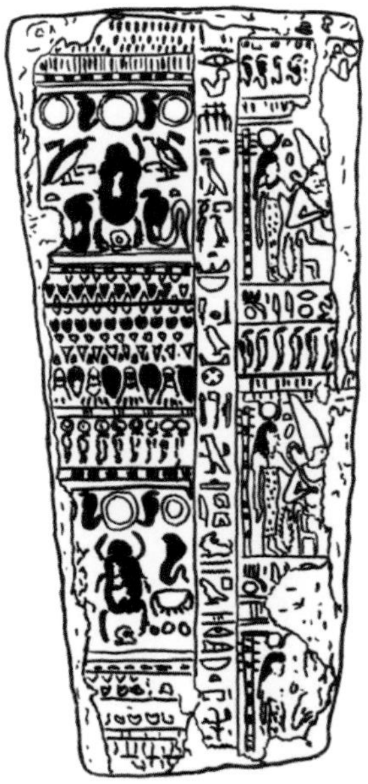

The vertical inscription on the Lviv mummy-cover is a part of a funerary formula, which is also found on the Turin CGT 10118 and Florence 2174 mummy-covers. These texts have similarities in mistakes and unusual forms of hieroglyphs. The only difference is the beginning (starting with a *ḥtp di nsw* formula) and the end of the text on the Florence example. The proto-graphic text could be restored as:

ḏd mdw in wsir-ḫntj-imntt nb ꜣbḏw nṯr ꜥꜣ ꜥꜣ (?) igr(·t) (?) wnn(-nfr) (?) <···> tꜣwj wsir nb·t pr šmꜥ·t n imn-rꜥ nsw-nṯrw N <···> nb n s·t mw·t

"Words spoken to Osiris-Hentiimentiu, Lord of Abydos, the Great God, the Head (?) (of) Iger(et), Unn(-nefer) (?) <...> Two Lands; Osiris, the mistress of the house, the chantress of Amun-Re, King of the Gods, N <...> Lord of the Place of Mut".

Two horizontal inscriptions have only parts of *imꜣḫy ḫr* + N formulas. The names of relevant deities are lost, and instead of *ḫr, rḫ* is written (cf.: Florence 2174, Turin CGT 10117, and 10119). The mummy-covers from Lviv, Turin, and Florence were off-the-peg products and belong to the same Theban workshop. The decoration of Lviv Ar–227 and Florence 2174 mummy-covers were probably painted by the same artist, or group of artists.

Tradition, innovation and archaism on Twenty-fifth and Twenty-sixth Dynasty coffins

Objects from the Liverpool World Museum Collection

Allison Williams

The ornate decoration schemes of the Twenty-fifth and Twenty-sixth Dynasty coffins blended elements of tradition, innovation and archaism. Images remained the core of decoration, highlighting and reproducing themes previously depicted on tomb walls, so continuing to surround the mummy with funerary rituals of the deceased. The relationship between the different fashions of design programmes (tradition, innovation and archaism) created a distinctive funerary object in a time of reunification. Tradition had always existed in ancient Egyptian funerary art, centring on all the fundamental rituals that surrounded life and death. Innovation allowed the Twenty-fifth and Twenty-sixth Dynasty Theban priesthood to mark their presence in the historical record of iconographic design with new concepts for the design programmes. The mobilisation of archaism was a reminder of what had been, with which successful elite of the past had integrated into ancient Egyptian art. The combination of these three fundamental aspects of artistic representation marked a time in ancient Egyptian history when coffin design demonstrated the need for elite funerary objects to convey a continuity, a stamp of originality and a distant reminder of the artistic past.

There are several collections in the northwest of England that contain coffins of the Twenty-fifth and Twenty-sixth dynasties. One such is the Liverpool World Museum, with a fairly substantial collection of Late Period coffins that illustrate these artistic design programmes of tradition, innovation and archaism. Tamutharibes (M14047), Ditamunpaseneb (24.11.81.5A+B), Pediamunnebnesuttawy (M14049), Pedneferhotep (39.4042.10) and Ta-aa (M13992), all demonstrate how the three design programmes were incorporated, often simultaneously depicted alongside each other, in a blending of image and text. Traditional iconography includes the vulture headdress, *wsḫ* collar, falcon terminals, winged Nut across the chest and the Abydos Fetish. Innovative features include a fringe along the wig, *nbw* under Nut, *wḏꜣt* eyes on the feet, the Apis bull under the feet and structural changes: the pedestal base and back plinth. Archaising trends include a false door/doorway underneath winged Nut and a palace façade pattern on the base. Some traditional elements from other media (tomb decoration and papyri) are newly integrated into coffin iconography, including the procession of deities in Book of the Dead spell 125, the vignettes of Book of the Dead spells 89, 151 and 85, and the *ꜥnḫ, wꜣs, nb* pattern on the base. All these iconographic elements, consciously put together, formed what we now know as the elaborate coffin designs of the Twenty-fifth and Twenty-sixth dynasties.

Fig. 135: Apis bull under the feet, inner coffin of Tamutharibes, Liverpool World Museum, M14047 (photo by author).

Three fragments of the wooden coffin of Osiris *pꜣ-ꜥꜥn* from the Al-Ashmunein magazine (1453 + 1395 + 1394)

Zeinab Zaghloul Abd El-azim and Mohamed Salah El-Kholi

The poster studies three wooden fragments which form the lid of the coffin of Osiris *pꜣ-ꜥꜥn*, which was found in the subterranean galleries of the sacred animal necropolis at Tuna el-Gebel during the excavations of the mission from Cairo University under the directorship of Dr S. Gabra (1931–1952). These fragments are currently stored in the magazine of Al-Ashmunein (inventory numbers 1453 + 1395 + 1394).

This presentation investigates the inscriptions and parallels from other periods, including a palaeographical study. Further, this presentation focusses on the cult of the god Osiris *pꜣ-ꜥꜥn*, i.e. Osiris baboon or the dead baboon.

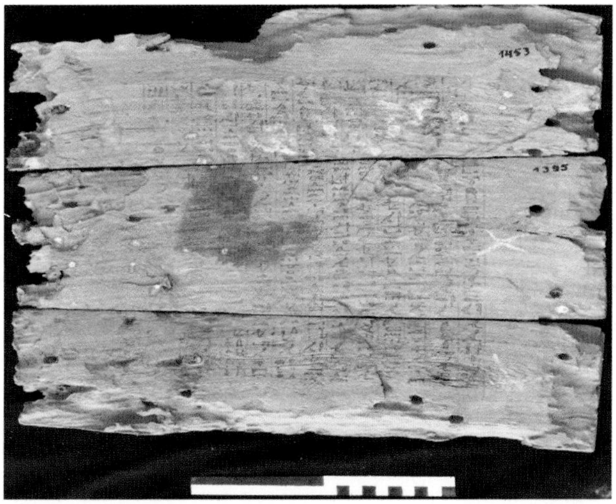

Documentation and conservation study of S.S 37, coffin and mummy cartonnage, The Egyptian Museum, Cairo

Eman H. Zidan, Rania El Atfy, Sabah A. Razek, Mohamed Gamal Rashed, Randa El Helw and Mohamed Hussien

A Late Period coffin set, comprised of an anthropoid wooden coffin and a cartonnage with an intact mummy, was found in the basement of The Egyptian Museum, Cairo during work in 2004. The only source of documentation (a report by Maspero in 1901) indicates that it entered the collection in 1900. It has remained unregistered since then. Maspero reports that it was excavated by Petrie in Lahun, Fayum. The report includes a black and white photograph taken at the time of discovery.

The type of coffin and cartonnage suggest it is from Middle Egypt, around the Third Intermediate to Late Period. The motifs of broad collar, pendants, rosettes and other decorative elements are Late Period in style. The central inscription, repeated on both the coffin and the cartonnage, contains an offering formula to Osiris. The name of the owner is lost.

The wooden coffin has multiple layers: wood, gesso, additives (under investigation) and a painted layer. The range of pigments used in the decoration of the coffin is as follows: white background covered with blue, red, black and yellow for inscription and decorations. The state of the wood is very poor, the coffin is in many pieces; some pieces are still joined together by wooden dowels. The head section has areas of loss, cracks and breaks, and areas that are detached.

The objects are suffering microbiological decay due to inadequate storage in the basement. After investigation, we found that the most predominant micro-organisms are bacteria in the mummy and cartonnage, which reach a count of 109 x 105, while the coffin bacteria are 67 x 105. Sterilisation was applied using natural chemical methods, in the form of plant extracts containing volatile oils, characterised as colourless, with a pungent smell, dissolved in alcohol, to reduce the growth of micro-organisms such as bacteria, fungi and yeasts.

The pigments and paint palette of the cartonnage are similar to that of the wooden coffin. The state of preservation appears to be moderately stable except in the lower parts, which have some losses and cracks. The foot area is severely damaged, with areas of loss, crumbling and distortion. It is covered with thick dust. Some black, greasy stains are located on the right side. It has an irregular surface, with slightly pushed-up areas possibly caused by the mummy inside. There are areas of abrasion, micro-cracks, and scratches in the painted layer. The pigments are lost in some parts of the cartonnage. There is severe damage to the foot area, with the textile layer exposed and the gesso layer and the painted layer almost completely lost except in a small part that is present but friable.

From observations through a crack in the head area, the mummy (154 cm) is much shorter than the cartonnage case (174 cm).

Further investigation and analysis will be performed later on the objects, using non-invasive techniques to identify the pigments. The mummy will be examined by X-radiography.

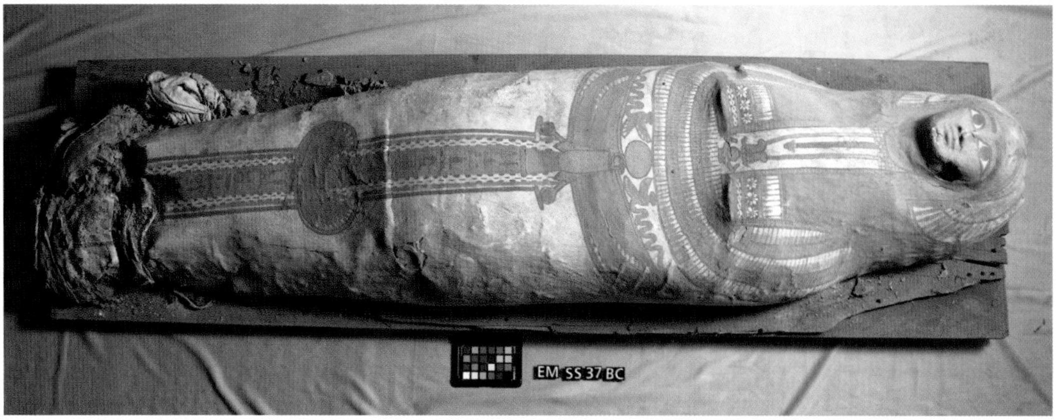

Contributors to this volume

Name	*Affiliation*
Mohamed Abd el-Rahman	Ministry of Antiquities, Egypt
Sabah Abd el-Razek	Director, Egyptian Museum, Cairo
Akram Abd el-Aziz	Egyptian Museum, Cairo
Averil Anderson	McManus Collections Unit, Dundee
Nour Mohamed Badr	Conservation Centre, Grand Egyptian Museum, Cairo
Yekaterina Barbash	Brooklyn Museum, New York
Ladislav Bareš	Czech Institute of Archaeology, Faculty of Arts, Charles University, Prague
Fruszina Bartos	Eötvös Loránd University, Budapest
Dana Bělohoubková	Czech Institute of Archaeology, Faculty of Arts, Charles University, Prague
Anders Bettum	University of Oslo
Isa Böhme	University of Leipzig
Lisa Bruno	Brooklyn Museum, New York
Paola Buscaglia	Conservation Laboratories, Centro Conservazione e Restauro "La Venaria Reale", Venaria Reale
Michela Cardinali	Director, Conservation Laboratories, Centro Conservazione e Restauro "La Venaria Reale", Venaria Reale
Caroline Cartwright	British Museum, London
Tiziana Cavaleri	Scientific Laboratory, Centro Conservazione e Restauro "La Venaria Reale", Venaria Reale
Anna Consonni	Centro di Egittologia F. Ballerini, Como
Kathlyn M. Cooney	UCLA, Los Angeles
Paola Croveri	Scientific Laboratory, Centro Conservazione e Restauro "La Venaria Reale", Venaria Reale
Sawsan Darwish	Conservation Department, Faculty of Archaeology, Cairo University
Yolanda de la Torre Robles	Universidad de Jaén
Nesrin El-Hadidi	Conservation Department, Faculty of Archaeology, Cairo University

Rania El Atfy	Egyptian Museum, Cairo
Randa El Helw	Egyptian Museum, Cairo
Jonathan P. Elias	Akhmim Mummy Studies Consortium
Trevor Emmett	Independent scholar, c/o The Fitzwilliam Museum, Cambridge
Gianna Ferraris di Celle	Conservation Laboratories, Centro Conservazione e Restauro "La Venaria Reale", Venaria Reale
Stéphane Fetler	Université Libre de Bruxelles
Mona Fouad Ali	Conservation Department, Faculty of Archaeology, Cairo University
Mohamed Gamal Rashed	Damietta University
Rainer Gerisch	Ancient Egypt Research Associates (AERA)
Geneva Griswold	de Young Museum, San Francisco
Dagmara Haladaj	Institute of Archaeology, University of Warsaw
Charlotte Hunkeler	University of Basel
Mohamed Hussien	Egyptian Museum, Cairo
Mohamed Ibrahim	Egyptian Museum, Cairo
Ahmed Ismail	Egyptian Museum, Cairo
Jiří Janák	Czech Institute of Archaeology, Faculty of Arts, Charles University, Prague
Salwa Kamel	Faculty of Archaeology, Cairo University
Sylvia Karner	Objects Conservation, Gröbliweg 4, 6844 Altach, Austria
Nika Lavrentyeva	Pushkin State Museum of Fine Arts, Moscow
Alessandro Lo Giudice	Department of Physics, University of Turin
Carter Lupton	Milwaukee Public Museum
Raphaële Meffre	Fondation Thiers / CNRS, Paris
Eid Mertah	Egyptian Museum, Cairo
Susanna Moser	Civic Museum of History and Art, Trieste
Hans-Hubertus Münch	University of Basel
Simone Musso	Stibbert Museum, Florence
Marco Nervo	Centro Conservazione e Restauro "La Venaria Reale", Venaria Reale
Marco Nicola	Director, ADAMANTIO Ltd, Turin
Andrzej Niwiński	University of Warsaw
Simone Petacchi	Stibbert Museum, Florence
Anna Piccirillo	Scientific Laboratory, Centro Conservazione e Restauro "La Venaria Reale", Venaria Reale
Marco Pisani	National Institute of Metrological Research (INRIM), Turin
Giovanna Prestipino	Egyptian Department, Vatican Museums
Tommaso Quirino	Centro di Egittologia F. Ballerini, Como
Mohamed Ragab	Conservation Center, The Grand Egyptian Museum, Ministry of Antiquities
Alessandro Re	Department of Physics, University of Turin
Patricia Rigault	Musee du Louvre, Paris

Corina Rogge	Museum of Fine Arts, Houston
Ibrahim Salah	Egyptian Museum, Cairo
Mohamed Salah El-Kholi	Department of Egyptology, Cairo University
Lisa Sartini	University of Pisa
Manon Schutz	Mansfield College, Oxford
Anna Serotta	The Metropolitan Museum of Art, New York
Cynthia May Sheikholeslami	American University in Cairo
Ruth Siddall	University College London
Uta Siffert	University of Vienna
Lucy-Anne Skinner	The Amarna Project
Anna Stevens	The Amarna Project
Marissa Stevens	UCLA, Los Angeles
Katharina Stövesand	German Archaeological Institute / Cologne University
Mykola Tarasenko	National Academy of Sciences, Ukraine
Allison Williams	University of Liverpool
Alexandra Winkels	Independent conservator, Freiburg
Zeinab Zaghloul Abd El-Azim	Department of Egyptology, Cairo University
Francesca Zenucchini	Conservation Laboratories, Centro Conservazione e Restauro "La Venaria Reale", Venaria Reale
Eman H. Zidan	Egyptian Museum, Cairo
Massimo Zucco	National Institute of Metrological Research (INRIM), Turin
Antje Zygalski	Cologne Institute of Sciences / Technical University of Cologne